Will China's Rise Be Peaceful?

Will China's Rise Be Peaceful?

Security, Stability, and Legitimacy

Edited by Asle Toje

OXFORD
UNIVERSITY PRESS

OXFORD
UNIVERSITY PRESS

Oxford University Press is a department of the University of Oxford. It furthers
the University's objective of excellence in research, scholarship, and education
by publishing worldwide. Oxford is a registered trade mark of Oxford University
Press in the UK and certain other countries.

Published in the United States of America by Oxford University Press
198 Madison Avenue, New York, NY 10016, United States of America.

© Oxford University Press 2018

All rights reserved. No part of this publication may be reproduced, stored in
a retrieval system, or transmitted, in any form or by any means, without the
prior permission in writing of Oxford University Press, or as expressly permitted
by law, by license, or under terms agreed with the appropriate reproduction
rights organization. Inquiries concerning reproduction outside the scope of the
above should be sent to the Rights Department, Oxford University Press, at the
address above.

You must not circulate this work in any other form
and you must impose this same condition on any acquirer.

CIP data is on file at the Library of Congress

ISBN 978–0–19–067539–4 (pbk)
ISBN 978–0–19–067538–7 (hbk)

CONTENTS

List of Contributors   ix

Asle Toje: Introduction   *1*
   Key Dimensions   *4*
   Security, Stability, and Legitimacy   *7*
   Structure   *8*

PART I. China and the International Order

1. Stephen M. Walt: Rising Powers and the Risks of War: *A Realist View of Sino-American Relations*   13
   Introduction   13
   The Balance of Power and the Risks of War   14
   The Historical Record   19
   China's Rise and the Future of Conflict in Asia   22
   Conclusion   28
2. G. John Ikenberry: A New Order of Things? China, America, and the Struggle over World Order   33
   Introduction   33
   Rising States and Power Transitions   36
   Rising States and Liberal International Order   40
   The Geopolitics of Sino-American Rivalry   43
   China and the World of Democracies   47
   Conclusions   51
3. William C. Wohlforth: Not Quite the Same as It Ever Was: Power Shifts and Contestation over the American-Led World Order   57
   Introduction   57
   No (Hegemonic) War and Change in World Politics   59
   Power Shift, Not Power Transition   65
   Institutions and Strategic Incentives   69
   Conclusion   73

4. Rosemary Foot: Restraints on Conflict in the China-US
   Relationship: Contesting Power Transition Theory   79
   Introduction   79
   Power Transition Theory   80
   The Return of Thucydides   84
   Regional State Preferences and the Shaping of Regional Order   87
   Economic Interdependence and Globalized Production
      Processes   90
   Domestic Economic and Political Priorities   93
   Conclusion   94

PART II. Historical Perspectives

5. Geir Lundestad: The Rise and Fall of Great Powers: The Uses
   of History   103
   Introduction   103
   Realism and the Rise of China   104
   Rise, Decline, and War   105
   The United States, China, and Cooperation   109
   Interdependence and War   111
   The United States Still Far Ahead   113
   Conclusion   116

6. Christopher Layne: The Sound of Distant Thunder: The Pre-World
   War I Anglo-German Rivalry as a Model for Sino-American Relations in
   the Early Twenty-First Century   123
   Introduction   123
   The Uses of Theory   125
   The Return of Power Politics   127
   The Difficulties of Rising Peacefully   127
   Bilateral Power Rivalries   130
   The United States and Stability   132
   The Carr Moment   135
   After Pax Americana   137

7. Odd Arne Westad: The Weight of the Past in China's Relations with Its
   Asian Neighbors   143
   Introduction   143
   The United States and China's Relations with Its Neighbors   144
   China and the Korean Question   146
   The Troublesome Ally   149
   China and the Challenge of Southeast Asian Integration   151
   The Promise of ASEAN   155
   Conclusion   155

PART III. Domestic Dimensions

8. Minxin Pei: The Rise and Fall of the China Model: Implications for World Peace   *163*
   - Introduction   *163*
   - Chinese Economic Growth   *166*
   - Patronage and Co-optation   *171*
   - Selective Repression   *174*
   - Manipulation of Nationalism   *176*
   - Concluding Thoughts   *179*
9. Johan Lagerkvist: Curtailing China's Rise before the Real Takeoff? Censorship, Social Protests, and Political Legitimacy   *185*
   - Introduction   *185*
   - Tightening Online Censorship   *190*
   - Climate of Compliance   *192*
   - Revisiting the Principal-Agent Dilemma   *195*
   - Social Protests in Rural Areas: The Wukan Incident   *197*
   - The Wukan Villagers' Effective Media Strategy   *199*
   - Conclusions and Implications   *201*

PART IV. Domestic Politics—International Policies

10. David Shambaugh: Is China a Global Power?   *211*
    - Introduction   *211*
    - China's Diplomatic Power   *214*
    - China's Military Power   *217*
    - China's Search for Soft Power   *219*
    - China's Economic Power   *221*
    - Still a Developing Country   *224*
    - Conclusion and Outlook   *225*
11. Zhang Ruizhuang: Despite the "New Assertiveness," China Is Not Up for Challenging the Global Order   *231*
    - Introduction: Is the Wolf Really Coming This Time?   *231*
    - The China Model   *232*
    - National Power: The Key Determinant   *236*
    - The Challenge of Domestic Stability   *237*
    - Changing the World Order from Within   *240*
    - Conclusion   *245*

PART V. China and Its Rivals

12. Liselotte Odgaard: Coexistence in China's Regional and Global Maritime Security Strategies: Revisionism by Defensive Means   *253*

Introduction   253
Coexistence and Legitimacy in International Political Change   256
The Diaoyu/Senkaku Dispute   258
Antipiracy Operations in the Gulf of Aden   264
Conclusion   268

13. Yoshihide Soeya: The Rise of China in Asia: Japan at the Nexus   277
Introduction   277
The Rise of China in Global and Asian Contexts   280
The Origin of the History Problem   283
The "Senkaku/Diaoyu" Dispute as a Paradigm Clash   285
China Policy of a "Normal" Japan   287
The Case for an Alternative Strategy   290
Conclusion   293

14. Jonathan Holslag: Can India Balance China in Asia?   299
Introduction   299
The Causes of Discord   300
Military Balancing   305
Diplomatic Balancing   310
Economic Competition   312
Conclusion   316

15. Michael Cox: Axis of Opposition: China, Russia, and the West   321
Introduction   321
United by History   327
Unipolarity and Its Dangers   330
China and Russia—International Cooperation   334
Conclusion: China, Russia, Ukraine, and Beyond   339

16. Steven E. Lobell: How Should the US Respond to a Rising China?   349
Introduction   349
Increasing Sino-American Competition   353
Offshore Balancing Versus Deep Engagement Strategies   355
New Model of Realist Major Power Relations (NMRMPR)   357
Disaggregate Power   358
Appropriate Elements of Power   361
Targeted Balancing   362
Conclusion   362

Index   369

CONTRIBUTORS

Michael Cox is professor emeritus of international relations at London School of Economics. His recent publications include *Soft Power and US Foreign Policy: Theoretical, Historical and Contemporary Perspectives* (coauthored, Routledge, 2010) and *The Global 1989: Continuity and Change in World Politics* (coauthored, Cambridge University Press, 2010).

Rosemary Foot, FBA, is professor emerita of international relations and a senior research fellow in the Department of Politics and International Relations, University of Oxford. Her latest publications include (with Andrew Walter) *China, the United States, and Global Order* (Cambridge University Press, 2011); *China across the Divide: The Domestic and Global in Politics and Society* (edited, Oxford University Press, 2013); and *The Oxford Handbook of the International Relations of Asia* (Oxford University Press, 2014), coedited with Saadia M. Pekkanen and John Ravenhill.

Jonathan Holslag is professor of international politics at the Free University of Brussels. His two latest books are *China and India: Prospects for Peace* (Columbia University Press, 2010) and *Trapped Giant* (IISS and Routledge, 2011).

G. John Ikenberry is the Albert G. Milbank Professor of Politics and International Affairs at Princeton University in the Department of Politics and the Woodrow Wilson School of Public and International Affairs. His recent works include *After Victory: Institutions, Strategic Restraint, and the Rebuilding of Order after Major Wars* (Princeton, 2001) and *Liberal Leviathan: The Origins, Crisis, and Transformation of the American System* (Princeton, 2011).

Johan Lagerkvist is senior research fellow in the East Asia Program of the Swedish Foreign Policy Institute and Professor of Chinese Language and Culture at SCORE (Stockholm Centre For Organizational Research) Stockholm University. He is the author of the widely acclaimed book *After* *the Internet, Before Democracy: Competing Norms in Chinese Media and Society*. (Princeton, 2010)

Christopher Layne is a University Distinguished Professor, Robert M. Gates Chair in National Security, and professor of international affairs at the Bush School of Government and Public Service at Texas A&M University. Professor Layne has written two books: *The Peace of Illusions: American Grand Strategy from 1940 to the Present* (Cornell University Press, 2006) and *American Empire* (Routledge, 2006).

Steven E. Lobell is professor of political science at the University of Utah. He is the author of *The Challenge of Hegemony* (University of Michigan Press, 2003); he is coeditor of *Neoclassical Realism, the State, and Foreign Policy* (Cambridge University Press, 2009), *Beyond Great Powers and Hegemons* (Stanford University Press, 2012), and *The Challenge of Grand Strategy* (Cambridge University Press, 2012); and he is co-author of *Neoclassical Realist Theory of International Politics* (Oxford University Press, 2016).

Geir Lundestad has been the director of the Norwegian Nobel Institute in Oslo and the secretary of the Norwegian Nobel Committee 1990–2014. Among his recent works are *The United States and Western Europe: From "Empire" by Invitation to Transatlantic Drift* (edited, Oxford University Press, 2003) and *International Relations since the End of the Cold War* (edited, Oxford University Press, 2013).

Liselotte Odgaard is an associate professor at the Royal Danish Defence College. Among her recent work are *China and Coexistence: Beijing's National Security Strategy for the 21st Century* (Woodrow Wilson Center Press/Johns Hopkins University Press, 2012); "Beijing's Quest for Stability in its Neighborhood: China's Relations with Russia in Central Asia," *Asian Security* 13, no. 1 (2017): 41–58; and *Strategy in NATO: Preparing for an Imperfect World* (Edited, Palgrave MacMillan, 2014).

Minxin Pei is the Tom and Margot Pritzker '72 Professor of Government and the director of the Keck Center for International and Strategic Studies at Claremont McKenna College. He is the author of *From Reform to Revolution: The Demise of Communism in China and the Soviet Union* (Harvard University Press, 1994) and *China's Trapped Transition: The Limits of Developmental Autocracy* (Harvard University Press, 2006).

Zhang Ruizhuang is professor of international relations and dean of the Academy of International Studies at Nankai University, Tianjin, China. He has published extensively in Chinese, with his latest book being *The*

Unharmonious World (Shanghai Peoples' Publishing House, 2010). A book chapter in *Global Giant: Is China Changing the Rules of the Game?* (Palgrave Macmillan, 2009) is his recent publication in English.

David Shambaugh is Gaston Sigur Professor of Asian Studies, Political science, and International Affairs and Director of the China Policy Program at George Washington University. His recent books include: *China's Future* (2016); *The China Reader: Rising Power* (2016); *Tangled Titans: The United States and China* (2013); and *China Goes Global: The Partial Power* (2013).

Yoshihide Soeya is professor of political science and international relations at the Faculty of Law of Keio University. His publications in English include *Japan's Economic Diplomacy with China, 1945–1978* (Clarendon Press, 1998) and *Japan as a 'Normal Country'?: A Country in Search of its Place in the World* (edited, University of Toronto Press, 2011).

Asle Toje is the research director at the Norwegian Nobel Institute in Oslo. His most recent publications include *The European Union as a Small Power: After the Post-Cold War* (Macmillan, 2010) and *Neoclassical Realism in Europe* (coedited, Manchester University Press, 2012).

Stephen M. Walt is the Robert and Renée Belfer Professor of International Affairs at Harvard University. His recent publications include *The Origins of Alliances* (Cornell University Press, 1987) and *Taming American Power: The Global Response to U.S. Primacy* (W. W. Norton, 2005).

Odd Arne Westad is professor of international history at the London School of Economics and Political Science. Professor Westad's most recent book is *Restless Empire: China and the World since 1750* (Random House, 2012). With Melvyn P. Leffler he coedited the three-volume *Cambridge History of the Cold War* (Cambridge University Press, 2010).

William C. Wohlforth is the Daniel Webster Professor of Government in the Dartmouth College Department of Government. He is the author of *Elusive Balance: Power and Perceptions during the Cold War* (Cornell, 1993); and editor of *Cold War Endgame: Oral History, Analysis, and Debates* (Penn State, 2003) and *World out of Balance: International Relations and the Challenge of American Primacy* (with S. G. Brooks, Princeton University Press, 2008).

Introduction

ASLE TOJE

"We do not want to place anyone into the shadow, we also claim our place in the sun." In a foreign policy debate in the German parliament on December 6. 1897 Secretary of State for Foreign Affairs, Bernhard von Bülow, articulated the foreign policy aspirations of the ascendant Wilhelmine Germany. This proved easier said than done. In 1907, Eyre Crowe of the British Foreign Office penned his famous memorandum where he accounted for "the present state of British relations with France and Germany." He concluded that Britain should meet imperial Germany with "unvarying courtesy and consideration" while maintaining "the most unbending determination to uphold British rights and interests in every part of the globe."[1] Crowe saw the rise of Germany in the international system as a threat to the British Empire, one that had to be balanced. Four decades later, George F. Kennan drew rather similar conclusions in his "long telegram" outlining the US containment strategy toward the Soviet Union.[2]

The lessons derived from these twin struggles for supremacy cast long shadows on contemporary international affairs. Similar debates today rage about how the rise of China should best be handled by the incumbent powers in general and the sole remaining superpower, the United States, in particular. The rise and fall of great powers continue to preoccupy scholars of all stripes. It has been the topic of some of the most enduring works of academia, from Thucydides via Edward Gibbon to modern scholars, among them Paul Kennedy, , Raymond Aron, Susan Strange and Graham Allison.

The previous wave of publications on this topic came a little more than two decades ago. At that time, the key question was how the international system would cope with the demise of the Soviet Union and with it the bipolar international system. What was perhaps most surprising about the collapse of the Soviet Union was just how little it affected the security, stability, and legitimacy in the international system. The reason why this question has gained fresh salience is, of course, due to a single event: the rapid ascension of the People's Republic of China (PRC). A number of measures can be employed, ranging from GDP statistics to industrial output, military strength and currency reserves; they all have in common that they are disputed and that they all tell the same story—one of rapid and sustained expansion.

So will the rise of China bring continuity or rupture? To answer this question, scholars from different branches of academia and from different corners of the globe have been invited to consider China's rise and its implications. To assess a topic as vast as this, it is important to define the terms employed. Will China's rise be peaceful? The term "peace" is a notoriously slippery one. Peace Studies as an academic subdiscipline tends to approach peace, not just as the absence of war—"negative peace"—but also the establishment of human development values and structures, or "positive peace." For scholars such as Johan Galtung, negative peace is seen to be a necessary but not a sufficient condition for positive peace, defined as "the integration of human society."[3] The assumption that globalization and conflict are mutually exclusive is far from self-evident, as history shows. In this volume, "peaceful" will, therefore, be understood as "negative peace" in general, and the absence of great power war in particular.

What is meant by the rise of China? Clearly we are talking about the PRC and not the Republic of China—which is referred to as Taiwan. Economists argue over if and when China will overtake the United States as the world's biggest national economy. While some of our contributors argue that the shift has already taken place, others are skeptical, arguing that Chinese growth figures leave a somewhat misleading impression due to a low starting point. Two statistics that illustrates this are that China is the world's largest exporter, with some 12 percent of the global total according to the International Monetary Fund; it has the largest energy consumption and carbon dioxide emissions in the world, outstripping the United States and the EU, according to the International Energy Agency; and it has lifted more than 500 million people out of poverty, as China's poverty rate fell from 88 percent in 1981 to 6.5 percent in 2012, according to the World Bank.[4]

The yardsticks by which scholars measure power vary in accordance with what they believe to be the most important power resources—economic, military, institutional, industrial, or "soft"—but most analytical pathways seem to end up in a broadly similar landscape. The economic strength and technological superiority that were the sources of Western primacy have become more evenly distributed during the first two decades on the 2000s, and China is a primary beneficiary of this age of globalization. For all this apparent ambition, Chinese leaders are not bent on global domination. They show limited interest in geopolitics beyond Asia, except perhaps in Africa, where China's power and reach are frequently overestimated.

"There are two ways of constructing an international order," Henry Kissinger wrote in 1957: "by will or by renunciation; by conquest or by legitimacy."[5] China cannot plausibly be said to pursue either. China's unilateral claims to disputed islands in the South China Sea, seeking to exploit oil resources in disputed waters, and attempting to unilaterally regulate airspace over contested waters have been carried out without any apparent strategy for how this is to be translated into regional primacy. China is neither a on a populist ideological mission nor is it a particularly successful "normative power," shaping the rules that others play by. The Beijing authorities' normative ambitions have been centred on owning the narrative of China's rise, cloaking it in peaceful euphemisms. China goes to great lengths to frame its ambitions in anything but realist terms, arguing that it's rise is essentially more benign than past power transitions. Others see in China's 'one belt, one road' -initiative the control of the Eurasian "heartland-theory" of Halford Mackinder and in the rapid development of a blue water navy, the imprint of Alfred Thayer Mahan's theory of sea power as the bedrock of hegemony.[6] Yet Chinese assertiveness in the near abroad has strained relations with some of its neighbors and with the United States. Steve Bannon, chief strategist to US President Donald Trump, claimed before the election in 2016, "We're going to war in the South China Sea in the next five to ten years."[7] Bannon perceives China as dangerously expansionist and increasingly militarized and confident.

The growth of Chinese power and the concern this causes among other powers point us to the crux of the matter. Peaceful power transitions are the exception in history.[8] Speaking on a visit to Washington in September 2013, Wang Yi, China's then foreign minister, referred to a study of fifteen historical cases of rising powers. In eleven of these cases, "confrontation and war have broken out between the emerging and established powers."[9] He did not present a list of which cases he was referring to. Graham Allison came to the rescue with his book on what he calls *Thucydides's Trap* where he examines sixteen cases since the 15th century when a rising power challenges an incumbent. Three quarters ended in war. Mr Allison concludes that war between China and the United States is "more likely than not."[10]

Others argue that peaceful transfers of power have after all taken place, as when the United States replaced Great Britain as the leading power. The rapid rise of Japan and Germany did not challenge the Cold War order, and the bipolar US-USSR rivalry also ended without war. In fact, all the wars Professor Allison examine took place before nuclear weapons were invented. China's rise coincides with an even larger phenomenon: globalization has made the world ever more integrated and interdependent, seemingly discouraging war between states in general and great powers in particular. This lends strength to the thesis illuminated by G. John Ikenberry in this volume: perhaps the stakes have grown too high and the potential rewards too limited? History, as so often is the case, offers no single lesson. The rise and fall of great powers may destabilize an international system, and they may not.

Thucydides pointed to the importance of regime type in his explanation of why actors behave a certain ways when dealing with other powers. E. H. Carr emphasized the role of public opinion; Hans Morgenthau looked to ideology and domestic politics; and George Kennan's most famous and influential work rooted the sources of Soviet conduct in the unique historical experience of Russia.[11] In his seminal study *Perception and Misperception in International Politics*, Robert Jervis argued that states may undertake what appear to be threatening actions for two very different reasons: fear or insecurity versus expansionist greed.[12] The problem is that depending on the nature of the perceived aggressive regime, two very different courses of action are prescribed—appeasement and accommodation works on the fearful, while the revisionist power only responds to strength and deterrence. The United States can, thus far, not be said to have pursued either strategy versus China.

The rise of China is set to be one of the grand events of the twenty-first century. But whether this story will be one of triumph or tragedy, and for whom, is yet to be determined. At the same time, a growing list of economic and territorial disputes seems to indicate that as Chinese power grows their corresponding interest increasingly come into direct competition with the interests of other actors in a strategic environment provided by the economic and military power of states, which they do not control.

KEY DIMENSIONS

The present volume sheds light on five core debates concerning China's rise. One is the question of whether it will seek to be a global power, or whether its aspirations are regional. A second question is the question of relative importance and permanence of economic and military strength in contemporary geopolitics. This leads on to the third question, that of the nature of the current international order. To what extent is it malleable enough to accommodate the rise of new major powers, and to what extent is it inseparable from American hegemony? This plays into the fourth of the overarching themes: can other powers accommodate China's rise, or will they more likely seek to balance and bandwagon for and against it? A final debate is the question of power transition and whether the best answers to the future trajectory of China are to be found in political science theory, or in the analysis of history.

Is China a regional or global power? Predicting China's rise to global hegemony has in recent years become somewhat of an academic cottage industry influenced by John Mearsheimer's dictum, that "potential hegemons [are] strongly inclined to become real hegemons."[13] The authors in the present volume question this assumption. While several of the contributors, led by Stephen Walt and Cristopher Layne, see a Chinese ambition for regional hegemony, none sees any such global ambitions, except, perhaps, in the long term. The authors in this volume agree that China is not, nor does it seek to be, a global peer competitor to the United States. China has no desire to build a far-flung empire. The appropriate level of analysis is thus regional. But, as Liselotte Odgaard points out, it is in its own region that China faces its most difficult strategic environment.

What sort of power is China? In a military sense, China remains predominantly a land power with a limited capacity to project power beyond its borders. Chinese military power is more comparable to that of Russia, India, or Japan than it is to that of the United States. This is not necessarily a debilitating weakness, since China compensates in terms of economic strength. Much of the literature on China's rise is nevertheless premised on a problematic assumption: that China will be able to maintain its impressive growth rates in the medium to long term. Several of the authors, led by David Shambaugh and Minxin Pei, question China's ability to outrun its "internal contradictions." Two other hegemons-in-waiting, Japan and the European Union, have—after all—failed to live up to their great power potential in the post-Cold War period. Out of the BRICS (Brasil, Russia, India, China, and South Africa) only China has delivered on its promise in the past decade. Bejing faces challenges ranging from a rapidly aging population to corruption, inequality, human rights abuses, and market failures that may hamper the projected growth pattern. Johan Lagerkvist and Zhang Ruizhuang offer insights into political, economic, and cultural challenges facing Chinese leaders.

The nature of the international system. Does the rise of China represent a threat to the liberal international order? If China espouses an alternative vision of world order, that would be the case. Perhaps to counter such concerns President Xi's speech to the Davos Conference in 2017 was a full-throated defense of the liberal international order.[14] Yet, shaping the norms and new rules of the order is the privilege of hegemony. Though often on opposing sides, G. John Ikenberry and William C. Wohlforth in this volume offer complementary views on international order being shaped by the established powers and of that order being favorable to its creators—prolonging their dominance. Powers that favor the status quo, most often those who participate in drawing up the "house rules," stand to benefit from these rules; revisionist powers tend to be dissatisfied with their place in the system and wish to revise the same rules to their own advantage.

This seems to be an apt summary of China, which, as Rosemary Foot points out, harbors a list of grievances that other powers have not taken very seriously. For this reason, Foot advises vigilant caution. Robert Gilpin has provided a blow-by-blow description of the breakdown of international order: rules are challenged by those who see the status quo as favoring established powers; the leading powers grow less willing to make sacrifices to maintain a system that is allowing other powers to rise. This breeds insecurity, uncertainty, and risk behavior that increase the chance of war.[15] In the present context, that could mean China in the future may attempt to make similar claims to the perceived "exceptionalism" the United States has granted itself in the aftermath of the Cold War. Rosemary Foot, William C. Wohlforth, and G. John Ikenberry—from different vantage points—argue that the current international order is both more malleable and robust than is sometimes assumed.

The response of other powers. There is another key variable in the equation of China's rise, namely the relative decline this entails for the incumbent hegemon, the United States. In 1987 Paul Kennedy published his seminal work, *The Rise and Fall of Great Powers*.[16] Much of the academic and popular fascination with that book was spun from the few pages toward the end under the subheading "The problem of number one in relative decline." What Kennedy argued, in effect was—as with all great thoughts—self-evident and deeply controversial: the United States of America is not exempt from history. Having grown accustomed to primacy in the international system, the United States experienced a period of uncharacteristic self-doubt in the 1980s that resonated with Kennedy's line of argument—that hegemons tend to get overstretched. Then, in apparent defiance of Kennedy's argument, America's main rival collapsed and a spurt of renewed growth lodged the country firmly, undisputedly as the world's leading power. Some even took to referring to the post-Cold War system as the Pax Americana. Christopher Layne and David Shambaugh both see this as a particular challenge; the latter predicts a "Teddy Roosevelt moment" as China moves politically on to the stages where it carries economic weight. Layne concludes that "China and the United States are on a collision course."

As long as China goes it alone, this challenge can be managed, but what if other secondary powers choose to balance and bandwagon for and against China, creating the conditions for regional conflict? The present volume gives a low probability of any such revisionist coalition arising. Yoshihide Soeya sees less inherent potential for conflict in Sino-Japanese relations, mainly because Japan lacks rival great power ambitions. Jonathan Holslag concludes that India has clear interests in balancing China, but remains woefully underequipped to do so. Michael Cox shows that shared opposition to a unipolar world has failed to translate into a genuine geopolitical partnership, due to many of the same reasons that hampered Sino-Russian relations during the Cold War.

The final discussion regarding the relative merits of political science theory and historical analysis in assessing the rise of China is a bone of contention among the contributors. While G. John Ikenberry, Stephen M. Walt, and Wiliam C. Wohlforth disagree about whether liberal realist theory offers the best insights into the rise of China, they share a conviction that theory can bring important insights to bear on this complex picture, insights that have policy implications. Geir Lundestad takes a different view. He points to how theory often is derived from historical examples, examples that he argues are frequently hand-picked to fit with a preferred conclusion. Lundestad is disparaging when it comes to the possibility using "lessons from history" to achieve or, indeed, avoid certain outcomes. He is countered by Odd Arne Westad and Christopher Layne, who attempt to demonstrate the relevance of the past in understanding contemporary China. In the final chapter, Steven Lobell takes up the gauntlet and presents a New Model of Realist Major Power Relations—a more finely tuned and more granular understanding of how state leaders gauge power relations and how they can balance against specific elements of China's power without triggering all-out rivalry.

SECURITY, STABILITY, AND LEGITIMACY

Many, perhaps most, edited volumes are less coherent than they purport to be. This volume is different in that regard. The spine of this book is made up by three key concepts: security, stability, and legitimacy. The question of security is understood narrowly as pertaining to questions of war and peace: will China's rise continue to be peaceful? A second set of questions considered by the authors is what sort of stability does a rising China provide for whom, and at what price? This concerns the resilience of the norms, institutions, and patterns underpinning the current order. How does the rise of China affect its own behavior, relations with and among other great powers, and the stability in the regions where Chinese power is most apparent? Although peace and stability are highly desirable, a third vital question is that of legitimacy. China, after all, is gaining in wealth, power, and prestige in an international system that is more norm and rule bound than any before it.

The rise of China will, for better or for worse, transform East Asian security and impact global security. As China's power and influence grows, so do its interests. China's outer rim is dotted with potential flashpoints, from the divided Korean peninsula to the Senkaku/Diaoyu dispute, to the question of Taiwan, not to mention dormant border disputes with India and Russia. American security guarantees to its friends and allies bring the world's most powerful state into several of these equations. The historical odds are, as mentioned, not necessarily favorable, but they are not insurmountable. This volume outlines the promises and pitfalls of a rising China.

A third aspect concerns legitimacy. Much has been written on the question of legitimacy in international affairs. It is not entirely certain how it is distinguished from acceptance or acquiescence. For all its nebulosity, the concept is nonetheless helpful. Some regimes are widely accepted; others are not. Legitimacy as it will be used in this volume is defined as "in accordance with established rules, principles or standards," in short, that a given state of affairs "can be justified."[17] This adds a moral dimension that distinguishes legitimacy from acceptance or, indeed, acquiescence. For instance, as is highlighted by Yoshihide Soeya, the Chinese position on maritime borders in the South China Sea may well be stated as fact, but this does not necessarily mean that the Chinese position is seen as just or legitimate, at least not by states that harbor contrary claims.

STRUCTURE

In analyzing the three sets of problems, the participants have been loosely grouped into four sections. In the first one, Stephen Walt and G. John Ikenberry deal with the political science perspectives on the rise and fall of great powers from a realist and liberal perspective, respectively. William C. Wohlforth and Rosemary Foot discuss the mechanics and implications of power transitions. This is followed by the historians. Geir Lundestad and Christopher Layne write on the uses of history, which historical examples are relevant, and which are not, while Odd Arne Westad offers insights on the weight of the past in China's relations with its Asian neighbors. The third section shifts attention to domestic perspectives, where Minxin Pei highlights the strengths and weaknesses of the "China model." His perspectives are contrasted by Johan Lagerkvist's analysis of patterns of cooperation and conflict among various groups in Chinese society. This plays into the dual questions of what role China wishes to play in the current global order, and what role the West sees for China. David Shambaugh and Zhang Ruizhuang take on the view from China. The final section addresses the responses to China's rise. Liselotte Odgaard offers an analysis of Chinese self-perceptions and responses to its policies in contested waters. Yoshihide Soeya, Jonathan Holslag, and Michael Cox present views from Japan, India, and Russia, respectively, while Steven Lobell elaborates the mechanics of the crucial Sino-American relationship.

It is our hope that the edited volume, which stems from the authors' collective endeavors that began with a Nobel Symposium held in Oslo in 2014, will serve three broad objectives. One is to provide a handy summing up of the status quo of the research into the patterns of great power conflict and cooperation in the present world order. This is, needless to say, a topic of great interest to a great many people. Our collective effort will be of help to students, scholars, policy makers, and the general public alike. If, by having succeeded in answering some questions, we have created new ones, that is all the more welcome. Different authors reach different conclusions; each is only to be held accountable for his or her own chapter. The third—and most important—ambition is to put forth a good read. As the editor, my goal with this book is to give readers some pleasant moments while giving them new perspectives and insights on this, the most pressing question of contemporary international politics.

NOTES

1. Eyre Crowe, "Memorandum on the Present State of British Relations with France and Germany, January 1, 1907," in *British Documents on the Origins of the War, 1898–1914*, ed. G. P. Gooch and Harold William Vazeille Temperley (London: H.M.S.O., 1928), The Testing of the Entente, 1904–6, 3: 419.
2. John Lewis Gaddis, *George F. Kennan: An American Life* (New York: Penguin Press, 2011), 201–25.
3. Johan Galtung, "An Editorial," *Journal of Peace Research* 1, no. 1 (1964): 1–4.
4. Sources: "International Trade Statistics 2015," World Trade Organization, 2015, www.wto.org/english/res_e/statis_e/its2015_e/its2015_e.pdf; "Energy and Climate Change: World Energy Outlook Special Report," International Energy Agency, 2015, www.iea.org/publications/freepublications/publication/WEO2015SpecialReportonEnergyandClimateChange.pdf; www.worldbank.org/en/country/china/overview#3.
5. Henry Kissinger, *A World Restored: Metternich, Castlereagh and the Problems of Peace* (Boston: Houghton Mifflin, 1957), 1, 172.
6. Mackinder, H.J., "The Geographical Pivot of History", The Geographical Journal, Vol. 23, No.4, (April 1904), 421–437; Mahan, A. T. 2010. The influence of sea power upon the French revolution and empire, 1793–1812. Cambridge: Cambridge University Press.

7. The quote stems from an online Breitbart radio show that was widely reported, inter alia by Benjamin Haas, *Guardian*, February 2, 2017.
8. Paul M. Kennedy, *The Rise and Fall of the Great Powers: Economic Change and Military Conflict from 1500 to 2000* (New York: Random House, 1987), 9.
9. Banyan, "One Model, Two Interpretations," *Economist*, September 28, 2013.
10. Graham T. Allison Destined for war: can America and China escape Thucydides's trap? Houghton Mifflin Harcourt, 2017.
11. Edward H. Carr, *The Twenty Years' Crisis, 1919–1939: An Introduction to the Study of International Relations* (Basingstoke: Palgrave, 2001); H. J. Morgenthau, *Politics among Nations: The Struggle for Power and Peace* (New York: Knopf, 1967); George Frost Kennan, *The Sources of Soviet Conduct* (New York: Council on Foreign Relations, 1947).
12. Robert Jervis, *Perception and Misperception in International Politics* (Princeton, NJ: Princeton University Press, 1967).
13. John J. Mearsheimer, "The Future of the American Pacifier," *Foreign Affairs*, September/October, 2001, 46–61.
14. "President Xi's Speech to Davos in Full," World Economic Forum, January 17, 2017, https://www.weforum.org/agenda/2017/01/full-text-of-xi-jinping-keynote-at-the-world-economic-forum.
15. Robert Gilpin, *War and Change in World Politics* (Cambridge: Cambridge University Press, 1982).
16. Paul M. Kennedy, *The Rise and Fall of the Great Powers: Economic Change and Military Conflict from 1500 to 2000* (London: Hyman, 1989), 514.
17. Geir Lundestad, *The Fall of Great Powers: Peace, Stability, and Legitimacy* (Oslo: Scandinavian University Press, 1994), xiv.

PART I
China and the International Order

CHAPTER 1
Rising Powers and the Risks of War

A Realist View of Sino-American Relations

STEPHEN M. WALT

INTRODUCTION

How will Sino-American relations evolve in the years ahead, and how will this relationship affect world politics? Optimists argue that a combination of global institutions, adroit diplomacy, and economic interdependence can limit the potential for rivalry and allow both sides to pursue a mostly cooperative path. By contrast, pessimists believe mutual fears and incompatible strategic objectives will doom the two countries to an increasingly intense competition.[1]

There are few global issues of greater significance. If relations between the United States and China remain positive, albeit with minor frictions, then prospects for regional stability in Asia will increase, cooperation on climate change, macroeconomic coordination, public health, and other global issues will be more likely, and citizens in both countries will lead more prosperous and secure lives. Only xenophobes and weapons manufacturers will be disappointed if this occurs.

But if Sino-American relations worsen and security competition intensifies, each will look for ways to take advantage of the other, cooperation will be more elusive, and the risk of war will increase. Sino-American rivalry might not reach the level of animosity of the Cold War, but it would still cast a dark shadow over world politics.

Which of these two scenarios is most likely? The issue is not what Sino-American relations will be tomorrow or next year; it is what they are likely to be over the next few decades, assuming China grows faster than the United States and the balance of power moves in Beijing's direction. To see what lies ahead, our best guide is a combination of theory and history.

Ever since Thucydides, the realist tradition in international relations has offered a clear and pessimistic answer to this question. Realist thinkers believe major shifts in the balance of power/threats are dangerous in a world lacking a central authority to preserve the peace, especially when a rising power is catching up to a previously dominant state. Such changes do not make war inevitable, but they increase the risk of war through several distinct causal paths.

Most importantly, realists believe these tendencies will be present whenever independent political units coexist in anarchy, irrespective of the cultural context, institutional setting, or other dimension of world order. Although diplomatic skill, shared political and cultural values, and adroit crisis management may mitigate these pressures and prevent open warfare from occurring, such features cannot eliminate the pressures for conflict that major power shifts invariably generate.

For realists, therefore, China's rise is not good news, and it is likely to have deleterious effects on global stability. If it continues, realist theory predicts growing suspicion between the United States and China, increased competition for allies and influence, and a heightened risk of war.

The rest of this chapter explores these issues at greater length. The first section presents the core logic of the realist perspective and explains why major changes in the balance of power make war more likely. The second section discusses a number of pertinent historical examples and shows that major shifts in the balance of power have led to trouble in the past in precisely the manner that realist theory predicts. The final section applies theory and history to the future of Sino-American relations, and explains why managing this relationship will be especially difficult.

THE BALANCE OF POWER AND THE RISKS OF WAR

Few sentences are more familiar to scholars of world politics than Thucydides's succinct explanation for the Peloponnesian War. "The growth of the power of Athens," he writes, "and the alarm which it inspired in Sparta, made war inevitable."[2] Scholars such as Robert Gilpin, Charles Doran, Dale Copeland, and A. F. K Organski and Jacek Kugler have elaborated on Thucydides's insight, and changing balances of power are both a key ingredient in John Mearsheimer's explanation for great power wars and central to his own pessimistic view of China's rise.[3]

Although these (and other) writers offer different accounts of the relationship between power and international conflict, each recognizes that international politics takes place in an anarchic order where no agency exists to protect states from one another and each must therefore rely upon its own resources and strategies to survive. In the resulting "self-help" system, behavior is driven by what Mearsheimer calls "the 911 problem: the absence of a central authority to which a threatened state can turn for help."[4] Anarchy does not make war inevitable by itself, but the lack of a legitimate central authority has a profound influence on relations between states. Because they cannot count on outside assistance or know for certain what others may do, states keep a keen eye on their own position vis-à-vis others.

But why do shifts in the balance of power make competition and war more likely? Realists identify four distinct causal pathways linking shifts in power to heightened competition and war.

Rising Powers Challenge the Status Quo to Enhance Security or Extract Benefits

Relations between states are regulated by a complex set of institutional arrangements. These arrangements can be as straightforward as mutually agreed borders or as complicated as the rules governing the World Trade Organization. These institutionalized understandings are a key element of international order and shape security arrangements between allies and adversaries alike. When these norms reflect the underlying balance of power and are accepted by the major powers, international stability increases. In this way, security, stability, and legitimacy are inextricably linked.[5]

Because powerful states have a greater capacity to shape these arrangements (or ignore them), the existing status quo invariably reflects the distribution of power at the time these arrangements were made. It will therefore reflect—albeit imperfectly—the interests of the strongest states.[6]

But such arrangements are not cast in stone. When new powers emerge, they will not passively accept arrangements established when they were weaker. They may embrace elements of the existing order that are compatible with their interests but choose to challenge any arrangements that place them at a disadvantage. The stronger a rising state becomes, the greater its capacity to modify those elements of the status quo it finds objectionable. Its goals may be limited to minor issues or may eventually entail a far-reaching challenge to the interests of the previously dominant powers.

If other states do not see the proposed revisions as undermining their own positions, a rising state's decision to challenge the status quo will not lead to conflict. Under these circumstances, proposed changes move the status quo to a more Pareto-optimal condition, leaving the rising state better off and no one else worse off.[7] But such benign outcomes are not guaranteed, and rising powers are likely to seek some changes that are in their own interest but not in the interest of others. When altering the status quo would harm other powerful countries and leave them in a weaker position in the future, a clash of national interests occurs.

Finally, although scholars have focused primarily on periods when a weaker power has risen to challenge the leading state(s), conflict can also occur when the balance of power shifts *in favor of* the most powerful state(s). Because the future is uncertain, even powerful and secure states may see a favorable shift as an opportunity to reduce lingering dangers, delay future challenges, and cement their privileged position for a longer period.[8] If they do, conflicts with the weaker powers now being disadvantaged will be more likely.

When the Soviet Union collapsed in 1992, for example, the United States did not simply declare victory and demobilize its vast national security establishment. Nor did it act as a "status quo" power. On the contrary, US leaders saw this "unipolar moment" as an opportunity to spread American ideals, overthrow or pressure recalcitrant "rogue states," and expand US influence. "Standing alone at the height of power," wrote former US national security advisor Brent Scowcroft, the United States "had the rarest opportunity to reshape the world."[9] Not surprisingly, the United States has been at war for two out of every three years since the end of the Cold War, in most instances seeking to remake other countries in accordance with US preferences.

In sum, significant changes in the balance of power lead to heightened conflicts of interest, as states with increased capabilities try to alter the status quo in their favor and as other states strive to prevent them.

Efforts to Change the Status Quo Encourage Malign Perceptions

In addition to expanding conflicts of interest, a powerful state's efforts to alter the status quo will lead other states to worry about its long-term intentions. Even if a rising power seeks only to correct unfair arrangements imposed on it when it was weak, other states are likely to wonder if its ambitions will grow as its capabilities increase.[10] Hardline elements among the status quo powers will be quick to interpret the rising power's actions as evidence of malign intent, eroding trust and making it more difficult to reach mutually acceptable compromises.

At the same time, the rising power is bound to interpret efforts to defend what it sees as an unfair status quo as part of a long-range effort to keep it weak or vulnerable. Because each state will see its own claims as legitimate and others' behavior as unwarranted, the potential for "spirals" of suspicion will increase.[11] Concerns for reputation and credibility will compound this tendency: because neither side can know how much its opponent wants, both will be tempted to engage in shows of resolve designed to to reinforce current claims and deter future challenges.

Shifts in the Balance of Power Encourage Preventive or Opportunistic Wars

Even when a rising power has not tried to alter the status quo, the fear that it may do so at a later date creates obvious incentives for preventive war. If a great power suspects that a rising state has or might eventually harbor revisionist aims, therefore, it will consider using force now to prevent or delay its rise.

Indeed, historian A. J. P. Taylor maintains that for the period 1848–1918, "every war between the great powers started out as a preventive war, not as a war of conquest."[12] This same logic led the Clinton administration to contemplate striking North Korea's nuclear facilities in 1994 and drove the Bush administration to invade Iraq in 2003. It was also routinely invoked by those who opposed the 2015 agreement limiting Iran's nuclear program, and who recommended the United States use force to destroy Iran's nuclear infrastructure instead.[13]

Rapid shifts in the balance of power can also encourage "wars of opportunity." Declining powers may be tempted to wage war to halt a rising power, but states whose enemies suddenly become weaker are often tempted to exploit a temporary advantage before it disappears. The wars that follow domestic revolutions sometimes take this form, if neighboring states see internal upheaval in a neighboring country as a chance to improve their own position.[14]

Preventive and/or opportunistic incentives increase even more when leaders believe the balance of power will fluctuate rapidly over time, because superiority today may vanish tomorrow and rivals will therefore be tempted to exploit any temporary advantage they are able to achieve. Moreover, the knowledge that both sides are facing similar incentives increases the temptation to strike whenever conditions are favorable. In this way, rapid and significant changes in the balance of power create recurring "windows of opportunity," and the fear of being the victim of aggression can convince even peacefully inclined leaders to be the aggressor instead. States do not always jump through these windows, but the more frequently they appear, the more that national leaders will consider opportunistic and/or preventive wars and the greater the long-term risk of conflict.[15]

Shifts in the Balance of Power Foster Miscalculation

Conflict and war are more likely when states disagree about their relative bargaining power. If two or more states do not know which one is stronger or more highly resolved, they are more likely to stumble into war, either because they exaggerate their own military prowess or because each believes others are less resolved and thus more likely to back down. By contrast, clarity about the balance of power or resolve reduces the danger of miscalculation: weaker states are less likely to challenge countries if they are far stronger and/or more resolute.[16]

It follows that major shifts in the balance of power encourage conflict by creating uncertainty about the outcome of a military clash. Such uncertainty does not necessarily mean that either side will deliberately start a war or provoke a crisis, but it makes it more likely that each side will take steps in a confrontation that increase the danger of war.

For example, Israel's decisive defeat of the Egyptian army during the 1956 Sinai War established a shared understanding of the balance of power between them and contributed to a decade of stability between the two states. Egypt's leaders understood Israel was militarily stronger and were careful not to cross Israel's "redlines." By the mid-1960s, however, Soviet arms shipments to Egypt, Syria, and Iraq had created greater uncertainty about the balance of power and made both Damascus and Cairo more inclined to take provocative positions vis-à-vis Tel Aviv. Although Egyptian leader Gamal Abdel Nasser did not seek war in May 1967, his foolhardy decision to expel the United Nations peacekeeping force, blockade the Straits of Tiran, and send Egyptian troops into the Sinai Peninsula in May 1967 reflected greater confidence about Egypt's ability to stand up to Israel in a protracted confrontation.[17] Nasser's costly blunder illustrates how the passage of time (and in this case, external military aid) increased uncertainty about the balance of power and induced less cautious behavior.[18]

Similarly, even when a rising power is clearly more capable than it used to be, neither its leaders nor its potential opponents can know for certain just how strong it has become. The degree of uncertainty will increase if the rising power is acquiring unfamiliar military technologies (such as a blue-water navy or sophisticated combined arms capabilities). Until its new capacities are tested in battle, no one can know who is stronger or by how much. Japan's decisive defeat of the Russian fleet at the Battle of Tsushima in 1904 illustrates this problem nicely: because Japan was a relative newcomer to modern naval warfare and the two adversaries had not fought each other at sea, neither Moscow nor Tokyo could anticipate the one-sided outcome in advance.[19]

For all these reasons, realism argues that major changes in the balance of power between states foster international competition and make war more likely. Interestingly, both offensive and defensive realists agree about the core logic embedded in the above propositions. Although defensive realists believe that incentives for conflict can be reduced by the development of defensive military postures and that security-seeking states can credibly signal benign intentions and avoid the spiral dynamics described above, they nonetheless recognize that major shifts in the balance of power are dangerous.[20]

To be sure, realist theory does not identify exactly how or why a specific dispute might arise or when it will escalate to war. Nor does realism provide reliable guidance about the precise timing of such disputes. For example, Mearsheimer's explanation for great power war relies on the logic of preventive war (i.e., in multipolar systems, great powers launch hegemonic wars when they gain a power advantage sufficient to take on the rest of the system), but he concedes that the timing of the resulting wars does not always correspond to his theory's predictions.[21]

THE HISTORICAL RECORD

Nonetheless, realism's emphasis on the central role of power and the destabilizing effects of change receives considerable support from the historical record. Since the emergence of the modern state system, in fact, rapid shifts in power—and especially the ascendance of new powers—are powerfully associated with conflict and war.

France was already a great power before the 1789 revolution began, but the social forces unleashed by the upheaval had profound effects on the European balance of power and ushered in more than two decades of recurrent warfare. In 1792, fears of revolutionary contagion and the belief that the revolution had weakened France's fighting capacity led Austria and Prussia to launch a half-hearted and feckless invasion, only to suffer an unexpected defeat at the battle of Valmy. Over the next decade, the mobilized forces of nationalism and patriotism produced *l'armée en masse* and a dramatic increase in France's military power, which Napoleon Bonaparte eventually used to conquer much of Europe. Misperception, ideological conflict, and personal ambition played key roles as well, but as Clausewitz recognized, shifts in power were critical to both the onset and continuation of these wars.[22]

Similarly, shifts in the balance of power played a key role in the onset of both World War I and World War II. In the former case, Germany's rapid rise spawned growing fears in France, Russia, and Great Britain. Repeated German efforts to adjust the international status quo led to increasingly malign views of German intentions and to the gradual formation of an anti-German Entente, developments that in turn reinforced German concerns about their long-term security position.[23] In particular, fears that Russia was beginning to develop its latent power potential convinced Germany's leaders they were in danger of falling behind and led them to launch an all-out bid for hegemony in 1914.[24]

In the latter case, a revanchist Nazi Germany abrogated the Versailles Treaty, rebuilt its military power, and launched a second attempt to subjugate Europe. Nazi ideology and Hitler's racist pathologies were obviously important, but so were German concerns about the long-term balance of power. In both 1914 and 1941, in short, German fears of Russia's greater power potential helped trigger a decision for war.

Japan's rise to great power status had similar effects. Japanese economic and military power rose dramatically following the Meiji Restoration, and Japan fought successful wars of expansion against China in 1895 and Russia in 1905. It tried unsuccessfully to take advantage of Russia's weakness after World War I and invaded Manchuria in 1931 as part of an ambitious attempt to establish a hegemonic position in Asia. Japan's leaders saw these decisions as necessary to ensure their long-term economic security and to reverse several centuries of Western domination in Asia.[25] Japan also sought to legitimate its regional dominance by portraying it as an assertion of Asian independence from European colonialism.

Unfortunately for Japan, its attempt to establish a "Greater East Asian Co-prosperity Sphere" put it on a collision course with the Roosevelt Administration, which was looking for a way to get the United States into World War II.[26] The result was Pearl Harbor and Japan's eventual defeat. Nonetheless, the entire course of relations in Asia from 1860 to 1945 is inextricably linked to Japan's rise, the ambitions its increased power encouraged, and the costly conflicts that resulted.

Rapid declines in power can cause trouble as well. The decline of British and French power after World War II was a permissive condition that sparked numerous anticolonial conflicts, as the depleted European powers were no longer strong enough to suppress movements for national liberation and colonial rule itself was no longer seen as legitimate. The collapse of the Soviet Union had a similar impact within the boundaries of Moscow's former empire and possibly in more distant areas (e.g., Africa) as well.

In anarchy, all states know nothing can prevent others from trying to improve their positions when the opportunity arises. Accordingly, the fear that others may seize an advantage tempts everyone to pursue such opportunities whenever they occur. In widely varying contexts, in short, the combination of fear, greed, and miscalculation fueled by shifts in power creates a potent recipe for trouble.

The Great Exception: America's Peaceful Rise

This brief glance at the historical record suggests realism's concerns about the impact of shifting power balances are well-founded. But there is an obvious exception: the United States. Beginning as thirteen weak and isolated colonies, the United States grew to be the world's largest economy by 1900 and established itself as a hegemonic power in the Western hemisphere. America's rise led to war with Mexico in 1846 and Spain in 1898, but it was never a direct cause of war with other great powers.

Instead, the United States supplanted Great Britain as the world's most powerful country without facing a serious risk of war with the British Empire. To be sure, relations between the United States and Great Britain were suspicious for much of the nineteenth century and London briefly considered intervening on the side of the Confederacy during the American Civil War. Yet as US power continued to rise, Britain gradually adopted a policy of appeasement, settled a series of territorial and commercial disputes in North and South America, and actively sought US entry into World War I.[27]

Democratic peace theorists attribute this anomaly to the pacifying effects of a shared liberal ideology,[28] but realism suggests a different explanation. Specifically, Britain chose to appease the United States because it was preoccupied by developments in Europe and especially the rise of German power on the continent. The United States was larger, wealthier, and had more latent power potential, but Germany had a large land army, an expanding Navy, revisionist ambitions, and was far closer to the British isles. Unlike the United States, Germany threatened to overturn the balance of power on the continent and establish itself as a European hegemon, precisely the outcome Britain had long sought to prevent.[29]

The United States, by contrast, was separated from the other great powers by two vast oceans. As a result, the other major powers worried far more about each other than about those bumptious upstarts in North America. As balance of threat theory explains, the United States eventually emerged as an ideal ally: it was strong enough to have a decisive impact on the Eurasian balance of power, but it was unlikely to try to conquer or colonize Eurasia itself.

As I have argued elsewhere, these features help explain the longevity of America's alliance networks in Europe and Asia, as well as the absence of any serious anti-American balancing coalition in the aftermath of the Cold War.[30] In brief, the United States is very powerful but not very threatening to most Eurasian states. And contrary to John Ikenberry's claim that this diminished level of threat is due mostly to the "self-binding" character of US-led liberal institutions, it is in fact largely the result of America's distant geographic position.[31]

The United States has also been an overly generous provider of security protection, either as part of its earlier strategy of containment or of discouraging other states from acquiring nuclear weapons. Thus, US allies in Europe and Asia do not bandwagon with American power because they are afraid of it; instead, they exploit American power to balance against various regional dangers. For these reasons, America's rise to world power did not have the same destabilizing effects that other major power shifts produced.

CHINA'S RISE AND THE FUTURE OF CONFLICT IN ASIA

If China's economic and military power continues to increase, realism predicts that the United States and China will increasingly see each other as rivals and will engage in more intense security competition.

The reasons are twofold. First, in anarchy, the two strongest states inevitably cast a wary eye on each other because each is the other's greatest potential threat. This tendency will be especially pronounced when neither state faces a more immediate threat to its security.

Second, as Mearsheimer has laid out in detail, China's rise poses a direct threat to the basic grand strategy that the United States has followed since becoming a great power.[32] Secretary of State John Kerry may have personally disavowed the Monroe Doctrine, but the United States still intends to remain the only great power in the Western hemisphere.[33] It also seeks to prevent any peer competitor from establishing hegemony in its own region. In practice, this goal means keeping other great powers out of the Western hemisphere and maintaining the political division of industrialized Eurasia. Together, these principles minimize direct threats to the US homeland and encourage other great powers to worry primarily about each other and not about the United States.

If China continues to rise, however, it will eventually seek to push the United States out of East Asia, much as Washington pushed Britain and France out of the Western hemisphere at the end of the nineteenth century. The motivation behind this goal is obvious: no great power wants its primary competitor to have close security alliances with many of its neighbors and to deploy powerful military forces on or near its borders.

China's unfavorable geographic circumstances and its restricted access to the world's oceans magnify these concerns. China has been a land power for most of its history, but it will not remain one because its economy increasingly depends on overseas resources and markets. To minimize the risk of blockades or other trade disruptions, Chinese leaders will want a greater capacity to shape events in regions on which they may depend (e.g., the Persian Gulf or Africa), and they do not want the United States to be in a position to thwart them.

Over time, therefore, realism predicts an intensifying security competition between Beijing and Washington. Instead of a direct clash of arms, however, this competition is likely to consist primarily of a competition for allies and influence.[34] China will try to persuade its Asian neighbors to distance themselves from Washington, while US leaders will seek to expand and reinforce their existing network of Asian allies.[35]

China's rise is already causing most of its neighbors to balance against it, usually via some form of association with the United States. Maintaining a successful balancing coalition will be more difficult in Asia than it was in Europe during the Cold War, however, and it will require adroit diplomacy on the part of Washington and its various Asian partners.

Levels of Threat

Why are Asian states balancing against China? Realism gives a straightforward answer to the question: as China becomes more powerful, its neighbors worry about how it might use its growing capabilities. To preserve their autonomy, they are forging closer security ties with each other and with the United States.

The vigor of these responses depends not just on China's aggregate power, however, but rather on the *level of threat* that China poses to others.[36] The level of threat, in turn, will be affected not just by China's overall capabilities (i.e., its GDP, defense spending, technological base, etc.) but also by (1) geography, (2) offensive military capabilities, and (3) perceived intentions.

To be more specific, states that are closer to China will be more concerned than states that lie some distance away. Because projecting power over oceans is difficult, states that border directly on China—such as Vietnam—have to fear China's rising power more than states that are separated from China by large bodies of water—such as Indonesia. Similarly, states that have specific territorial disputes with China—such as Japan—will be more concerned than states that do not, such as Australia. Taiwan is a special case, given its proximity to the mainland and the tangled history of cross-strait relations.

The level of threat China poses will also depend on how it chooses to employ its growing wealth. If it acquires military forces and adopts military doctrines designed primarily for the defense of its own territory, China's neighbors will feel less threatened and be less inclined to balance vigorously. But if China continues to develop the power projection capabilities typical of other world powers (i.e., large naval and air forces, long-range missiles, amphibious capabilities, etc.), its neighbors will worry about how China's capabilities might be used and be more likely to join forces with each other and the United States.

Finally, the level of threat will also be affected by whether China is perceived as an ambitious revisionist power, or as a state committed to preserving the central features of the regional status quo. In terms of the framework set forth in the introduction to this volume: is China trying to maximize stability and legitimacy, or will its pursuit of security depend on destabilizing the existing arrangements and trying to legitimize a very different regional order?

Here China's shift to a more assertive regional diplomacy—expanding its territorial claims in the South China Sea, building up contested islands and reefs to consolidate those claims, overreacting to Japan's seizure of a fishing trawler in 2010, or declaring an "air defense security zone" in the East China Sea—stand in obvious contrast to its earlier emphasis on pursuing a "peaceful rise." But the more sharp elbows Beijing throws, the more mutual support others will seek and provide.[37] In April 2016, for example, US defense secretary Ashton Carter completed new defense cooperation agreements with the Philippines and with India, clearly inspired by mutual concerns about Chinese assertiveness.[38]

Obstacles to Effective Balancing Behavior

The decision to "rebalance" US foreign policy and military resources toward Asia suggests Washington is determined to prevent China from establishing hegemony there. And at first glance, prospects for successful balancing appear reasonably good. Although China has the greatest power potential in Asia, most of its neighbors are not so weak that they have little choice but to bandwagon with Beijing. Japan has the world's third-largest economy, a powerful national identity, a latent nuclear weapons capability, and significant military power of its own. Despite an aging population, Tokyo will be hard to intimidate unless it becomes completely isolated. Vietnam is never a pushover, India has a billion people, a growing navy, and its own nuclear arsenal, and states like Indonesia, the Philippines, and Singapore control strategically significant real estate and, in the case of Singapore, military strength disproportionate to their size. Last but not least, the Republic of Korea is now an impressive industrial power with significant military capabilities and an increasingly active diplomatic presence.

Furthermore, even a vastly more powerful China would have difficulty projecting significant power against most of its neighbors, because it would have to do so in the air and on the seas, realms where the United States still enjoys impressive advantages.[39] Given the US interest in preventing China from exercising regional hegemony, the potential targets of a Chinese drive for regional dominance would have a powerful ally ready to back them up.

For the United States and its Asian partners, this is good news. They can also take heart from the domestic challenges that are likely to slow China's rise and focus its leaders' attention inward.

These features have led some analysts to conclude that the danger of a hegemonic challenge, let alone a hegemonic war, is slight. In their contributions to this volume, for example, John Ikenberry, William Wohlforth, and Rosemary Foot all suggest that the sort of system-altering hegemonic challenge depicted in Robert Gilpin's *War and Change in World Politics* remains unlikely. Wohlforth reminds us that China's aggregate power will trail the United States for many years, and all three writers believe today's liberal world order still enjoys considerable legitimacy and that it would be difficult for even a far more powerful China to disrupt it. Nuclear weapons make a great power war even less likely, and economic interdependence gives Beijing a large stake in many aspects of the existing order. Accordingly, Ikenberry believes China's revisionist aims will be limited and sees no sign that Beijing seeks to replace today's international order with a radically different set of institutional arrangements.[40]

There is some truth in these assertions, and one can only hope their optimistic forecasts are correct. Nonetheless, there are good reasons to be skeptical. Even if China cannot match America's more diverse portfolio of power, it may become strong enough to challenge the existing security order in Asia, especially if the United States is unable to extricate itself from other international burdens. Beijing may have no reason to overturn the *entire* international order (i.e., the United Nations, World Bank, World Trade Organization, etc.), but a sustained challenge to US dominance in Asia would be trouble enough.

Moreover, once a low-level rivalry begins, it can easily take on a life of its own. Hegemonic conflicts do not always arise from a premeditated campaign to provoke one: the wars of the French Revolution began with a half-hearted Prussian and Austrian intervention on behalf of Louis XVI, but they eventually escalated to more than two decades of war on several continents. In the years ahead, what might begin as a limited skirmish over the South China Sea, Senkaku/Diaoyu Islands, Taiwan, or the two Koreas could easily turn into a far more dangerous test of strength.

Even if the United States and China avoid a Gilpinian struggle for hegemony, one can still foresee plenty of trouble. Because the US homeland is an ocean away, Washington's ability to maintain its present position in Asia depends on maintaining a reliable set of regional allies. Although the prerequisites for a strong balancing coalition are present, balancing does not always take place efficiently even when the level of threat is rising. And when balancing failures occur, the odds of miscalculation and predation increase.

Unfortunately, US efforts to maintain a credible balancing coalition in Asia will face significant obstacles. For starters, this coalition faces the usual dilemmas of collective action. Asian states may worry about a rising threat from China, but they will also be tempted to get others to bear as much of the burden as possible and to free or "cheap"-ride on the United States. There are worrisome signs of this tendency already: despite evident concerns about Chinese power, its Asian neighbors continue to spend remarkably low percentages of GDP on defense.[41]

Second, many of China's neighbors now have extensive economic ties with China and will be reluctant to jeopardize them. This situation stands in sharp contrast to the US-Soviet Cold War, where economic and security ties were almost perfectly aligned. The extensive economic ties between China and the United States complicate matters even more, recently leading Australian scholar Hugh White to see Chinese pressure on its neighbors as intended "to demonstrate the unsustainability of the American position of having a good relationship with China and maintaining its alliances in Asia."[42]

Third, there are still lingering historical resentments between some potential allies (most notably Japan and South Korea), compounded by territorial issues such as the continuing dispute over the Liancourt Rocks. Such frictions can interfere with efforts to promote closer security cooperation, as when South Korea backed away from an agreement for closer military and intelligence cooperation with Japan in 2012.[43]

Fourth, a balancing alliance in Asia requires the member-states to coordinate commitments across a vast geographic area. It is nearly three thousand miles by air from New Delhi to Taiwan, and some five thousand miles from Sydney to Seoul. If one country in Asia faced direct pressure from China, others will be tempted to look the other way and pretend their interests are not affected. Once again, a comparison with NATO is instructive: because distances in Europe were quite small (e.g., the distance from Paris to Bonn was a mere 250 miles), European leaders understood they faced a common threat from Soviet power, and Moscow could not play a effective strategy of "divide and conquer."

Fifth, these problems will encourage intense intra-alliance bargaining and could easily encourage resentment and disharmony. The Trump administration has sought to discourage free-riding by threatening to disengage if key allies do not do more, while states like South Korea, Japan, or Singapore have expressed doubts about US credibility and may threaten to bandwagon with Beijing if Washington tries to reduce its role. Both sides may be (mostly) bluffing, but such posturing can erode the trust and sense of common purpose needed to sustain effective partnerships. Policy makers will have to walk a fine line: providing enough reassurance to convince their partners that balancing will work, but not so much that they are taken for granted or exploited. And that will be a very fine line indeed.

Given these various obstacles, managing alliance relations in Asia will require more diplomatic effort and skill than it took to manage relations in Europe during the Cold War. Haphazard or inefficient balancing behavior is especially worrisome in this case, because it could undermine efforts to deter future Chinese provocations and make crises and/or the use of force more likely.

In short, realism offers a gloomy forecast for the future of Sino-American relations and the future of Asian security. As discussed above, major shifts in the balance of power tend to make international conflict more likely, for several different and mutually reinforcing reasons. At the same time, the particular features of Asia's geopolitics will make it harder to maintain the same kind of stable and tightly unified alliance network that helped keep the peace in Europe during the height of the Cold War. Neither factor augurs well for the future.

CONCLUSION

Since 2009, a growing number of experts have recognized the potential for serious Sino-American rivalry and begun to sound more worried notes. Nonetheless, well-qualified observers still believe a serious clash is not inevitable and that Sino-American relations can be "managed." In particular, they maintain that wise statecraft and sophisticated diplomacy could allow the two countries to avoid "Thucydides' trap."[44]

Such assertions are to some extent tautological: if all future tensions are managed "successfully," then by definition conflict was not inevitable. But we should not take much comfort from such truisms. If China's current and future leaders are consistently wise, sensible, mature, restrained, and in reliable control of contending political forces inside their country, then they may indeed act in ways that keep potential conflicts within bounds. Similarly, if all American officials are equally wise, mature, sensible, and restrained in the decades ahead, then they too will avoid needless provocations and help keep Sino-American relations on a (mostly) even keel. If we are lucky, other Asian leaders will act sensibly too. In short, if leaders in all the relevant capitals are prudent, enlightened, far-sighted, and peace-loving—not just now but for many years to come—then relations between these two great countries could remain tranquil and mutually beneficial.

But given all we know about politics and history, is it likely that paragons of the sort just described will always be in charge? Is it not more likely that at some point the government in Beijing or Washington or Tokyo or Seoul will be led by politicians and advisors who are ill-informed, impulsive, xenophobic, jingoistic, or just not very competent? Might that in fact be the situation we face today? We may even see a situation where leaders with these disturbing qualities are in power in several capitals simultaneously, raising serious doubts about their ability to "manage" the rivalry effectively.

What, therefore, is to be done? Realism offers no guarantees, alas, but it does suggest several possible courses of action. First, to the limited extent that they can, the United States (and others) should seek to slow the growth of Chinese power and especially its military elements. China's rise is probably impossible to prevent, but that rise will be easier for the rest of the world to accommodate if it occurs more gradually. Implementing this prescription will be hard, however, because neither Europe, Asia, nor the United States is likely to forego short-term economic benefits for the sake of the long-term balance of power. Moreover, limiting Chinese economic growth would be exceedingly hard to do without simultaneously provoking bitter Chinese resentment.

A slightly more promising step would be to clarify US and Chinese interests and set clearer redlines on issues such as Taiwan, the Korean Peninsula, and the increasingly vexing territorial issues in the South and East China Seas. Clarity could prevent miscalculation and discourage further Chinese encroachments, but achieving any sort of enduring understanding on these issues will not be easy, and any agreements that are reached will be subject to revision if the balance of power shifts further.

Third, the United States and China could pursue an agenda of confidence-building and crisis-management measures similar to the arrangements that helped stabilize US-Soviet relations during the Cold War. Agreements to avoid accidental encounters between air and naval forces fit under this heading and could be especially valuable if relations deteriorate. But such measures are no panacea, and it is hard to imagine either country halting all activities that could create the short-term frictions, such as US reconnaissance activities near China's shores and Chinese hacking of US computer sites.

None of these proposals would prevent a Sino-American rivalry, which underscores how difficult it will be to prevent China's rise from affecting Sino-American relations and the rest of world politics adversely. Given the likelihood of rising regional competition—which most of the authors in this volume anticipate—the United States should do more to nurture its existing alliance partners and strive to make its Asian alliance network work as effectively and efficiently as possible. In the decades ahead, effective alliance management offers the best chance for preserving a modicum of regional stability and avoiding a direct test of strength that would benefit no one.

Realism cannot predict the exact date serious trouble may arise or the precise circumstances under which it will occur. But it warns us that the potential for trouble is growing, that this trend will place new demands on national leaders, and that only a fool or a knave would count on human wisdom, clever diplomacy, or weak and contested international institutions to see us through safely.

NOTES

1. For optimistic liberal views, see David Lampton, *The Three Faces of Chinese Power: Might, Money and Minds* (Berkeley: University of California Press, 2008); and G. John Ikenberry, "Asian Regionalism and the Future of U.S. Strategic Engagement with China," in *China's Arrival: A Strategy Framework for a Global Relationship*, ed. Abraham Denmark and Nirav Patel (Washington, DC: Center for New American Security, 2009), 95–108. A cautiously optimistic realist forecast is

Charles L. Glaser, "Will China's Rise Lead to War?: Why Realism Does Not Mean Pessimism," *Foreign Affairs*, March/April 2011, 80–91. Henry Kissinger, *On China* (New York: Penguin, 2012), provides much evidence for why one should expect trouble in the future, but he reaches a surprisingly optimistic conclusion. For more pessimistic forecasts, see John J. Mearsheimer, *The Tragedy of Great Power Politics*, 2nd. ed. (New York: W. W. Norton, 2014), chap. 10; and Aaron Friedberg, *A Contest for Supremacy: China, America, and the Struggle for Mastery in Asia* (New York: W. W. Norton, 2012). For background, see Thomas C. Christensen, "Fostering Stability or Creating a Monster?: The Rise of China and U.S. Policy toward East Asia," *International Security* 31, no. 1 (Summer 2006): 81–126; and Yuen Foong Khong, "Primacy or World Order?: The United States and China's Rise," *International Security* 38, no. 3 (Winter 2013–2014): 153–75.

2. Robert Strassler, ed., *The Landmark Thucydides: A Comprehensive Guide to the Peloponnesian War* (New York: Simon & Schuster, 1996), 16.
3. See Robert Gilpin, *War and Change in World Politics* (New York: Cambridge University Press, 1981); Charles Doran, *Systems in Crisis: New Imperatives of High Politics at Century's End* (Cambridge: Cambridge University Press, 1991); Dale C. Copeland, *The Origins of Major Wars* (Ithaca, NY: Cornell University Press, 2000); A. F. K. Organski and Jacek Kugler, *The War Ledger* (Chicago: University of Chicago Press, 1980); *Power Transitions: Strategies for the 21st Century*, ed. Ronald Tammen (New York: Chatham House, 2000); and Mearsheimer, *Tragedy of Great Power Politics*, chaps. 9–10. The most recent attempt to apply Thucydides' insight to the issue of Sino-American relations is Graham T. Allison, *Destined for War?: Can America and China Escape Thucydides' Trap?* (New York: Houghton Mifflin, 2017).
4. Mearsheimer, *Tragedy of Great Power Politics*, 32; also see Kenneth N. Waltz, *Theory of International Politics* (Reading, MA: Addison-Wesley, 1979), 111–14.
5. The chapters by Asle Toje, Martha Finnemore, John Ikenberry, and Rosemary Foot in this volume all highlight this role of international institutions.
6. See in particular Lloyd Gruber, *Ruling the World: Power Politics and the Rise of Supranational Institutions* (Princeton, NJ: Princeton University Press, 2001).
7. See Stephen D. Krasner, "Global Communications and National Power: Life on the Pareto Frontier," *World Politics* 43, no. 3 (1991): 336–66.
8. See Nuno Monteiro, *Theory of Unipolar Politics* (Cambridge: Cambridge University Press, 2014).
9. George W. Bush and Brent Scowcroft, *A World Transformed* (New York: Alfred A. Knopf, 1998), 564.
10. For example, the United States began as thirteen vulnerable colonies seeking to stay out of global quarrels, but it eventually became a mighty global power with far-flung "vital interests."
11. On the so-called spiral model, see Robert Jervis, *Perception and Misperception in International Politics* (Princeton, NJ: Princeton University Press, 1976), chap. 3; and Charles Glaser, "The Security Dilemma Revisited," *World Politics* 50, no. 1 (October 1997): 171–201.
12. A. J. P. Taylor, *The Struggle for Mastery in Europe 1848–1918* (London: Oxford University Press, 1966), 166.
13. See Matthew Kroenig, "Time to Attack Iran," *Foreign Affairs* 91, no. 1 (January/February 2012): 76–86; and Alan J. Kuperman, "There's Only One Way to Stop Iran," *New York Times*, December 23, 2009.

14. On "opportunistic wars," see Geoffrey Blainey, *The Causes of War*, 3rd ed. (New York: Free Press, 1988), chap 8. On the relationship between domestic revolution and opportunistic wars, see Stephen M. Walt, *Revolution and War* (Ithaca, NY: Cornell University Press, 1996), 32–33.
15. On "windows of opportunity," see Stephen Van Evera, *Causes of War: Power and the Roots of Conflict* (Ithaca, NY: Cornell University Press, 1999), chap. 4; Richard Ned Lebow, "Windows of Opportunity: Do States Jump Through Them?," *International Security* 9, no. 1 (Summer 1984): 147–86; and Michael Shane Smith, "Windows of Opportunity and Military Escalation: Bringing Diplomatic Factors Back In" (PhD diss., University of Colorado, 2003).
16. See Blainey, *Causes of War*; and also James D. Fearon, "Rationalist Explanations for War," *International Organization* 49, no. 3 (Summer 1995): 379–414.
17. See in particular Roland Popp, "Stumbling Decidedly into the Six Day War," *Middle East Journal* 60, no. 2 (Spring 2006): 281–309.
18. See Elli Lieberman, "What Makes Deterrence Work?: Lessons from Egyptian-Israeli Enduring Rivalry," *Security Studies* 4, no. 4 (Summer 1995): 851–910.
19. Japan's decision for war in 1904 was also based on fears that Russian power in the Far East was increasing rapidly. According to Ian Nish, "[T]he Japanese feared the increase in Russian power in east Asia since 1900 . . . . Some Russians did record Japan's military growth but the general reaction of the Russian military seems to have been to discount her army and navy." See *The Origins of the Russo-Japanese War* (London: Longman, 1985), 256.
20. On the ability of states to signal peaceful intentions, see Charles L. Glaser, *Rational Theory of International Politics: The Logic of Cooperation and Competition* (Princeton, NJ: Princeton University Press, 2010). For a critique, see Sebastian Rosato, "The Inscrutable Intentions of Great Powers," *International Security* 39, no. 3 (Winter 2014–2015): 48–88.
21. Mearsheimer's theory implies Wilhemine Germany should have launched its bid for hegemony in 1905, when its relative power position was at its peak, rather than in 1914. See *Tragedy of Great Power Politics*, 216.
22. See Walt, *Revolution and War*, chap. 3. As Clausewitz notes, "[N]ot until statesmen had at last grasped the nature of the forces that had emerged in France . . . could they foresee the broad effects all this would have on war." See Carl von Clausewitz, *On War*, trans. M. Howard and P. Paret (Princeton, NJ: Princeton University Press, 1976), 609.
23. See Paul M. Kennedy, *The Rise of Anglo-German Antagonism, 1860–1914* (London: Allen & Unwin, 1980); Imanuel Geiss, *German Foreign Policy: 1871–1914* (London: Routledge and Kegan Paul, 1976), chaps. 10–12.
24. This interpretation follows Copeland, *Origins of Major War*, chaps. 3 and 4.
25. See Michael Barnhart, *Japan Prepares for Total War, 1919–1941* (Ithaca, NY: Cornell University Press, 1988).
26. See Marc Trachtenberg, "Developing an Interpretation through Textual Analysis: The 1941 Case," chap. 4 in *The Craft of International History: A Guide to Method* (Princeton, NJ: Princeton University Press, 2006).
27. See Bradford Perkins, *The Great Rapprochement: England and the United States, 1895–1914* (New York: Atheneum, 1968).
28. See especially John M. Owen IV, *Liberal Peace, Liberal War* (Ithaca, NY: Cornell University Press, 2000); and "How Liberalism Produces Democratic Peace," *International Security* 19, no. 2 (Fall 1994): 87–125.

29. As Winston Churchill put it, "For four hundred years the foreign policy of England has been to oppose the strongest, most aggressive, most dominating power on the Continent." See his *The Second World War*, vol. 1, *The Gathering Storm* (Boston: Houghton Mifflin, 1948), 207–8.
30. See Stephen M. Walt, *The Origins of Alliances* (Ithaca, NY: Cornell University Press, 1987), chap. 8; "Keeping the World 'Off-Balance': Self-Restraint and U.S. Foreign Policy," in *America Unrivaled: The Future of the Balance of Power*, ed. G. John Ikenberry (Ithaca, NY: Cornell University Press, 2002), 121–54; *Taming American Power: The Global Response to U.S. Primacy* (New York: W. W. Norton, 2005), chap. 4; and "Alliances in a Unipolar World, *World Politics* 61, no. 1 (January 2009): 86–120.
31. John Ikenberry argues the key to US liberal hegemony after 1945 was its willingness to "self-bind" within various multilateral institutions. See his *After Victory: Institutions, Strategic Restraint, and the Rebuilding of Order after Major Wars* (Princeton NJ: Princeton University Press, 2000). "Self-binding" was highly selective, however, and Washington ignored these institutions whenever they got in the way of what US leaders wanted to do.
32. See Mearsheimer, *Tragedy of Great Power Politics*, chap. 10.
33. See Joshua Keating, "Kerry: 'The Monroe Doctrine Is Over,'" *Slate*, November 19, 2013, http://www.slate.com/blogs/the_world_/2013/11/19/kerry_the_monroe_doctrine_is_over.html.
34. See Helene Cooper and Jane Perlez, "US Sway in Asia Imperiled as China Challenges Alliances," *New York Times*, May 31, 2014.
35. As Kissinger rightly observes, "America's fear, sometimes only indirectly expressed, is of being pushed out of Asia by an exclusionary bloc." See *On China*, 541.
36. On the distinction between power and threat, see Walt, *The Origins of Alliances*, chap. 2.
37. In May 2014, for example, Japanese Prime Minister Shinzo Abe pledged to support other Asian nations engaged in territorial disputes with China. See Martin Fackler, "Japan Offers Support for Nations in Disputes with China," *New York Times*, May 30, 2014.
38. See Michael S. Schmidt, "In South China Sea Visit, U.S. Defense Chief Flexes Military Muscle," *New York Times*, April 16, 2016.
39. See Barry R. Posen, *Restraint: A New Foundation for U.S. Grand Strategy* (Ithaca, NY: Cornell University Press, 2014), chap. 3
40. See the chapters by Rosemary Foot, John Ikenberry, and William Wohlforth in this volume.
41. David Kang, "A Looming Arms Race in East Asia?," *The National Interest* (online), May 14, 2014, at http://nationalinterest.org/feature/looming-arms-race-east-asia-10461; and Dave Kang, "Military Spending in Asia Is Lower than You Think," *Robert Kelly—Asian Security Blog*, May 14, 2014, http://asiansecurityblog.wordpress.com/2014/05/14/guest-post-dave-kang-military-spending-in-east-asia-is-lower-than-you-think/.
42. Quoted in Cooper and Perlez, "US Sway in Asia Is Imperiled."
43. See "South Korea Postpones Historic Military Pact with Japan," *BBC News*, June 29, 2012, http://www.bbc.com/news/world-asia-18640476.
44. See Robert Zoellick, "US, China and Thucydides," *The National Interest*, no. 126 (July/August 2013): 22–30: and Kissinger, *On China*, 529.

CHAPTER 2

A New Order of Things?

China, America, and the Struggle over World Order

G. JOHN IKENBERRY

INTRODUCTION

Over the centuries, world politics has been shaped and reshaped by the rise and decline of states and their struggles over international order. It is a drama that has repeated itself across ancient and modern eras. Great powers have risen and commanded the global stage, endeavoring to establish, in one way or another, relations of order. Over time, however, the leading state's power and wealth decline, and new challengers emerge. Conflict and fragmentation ensue as the old order enters into crisis and rising and declining great powers compete for mastery of the global system. Out of the crisis, a newly powerful state steps forward to command the relations among states, seized with the capabilities and opportunities to reorganize international order.

It is this grand narrative of power transition and the reshaping of the world order that is increasingly invoked by observers as the world watches the rise of China. If the world is indeed in the midst of a global power transition, the implications are far reaching. The most basic questions of world politics are thrust to the fore. Who will dominate the global system, and how will that dominance be manifest? It throws into question the future of America's leadership position in the global system and the fate of the liberal international order. Most of all, it throws into question the terms of peace and stability themselves. The classic dilemmas and dangers of power transitions will once again be at the heart of world politics. This is what Robert Gilpin had in mind when he argued that shifts from one leading state to another pose the most fraught and dangerous moments in international relations.[1] The rise of post-Bismarck Germany in the late nineteenth century—and the ensuing great power rivalry, arms races, realignments, and thirty-year war between Great Britain and Germany—is the classic case that shows how dangerous and violent power transitions can be.

But does this grand narrative of power transitions illuminate or obscure the logic of the coming struggles between China and the United States? Power transitions are indeed dangerous moments in world politics—and power shifts in East Asia are generating security competition and conflict across the region. The United States and China seem destined to compete as geopolitical rivals. But it is less certain that the power shifts underway today will trigger hegemonic war and the remaking of global order under Chinese auspices. To be sure, the distribution of material capabilities—and its shifts over time—provides the setting and resources for states as they struggle over the terms of the world order. But the wider world-historical setting of power transitions has continuously evolved, driven by long-term shifts in the character of states, societies, capitalism, technologies, violence, and ideas. This means that the future is never simply a reproduction of the past—not least when it comes to struggles over international order.

Indeed what is most striking is the variation in the way in which power transitions have played out. Not all power transitions have generated security competition or war or overturned the old international order. Britain ceded power to a rapidly growing America in the early decades of the twentieth century without war or a rupture in relations. Japan grew from 5 percent of the American GNP in the late 1940s to over 60 percent of its size in the early 1990s without challenging the existing order. Other great powers have risen up and sought to challenge the existing order, such as post-Bismarck Germany. Clearly there are different types of great powers, great power ascents, and power transitions.

What is missing in the cyclical theories of power and order is an understanding of the "existing order" that rising states confront on their path upward. Rising states across eras have not all been greeted by the same sort of order. These orders have differed in their logic and character—and they have differed in their weight and durability. In this regard, China faces a very different type of status quo international order than past rising states. The old American-led international order is a wider and deeper political order than any other built in the past. In the decades since 1945, the United States led the way in constructing a liberal international order—a far-flung system of alliances, open trade, multilateral institutions, and political partnerships. This order tied the United States to other liberal democracies, backed by a vision of order that enshrined democracy, capitalism, openness, cooperative security, the rule of law, and human rights. It is an order that has made American power more legitimate, durable, and far-reaching, while at the same time creating capacities, partners, and principles with which to confront and deter illiberal great power rivals.

In the background, two other developments have added to the durability of the old US-led international order—nuclear weapons and the spread of democratic states. Nuclear weapons have radically reduced the ability of a rising state—such as China—to overturn the old international order through a great power war. A world of democracies has shifted the geopolitical playing field in America's favor and made it harder for China to use old-fashioned coercion to dominate its neighborhood. China finds a complex array of constraints and incentives as it faces the existing international order. It has incentives and opportunities to operate within that order, while its ability to use its power to usher in a different international order is surprisingly limited. In short, the international order today is, compared to past orders, easier to join and harder to overturn.

In this chapter, I look first at power transition theory, and I identify the various types and pathways of power transition and relate them to the specific problem of the rise of China. Following others, I look at the types of clashes or challenges that rising states might bring to struggles over international order—traditional power struggles over territory and political dominance within regions, struggles over authority and privileges within the international order, and more fundamental struggles over the basic principles and values that guide rule and governance within the order. Out of these distinctions we can depict rising great power in various ways—as revisionist states that seek to overturn the existing international order, spoilers and free riders that operate on the edges of that order, or stakeholder states that seek to accommodate themselves to the existing order, even as they attempt to gain new advantages within it.

Second, I look at the distinctive character of the American-led liberal order and the ways in which this existing order creates constraints and incentives for a rising China. The American-led liberal international order has a variety of features that distinguish it from past international orders, and that makes it both more durable and easier for rising states to achieve their goals within it. Compared with past international orders, it has great capacities for integration, shared leadership, distribution of economic gains, and accommodation of diversity. This has created a more expansive and complex international order than any rising state in world history has ever faced. It is an order that China is already a part of, and indeed it is enjoying the rights and privileges that flow from participation in this order. But also, because this order is not simply an American-owned and operated order, the scale and scope of the "old order" makes a Chinese effort to oppose and overturn that order all the more difficult. Past rising states have faced specific great powers and imperial orders. China is the first rising states to face a postimperial global order—an order with more universal-style rules and principles of order.

Third, I look at the wider geopolitical setting in which China is situated. The United States, its allies, and the wider liberal international order they inhabit, have considerable advantages over China. The United States is geographically remote from the other great powers, while China is rising up in a crowded neighborhood. China increasingly is trapped in a region that is dominated by democracies and countries allied with the United States. States in the region worry about Chinese domination and American abandonment. These geopolitical circumstances create an unequal playing field that favors the United States—even if it is declining in relative terms—over China.

Fourth, I argue that even as China faces constraints on the pursuit of a revisionist agenda, it is finding incentives to operate within a liberal-oriented international order. It seeks greater authority—rights and privileges—within the existing order, even as it resists American hegemony and acts to assert its dominance within its region. In a fundamental sense, China is not a revisionist great power. Its economic goals of gaining political influence within global leadership forums and strengthening the international role for its currency are drawing China into rather than away from the world economic order.

China and the United States seem destined to clash over the terms of order in East Asia. But it is a clash that will unfold in a different world-historical setting than past power transitions. Liberal international order and the rise of liberal democracy around the world create distinctive circumstances that alter the way in which power is expressed, security dilemmas are manifest, and geopolitics play out. The rise of China may bring to an end the era of American hegemony—but it will be harder, if not impossible, for China to bring to an end the liberal world order that the American era wrought.

RISING STATES AND POWER TRANSITIONS

The rise and decline of great powers and convulsive shifts in international order have played out many times over the centuries. In past eras, states have risen up, fought wars, and built international order. Spain, France, Great Britain, Germany—each of these states grew in power in a past century, surpassed rival great powers, and made a bid to dominate Europe or the wider world. In turn, each declined or was defeated in war, triggering a renewal of global struggle over leadership and the organizing rules and arrangements of global order. In this way, world politics can be understood to be driven by grand cycles of rise and decline, in which powerful states emerge from geopolitical struggle to impose or build international order. History may not repeat itself, but when it comes to the rise and decline of states and order, it does, as Mark Twain noted, rhyme.[2]

Robert Gilpin's *War and Change in World Politics* provides the most systematic statement of this perspective. International relations are marked by a succession of ordered systems created by leading—or hegemonic—states that emerge after war with the opportunities and capacities to organize the rules and arrangements of interstate relations. As Gilpin argues, "[T]he evolution of any system has been characterized by successive rises of powerful states that have governed the system and have determined the patterns of international interactions and established the rules of the system."[3] Steady and inevitable shifts in the distribution of power among states give rise to new challenger states who eventually engage the leading state in hegemonic war, which in turn gives rise to a new hegemonic state that uses its dominant position to establish an order favorable to its interests.[4]

Gilpin's theory offers a way of thinking about the relationship between power and order. The most powerful states in the system are driven to secure and advance their interests through the establishment of institutions and regularized relationships. The resulting political order serves the interests of the leading actors. Indeed, it is established precisely for this purpose. This is what happens in international relations. A powerful state rises up in the system and creates order, doing so to protect and advance its interests. Over time, however, the distribution of power and wealth change, driven by the diffusion of technology and production. The old order still exists, but the underlying distribution of material capabilities that supported it has eroded. In Gilpin's language, a "disequilibrium" emerges between the international order and the underlying distribution of power and interests. Eventually, the state or states that are growing more powerful and wealthy will seek to change the order to reflect their interests. At great historical junctures, this change is brought on by hegemonic wars in which a rising state violently takes command of the global system and overturns the old order. The resulting order reflects a new equilibrium between power and interests. As Gilpin puts it, "[T]he process of international political change ultimately reflects the efforts of individuals or groups to transform institutions and systems in order to advance their interests."[5]

The most dangerous moments in world politics occur when the declining lead state is no longer able to enforce the rules of the old order. The "governance institutions" of the old order go into crisis. They lose legitimacy. The disparities in power between the old hegemonic state and rising great powers close, and this creates uncertainty, insecurity, shifting ambitions, and risk taking. These circumstances have often culminated in "hegemonic war," which creates winners and losers, shifting disparities of power, and the emergence of a new lead state or group of states that, in one way or another, establishes a new international order. As Gilpin argues, these periodic wars "resolve the question of which state will govern the system, as well as what ideas and values will predominate."[6] The iconic order-building moments, of course, are the European and World War settlements—1648, 1713, 1815, 1919, and 1945. These are not just wars over territory and borders. At stake in these major conflicts is the governance of world politics.

Gilpin and other power transition theorists provide a striking image of power and order in world politics. Powerful states build hierarchical orders that can persist for decades and even centuries. But, eventually, material conditions of power shift and transform, and the hierarchies of world politics break apart, sometimes quite violently. This narrative is a useful starting point for thinking about power shifts and struggles over order. It allows us to look across centuries and eras to find recurring patterns—and to compare and contrast different episodes of rise and decline of states and orders. It also illuminates the dynamic connections between the distribution of material capabilities—the "base"—and the political formations that are built on top of these power capabilities—the "superstructure."

But power transition theory offers little guidance in understanding how these epic cycles of change have varied or evolved over the centuries. In fact, power transitions have unfolded in a wide variety of ways. First, their scale and scope have varied. The early modern episodes were confined to Europe, while the twentieth-century power transitions were global. Some power shifts have resulted in full-scale contests between major states seeking to establish leadership or hegemonic control over the wider system—such as the Hapsburg Empire and France in the seventeenth century, Napoleonic France and Britain in the nineteenth century, and Britain and post-Bismarck Germany in the first half of the twentieth century. Other power shifts—between France and Britain in the 1930s and Japan and the United States after World War II—did not generate power disparities sufficient to put control of the international order in play. Second, the outcomes of these power transitions varied. Most strikingly, both Germany and the United

States were rising states facing a declining Britain in the early twentieth century. But the terms of their "dissatisfaction" differed, and the ways that they sought to project power and reshape the global order differed. Third, the political character of the states involved in the power transition—and the character of the "old" international order—mattered in shaping outcomes. It is notable that rising democratic states have not launched wars against declining democratic states—as the British-American hegemonic transition suggests. Likewise, when a declining democratic state has faced a rising and potentially threatening nondemocratic challenger, it has tended to form counterbalancing alliances. This was Britain's strategy as it faced Germany before the World Wars, France's strategy in 1933–1936 as it faced Germany, and the United States' strategy as it faced the Soviet Union in the Cold War. Rising states have differed in their character, risen up in different ways, and confronted different types of international orders.[7]

To get at these variations, we need to ask more questions. We need to ask what precisely rising states "want" and what they can "get" in terms of the reordering of global rules and institutions. A rising state might want to extend its influence over other states and territories. It might want to control or have greater influence over the operation of the world economy—including the terms of trade, flow of resources, and monetary relations. It might want to control or have greater influence over the governance arrangements of the international order—the rules, rights, and principles of order. It might want to seek greater prestige or status within the international order to accord with its rising power. Rising states might seek to pursue all or only some of these goals. Pursuing these goals might entail gaining authority and a voice within the existing international order—or it might entail more revisionist efforts to overturn and remake the international order.

China clearly wants to expand its influence—and domination—within its region. Indeed, this goal is almost inevitable given its growing economic and military power. But it remains uncertain what sort of influence and domination it might seek to establish. Does it want to dominate through old-style coercion or build an order where its influence is extended through more consensual and agreed-upon regional rules and institutions? Does it want to "push" the United States out of the region or seek a more open and multipolar regional order? Beyond East Asia, does China want to gain greater authority and status within existing international governance institutions or seek to overturn the liberal-oriented global system? If it seeks to diminish—or even destroy—American hegemonic leadership within this liberal international order, does it also seek to oppose and undermine the wider open and rule-based international order? Answers to these questions depend not only on whether China is a "revisionist" state, but also on the constraints, incentives, and opportunities generated by the existing international order.

RISING STATES AND LIBERAL INTERNATIONAL ORDER

Rising states have a choice between joining or opposing the existing international order. They can rise up within that order or seek to oppose and overturn it. They can act to gain more rights and authority within that order—that is, to move up within the existing political hierarchy—or they can become revisionist powers that contest the deep rules and principles of the order. Of course, it is also possible for states to operate between these extremes. But whatever rising states might seek to do, their choices presumably hinge in part on the character of the existing international order. As John Ruggie has argued, using a counterfactual, if Nazi Germany had won World War II, the international order would look very different than the US-led postwar order. It would have been more imperial and less open and multilateral.[8] This outcomes would have had implications for how other great powers made choices about whether and to what extent they decided to acquiesce and integrate into that order or, as their power grew, endeavored to challenge and overturn it.

International orders can differ in many ways. They can be more or less global in scope, more or less open, more or less rule based, more or less institutionalized, and more or less hierarchical. Generally speaking, international orders have ranged from imperial to liberal. Empires have come in many varieties—direct, indirect, informal, and so forth. It is a form of organized domination in which the imperial state exercises despotic rule and maintains order, at least in the last resort, through coercion. Liberal international order is a system organized around open and at least loosely rule-based relations. Power does not disappear but is embedded in agreed-upon rules and institutions. Hegemonic orders are a mixed system in which a leading state dominates but does so indirectly. It is still a system based on domination, in which the hegemonic state plays a disproportionate role—a hegemonic role—in setting the terms of order, but it also operates more or less within the rules and institutions. States are not coerced, strictly speaking, to join the order. They join the order seeking benefits. Hegemonic order is less despotic than empire, and where rules and institutions do in fact hold sway, the order takes on liberal characteristics.[9]

A general proposition follows from these observations. The more closed and despotic the existing order is, the more incentives rising states will have to oppose and seek to overturn that order. Likewise, the more open and liberal-oriented that order is, the more incentives—and opportunities—rising states will have to join and rise up within it. A liberal international order has more points of access than imperial orders. It is less hierarchical, and there are more opportunities for a wide variety of states to use the prevailing rules and institutions to secure rights and privileges and advance their interests. There are more functional and universal-style rules and institutions that provide frameworks for pursing mutually beneficial relations with other states. Rising states are presumably more ambivalent about hegemonic orders. Hegemony gives the old and declining lead state disproportional rights and authority, so rising states might want to redistribute rights and privileges to favor themselves. But they may also want to preserve and build upon the wider array of liberal internationalist rules and institutions, which have, after all, provided the setting for their rise.

Seen in this light, China faces a very different international order than past rising states. It is more formidable and durable than past orders, but it is also one that offers attractions and opportunities for many states, including China. It is more global than past orders—a sprawling system of rules, institutions, partnerships, and functional arrangements that are deeply embedded in the societies and economies of states around the world. China does not face an empire. It is a more complex and multidimensional order than empire—traditional, indirect, informal, or otherwise. Nor it is simply an "American order." It is not simply a hegemonic system in which the United States leads. It is a complex and multilayered political formation. It is an order that bears the marks of empire, hegemony, and liberal internationalism. It is not just the crystallization of the distribution of power—it is constituted with authority relations, shared expectations, and settled practices through which states do business. Order is indeed built on the structured asymmetry of power. The most powerful states dominate—or try to—and seek to impose their ideas and interests. It is marked not by empire, but by politics and institutions. There is give and take. It is a political order with a hegemonic leader, differential roles, rules and norms, and complex moving parts.

There are several features to this order that underscore its postimperial or liberal hegemonic character. One is simply its integrative tendencies. States of various sizes and types have found pathways into this loosely organized order. Germany and Japan were the first major states to reconstitute themselves and integrate into postwar security and economic institutions. Some states joined the order as client states or frontline allies during the Cold War. After the Cold War, many of the post-Soviet states and some of the former Soviet republics joined the European Union and NATO. Many countries integrated into the order by making political and economic transitions. One can see this in the steady expansion of the Organization for Economic Cooperation and Development—a club of the developed market economies—which has grown from twenty countries at its founding in 1960 to thirty-four countries today. The point is that a wide range of states outside the West have sought to get into this order, to rise up and seek gains within it. The institutions and ideology of this order—hegemonic and liberal internationalist—seem to facilitate this integration.

A second characteristic is shared leadership. Hierarchical orders can differ in terms of the presence or absence of coalitions of states and stakeholders. That is, order can be more or less dominated by a single state. A leading state can organize and dominate the international order, standing above other states. Alternatively, the order might be made up of a wider coalition of major states that cooperate together—and lead the order—in various ways. In this regard, the existing international order is not really an order in which one state "rules." It is an order organized around an array of great powers, junior partners, client states, and other stakeholders. In the economic realm, authority and decision making is shared. This is true for the formal multilateral institutions—the International Monetary Fund (IMF), World Bank, and World Trade Organization (WTO). It is also true for the informal leadership groups, such as the G-7 and the G-20. These are still hierarchical institutions, but they are inhabited by a coalition of leading states. The United States and Western Europe remain overrepresented in many of these organizations, but they are not based on fixed membership or voting rights.[10] Doors are open, and bargains are on the table. The movement of activity from the G-7 to the G-20 also suggests ways that leadership mechanisms are evolving as power shifts away from the old Western great powers.

A third characteristic is the way economic gains are spread across the international order. Orders can differ in the way that economic and other material rewards are distributed across states. The economic gains from the order can accrue disproportionately to the leading state, or those gains can be shared more widely. In traditional imperial orders, the profits and gains flowed overwhelmingly to the imperial core. In colonial and informal empires, economic gains flowed disproportionately to the wealthy and powerful states, classes, and societal groupings that organize and run the order. In the existing order, with its system of open trade and investment, the profits and economic gains seem to be more widely shared.[11] In the case of the American-led postwar order, trade and investment across the system allowed states near and far to grow and advance, often outpacing the United States or its Western partners. States in all regions of the world over the last half century have made systematic efforts to integrate into this American-led order in pursuit of trade and growth.

A fourth characteristic of order is the degree to which it accommodates diversity of models of capitalism and strategies of development. In this regard, the postwar global order has been—in practice if not in ideology—remarkably broad-minded. There have been three general types of capitalist models. One is the Anglo-American neoliberal or fundamentalist model. This takes center stage beginning in the 1980s and dominates thinking in Western capitals into and past the 2008 global financial crisis. A second is the older postwar model of "embedded liberalism," which is more social democratic in its emphasis on the social welfare state and "managed" openness. A third is the statist development model that has been pursued throughout East Asia and the developing world.[12] What is interesting is that these different models have tended to coexist.

These aspects of the American-led order reflect its hegemonic and liberal internationalist character. Integrative tendencies, shared leadership, distribution of economic gains, tolerance of diversity—these are features or dimensions of international order. The argument is not that the existing global order conforms to some ideal type of liberal hegemonic system. Rather, it is that orders can be compared along these dimensions—and the current order seems to have more integrative tendencies, shared leadership, distribution of economic gains, and tolerance for diversity than past international orders. The sharp edges and steep hierarchies of empire seem to be missing in today's global order. These aspects of the current international order make it harder for China to overturn it, even as it creates incentives to seek authority and a voice within it.

THE GEOPOLITICS OF SINO-AMERICAN RIVALRY

Even if China does not have the incentives or capacity to overturn the existing global order, it will certainly compete with the United States for influence and leadership. As China grows more powerful, it will want to expand its political reach and sphere of influence—and this will inevitably unsettle old relationships within the region and fuel rivalry with the United States. East Asia is already a region increasingly marked by security competition and balance of power politics—and it will probably get worse. But this emerging Sino-American rivalry will be shaped and constrained by its wider geopolitical setting and international liberal order. It is a global setting that provides advantages to the United States as the status quo power and creates incentives for China—as well as the United States—to exercise restraint.

If China continues to grow quickly, it will surely pass the United States and become the largest economy in the world. In this narrow sense, China will become a peer global power, and the global power transition will be in full swing. But if power is seen in a wider sense—defined by geography, demography, politics, economics, allies, and ideas—the United States will continue to have decisive advantages over China for decades to come, influencing the way China rises.

The starting point is America's global political and security relationships. The United States may not be growing as quickly at China, but it will continue to have the economic capacity, backed by massive new energy resources, to maintain a global military presence and security commitments. Indeed, it is the American alliance system that is particularly formidable. In one study, the United States has military partnerships with over sixty countries, while China has one alliance partner and Russia has eight.[13] This is a remarkable aspect of the United States as a global power: its seemingly unique willingness and ability to build security partnerships. In contrast, China does not exhibit such willingness or capability. As a British diplomat noted recently at an international gathering—"the Chinese do not do alliances." But the United States does, and they provide a double dividend. On the one hand, they provide a global framework for the projection of American power, making that power more stable, welcome, and expansive. On the other hand, the alliance partners share in providing security, in effect leveraging American power. There are dangers that allies will free ride on America's provision of security, but the amount of military capability aggregated within this American-led alliance system overshadows anything that China—or Russia—might generate for many decades to come.

The composition of power also matters, in particular the presence of nuclear weapons. These weapons—which are in the hands of Russia, China, and the United States—also have a double effect. On the one hand, they radically reduce the likelihood of a great power war, which is the sort of upheaval in the global system that has provided the opportunities for past great powers, including the United States after World War II, to build and entrench an international order. China will not have this opportunity. But nuclear weapons also make China and Russia more secure. They know that the United States will not invade them. Nuclear weapons reduce the fear of American domination through conquest.[14]

Geography reinforces this American advantage. The United States is unique in that it is the only great power that is not neighbored by other great powers—and it emerged in these remote geographical circumstances as a "late developing" great power. This has had several implications. First, geographical insularity made the rise of American power during the twentieth century less threatening. Remarkably, the United States became the world's leading power without triggering war or balancing behavior. Indeed, even after the Cold War, when the United States was truly unipolar, other great powers—who were oceans away—did not balance against it.[15] None of the other major states—including Great Britain, France, Germany, Japan, and China—have this geographical advantage. Each lives in a crowded geopolitical neighborhood where shifts in power are routinely met by counterbalancing. China is discovering this today as its growing power is greeted by hedging and balancing reactions, manifest as surrounding states engage in military modernization and the reinforcement of alliances.

Second, America's geographical remoteness has reinforced its incentives to champion universal principles that allowed it access to the various regions of the world. This is an observation about geography and historical timing. The United States emerged as a great power relatively late—only in the first half of the twentieth century. By the 1930s, the United States confronted a situation where most of the regions of the world were closed, divided into empires, blocs, and spheres of influence. At the end of World War II, the underlying judgment that the United States acted on was that the size of the "grand area" necessary for its viability as a major state needed to be global. The United States needed to open up and gain access to the world's regions. So the United States championed global rules and institutions rather than old-style imperial organizing ideas. It championed the open door, self-determination, and anticolonialism, not for idealist reasons but because of the practical need to get Europe, Asia, and other regions open for trade, investment, and diplomacy.[16] In this sense, geography and its late arrival as a great power are what launched the United States on its project to organize a global order. It was globally oriented because it needed to open up and link itself to the major regions of the world. This, in turn, gave it incentives to articulate anti-imperial principles and rules, such as openness, nondiscrimination, and self-determination. If the United States built the first "global empire," it did so by elevating universal principles and multilateral rules and institutions. It had to turn the old organizational logic of empire on its head.

Third, America's offshore geographical position also turned on its head the way many states in Europe and East Asia thought about American power. They worried more about abandonment than domination. States in postwar Europe and East Asia sought to draw the United States into playing economic and security roles within their regions. They looked for ways for American military commitments to help solve regional security problems. For example, France and Great Britain wanted an ongoing American security commitment as part of a wider regional system that would help restrain and integrate West Germany into Europe. Japan was also able to use the alliance with the United States to solve its security problems and find a pathway back to growth and modernization. It was America's distance from these regions that made it less threatening. The result is what the historian Geir Lundestad has called an "empire by invitation."[17] This dynamic is clearly in evidence today in Asia, where China is seen as a greater potential security danger—because of its proximity, if nothing else—than the United States.

Fourth, America's geopolitical setting also reinforced its incentives to support various sorts of national movements toward statehood and self-rule. Again, this is an anti-imperial-order building impulse. It has a realist-style logic. If a great power cannot directly dominate a weaker state, its second-best option is to support that state's sovereignty and independence, precisely so that it will not be dominated by a rival great power. Ian Chong, for example, argues that the United States championed sovereignty and self-determination in East Asia as a way to avoid being excluded. Chong argues that great powers do prefer outright domination if they can get away with it. But within East Asia—and for most of the world, except the Western Hemisphere—this was not a realistic option. So in postwar states such as China, Indonesia, and Thailand, the United States eventually put its weight behind movements toward national self-determination.[18] In Chong's view, the United States is not unique in pursuing this *second-best* strategy. Great Britain and other European powers have promoted state building—that is, self-determination and sovereign independence—in various parts the developing world to undercut bids by rival great powers for regional domination.[19] But geography and historical timing made this a dominant American postwar strategy of order building.

The way the United States rose up and shaped the twentieth-century international order was unique. It grew powerful in relative isolation from the other major powers. It became a world power during the high tide of great power empire. It did not become a great power through conquest. It stepped into vacuums and postwar moments to shape the geopolitical settlements. In one sense, it was like Great Britain in an earlier era. It tried to shape events as an "offshore" power. It did not seek to become a continental power. Its comparative advantage was in offering other countries security protection, undercutting bids for dominance by land powers in Asia and Europe. Unlike Great Britain, the United States did this through a system of alliances and client states. In seeking to build a global order, it advanced universal-style principles and multilateral rules and institutions. These tools of domination made the order more hegemonic and less imperial—a more open and pluralistic international order with far-flung constituencies and vested interests that favor its continuation.

These geopolitical advantages and order-building impulses will not disappear soon, even as China rises in power. China will have a much harder time than the United States in projecting power, building alliances, and making its power acceptable to other states. These advantages do not just reflect the distribution of material power capabilities but more deeply rooted circumstances reflecting geography, history, technology, and modernity.

CHINA AND THE WORLD OF DEMOCRACIES

The rise of China is the most dramatic aspect of today's global power transition. But to focus on China's growing power is to miss wider shifts in global politics and economics that are shaping international power balances and the terms of Sino-American conflict. Indeed, the most profound global power transition at work over the last three decades is arguably not the rise of China but the rise and spread of liberal capitalist democracy. To be sure, many liberal democracies are struggling—plagued by slow economic growth, social inequality, and political instability. But the remarkable spread of liberal democracy throughout the world, beginning in the late 1970s and accelerating after the Cold War, has radically shifted the world power balances—strengthening America's position, creating new constituencies for liberal international order, and tightening the geopolitical circle around China and other illiberal states, including Russia.[20]

We forget how exceptional liberal democracy has been in the modern world until the twentieth century, confined to the West and parts of Latin America. After World War II, democracy began to spread to the non-West, as former British colonies and newly independent states established self-rule. During these Cold War decades, military coups and the revival of authoritarianism put limits on democratic transitions. The most dramatic moments toward liberal democracy began in the late 1970s, in what Samuel Huntington has famously described as the third great "wave" of democratization. In Southern Europe, Latin America, and East Asia, a wide variety of states made transitions from military to democratic rule.[21] The end of the Cold War brought another cohort of post-Communist states in Eastern Europe into the democratic fold.

What is striking is how far and wide liberal democracy has spread. As Daniel Deudney and I have argue elsewhere, "The democratic world is no longer primarily Anglo-American or even Western. It now includes countries in every region of the world, spanning civilizational lines (Japan, South Korea, India, and Turkey), former rivals (Germany and Japan), historical allies (Canada, Britain, and France), former colonial states (India, Indonesia, Ghana, and South Africa), and hemispheric neighbors (Mexico, Brazil, and Argentina). Democracies are new and old, Western and non-Western, colonial and post-colonial, and highly developed, rapidly developing, and underdeveloped."[22]

The high tide of this worldwide democratic movement was reached in the late 1990s when fully 60 percent of states had become democratic. Some reversals have occurred—in countries such as Pakistan, Nigeria, Venezuela, and Russia. But it is the wider global transformation in politics and economics that is geopolitically significant. There is a lot of attention given to the so-called BRICs—Brazil, Russia, India, and China. But the transformation goes beyond these states. A sort of global democratic "middle class" of states has emerged. India and Brazil are part of this middle class, but it includes other middle states as well—Mexico, Indonesia, South Korea, Turkey, and Australia. These are all states that are part of a global power transition. They are all rising up and seeking voice within the global system. In one way or another, they are all pursuing "stakeholder" strategies: pushing for multilateral cooperation, seeking greater rights and responsibilities, and exercising influence in world politics through agenda setting, bridge-building, and coalition diplomacy. South Korea is perhaps the best example of this new type of rising state in the global middle class. It has fashioned an identity as "Global Korea," stepping forward to host the G-20 summit, the nuclear safety summit, and various development and human security forums.[23]

It is this global middle class of democratic states that gives the existing liberal-oriented world order new geopolitical weight. As Larry Diamond indicates, if G-20 countries such as Indonesia, Argentina, Turkey, and South Africa, together with Brazil and India, regain their economic footing and stabilize democratic rule, the G-20 forum—which includes the United States and European countries—"will have become a strong 'club of democracies,' with only Russia, China, and Saudi Arabia holding out." Indeed, the rise of a world democratic middle class has turned illiberal states, such as China and Russia, into outliers. These liberal democracies are not all allies—or even close partners of the United States—and indeed, many non-Western democracies are quite suspicious of the United States and the "dark side" of American postwar foreign policy. But none of these states actively balances against the United States, and most of them seek some sort of reformed and updated liberal international order.

This democratic upsurge has helped shape the environment in which China navigates its rise. The presence of this loosely defined global "middle class" of liberal democracies makes it harder for China to assemble a countercoalition of states that would work as a group to oppose and undermine the existing international order. There are also more immediate implications for China's options within its own region. Indeed, within East Asia, China is surrounded by democracies. In the mid-1980s, India and Japan were the only Asian democracies. But democratic transitions in the Philippines, South Korea, Taiwan, Thailand, Mongolia, and Indonesia have transformed the region. Burma has also made cautious steps toward multiparty government. Not all of these countries are strong and stable democracies, to say the least. But they have, together with Australia and New Zealand, tilted China's neighborhood decidedly in the direction of liberal democracy.

China's predicament is illustrated by its chronic problem with Taiwan. Chinese leaders sincerely believe that Taiwan is part of China. But the problem is that the Taiwanese do not agree—and the democratic transition in Taiwan makes their contrary claims more deeply felt and legitimate. According to one survey in 1992, only about 17 percent of people living in Taiwan identified themselves as Taiwanese. But twenty years later, in June 2013, that number had grown to 57 percent.[24] Similarly, a 2011 Taiwan National Security Survey found that if they could be assured that China would not attack Taiwan if it declared independence, fully 80 percent of Taiwanese would opt for independence. China may seek to extend its geopolitical control over its neighborhood. But the spread of democracy to all corners of Asia makes old-style coercive domination its only option, albeit one that is extraordinarily costly and ultimately self-defeating.

China's most obvious potential partner in an effort to confront and overturn existing global rules and institutions is Russia. But Russia faces the same dilemma as China—it is surrounded by liberal democracies and countries seeking closer ties with the West. In Eastern and Central Europe—Russia's near abroad—post-Soviet states and old allies have made democratic transitions and integrated into Western and global order. As worrisome as Putin's moves in Ukraine are, they are a reflection of geopolitical weakness and vulnerability—not strength. Over the last two decades, the Western democratic world has moved ever closer to Russia. Poland, Hungary, and the Czech Republic entered NATO in 1997. In 2004, seven more former Soviet bloc countries joined the Western security organization, including the three Baltic states—Lithuania, Latvia, and Estonia—who were part of the Soviet Union. In 2009, Croatia and Albania joined NATO. In the meantime, six former Soviet republics—Ukraine, Georgia,

Moldova, Kazakhstan, Armenia, and Azerbaijan—are now linked to NATO through the "Partnership for Peace" program. Russia is not in the midst of a great geopolitical advance. Quite the contrary, Putin's Russia is experiencing one of the greatest geopolitical contractions that any major state has experienced in the modern era. Russia and China may both seek to expand their regional spheres of influence. But doing so risks backlash and self-encirclement by states—many of them democracies—that do not want to be put under the thumb of an illiberal regional great power.

The larger significance of a world of democracies is that America's global security environment is remarkably benign. China may be America's security rival—but this rivalry exists in a world where the United States has overwhelmingly more friends and allies, and certainly the most capable ones. One can see this in the distribution of military power. The United States and its allies generate fully 75 percent of global military spending. Indeed, in the first decade after the Cold War, the world's democracies generated a remarkable 90 percent of global military capabilities. To be sure, this total has come down a bit, but only slowly, and today military spending by democracies still constitutes roughly 85 percent of the world total.[25]

The world of democracies does not need to operate as a global alliance or even a political bloc to have a profound global impact on China's options. They simply need to—in the aggregate—resist domination and seek peaceful change by working through the far-flung system of rules, institutions, and partnerships. This is, overwhelmingly, how they are operating today. Of course, it is possible that liberal democracy as a form of governance will enter into a deep crisis, giving way to a new global wave of political transitions to authoritarian rule. Some argue that this is indeed happening today—a sort of "global Weimar." It might be that the current dysfunctions of democracy around the world become so severe that more statist and authoritarian models—such as those pioneered by China and Singapore—drive a global transition away from old Western forms of governance.[26] Indeed, it may well be that 2008 was a sort of world historical turning point in which the United States has lost its vanguard role in modernization and economic advancement. Yet even if this is true, it is not clear that China offers the world a new model of modernity—or an alternative grand vision of global order.

Although China is committed to an illiberal form of rule, it still embraces the deeper organizing logic of an open and loosely rule-based international order. And indeed it has reasons to do so. A liberal-oriented open international system gives it access to other societies—for trade, investment, and technology. A rule-based system gives it tools to protect its sovereignty and interests. Despite controversies over new ideas about the "responsibility to protect," the existing international order enshrines old norms of state sovereignty, nondiscrimination, and nonintervention. These Westphalian principles remain the bedrock of world politics—and China has tied its national interest to them.

In fact, China is deeply integrated in the existing global system. It is a permanent member of the UN Security Council. It is a participant in the WTO and plays a role in the IMF, World Bank, and the G-20.[27] Indeed, in its ideology and vision, China has slowly moved away from earlier calls for a "new international order," found in party and government documents in pasts decades and has, beginning in 2007, given way to calls for modest reforms. The discourse now is more about fairness and justice in the organization of the global order—and this means, fundamentally, giving China itself more voice in the running of existing global institutions. Reform efforts seek to make the international order "more reasonable," which more specifically means giving China a larger role in the IMF and World Bank, more voice in international leadership forums such as the G-20, and, over the longer term, the internationalization of the Chinese currency. These reforms all point toward a Chinese movement toward the center of the existing international economic order, and not in a revisionist move away from it.

The world of democracies occupies the core of world politics today. Many democratic states are struggling, but grand alternatives to democracy and the rule of law do not appear to exist. Indeed, across a wide array of global rules and institutions, China acts more like an established great power than a revisionist. It is frequently a reluctant participant in global multilateral affairs. But so too is the United States. Both the United States and China make pragmatic use of global rules and institutions to advance their interests and protect their sovereignty. China and the United States may be drawn into dangerous security conflicts within East Asia. But at the global level, China's struggles with the United States are primarily about gaining a voice within global institutions and manipulating the rules and regimes to suit their interests. China is seeking to revise the political hierarchy and enhance its position and status within the global system. But it is not engaged in world-scale revisionist struggles over rival models of modernity or even divergent ideologies of an international order.

CONCLUSIONS

The world has moved through cycles of rise and fall of great powersand epic struggles over international order. It is a familiar story—old leading powers lose their grip on the global system, while rising states seek to establish their mastery over it. But international orders do not just come and go; they also evolve, adapt, expand, and deepen. In the modern era, great powers have found themselves positioned—even after hegemonic wars—in a larger historical setting defined in terms of the Westphalian system and the liberal ascendancy. The Westphalian system has evolved as leading states have built upon and adapted its rules and norms. The rise to dominance of liberal democracies has provided another layer to order building over the last two hundred years. Powerful states dominate the global system, but their choices and options depend heavily on what has come before them. This is particularly true for China, as it rises up and faces the most formidable and entrenched international order the world has yet seen.

The "old" international order is a massive political formation that has within it powerful constituencies for its preservation—and, indeed, for its extension. It is an order that has distinctive features—it has capacities for integration, shared leadership, shared economic gains, and toleration of diversity. It is more than simply the United States or the West. It is a world of liberalism, capitalism, nationalism, and democracy. It is also a world of extended security alliances, client states, and other fellow travelers. If China intends to rise up and challenge the existing order, it has a much more daunting task than simply confronting the United States and grabbing control of the system. American hegemony may come and go, but the wider system is not reducible to American power and rule—it has its own features and laws of motion. To depose the United States from the apex of this hierarchical order is not to dislodge liberal international order as the dominating logic of twenty-first-century world politics.

These structural conditions will inevitably influence how China thinks about the costs and benefits of strategies of integration and contestation. The sheer weight and complexity of the liberal international order makes it hard to overturn. Nuclear weapons radically reduce the probability of a hegemonic order—and if war does not destroy the existing order, it is unlikely that China can overturn it through economic power and coercive threats. The type of power transition that China triggers will be shaped by its interests and capacities. China may have an interest in contesting American hegemony and establishing its dominance in East Asia. But it also has an interest in the stability of a functioning international order, one that is open and organized around rules and institutions that protect its sovereignty and equities. China no doubt has an interest in acquiring greater authority and leadership within the global system. But it cannot acquire authority and leadership simply through the barrel of a gun. It needs to work with existing rules and institutions and find ways to make friends and allies.

Even if China does not attempt to contest global rules and institutions, it may seek to dominate East Asia. It may even try to push the United States out of the region. The United States, in turn, will try to remain the region's leading security provider, working to balance against growing Chinese power. It is difficult to see how China and the United States can avoid a grand struggle over leadership and influence in East Asia. The dangers of security competition, arms races, and armed conflict are real. The question is whether the United States and China can exercise sufficient restraint to avoid war. It is here that the wider global and regional context matters. The source of Chinese restraint is the danger of self-encirclement—the risk that its growing power and belligerence will be greeted by balancing and a tightening of the American-led alliance system around China. The states that surround China—many of whom are democracies—will not be easy to subdue or subordinate. China will need to look for ways to signal restraint and peaceful intentions. The source of American restraint is the fact that all of its regional allies are tied to China for trade and investment. The United States will need to pursue a "not too hot and not too cold" strategy—showing firmness and alliance credibility without provoking China. The peaceful navigation of today's global power transition is not inevitable. But it is made more likely because it is occurring in an era when revisionism is costly and ultimately self-defeating, while the constituencies for open and rule-based order are growing.

NOTES

1. Robert Gilpin, *War and Change in World Politics* (New York: Cambridge University Press, 1981).
2. For explorations of this theme, see the chapters in G. John Ikenberry, ed., *Power, Order, and Change in World Politics* (New York: Cambridge University Press, 2014).
3. Gilpin, *War and Change in World Politics*, 42–43.
4. The focus of *War and Change in World Politics* on recurring cycles of power and order places it in the company of several large literatures. On power transitions, see A. F. K. Organski, *World Politics* (New York: Knopf, 1958); and A. F. K. Organski and Jacek Kugler, *The War Ledger* (Chicago: University of Chicago Press, 1980). On long cycles, see George Modelski, *Long Cycles in World Politics* (Seattle: University of Washington Press, 1987); George Modelski, ed., *Exploring Long Cycles* (Boulder, CO: Lynne Rienner Publishers, 1987); and William R. Thompson, *On Global War: Historical-Structural Approaches to World Politics* (Columbia: University of South Carolina Press, 1988). On hegemonic stability theory, see Charles Kindleberger, *The World in Depression, 1929–39* (Berkeley: University of California Press, 1974). See also Paul Kennedy's

magisterial *The Rise and Fall of the Great Powers: Economic Change and Military Conflict from 1500 to 2000* (New York: Random House, 1987).
5. Gilpin, *War and Change in World Politics*, 10.
6. Gilpin, *War and Change in World Politics*, 203.
7. For a discussion of variations in great power ascents, see Randall L. Schweller, "Managing the Rise of Great Powers: History and Theory," in *Engaging China: The Management of an Emerging Power*, ed. Alastair Iain Johnston and Robert S. Ross (New York: Routledge, 1999), 1–31.
8. John Gerard Ruggie, *Multilateralism Matters: The Theory and Praxis of an Institutional Form* (New York: Columbia University Press, 1993).
9. This formulation is offered in G. John Ikenberry, *Liberal Leviathan: The Origins, Crisis, and Transformation of the American World Order* (Princeton, NJ: Princeton University Press, 2011), xi–xiii
10. On the difficulties of accommodating rising non-Western states in global institutions, see Robert Wade, "Protecting Power: Western States in Global Organization," in *Global Governance at Risk*, ed. David Held and Charles Roger (Cambridge: Polity Press, 2013), 77–110.
11. There is a literature that explores "who benefitted" from empire. But there is less systematic work that explores the distribution of economic gains across the wider global and regional orders in different historical eras. D. K. Fieldhouse has done some of the best work on the economics of empire. See Fieldhouse, *Economics and Empire, 1830–1914* (London: Weidenfield and Nicolson, 1973); and *The West and the Third World: Trade, Colonialism, Dependence and Development* (Oxford: Blackwell, 1999). On the American case, see William Woodruff, *America's Impact on the World: A Study of the Role of the United States in the World Economy, 1750–1970* (London: Macmillan, 1975).
12. See Alice H. Amsden, *The Rise of "The Rest": Challenges to the West from Late-Industrializing Economies* (Oxford: Oxford University Press, 2001). For a discussion of the struggles between the United States and developing countries' overdevelopment and economic policies, see Alice H. Amsden, *Escape from Empire: The Developing World's Journey through Heaven and Hell* (Cambridge, MA: MIT Press, 2007).
13. See Brett Ashley Leeds, Jeffrey M. Ritter, Sara McLaughlin, and Andrew G. Long, "Alliance Treaty Obligations and Provisions, 1915–1944," *International Interactions* 28 (2002): 23–26.
14. Robert Gilpin notes that nuclear weapons might be a revolutionary factor that alters the age-old process of the rise and decline of states and the overturning of international order. See Gilpin, *War and Change in World Politics*. See also Daniel Deudney, "System and Systemic Change: Nuclear Deterrence, Hegemony, and Liberal Hegemony," in Ikenberry, *Power, Order, and Change in World Politics*, ed. G. John Ikenberry (New York: Cambridge University Press, 2014), 195–232.
15. For elaborations, see G. John Ikenberry, ed., *American Unrivaled: The Future of the Balance of Power* (Ithaca, NY: Cornell University Press, 2002); and G. John Ikenberry, Michael Mastanduno, and William Wohlforth, eds., *International Relations Theory and the Consequences of Unipolarity* (New York: Cambridge University Press, 2011).
16. See Nicholas John Spykman's *America's Strategy in World Politics: The United States and the Balance of Power* (New York: Harcourt, Brace, 1942). For a detailed discussion, see Carlo Maria Santoro, *Diffidence and Ambition: The Intellectual Sources of U.S. Foreign Policy* (Boulder, CO: Westview, 1992).

17. Geir Lundestad, *"Empire" by Invitation: The United States and European Integration, 1945–1997* (New York: Oxford University Press, 1998).
18. Ian Chong, *External Intervention and the Politics of State Formation: China, Indonesia, and Thailand, 1893–1952* (Cambridge: Cambridge University Press, 2012), 135–152.
19. See Robert H. Jackson, *Quasi-States: Sovereignty, International Relations, and the Third World* (New York: Cambridge University Press, 1990).
20. This section draws on Ikenberry, "Illusion of Geopolitics: The Enduring Strength of Liberal Order," *Foreign Affairs*, May/June 2014, 80–90.
21. Samuel P. Huntington, *The Third Wave: Democratization in the Late 20th Century* (Norman: University of Oklahoma Press, 1993).
22. Daniel Deudney and G. John Ikenberry, "Democratic Internationalism: An American Grand Strategy for a Post-Exceptionalist Era," New York, Council on Foreign Relations, International Institutions and Global Governance Program, Working Paper, November 2012, 6.
23. G. John Ikenberry and Jongryn Mo, *The Rise of Korean Leadership: Emerging Powers and Liberal International Order* (New York: Palgrave Macmillan, 2013).
24. National Chengchi University: Election Study Center poll, 2014.
25. See Dinah Walker, "Trends in US Military Spending," Council on Foreign Relations report, July 30, 2013, http://www.europarl.europa.eu/RegData/etudes/IDAN/2016/570464/EXPO_IDA(2016)570464_EN.pdf; accessed 20 July, 2017.
26. See John Micklethwait and Adrian Woodridge, *The Fourth Revolution: The Global Race to Reinvent the State* (London: Penguin, 2014).
27. See Rosemary Foot and Andrew Walter, *China, the United States, and Global Order* (New York: Cambridge University Press, 2011).

CHAPTER 3

Not Quite the Same as It Ever Was

Power Shifts and Contestation over the American-Led World Order

WILLIAM C. WOHLFORTH

INTRODUCTION

A narrative has taken hold around the world that is directly relevant to this volume: that the material capabilities standing behind the dominant order are in relative decline, and, as a result, contestation—sometimes violent—over basic rules and institutions is on the rise. Legitimacy ultimately rests on power, the argument goes, and so rising powers will seek to undermine the legitimacy of the current order and establish new rules. If the status quo states resist, the result will be instability and hence insecurity.

The narrative dominates punditry but also reflects the official policy and concrete, costly behavior of major powers. Putin's Russia has forcefully toppled one of the foundational pillars of the 1991 settlement: respect for the territorial status quo in Eurasia. China's neighbors accuse it of raising the specter of a forceful resolution of maritime boundary disputes in contravention of widely agreed regional norms and principles of international law. Both countries continue to increase military expenditures, in Russia's case shouldering a greater relative burden than the United States (4.2 vs. 3.8 percent of GDP). The BRICS (Brazil, Russia, India, China and South Africa) grouping and its fellow travelers push back against Western-sponsored expansions of norms regarding human rights and legal armed intervention in sovereign states under the "responsibility to protect" (R2P) rubric. On global economic governance, rising powers seek greater roles in existing institutions or periodically work to create nascent regional alternatives. Not surprisingly, attempts to measure the effectiveness of institutionalized cooperation on a large range of key global issues find a depressing downward trend.[1]

Where is this headed? Many analysts portray current contestation as the leading edge of a full-blown conflict over the US-led global order. Ably represented in this collection by Christopher Layne's chapter, their arguments often feature the use of terminology that suggests system-altering changes are afoot, for example, the claim that the unipolar era is over or a new multi- or bipolar world is nigh. Another indicator of this view is the popularity of the 1914 analogy: that China's rise and its dissatisfaction with the status quo are like Wilhelmine Germany's, raising similar risks of escalation and major military conflict.[2] Against this view is the position championed in this volume most notably by John Ikenberry and Rosemary Foot, arguing that the current order is far more robust and resilient than the pessimists contend. In this view, while contestation grabs the headlines, the main underlying trend is adaptation and accommodation.[3]

In this chapter, I address this question using the classical Gilpinian framework as well as more recent rise-and-decline scholarship.[4] I argue that the balance of theory and evidence points to a more nuanced position: we are in for increased competitiveness and contestation; a harder-to-manage world had indeed arrived, but the essential structural imperatives that have operated for the last two decades are likely to remain in place. The pessimists overstate the scale and significance of change; the optimists understate the levels of dissatisfaction and the challenge of accommodation.

I consider the implications of three key ways in which the current power shift differs from the canonical historical cases that inform much scholarship and commentary. In each case, there is a big implication and a qualifier. The big implication is that each change favors the status quo states and makes revisionism harder. The qualifier is that each also allows lower-level competition by creating incentives for challengers to challenge and status quo states to stick to current commitments. The three changes, considered in the sections that follow, are these:

1. the near certainty that all-out systemic war is off the table as a mechanism for hegemonic transition;
2. the fact that the rising challenger to the system's dominant state is credibly approaching peer status on only one dimension of state capability, gross economic output; and

3. the historically unprecedented degree of institutionalization in world politics coupled with the uniquely central role institutions play in the dominant power's grand strategy.

NO (HEGEMONIC) WAR AND CHANGE IN WORLD POLITICS

A "hegemonic war is characterized by the unlimited means employed and by the general scope of the warfare," Robert Gilpin wrote over thirty years ago.[5] "Because all parties are drawn into the war and the stakes involved are high, few limitations, if any, are observed with respect to the means employed."[6] Such a war is exceedingly unlikely to emerge among states armed with secure second-strike nuclear forces, whose core security, future power, and economic prosperity do not hinge on the physical control of others' territory. We need to know what function these wars served in the past to assess the full implications of their expected absence in the future. Needless to say, there is no scholarly consensus on this question. Here I shall focus specifically on the main theories that assign this type of war an important role in explaining international politics, setting aside for now the many approaches that deny any special functional implications to especially large or costly wars.[7]

Two functional arguments are most prominent in the literature. For Gilpin, as for many theorists in the power-cycle tradition, the core function of hegemonic war is to resolve the contradiction between the underlying distribution of capabilities in the system and the hierarchy of prestige. His theory relies on a major lag between the diffusion of system capabilities away from the hegemon, on the one hand, and states' ability to revise the international order accordingly, on the other hand. As capabilities shift to rising states, their dissatisfaction increases, as does their putative bargaining power, but the dominant state faces incentives to hold fast defending the existing order. The gap between the system's material "base" and its governance superstructure is resolved by a major war, which clarifies the distribution of capabilities and prestige, setting the stage for efficient bargaining over a new order.[8] John Ikenberry stresses a second function: "Major or great-power war is a uniquely powerful agent of change in world politics because it tends to destroy and discredit old institutions and force the emergence of a new leading or hegemonic state."[9] The first part of Ikenberry's argument seems intuitive, but it is not clear exactly how war "forces the emergence" of a new hegemon.

Randall Schweller has most recently and fulsomely developed the core arguments for why hegemonic war alone can perform these functions.

Other destructive events one can imagine, such as a global economic crash, pandemic, or environmental catastrophe, may wreak widespread destruction, but they are not driven by political logics and so cannot perform certain political functions. As Schweller argues, "[I]t is precisely the political ends of hegemonic wars that distinguish them and the crucial international-political functions they perform—most important, crowning a new hegemonic king and wiping the global institutional slate clean—from mere cataclysmic global events."[10] On his view, only hegemonic war can force the emergence of a new hegemon, clarify power relations, and wipe the interstate institutional structure clean, leaving a tabula rasa for the newly anointed hegemon to write new rules. "The distasteful truth of history," Schweller writes, "is that violent conflict not only cures the ill effects of political inertia and economic stagnation but is often the key that unlocks all the doors to radical and progressive historical change."[11]

But this distasteful truth rests on an assumption: that war is indeed governed by political logic, while other kinds of global events (or states' reactions to them) are not. And Clausewitz's famous thesis that war is a continuation of politics[12] has always been in tension with the antithesis also highlighted by the Prussian theorist: war's inherent tendency to escape control. The argument that hegemonic wars are at root powerful political processes has yet to be subjected to focused empirical studies. For his part, Gilpin ignored the actual processes wrought by war, focusing almost exclusively on causes. Ikenberry's narrative studies of postwar order building implicitly refer back to his arguments about war's effect, but they are not structured around an investigation of these processes. And Schweller's claim that hegemonic wars are necessary to prevent the degenerative "entropy" of international politics rests entirely on contemporary evidence of disorder, ungovernability, dissolution, and dissipation rather than concrete evidence that hegemonic wars prevented these processes from occurring in the past.

An initial review yields some evidence for these scholars' arguments, but the major implication is that the conditions for hegemonic emergence are very hard to produce. Over the last two centuries, such conditions only truly obtained once, and, while it took a cataclysmic war to create them, neither Gilpin's nor Ikenberry's nor Schweller's arguments fully capture the major mechanisms leading to American hegemony and the creation of a new institutional order. Consider four "ordering moments": 1815, 1914, 1945, and 1991.

After 1815, Russia was preeminent on land, and Britain ruled the seas and dominated global finance. Nearly a quarter century's fighting in the wars of the French Revolution and Napoleon failed to clarify the relation between these elements of power.[13] The war, in short, did not "force the emergence of a new leading or hegemonic state," as Ikenberry puts it, but rather clarified the emergence of two cohegemons whose comparative strength was not tested until the Crimean War a generation later: the British and Russian Empires. While detailed reconstructions of the Vienna negotiations and the Concert's functions do show how London's financial and naval power gave it bargaining leverage over some negotiations, it had to defer to St. Petersburg on core continental questions. Moreover, if the Napoleonic Wars had yielded one clear lesson, it was that it took grand coalitions of all the other powers to beat France, which was left intact and ready to vie with St. Petersburg or London for hegemonic status. Hence, the Concert bargaining was muddled by the existence of two empires in a special but unacknowledged class of "cohegemons," each in possession of a different mix of power resources whose ultimate superiority had not been tested, and both perilously close in power to the next lower-ranked state.

A generation of war quite simply failed to settle the power and status hierarchy and to clarify bargaining among the key actors. As to sweeping clean the institutional slate by destroying or discrediting the old order, this, too, remained ambiguous. After all, the main discredited order was that of Napoleon and the very idea of any state seeking singular as opposed to shared hegemony—not a propitious normative setting for any state seeking singular hegemony.[14] True, as Paul Schroeder has argued, eighteenth-century norms about how sovereigns ought to compete were indeed discredited for a time, but that negative conclusion could not lead to positive consensus on anything other than highly constrained new institutional order.[15] As Ikenberry observes, "[T]he institutional arrangements were of dramatically less breadth and depth than those that were proposed or employed after 1919 and 1945."[16]

World War I did a more effective job of discrediting old institutions and practices—particularly the classical nineteenth-century approach to the balance of power and alliances—but it is justly famous among scholars for its failure to settle European power relations. As E. H. Carr stressed, Germany and the Soviet Union were knocked down but not out—each retained fearsome power potential and was poised to grow fast and stake claims to revise the order.[17] Even worse, the United States was by far the world's greatest industrial and economic power, but its role in the actual fighting was minimal and its military and naval capabilities comparatively modest.[18] Woodrow Wilson cut a large figure at Versailles, and the United States was the only major power whose overall capabilities were actually increased by the war, but a recurrent theme of accounts of the negotiations in Paris is the massive gap between the US president's expectations and the actual influence he wielded.[19]

Even had domestic politics not intervened to thwart Wilson's vision for postwar order, the underlying power asymmetry would have frustrated bargaining. American power was simply not perceived in 1919 in the way it began to be thought of in the Cold War—as relevant to the actual workings of European and Eurasian security. As Ikenberry notes, "Wilson wanted to transform European politics without getting too involved in actually working with or protecting Europe."[20] Even an unambiguous and consistent American posture backed by a united domestic political scene would not have been effective without credible security guarantees to European partners for which the United States lacked not only the will but also the means. Thus, the World War I at least partially fulfilled Ikenberry's function of discrediting past institutions and creating demands for new ones, but it failed utterly to "force the emergence" of a hegemon.[21] And the most comprehensive war the world had known also failed to perform Gilpin's function of settling power relations and establishing a new hierarchy of power and prestige. The result of strongly discredited old institutions coupled with deep power asymmetries and resultant bargaining problems was the well-known story of the fatally compromised implementation of lofty postwar visions.

World War II is widely seen as the most destructive of modern history. Less widely recognized is the fact that while it knocked several great powers down, it yielded ambiguous lessons concerning the relative importance of American sea, air, and economic capabilities versus the Soviet Union's proven conventional military superiority in Eurasia.[22] The war's failure to clarify power and bargaining relations between the two superpowers and the resultant struggle for security and prestige constitute the key backdrop of the postwar American order-building project. Postwar American hegemony was inextricably intertwined with the bipolar Cold War struggle.[23] It was the war's manifest *failure* to clarify the US-Soviet power balance that aided and abetted the creation of the Pax Americana.

At the same time, the war wrought a series of other changes that cumulatively created hothouse conditions for forcing the emergence of the United States as the hegemon of its portion of the world. Consider the features it possessed that the other major wars lacked:

- Though it failed to clarify relative US and Soviet military power, it radically increased the economic gap in the United States' favor not only by giving it history's greatest Keynesian boost but also by physically destroying or gravely wounding all of the world's other major economies.

- It created the preconditions for the Cold War, without which America's order-building project could never have been as elaborate and extensive. It left the Soviet Union's armies in the center of Europe, creating the conditions for a plausible threat of Eurasian hegemony. This in turn enabled history's most deeply institutionalized and long-lasting counterhegemonic coalition—NATO—by giving Washington the incentive to overcome domestic resistance to the costs of building hegemony while conferring unprecedented US leverage over its allies to bend them to its will.
- It left in its wake unprecedented humanitarian and economic crises that only the United States had the means to address in a timely fashion.

The Second World War, in sum, did indeed foster a Gilpin/Ikenberry order-building moment, but for reasons lying outside either thinker's theoretical setup. Precisely because it did not clarify power relations, it did not create a truly global order in the Gilpin/Ikenberry sense. Rather, it yielded a roughly bipolar distribution that created perfect conditions for a Gilpin/Ikenberry-style order in one part of the world. The Cold War and American hegemony over its part of the world were inextricably linked.

It is impossible to assess the relationship between hegemonic war and the emergence of hegemony without examining cases that do not feature a major war. Hegemony may emerge as a result of processes other than hegemonic war, such as smaller wars or even peaceful changes.[24] After all, past hegemonic order-building moments were grounded in war outcomes that were much more ambiguous than traditional rise-and-decline, hegemonic war scholarship allows. Perhaps other kinds of phenomena perform functions scholars such as Ikenberry and Gilpin attribute to war? 1991 is a case in point. John Mueller described the changes of 1989–1991 as "the functional equivalent of World War III."[25] As Mary Elise Sarotte shows, many policymakers and observers outside the corridors of power sensed that the circumstances were ripe for constructing a new order.[26]

I have established elsewhere that, despite their comparatively peaceful nature, the events that gave rise to the current hierarchy were unusually diagnostic for power relationships.[27] Only Germany and Japan in the Second World War suffered as unambiguous a decline as the Soviet Union after 1989. The gap between the power and status of the superpowers, on the one hand, and all other major powers, on the other hand, was greater in the Cold War than any analogous gap in the history of the European states system. Since the United States and the Soviet Union were so clearly in a class by themselves, the fall of one from superpower status left the other much more unambiguously "number one" than at any other time since 1800.

Thus, the comparatively peaceful events of 1989–1991 yielded an interstate power hierarchy that was unusually clear.[28] Yet no ordering moment occurred.[29] The reason that leaps from the pages of the documents and other evidence of the period is that while the Gilpin conditions (clarity of power relations) were in place, Ikenberry's were not. Far from sweeping away and discrediting the old order, the events of 1989–1991 seemed to those decision makers with the most power to be a stunning affirmation of the order's essential robustness and rightness.[30]

Despite decades of research, many scholars do not know about the relationship between war and the emergence of hegemony. Further study may yet yield subtler processes or events that yield hegemonic authority, or ways in which hegemony can emerge slowly and subtly rather than at the dramatic junctures that have attracted scholars' attention. Yet it is hard to identify better candidates for hegemonic ordering moments over the last two centuries than those discussed here. And this admittedly preliminary examination suggests that most comprehensive hegemonic wars in history routinely perform the functions of discrediting the old order and clarifying relations of power much less effectively than existing scholarship would lead one to believe.

If Gilpin was right that "hegemonic war historically has been the basic mechanism of systemic change in world politics," and if most scholars are right that such a war is exceedingly unlikely in the nuclear age, then systemic change is much harder now than in the past. With world-war-scale violence off the table, any order presumably becomes harder to overthrow.

It follows that scholarly and popular discussions radically underestimate the difficulty of hegemonic emergence and therefore overestimate the fragility of American hegemony. Standard treatments of hegemonic emergence do not capture crucial effects that conspired to facilitate the current hegemonic order that emerged under US auspices. Uniquely in modern history, World War II yielded a combination of the Gilpin/Ikenberry conditions (destroying old order, clarifying power relations between hegemon and allies) and the Waltzian condition (a credible Soviet threat of hegemony producing unusually strong counterbalancing imperative). If even some of the most destructive wars in human history failed to establish key preconditions for hegemonic emergence, it is difficult to imagine what sort of event might generate such conditions under contemporary circumstances. In this light, expectations of a coming "Chinese century" or "Pax Sinica" seem fanciful.

POWER SHIFT, NOT POWER TRANSITION

Successfully challenging a settled interstate order is extremely hard even with major war as an option, it is even harder with such wars off the table, and it is harder yet if the reigning hegemon retains decisive power advantages. The distribution of capabilities is changing, as it always is. The question is how to describe the change. It has become commonplace to claim that the unipolar era is over or fast winding down. As Christopher Layne puts it, "The international system is in the midst of a transition away from unipolarity. As US dominance wanes, the post-1945 international order—the *Pax Americana*—will give way to new but as yet undefined international order."[31] Setting aside academic quibbles concerning the definition and measurement of polarity, this way of phrasing the power shift implies momentous, system-altering change.[32] The reality is subtler. As figure 3.1 shows, since the mid-1990s, the United States' share of global GDP has declined gradually. The far more significant shifts, however, have been the economic rise of China and the decline of US allies.[33]

In other words, the power shift that has captured the imaginations of politicians and pundits alike boils down to China's rapid economic growth. As figure 3.2 (below) indicates, if China did not exist, or if China's economic growth rates had mimicked Japan's since 1990, there would be no talk of US decline. The issue is not rising powers or BRICS or the rise of the East or the rise of the rest. It is China's rapid GDP growth. China is in a class by itself—it stands above all other so-called rising or great powers as the only one with a plausible chance of achieving superpower status in the decades to come. For the moment, however, the only transition on the horizon is in gross GDP. Only on this one dimension of state capability is China set to become a peer.

This warrants talk of polarity shifts and hegemonic transitions only if gross economic output is readily convertible into other key elements of state power. Based on the experience of past challengers, many scholars and commentators appear to think that the GDP→Power conversion rate has remained constant over time, so that China, like Wilhelmine or Nazi Germany or the Soviet Union in the twentieth century, might choose to ramp up to superpower status and succeed in relatively short order. Indeed, the China/Wilhelmine Germany analogy is even more popular than the unipolarity-is-ending line. Chris Layne's chapter in this volume resonates with the work of scores of analysts who explore China's dissatisfaction with the status quo and possible US responses via comparisons with Germany's rise of a century ago.[34]

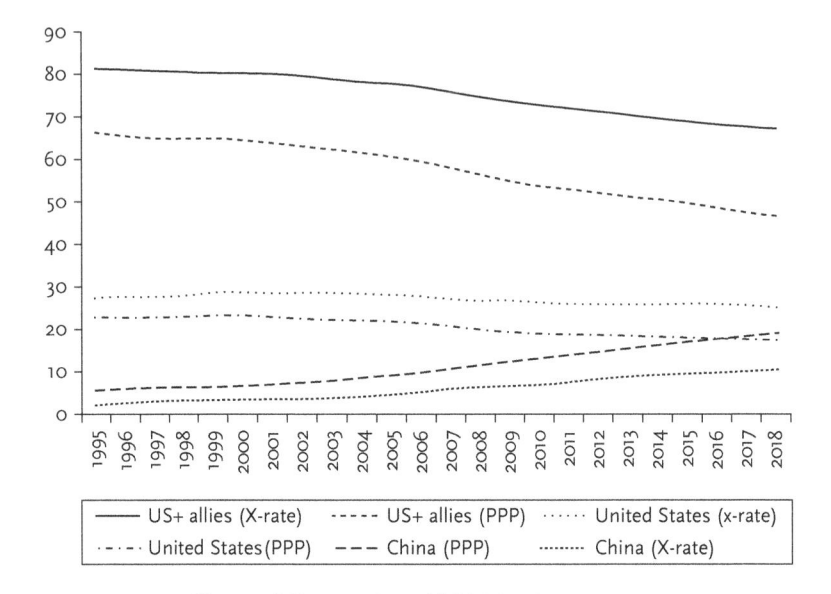

Figure 3.1 US, US+Allies, and China as % World GDP, 1995–2018
Notes: 2013–2018 USDA and IMF estimates. Allies = NATO, non-NATO EU, and West Europe; Japan, Republic of Korea, Australia, New Zealand; Israel, Saudi Arabia.
Sources: USDA ERS (http://www.ers.usda.gov/data-products/international-macroeconomic-data-set.aspx#.Un0IFY2p3yd), IMF *World Economic Outlook*.

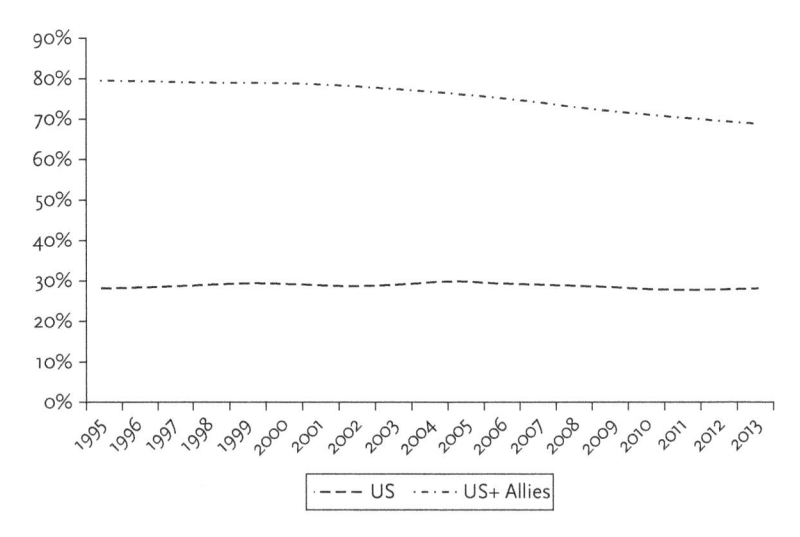

Figure 3.2 US, US+Allies as % World GDP China.
Notes: X-rate measure. 2013–2018 USDA estimates. Allies = NATO, non-NATO EU, and West Europe; Japan, Republic of Korea, Australia, New Zealand; Israel, Saudi Arabia.
Source: USDA ERS (http://www.ers.usda.gov/data-products/international-macroeconomic-data-set.aspx#.Un0IFY2p3yd).

But as Steve Brooks and I detail elsewhere, this is misleading on two counts.[35] First, past challengers were roughly comparable in population to the dominant power. When their gross economic output came within range of the dominant state's, their relative wealth and technological prowess followed suit, either surpassing, matching, or at least approaching the hegemon's. When it came to be seen as a challenger to Britain's world position, Wilhelmine Germany, for example, was richer, more technologically advanced in key areas, and had a larger economy than Britain. By comparison, China's huge population dictates that its economy can match US output while still being dramatically poorer and less advanced. Even the Soviet Union, which used totalitarianism to compensate for relative backwardness, was much richer vis-à-vis the United States during the Cold War peak than China is today.[36] And for the initial phases of the Cold War, Moscow matched or even surpassed the United States in key, strategically significant technological areas. As Odd Arne Westad and David Shambaugh detail in this book, China still has a long way to go before presenting a challenge of that nature.

Second, for a variety of reasons Brooks and I detail, it is much harder today to translate raw GDP into other elements of state capability—especially military capacity —than it was in the mid-twentieth century. Modern weapons systems are orders of magnitude harder to develop and learn to use effectively than their mid-twentieth-century predecessors. China thus confronts a higher bar for peer competitor status than did earlier challengers from position of less wealth and lower indigenous technological capacity. As a result, the best estimate is that China will long remain in its current status as a potential superpower.

How is this likely to affect contestation over the status quo? The standard answer is that China will pursue a quiescent "peaceful rise" strategy until its leadership decides that it can amass the full-spectrum capabilities needed for full emergence as a superpower peer. But this runs up against recent research positing that contestation becomes more likely the more uncertain each state is of its position. In this view, satisfaction with a given status quo is not wholly reducible to its material costs and benefits. Abundant research shows that leaders and citizens place some value on their state's standing in international affairs.[37] The politics of interstate status or prestige is ubiquitous and usually harmless. It becomes a problem when one state seeks to enhance its standing at another's expense, and that second states resists, raising the potential for foregone cooperation, costly competition, and militarized rivalry. For this to occur, the riser has to think a revision of its status is warranted and possible, and the dominant status quo state must simultaneously think that it has ample means to defend its position.

China's meteoric rise is setting up just such a scenario. The stability of a state's dominance is partly a function of the robustness of the material foundations on which it rests. Uneven capability portfolios—when key states excel in different kinds of power—raise uncertainty about relative rank and thus increase the probability of competition over status. In other research, I have found evidence of this dynamic at work in the nineteenth and twentieth centuries, most recently in the Cold War, when the Soviet Union matched the US militarily but not in other dimensions.[38] When an actor possesses some attributes of high status but not others, uncertainty and status inconsistency are likely. The more a subordinate state matches its superior in some but not all key material dimensions of status, the more likely it is to conceive an interest in contesting its rank and the more likely the higher-ranked state is to resist. Thus, status competition is more likely to plague relations between leading states whose portfolios of capabilities are not only close but also mismatched.

While the United States remains dominant on most dimensions of state capability—military power, global reach, technological capacity, wealth—the "full spectrum preeminence" it has enjoyed since 1991 is projected to end relatively soon when China's GDP surpasses America's. And there is, at least, circumstantial evidence that this shift is already having the predicted effect. In the wake of the 2008 financial crisis, most observers detected a new assertiveness on the part of China concerning both the deference it expected from smaller neighbors on key security and economic issues and the degree of resentment at America's continued dominance in the region. As Ikenberry, Foot, and Odgaard show in this volume, the "China challenge" to the order is complex, with significant strains of policy endorsing the status quo. Hence, the degree of Beijing's revisionism remains debatable.[39]

But there is no question the passage of time has generated increased evidence of China's dissatisfaction, especially with US dominance in its region. Leadership statements as well as commentary by China's foreign policy analysts and the informed public were consistent with the analysis here.[40] Regional arrangements that were endured when China was weaker become intolerable for a country with the world's second-largest economy. For its part, the United States remains committed to the overall regional status quo. And why not? By most estimates, the United States and its allies have the capacity to sustain it. The mere fact that China's gross economic output has increased does not immediately invalidate those assessments.

The result is a nascent competition for position in Asia. It is still attenuated by a very large set of countervailing factors that augur for cooperation, not least the huge economic costs each side (but especially China) would have to bear if competition escalated. But the incipient rivalry is sufficiently worrisome to have generated a cottage industry of expert analyses warning of dangers and advising policies to avoid them.[41] What is striking is that there is even this much evidence of incipient status competition even though the changes in the overall global power structure are subtle. Not only is China approaching the United States only in one major dimension (GDP), and that only according one measure (PPP), but, as figure 3.1 above shows, Washington is still allied to most of the world's largest and most technologically advanced economies as well as most of its most formidable military powers. The global status quo is still buttressed by a daunting preponderance of interstate power. And yet a comparatively slight increase in uncertainty occasioned chiefly by global economic shifts may well have helped generate a measurable increase in dissatisfaction and competitiveness.

INSTITUTIONS AND STRATEGIC INCENTIVES

The analysis so far suggests that the pessimists radically overstate the dangers presented by current rise-and-decline dynamics, but they are right that China's rise generates more incentives for contestation than was the post-1991 norm. Why cannot the system leader simply adjust via careful retrenchment and accommodation? If the analysis here is right, the problem is real but, in theory, easily manageable. Given that overall system leadership is not at issue, adjustments should be straightforward. At issue is US preeminence in China's region, as well as some of the basic rules and institutions that Beijing currently finds nettlesome. This zeroes in on an undertheorized part of Gilpin's original framework, as well as other rise-and-decline theories. Why must a lag develop between underlying distribution of capabilities and the rules and institutions governing the interstate system? Why cannot the order be revised incrementally as underlying power shifts?

Half the answer has already been established: capabilities shift unevenly and are hard to measure. In previous transitions, the problem was rising powers that created outsized military postures. In the current setting, this is reversed: it is the dominant power that remains the military behemoth while the challenger racks up economic gains. While this difference creates interesting shifts in strategic incentives, the immediate implication is to generate uncertainty, allowing challenger and defender simultaneously to think that the order can be challenged and defended.

But today's international system is far more thickly institutionalized than those in which previous power shifts occurred, and institutions play a far more salient role in the US grand strategy than was the case for its predecessors at the top of the interstate heap. There are good reasons to worry that this may induce rigidity the system. And if that is so, then today's order may well be far less amenable to accommodation than its defenders argue. Key here is the close interaction between institutions and grand strategy.

Woven through the speeches of President Obama and other top US officials is a robust restatement of the traditional US commitment to multilateral institutions as a key plank in a grand strategy of global leadership. Even as the president sought to carve out a somewhat more restrained vision for US grand strategy in his recent West Point Commencement speech, the emphasis on American leadership of the current institutional and rule-based order remained as pronounced as ever. With some oversimplification, this approach can be summarized in a few core propositions:

1. US leadership is a necessary condition of institutionalized cooperation to address classical and new security challenges, which is, in turn, a necessary condition of US security.
2. The maintenance of US security commitments to partners and allies in Europe and Asia is a necessary condition of US leadership. Without the commitments, US leverage for leadership declines.
3. The leverage the United States obtains by being a security provider for scores of countries spills over into other functional areas, notably economics.
4. Embedding US leadership in formal institutions often has major benefits for Washington and its partners: the classical functional benefits (focal point, reduced transaction costs, monitoring, etc.); and political and legitimacy benefits (mitigating politically awkward aspects of hegemony). Because the United States is not meaningfully constrained by its institutional commitments, the benefits far outweigh the costs.
5. Embedding US leadership in less formal institutions—for example, international law and other rules—also often pays in more diffuse ways. It is easier to pursue a national interest when it can be expressed as a rule or principle to which others have formally subscribed. Again, because the United States itself is not meaningfully constrained by rules, the benefits outweigh the costs.

According to US foreign policy elites—and reams of political science research on institutions—the focus on leadership and institutions brings benefits to the United States from institutionalized cooperation to address a wide range of problems.[42] There is wide agreement that a stable, open, and loosely rule-based international order serves the interests of the United States. Most scholars and policy makers agree that such an interstate order better serves American interests than a world that is closed—that is, built around blocs and spheres of influence—and devoid of basic agreed-upon rules and institutions. As scholars have long argued, under conditions of interdependence—and especially rising complex interdependence—states often can benefit from institutionalized cooperation.

And there is substantial evidence for the idea that US leadership increases the prospects that such cooperation will emerge in a manner relatively favorable to American interests. Of course, the prospects for cooperation are partly a function of compatible interests. Yet even when interests overlap, scholars of all theoretical stripes have established that institutionalized cooperation does not effortlessly emerge: generating agreement on the particular cooperative solution can often be elusive. And when interests do not overlap, the bargaining becomes yet tougher: not just how, but whether cooperation will occur is on the table. Many factors affect the initiation of cooperation, and under various conditions states can and have cooperated without hegemonic leadership.[43] But scholars acknowledge that the likelihood of overcoming problems of collective action, relative gains, and incomplete information drops in the absence of leadership.[44]

Arguably the biggest benefit is that a complex web of settled rules and institutions is a major bulwark of the status quo. Over a century of social science scholarship stands behind Ikenberry's signature claim about the "lock in" effects of institutions.[45] Path dependence, routinization, socialization, internalization, and many other causal mechanisms underlie institutions' famed "stickiness." These stand as important allies of status quo oriented actors—and major adversaries of revisionists. They radically raise the costs of overturning any given institutional arrangement and provide strong incentives for mildly dissatisfied actors to accept the given arrangements even though they are suboptimal from their perspective. Needless to say, this same stickiness can vex those who like the status quo in general but might want to revise rules—as in the case of Europe's and to a lesser extent the United States' efforts to alter norms of lawful military intervention in sovereign states. Or, consider the United Nations Security Council—many (perhaps even including the United States) might prefer a revised set of permanent members, but the political and other costs of trying to achieve that outcome appear to outweigh expected benefits. And, as Liselotte Odgaard shows in her chapter herein, dissatisfied powers like China can use existing rules to push back against changes they dislike, and they can exploit ambiguities in the normative order to defend their prerogatives. But given that the United States remains essentially a status quo power and that the existing institutional order reflects its core preferences, overall the stickiness of institutions works to its advantage and is a major argument for defending the order.

In sum, the incentives for the United States to foster and lead the institutional order are strong. The benefits appear large, and US policymakers reject neoconservative, institutionalist, and constructivist arguments about the costs of embedding their leadership grand strategy in institutions and rules. To neoconservatives, US officials reply that institutions do not sap US sovereignty and do provide net efficiency and legitimacy gains. To institutionalists and constructivists, US officials would say (off the record) that Washington does not actually have to bind itself via rules to reap some of their benefits. American leaders repeatedly promise their people that they will never allow foreigners a veto on any action they deem necessary for US interests, and I think they mean it. As far as I can tell, the United States ignores most rules that get in its way.[46]

But that does not mean that there are no downsides. Even if the United States is not tightly constrained by the specific rules and norms of the institutional order, embedding its grand strategy in institutions may curtail options and reduce flexibility in other ways. First is the problem of exclusion. Foundational elements of the US grand strategy of leadership are exclusionary by nature. As noted, US officials believe that the maintenance of US security commitments to partners and allies in Europe and Asia is a necessary condition of US leadership. And those commitments are exclusionary by definition. As long as those commitments remain the bedrock of the US global position, states against which those commitments are directed—especially China and Russia—can never be wholly integrated into the order. The result is to foreclose an alternative grand strategy of great power concert. Securing the gains of institutionalized cooperation today may come at the price of having alienated potential partners tomorrow. This problem grows with the power and dissatisfaction of excluded states

Second and more speculatively, US policymakers may confront another set of constraints in the longer term. Key here is the article of faith among US policymakers that all the parts of the US grand strategy are interdependent: US security commitments are necessary for leadership that is necessary for cooperation that is necessary for security and for US leadership in other important realms. The result is to create apparently potent disincentives to disengaging from any single commitment. Pulling back from US security guarantees to South Korea or Taiwan or NATO may make sense when each of these cases is considered individually. But if scaling back anywhere saps US leadership capacity everywhere, any individual step toward retrenchment will be extremely hard to take. When US officials are confronted with arguments for retrenchment, these concerns frequently come to the fore.[47]

In sum, while Ikenberry is right to stress the institutional order's resilience, and Foot is right to stress the degree to which China accepts key elements of it, neither scholar investigates the rigidity it fosters in US grand strategy and the ways in which it might inhibit optimal rebalancing to accommodate China's rise. These effects were strongly in evidence in the crisis over Ukraine. NATO's exclusionary essence was an important driver of Russian policy. Political and organizational incentives within the institution, moreover, made it very hard to agree formally to close the door to further expansion to Ukraine and Georgia even when many NATO allies supported such a move. The result appeared to be a case in which the incentives intrinsic to the institution pushed toward conflict with a major power. The ability to accommodate rising (or, in Russia's case, assertively dissatisfied) powers appears to be constrained by the central role institutions play in the leading state's grand strategy. Similarly, Washington's ability to give way to Beijing on some of its maritime claims is strongly constrained by worries of follow-on effects. If China succeeds in overturning key freedom-of-the-seas norms in the East and South China seas, other littoral states in other regions may follow suit, creating a cascade that might threaten America's command of the commons. Thus, the highly ramified institutional order may foreclose potentially optimal deals to defuse tensions with rising and/or dissatisfied powers.

CONCLUSION

Change in world politics tends to be gradual in the absence of major catalysts. Historically, major hegemonic wars played this role. I provided initial evidence to the effect that even some of history's most devastating wars performed this function poorly. Even with all-out great power wars as a mechanism, displacing hegemonic leadership is very hard to do. Yet Schweller makes a strong case that other major events lack the political mechanisms required to reorder the international political system. The net implication is that displacing the current US-dominated interstate order is much, much harder than much current commentary allows. If that were not enough, the power shift currently underway is far more modest than the hyperbolic rhetoric used to describe it. It amounts to China reaching peer status in terms of gross economic size. Yet for a number of reasons

Beijing faces a higher bar for translating that economic output into the other requisites of superpowerdom, not least because it is comparably poor relative to the system leader and barriers to entry in the top-end military competition are higher than ever. And if all *that* were not enough, China confronts a settled, ramified institutional order that stacks the deck against revisionism.

But the analysis presented here is hardly Panglossian. The shifting scales of world power are already generating incentives for militarized contestation. China's rise appears to have generated dissonance in Beijing sufficient to propel a more pugnacious policy of pushback against US preeminence in its region. Because US dominance is most pronounced in the military area, and because security relationships are so central to its grand strategy—even in its institutional and economic manifestations—Washington faces increased incentives to rely on its security relationships in system management. And given the large role of institutions in its grand strategy and perennial fears that backing down in any area will compromise the stability of other areas, the United States faces strong incentives to double down on most if not all of its current commitments. This makes rational adjustment of the status quo in tandem with shifting power balances even harder than when E. H. Carr first theorized that approach to peaceful change in the mid-twentieth century.

For their part, rising and more assertive powers face incentives for "salami tactics," subtle moves that seek to effect change one small slice at a time. A full-scale assault on the order is out of the question, but subtle power plays and faits accomplis may well satisfy near-term aspirations, as Vladimir Putin may have demonstrated in his neighborhood. Great power tensions are thus likely to assume a salience in world politics that was absent in the first fifteen years of unipolarity. The security effects discussed here are manageable. Indeed, the security ramifications of emerging markets' rise might be more benign than at least some forms of decline. Most China watchers, for example, are more worried about the security downsides of a hard landing for China's economy than its continued rise. But these security effects do portend a world that is harder to manage than it was when the United States and its allies represented 70–80 percent of global GDP. It is far easier to use economic leverage and incentives in economic bargaining than to deploy security leverage, which can be a blunt instrument. And it is far easier to manage the status aspirations of rising powers from a position of full-spectrum preeminence than from the marginally less robust position that is already emerging.

NOTES

1. Council on Foreign Relations, *Global Governance Report Card 2014*, June 2014, http://www.cfr.org/thinktank/iigg/reportcard/.
2. See Christopher Layne, "The Sound of Distant Thunder: The Pre-World War I Anglo-German Rivalry as a Model for Sino-American Relations in the Early Twenty-First Century," this volume. And, for a comprehensive accounting of many such analogies, see Steven Ward, *Status and Revisionism* (unpublished book manuscript, Cornell University, 2014).
3. See G. John Ikenberry, "A New Order of Things? China, the United States, and the Struggle over World Order," and Foot, "Restraints on Conflict in the China-US Relationship: Contesting Power Transition Theory," this volume.
4. Robert Gilpin, *War and Change in World Politics* (Cambridge: Cambridge University Press, 1982).
5. Some of the material in this section first appeared in William C. Wohlforth, "The Future of War as the *Ultima Ratio*," in Ken Booth and Toni Erskine, eds., *International Relations Theory Today* (2nd ed.) (Polity 2016).
6. Gilpin *War and Change*, 200.
7. Many see a kind of hindsight bias in the scholarship I am about to discuss, on account of its assumption that big and costly wars must have profound causes and major effects. See, e.g., R. Ned Lebow, *Forbidden Fruit: Counterfactuals and International Relations* (Princeton, NJ: Princeton University Press, 2010); R. Ned Lebow and Benjamin Valentino, "Lost in Transition: A Critical Analysis of Power Transition Theory," *International Relations* 23 (2009): 389–410; Bruce Bueno de Mesquita, "Pride of Place: The Origins of German Hegemony," *World Politics* 43 (1990): 28–52.
8. Gilpin *War and Changee*, chap. 5.
9. G. John Ikenberry, *After Victory: Institutions, Strategic Restraint, and the Rebuilding of Order after Major Wars* (Princeton, NJ: Princeton University Press, 2000), 254n134.
10. Randall L. Schweller, *Maxwell's Demon and the Silver Hammer* (Baltimore: Johns Hopkins University Press, 2014), 143.
11. Ibid., 107.
12. Carl von Clausewitz, 1984. *On war*. Princeton, NJ: Princeton University Press, Chapter 1, Section 24.
13. For these generalizations, I rely most on Paul W. Schroeder, "The 19th-Century International System: Changes in the Structure," *World Politics* 39 (1986): 1–26; "Did the Vienna Settlement Rest on a Balance of Power?," *The American Historical Review* 97 (1992): 683–706; and *The Transformation of European Politics* (London: Oxford University Press, 1993). See also Paul M. Kennedy, *The Rise and Fall of the Great Powers* (New York: Random House, 1987); Adam Watson, *The Evolution of International Society: A Comparative Historical Analysis* (London: Routledge, 1983); Ikenberry, *After Victory*; Ian Clark, *Hegemony in International Society* (Cambridge: Cambridge University Press, 2011); and Richard Elrod, "The Concert of Europe: A Fresh Look at an International System," *World Politics* 28 (1976): 159–74.
14. Clark, *Hegemony*, 74.
15. Schroeder, *Transformation*, 244.
16. Ikenberry, *After Victory*, 81.

17. Edward Hallet Carr, *The Twenty Years' Crisis: 1919–1939: An Introduction to the Study of International Relations* (London: Macmillan, 1951).
18. Kennedy, *Rise and Fall*, chap. 6.
19. See, e.g., Alan Sharp, *The Versailles Settlement: Peacemaking in Paris, 1919* (Basingstoke: Macmillan, 1991); Harold Nicolson, *Peacemaking 1919* (London: Houghton Mifflin, 1933).
20. Ikenberry, *After Victory*, 139.
21. G. John Ikenberry. 2017. *After Victory: Institutions, Strategic Restraint, and the Rebuilding of Order after Major Wars*, 254, n. 134.
22. William C. Wohlforth, *Elusive Balance: Power and Perceptions in the Cold War* (Ithaca, NY: Cornell University Press, 1993).
23. Analyzed in detail in Wohlforth, *Elusive Balance*, and Simon Bromley, *American Power and the Prospects for International Order* (Cambridge: Cambridge University Press, 2008).
24. R. Ned Lebow, *Why Nations Fight* (Cambridge: Cambridge University Press, 2010"; Bruce Bueno de Mesquita, "Price of Place: The Origins of German Hegemony," *World Politics* 43: 1 (1990): 28–52.
25. John Mueller, *Quiet Cataclysm: Reflections on the Recent Transformation of World Politics* (New York: HarperCollins, 1995), 1.
26. Mary Elise Sarotte, *1989: The Struggle to Create Post-Cold War Europe* (Princeton, NJ: Princeton University Press, 2009), 64–72.
27. William C. Wohlforth, "The Stability of a Unipolar World," *International Security* 21 (1999): 5–41.
28. William C. Wohlforth, "Unipolarity, Status Competition and Great Power War," *World Politics* 61 (2009): 28–57.
29. Mary Elise Sarotte, "Perpetuating U.S. Preeminence: The 1990 Deals to 'Bribe the Soviets Out' and Move NATO In," *International Security* 35 (2010): 110–37; Daniel Deudney and G. John Ikenberry, "The Unraveling of the Cold War Settlement," *Survival* 51 (2010): 39–62.
30. In addition to Sarotte's *1989*, see James Davis and William C. Wohlforth, "German Unification," in *Ending the Cold War: Interpretations, Causation, and the Study of International Relations*, ed. Richard K. Herrmann and Richard Ned Lebow (New York: Palgrave, 2004), 47–51; and William C. Wohlforth, "German Reunification: A Reassessment," in *The Cold War—Reassessments*, ed. Arthur L. Rosenbaum and Chae-Jin Lee (Claremont, CA: The Keck Center for International and Strategic Studies, 2000), 131–57.
31. Layne, "The Sound of Distant Thunder," 137. See also Layne, "This Time It's Real: The End of Unipolarity and the *Pax Americana*," *International Studies Quarterly* 56 (2012): 203–13; T. A. Shakleina and A. A. Baykov, eds., *Megatrendy: osnovnye traektory evoliutsii mirovogo poriadka v XXI veke* (Moscow: Aspekt Peess, 2013); National Intelligence Council (2012), *Global Trends 2030: Alternative Worlds*, https://www.dni.gov/files/documents/GlobalTrends_2030.pdf.
32. William C. Wohlforth, "How Not to Evaluate Theories," *International Studies Quarterly* 56 (2012): 219–22.
33. US allies as defined in figure 1 declined from 54 percent of world GDP in 1995 to 44 percent in 2013. Major forecasts converge on the expectation that this trend will continue.
34. See Ward, *Status and Revisionism*, chap. 1.

35. Stephen G. Brooks and William C. Wohlforth, "The Rise and Fall of Great Powers in the 21st Century: China's Rise and the Fate of America's Global Position," *International Security* 40, no. 3 (Winter 2015–2016): 7–53; and *America Abroad: The United States' Global Role in the 21st Century* (Oxford: Oxford University Press, 2016).
36. By Maddison's estimates, in 1960, the Union of Soviet Socialist Republics's per capita GDP was 35 percent of US; today, by World Bank estimates, China's per capita GDP is 11 percent of US in exchange-rate conversion and 18 percent by PPP conversion.
37. For details, see Deborah Larson, T. V. Paul, and William C. Wohlforth, eds., *Status and World Order* (Cambridge: Cambridge University Press, 2014).
38. See William C. Wohlforth, "Unipolarity, Status and Great Power War," *World Politics* 61:1 (January 2009): 28–57; and "Status Dilemmas and Inter-State Conflict," in *Status and World Politics*, ed. T. V. Paul, Deborah Welch Larson and William C. Wohlforth (Cambridge: Cambridge University Press, 2014), 115–40.
39. See, e.g., A. I. Johnston, "How New and Assertive Is China's New Assertiveness?," *International Security* 37 (2013): 7–48.
40. For more, see discussion in D. W. Drezner, "Military Primacy Doesn't Pay (Nearly As Much As You Think)" *International Security* 38 (2013): 52–79.
41. See, e.g., Hugh White, *The China Choice: Why America Should Share Power* (Colingwood: Black, 2012); A. L. Friedberg, *A Contest for Supremacy: China, America and the Struggle for Mastery in Asia* (New York: Norton, 2011); Avery Goldstein, "First Things First: The Pressing Danger of Crisis Instability in US-China Relations," *International Security* 37 (2013): 49–89.
42. S. G. Brooks, G. J. Ikenberry, and W. C. Wohlforth, "Don't Come Home, America: The Case Against Retrenchment," *International Security* 37 (2012–2013): 7–51.
43. See Robert O. Keohane, *After Hegemony* (Princeton, NJ: Princeton University Press, 1982); and Robert Axelrod, *The Evolution of Cooperation* (New York: Basic Books, 1984).
44. See Robert Keohane, "Hegemony and After: What Can Be Said About the Future of American Global Leadership?," *Foreign Affairs* July/August 2012, 1–5.
45. Ikenberry, After Victory.
46. For evidence, see S. G. Brooks and W. W. Wohlforth, *World out of Balance: International Relations and the Challenge of American Primacy* (Princeton, NJ: Princeton University Press, 2008).
47. Important strains of scholarly research question this assumption of interdependence, finding either that reputations never form across issues or cases or that reputations are separable and so reneging on a commitment in one region or functional area need not affect assessments of credibility in other regions or areas. But sincere and intense conviction on the part of policy makers that commitments are interdependent appears endemic to the institutionalized grand strategy.

CHAPTER 4
Restraints on Conflict in the China-US Relationship

Contesting Power Transition Theory

ROSEMARY FOOT

INTRODUCTION

As with the study of China itself, those who have worked with various versions of power transition theory have found increased scholarly and media interest in their ideas. In the last few years, China has emerged as the world's second-largest economy, has become the leading exporter of goods, and has acquired the world's second-largest military budget. Over a similar time period, we have witnessed the United States sustain and only slowly recover from economic losses as a result of the impact of the 2007–2008 global financial crisis, as well as the effects of its overextension in wars in Afghanistan and the wider Middle East. Inevitably, perhaps, these shifts in relative power between Beijing and Washington have led to a revival of interest in the argument that the probability of major war increases when a dissatisfied rising power begins to displace a declining hegemon from a position of preeminence that it had previously held. Notwithstanding criticisms of this argument based on the complexities associated with measuring power transition, the unhelpful emphasis on gross material attributes rather than the social or wider dimensions of power, as well as the difficulties of determining who is a dissatisfied or status quo state in this and other dyads, discussion of the Sino-American relationship continues often to be conducted in material power distribution terms.[1]

This chapter offers a critique of the major arguments that those interested in this structural redistribution of power advance to explain the current tensions and, in their view, likely future conflict between China and the United States.[2] However, its main aim is to put the focus on group and state agency, and to consider the arguments that impose some restraints on political actors as they contemplate a regional and global order undergoing significant change. The chapter does not discuss at any length conventional or nuclear deterrence, including recent evidence of US strengthening of its alliances with, for example, Australia, Japan, and South Korea, together with the deepening of America's informal ties with Indonesia, Malaysia, Singapore, and Vietnam. Neither does it discuss China's efforts at internal military balancing, leaving those points for elsewhere in this volume. Instead, four less-often remarked upon themes will receive attention. These are

- historical awareness of the so-called Thucydides trap;
- regional state action designed to shape and subdue major state rivalries;
- new forms of economic interdependence that have promoted regional and global economic integration; and
- China's and America's domestic political-economic priorities.

While these restraints certainly do not guarantee peaceful cooperation between the two central protagonists in an era of change, they do place some bounds on the conflictual elements of that relationship.[3] If these restraints turn out not to be enough to avert conflict, I argue it is not transitions in material power that best explain this outcome, but rather the difficulties of promoting clear and sustained strategic goals in a global order of great complexity and that has seen a collapse of any well-defined boundaries between the domestic and global policy realms. I explore these ideas in relation to US and Chinese policies toward the Asia-Pacific region because it is here that the relationship faces its greatest tests, and also where the power transition literature has turned its primary attention.

POWER TRANSITION THEORY

Power transition theory in its classical formulation argues that shifts in power, most likely caused by rapid economic growth in one party relative to another in a dyadic relationship, are likely to lead to war. The probability of major war is deemed to be greatest at the moment that the declining hegemon is about to be overtaken by a rising, dissatisfied power. Either the declining hegemon initiates a preventive war to avert being overtaken by the upstart, or the rising challenger initiates fighting so that its newfound status is reflected in the distributional benefits that the international system accords it. As G. John Ikenberry reminds us in his chapter in this volume, Robert Gilpin's classic formulation notes that states that are growing in power will seek to move a "disequilibrium" in international order to "equilibrium" through hegemonic war. Such a war has the effect of overturning the old order, thereby bringing about a correspondence between the interests of the resurgent state and the new international order that is created by hegemonic war.[4]

These insights are reflected to lesser or greater degrees in a number of more recent analyses focusing on contemporary changes in the distribution of power between China and the United States. Graham Allison has popularized the notion of the dangers of power transition beyond the academy by referring to what he describes as the "Thucydides trap"— that is, the argument made by the Athenian historian and general, Thucydides, that the cause of the Peloponnesian War in the fifth century BC was the rise of Athens and the fear it inspired in Sparta. Allison, among many others, has also made use of the hundredth anniversary of World War I to remind us that that particular conflagration was sparked by a dissatisfied Germany whose leaders chose to challenge a declining hegemon, Britain.[5]

Other scholarly analyses of this type have also received a great deal of attention in the contemporary discussion of Sino-American relations. Aaron L. Friedberg, John J. Mearsheimer, and Hugh White have each produced extended treatments of the US-China relationship and have framed their arguments broadly in power transition or structural realist terms.[6] They have each argued that the intensity of the rivalry between these two states is likely to increase as China grows richer and stronger because, among other things, Beijing will work harder to eject the US presence from a region where America has long enjoyed preponderance. While Friedberg points out how China's authoritarian system sharpens the effects and heightens the stakes of the power transition, Mearsheimer, from his offensive realist position, de-emphasizes political regime type (though he highlights the power of nationalism). Instead, he argues that states seek power and ultimately regional hegemony in order "to survive under international anarchy." Thus, "if China continues to grow economically, it will attempt to dominate Asia the way the United States dominates the Western Hemisphere."[7]

Of these three analyses (or four if we include Allison in the mix), it is Mearsheimer who—in part through the boldness of his message, together with the titles he chooses for his articles and other contributions—promotes particularly starkly the near certainty of conflict. In outlets as varied as *Global Times, Current History*, and *The Chinese Journal of International Politics*, together with the new and extended treatment of his argument in the final chapter of the second edition of *The Tragedy of Great Power Politics*[8] Mearsheimer has stated that he is "quite certain that China cannot rise peacefully," predicting that "there is a reasonable chance that the US and China will end up in a shooting war over the next 30 or 40 years."[9] Moreover, he states that the prospects for a Sino-American war breaking out over the longer term is "more likely than a war between the superpowers was during the Cold War."[10]

Mearsheimer's offensive realist approach, referenced also in the chapter by Stephen Walt in this volume, is based on several assumptions: states are the main actors in international politics, and they operate in an anarchical system with no central authority able to provide a guarantee of security. States should be viewed as rational actors, capable of designing strategies that bolster their security. Thus, great powers, for security reasons, will seek hegemony within their own region and seek to ensure that all other regions are not dominated by a rival great power. Every great power will seek to maximize power in order to protect its core goal of survival, which "when push comes to shove ... trumps all other goals." In order to improve its chances for survival, the state will turn its economic strength into military capabilities. The acquired military capabilities will be difficult to interpret as either offensive or defensive, and anyway the intentions of states are difficult to read. Thus it is prudent to assume the worst. Economic interdependence will not operate as a constraint on behavior when survival is at stake because all other goals are subordinate to that overriding survival goal. Diplomacy is not much of a constraint because great powers will expect other great powers to behave in a similar self-regarding way, and, thus, protestations of peaceful coexistence to the contrary, such words or treaty commitments cannot, indeed should not, be relied upon. With respect to China and the United States, the presence of nuclear weapons will not keep the lid on things either, in part because of the low stakes involved in each Asia-Pacific crisis compared with the European theatre during the Cold War.[11]

These assumptions have been subjected to several critiques since Mearsheimer first elaborated them in 2001.[12] Jonathan Kirshner, from a classical realist perspective, has provided a powerful attack on the logic of Mearsheimer's arguments as well as on the historical lessons to be derived from past cases of power transition. Ikenberry and Wohlforth's chapters in this volume also note the historical exceptions, taking issue with the notion of epic cycles in world politics, placing emphasis instead on evolutionary change.[13] Kirshner, focusing on historical lessons, argues that bidding for hegemony (rather than having hegemony) is a dangerous occupation and historically has proven to be "one of the few and rare paths *to* destruction for a great power." Kirshner further notes that apart from the United States, states that have bid for hegemony have not succeeded (Wilhelmine Germany and imperial Japan spring most readily to mind here). If they follow offensive realist logic, then we can assume that states like China, while operating on rationalist premises, have learnt nothing from history.[14] In addition, there is the matter of whether actual survival is really at stake in this relationship given America's and China's "military establishments, their nuclear deterrents, their economic might, their continental size, and their vast populations." In the absence of that existential threat to their survival, why would they rationally imperil it all by adopting an offensive realist strategy?[15] Surely, they are more likely to try to navigate their way through these dangerous waters, seeking to find a way to coexist, even occasionally to cooperate.

Kirshner, like Steve Chan before him, argues instead for an approach that allows for state agency over structuralism, and the working through of politics both domestic and international: as Chan has put it, "[S]tates make strategic choices, and officials and scholars construct realities."[16] What Mearsheimer's account neglects are some of the consequences of a world and regional order that render discussions of power in the current international system as more complex. Neither does his approach seek out evidence that shows attempts to develop the cooperative areas in this often fraught Sino-American relationship and that demonstrate both strategic rivalry as well as various forms of interdependence. Mearsheimer is right to note that we are operating in a difficult period of adjustment in the security order in the Asia-Pacific that is generating high levels of tension. Nationalist sentiment is also disturbingly high and complicating decision-making. Long-standing sovereignty disputes are notorious for their ability to generate conflict.[17] But to predict a shooting war in thirty to forty years in its starkness obscures the range of choices that decision-makers face in the short to medium term and that will shape the future. Moreover, as he also notes, thirty to forty years is a dangerously long time span for theories of international politics that have a limited ability to predict the future and represent only "rather crude instruments."[18]

As Ikenberrry has argued, and as US and Chinese official statements have underlined (as detailed below), the structural realist account fails to take seriously that US-China rivalry is played out in a situation where both great powers are not just competitors but also deeply interdependent. Ikenberry rightly notes "There are deep sources of conflict and mistrust generated by the anarchic and competitive structures of world politics. But there are also deep sources of stability and cooperation generated by the interdependence and mutual vulnerability that come with living in the modern era."[19] Andrew Hurrell has put it somewhat similarly,[20] noting also that while power is shifting to the emerging powers, this is part of a much more general diffusion of power, "often linked to technological changes, to changes in the global economy, and to new forms of social and political mobilization."[21]

Those depictions of world politics suggest that we need to investigate the full spectrum of concerns—domestic as well as external—that governments face when they determine their policies in this hybrid world order. A "just you wait" form of argumentation based solely on changes in the distribution of power between the two leading states in the global system draws our attention away from the short to mid-term strategies that both China and the United States choose to engage in and that may depend on different underlying logics in response to a more complex set of pressures typically ignored by parsimonious structural realist theories. In what follows, I flesh out four main ways in which restraints are operating and shaping both Chinese and US decision-making, beginning first with the historical references to the so-called Thucydides trap.

THE RETURN OF THUCYDIDES

When Chinese and US officials meet, as they have been doing on several dozen occasions each year, they often refer explicitly to the academically rooted idea of the Thucydides trap. For example, Hu Jintao, when president, stated in the Sino-American Strategic and Economic Dialogue of 2012, "We should prove that the traditional belief that big powers are bound to enter into conflict is wrong, and seek new ways of developing relations between major countries in the era of economic globalization."[22] At the Brookings Institution in September 2013, where he spoke of China's "new model of major-country relations between China and the United States," Foreign Minister Wang Yi also referred to the fifteen cases of rising powers and the eleven cases where this has purportedly resulted in war between the emerging and the established state. The United States and China, he stated, needed to work to avoid that outcome.[23] Again at Davos in January 2014, Wang made explicit reference to the need to free the China-US relationship "from the so-called Thucydides trap," with war not seen in zero-sum terms but as a "lose-lose" outcome for two countries that are so closely integrated. Wang also suggested that this type of thinking "is the prime feature of the proposed new model of major-country relationship [sic]."[24] His cooperation agenda included topics such as counterterrorism, cyber security, nuclear nonproliferation, climate change, peace in the Middle East, and Africa's development.[25]

These historical references are more than matched on the US side. Former US secretary of state Hillary Clinton in March 2012, shortly after the fortieth anniversary of President Nixon's visit to China, put it thus: "We've gone from being two nations with hardly any ties to speak of, little bearing on each other, to being thoroughly, inescapably interdependent. For two nations with long traditions of independence, deeply rooted in our cultures and our histories, these are unusual circumstances to say the least. They require adjustments in our thinking and our actions, on both sides of the Pacific. And so, how do we respond to what is not just a new challenge to our two countries, but I would argue, an unprecedented challenge in history?"

Clinton went on to refer directly to power transition arguments:

> We are now trying to find an answer, a new answer to the ancient question of what happens when an established power and a rising power meet. We need a new answer. We don't have a choice. Interdependence means that one of us cannot succeed unless the other does as well. We need to write a future that looks entirely different from the past. This is, by definition, incredibly difficult. But we have done difficult things before.[26]

These types of comments were also continually made in the second-term Obama administration. Kurt Campbell, former US Assistant Secretary of State for East Asian and Pacific Affairs, affirmed in 2014 (referencing Thucydides once again) that the Obama administration objectives had been to "try to go at this idea that the United States and China were destined for conflict, and that it was almost preordained." He went on to stress that a major effort was underway "to learn from the lessons of history, the very difficult lessons of history, and to apply different mechanisms and different approaches."[27] Daniel Russel, Campbell's successor, spelled things out even more clearly, criticizing the view that the United States and China were engaged in a "zero-sum struggle for supremacy, if not conflict." In his view, this "deterministic analysis overlooks the role of leaders to have the ability to set policy and to shape relationships. It gives short shrift to the fact that our two economies are becoming increasingly intertwined, which increases each side's stake in the success of the other. It undervalues the fact that leaders in Washington and Beijing are fully cognizant of the risk of unintended strategic rivalry between an emerging power and an established power and have agreed to take deliberate actions to prevent such an outcome. And it ignores the reality of the past 35 years—that, in spite of our differences, U.S.-China relations have steadily grown deeper and stronger–and in doing so, we have built a very resilient relationship."[28]

Again in 2016, and despite the rise in Sino-American tensions as a result of developments in the South China Sea, Russel claimed that the US had "avoided not only the 'Thucydides trap,' but also the accommodationist trap where accepting China's 'core interests' is the price for trade benefits and global cooperation."[29]

These understandings could, of course, be disrupted. At the time of writing, we still await the full fleshing out of the Trump administration's China policy, and there are many Asia-related official appointments still to be made. Certainly, President Trump has been harshly critical of the US-China economic relationship, casting interdependence not as a mutual benefit but as a relationship benefitting only China. However, as of February 2017, Trump still has not acted decisively on China. Moreover, despite criticisms of Chinese assertiveness in the South China Sea, it is notable that US Defense Secretary James Mattis affirmed during his trip to Tokyo in February 2017 that diplomacy would remain the priority and that major US military action against China's claims in that region were not being considered.[30]

During Obama-Xi exchanges, and in order to demonstrate to Asia-Pacific states, in particular, that the United States and China had both cooperative as well as competitive elements in their relationship, the two governments tried to make good on this "new era" language. In June 2013, Presidents Obama and Xi met for an informal summit in California (Sunnylands) and laid out a full agenda for regular discussion.[31] In 2014, Obama and Xi met for ninety minutes at the Nuclear Security Summit, where they held discussions on North Korea, Iran, climate change, cyber security, Russia's annexation of Crimea, human rights, and the need to deepen bilateral military engagement. November 2014 saw Obama in Beijing, and in September 2015 President Xi Jinping made a return visit to Washington. The two met again at the 2016 Nuclear Security Summit, where North Korea's January nuclear test formed the major item of discussion. Indeed, Presidents Obama and Xi met over twenty times during the period of their terms in office.

The bilateral military relationship also notably advanced during the Obama period, partly because of President Xi's firm directive to the People's Liberation Army to seek to improve these ties.[32] Secretary of Defense Chuck

Hagel's first visit to China included a tour of China's one aircraft carrier, and meetings with China's Defense Minister as well as with President Xi. Where the latter emphasized the need to manage and control differences, Hagel suggested proceeding along tracks that would lead to substantive discussion, practical cooperation, and greater openness. Agreements reached, amid much sparring over Japan, the South China Sea, and Taiwan, included further discussions on Xi's initiative—first proposed at the Sunnylands Summit—to establish a military notification mechanism; to set standards of behavior to ensure safety at sea; and to convene an Asia-Pacific security dialogue. China participated in 2014 and in 2016 in the US-led Rim of the Pacific (RIMPAC) exercise.

These attempts at dialogue and at routinizing the discussions of difficult issues between these two states may well prove impossible to bring to a satisfactory conclusion. Neither do we have any indication that these regular meetings will continue during President Trump's period in office. However, they do indicate at least some past appreciation of the high stakes involved and a willingness to keep talking about the serious topics that often divide these two states. Other forms of behavior reflect a realization that states in the Asia-Pacific region, concerned about polarization, are also actors important to the shaping of the security order. In this sense, they reinforce a point made in Ikenberry's chapter, that the international order is "not simply an American owned and operated order." I turn to this topic next.

REGIONAL STATE PREFERENCES AND THE SHAPING OF REGIONAL ORDER

There has been constant reference in many Asia-Pacific states over several years to not having to choose between China and the United States in any contest between these two states.[33] Most states in the region do not want this area to become polarized in such a way that this choice is forced upon them. A combination of security and economic interests underpin this regional policy.

These local state preferences have become better understood in the United States: the Obama administration, for example, took note of the fact that most regional states did not want his administration's policy of a "pivot" or "rebalance" to Asia to be mainly military in intent, or one that tipped toward containment of a resurgent China. Thus, his administration tried to round out its rebalancing strategy. The emphasis on the Trans-Pacific Partnership agreement, the constant visits by high-level officials to the region, the US appointment of an ambassador to the Association of

Southeast Asian Nations (ASEAN), and the signature of ASEAN's Treaty of Amity and Cooperation were some of the ways in which it tried to recast its Asian strategy as multidimensional, and not simply militaristic in form. High-level official speeches—including notably those by the president himself during his April 2014 visit to Japan, the Republic of Korea, the Philippines, and Malaysia—each contained statements about the cooperative elements in the US-China relationship. While this emphasis on areas of cooperation with China often appeared alongside statements of a clear deterrent nature—particularly in the case of Japan, where the United States confirmed that any Chinese use of force with respect to the disputed Senkaku Islands would be covered by Article 5 of the US-Japan security treaty—the outlining of areas of constructive partnership with Beijing was generally made a part of the diplomatic package.

This combination of both deterrent statements and those stressing elements of cooperation in the Sino-American relationship were designed not only to send signals to the Chinese government but also to reassure the regional states that are most concerned about the prospects of polarizing rivalry. Local preferences, then, in the past have placed some restraints on US policy toward China and have slowed down the development of an all-out Cold War style containment policy toward the People's Republic of China (PRC). These regional state preferences may continue to exert a stabilizing role in the future. Knowledge and wariness of the Thucydides trap in the Obama administration added weight to the direction of this US strategy.

At the same time, the US presence in the region has been bolstered by another long-standing meme: that Washington has acted as a benign hegemon that, unlike China, has no territorial ambitions and can act as a stabilizing force that allows the serious business of economic development to continue without distraction. US governments under President Obama as well as earlier administrations have constantly reminded the local states that, above all, it has been Washington that has offered public security and economic goods that have allowed the states to prosper. As US Secretary of State John Kerry put it in September 2015 on the seventieth anniversary of the ending of World War II, the United States "has been a proud partner in the Asia-Pacific region's astonishing rise from the devastation of war" to a region that is the "engine for global economic growth" and that has "lifted hundreds of millions out of poverty."[34] Many Southeast Asian governmental elites appear to have accepted this depiction of the US role as essentially benign and stabilizing.[35] However, this message, if it is to continue to resonate, also requires the United States to live up to this role of stabilizer, and not operate as a country intent on trying to line up allies and enemies in the region in order to contain a resurgent China.

Finally, Washington has also been working to find the balance between support of its treaty allies and not becoming entrapped by them. The Obama administration reminded its various audiences that it took no position on the sovereignty disputes in the South China Sea, emphasizing its main concern was with freedom of navigation and of overflight. It also placed great stress on the benefits of taking sovereignty disputes to international adjudication. Even with its treaty ally, Japan, it restated its formal alliance commitments but also put pressure on the government to water down its historically revisionist rhetoric and undertake to improve its relations with the Republic of Korea (ROK) and also with China.

China is less responsive to these regional signals; it perceives the US rebalance to Asia as destabilizing and as creating conditions where local states are emboldened rather than constrained by the US presence. A combination of perceived victim status, the belief that its sovereignty claims are solid, and that its strengths should command respect through acquiescence is hampering the maintenance of what was once a more subtle and sensitive approach. The earlier "peaceful rise" policy, including participation in ASEAN-promoted regional multilateral enterprises, was an attempt to reassure regional neighbors. Beijing also has taken seriously in the past ASEAN rhetoric that may sound indirect and nonconfrontational, but which was designed to signal to China that it is generating discord with all ASEAN members over its behavior in the South China Sea.[36] Now, as Zhang Yunling of the Chinese Academy of Social Sciences has admitted, "As China's influence rises, its neighbours' distrust grows." He added, "[S]ome of them worry that China harbours ambitions for regional hegemony."[37]

However, China's earlier emphasis on a peaceful rise has not entirely been put aside. The Chinese leadership still stresses the need for a stable and peaceful environment to aid China's and the region's rise, and under President Xi there is more fleshing out of what that implies over the longer term. At a work forum on diplomacy held in October 2013, Xi laid out China's mid- to long-term strategy and the "extreme strategic importance" of the region of which China is a part. Xi spoke of the need to develop "comprehensive relations" with regional states and also to "consolidate friendly relations." He argued that this would mean strengthening diplomatic, security, and economic ties with the regional states in order to cultivate good will and increase the identification of these states with China.[38] The current list of Chinese initiatives is long, including Xi's signature infrastructure and connectivity development policy at first labeled "One Belt, One Road," and now called the "Belt and Road Initiative," a China-ASEAN 2 + 7 cooperation framework, and the establishment in 2015 of the Asian Infrastructure Investment Bank (AIIB).[39] In addition, the Chinese leadership signaled the need to manage the maritime sovereignty disputes and to ensure that crisis management mechanisms are effective.[40]

Yet, pushing in the other direction, President Xi has also put great emphasis on the need to protect China's core interests relating to the contests over territory that have roiled relations in the region. His stance is firm and seemingly uncompromising on these points, reportedly sending out the instruction that "while firmly committed to peaceful development, we definitely must not forsake our legitimate interests or compromise our core national interests." Neither should any country expect China to "swallow the bitter fruit that undermines our sovereignty, security and development interests."[41] The leadership appears to believe its sovereign territorial claims are as strong or stronger than those of other states in the region, and that it is playing catch-up to other states that have taken advantage of its relative quiescence over these issues until the last few years.[42] China's "victim mentality" and rivalries among Beijing's leaders may well play into this uncompromising stance. Christopher K. Johnson has argued that "maintaining a modest level of tension, both domestically and externally, is essential to achieving [Xi's broader] policy goals."[43] What is plain, however, is that these two policies of good neighborliness and protection of core interests are incompatible and that a "modest level of tension" seems not quite to capture the current levels of anxiety that China's behavior has generated. Chinese land reclamation that has turned reefs into islands and a stronger paramilitary naval presence have heightened strategic uncertainty, leading some states in the region to welcome a continuing American presence.

Perhaps even more than with US objectives in the Asia-Pacific, holding to the goal of consolidating regional ties in the context of a message also to protect China's sovereign claims has led to a deterioration in relations with Washington and with Asia-Pacific states. Strident nationalism and miscalculation also heighten the risk of conflict. However, we could see Beijing's incrementalist approach as primarily a strategy that is (perhaps poorly) designed to manage these territorial disputes in the short and medium term, and control the risks of escalation, as Chinese leaders have stated is the aim. We should be less sure that this approach portends a willingness to contemplate outright conflict with the United States as power transition theorists have been arguing.

ECONOMIC INTERDEPENDENCE AND GLOBALIZED PRODUCTION PROCESSES

The relationship between economic interdependence and reductions in international conflict has always been controversial in the academic literature. Not least are the concerns that asymmetrical economic interdependence provides coercive leverage to those that dominate economically. However, there is little doubt that the economic relationship between China and the United States is vital to both parties. The United States remains China's major export market and its largest trading partner. China is the largest foreign holder of US treasury bills and America's third-largest export trading partner. The US-China Business Council estimates that US exports to China will rise from $165 billion in goods and services in 2015 to about $525 billion in 2030,[44] and despite a difficult and sometimes hostile US market for Chinese investment, cumulative investment has gone from virtually nothing in 2000 to over $100 billion in 2016.[45] China has long operated as the fastest growing export market for US companies. For example, "between 2000 and 2011, U.S. exports to China grew by 542% compared to 80% export growth with the rest of the world."[46]

However, while these bilateral economic ties are important, they do tend to obscure a more complex form of interdependence that considerably raises the costs of conflict. China and the United States, together with many other economies (including Taiwan's) in the Asia-Pacific region, are linked in dense and complex ways through global production chains.

As is well understood, the Asia-Pacific has relied extensively on export growth to facilitate its emergence as the most dynamic region in the global economy. Much of that export trade has been in the form of networked trade, making the region the center of the globalization of production. Globalized production takes account of the fragmentation of the production process that can be achieved in areas such as electronics and technology, automobiles, footwear, toys, and so on.[47] Networked trade makes use of the revolution in communications and transportation to break the value chain into various components.[48] The share of network trade in the Asia-Pacific region is high, and China is more heavily engaged in these networks than other countries, its share in this type of activity from 2009 topping the world average. The PRC has had a core role in assembling final products made up of parts and components that derive from elsewhere in the region and that then go on to be sold in the US and other developed country markets. For example, in 2016, one-third of the content that China exported was foreign. If we adjusted the US-China trade balance to take account of the value-added content, that trade deficit would be cut in half for the United States.[49]

The implications of this networked production for the outbreak of conflict are potentially profound: not only would there be damage to or loss of access to export markets, but also loss of access to inputs that, as John Ravenhill has put it, are "critical to international competitiveness." These losses would negatively affect the whole economic development model of the state or states in question. Ravenhill goes on to argue, "To compare contemporary economic interdependence with that of previous eras is very much a matter of placing different objects in the same category: there have been qualitative changes in the character of interdependence as well as quantitative changes." Countries depend on these linkages for "critical inputs into their products; the networks also give them access to distribution and marketing channels and to brand names. Not only is this a world in which the costs of territorial conquest far outweigh any conceivable gains, but the potential costs of severing links with the global economy have also never been greater." All this adds up to a significant change in the way that the costs and benefits of going to war are calculated.[50] Interdependence in 2014 was not the same as interdependence in 1914.

Perhaps this is why the China-Japan economic relationship has not suffered as much as expected. Japan's exports to China rose 11 percent over the year 2012 to 2013—a time of high political tension—and Japan's imports from China increased more than 30 percent over the same period. The value of two-way trade has reached more than $300 billion, and while trade values are declining now, that relates mostly to a decrease in the value of the Yen and a slowing of China's growth rate.

Richard Katz has described the economic interdependence between China and Japan as an economic version of mutual deterrence helping to preserve the "uneasy status quo." He went on to note that some "60–70% of the goods that China imports from Japan are the machinery and parts that China needs to make its own products," products that it mainly sells to the developed world and particularly to the United States.[51] In the eruption of violence in Vietnam in May 2014 in response to China's stationing of an oil rig in waters that Vietnam claims as its own, we saw too how this led international companies to call on the Vietnamese authorities to clamp down on the public protests that resulted in factory shutdowns in a country that has established itself as a global manufacturing hub. In response, a mass text message sent to mobile phone users passed on the news that the Vietnamese prime minister had ordered the security forces to stop the protestors' "illegal acts," and the demonstrations were brought to a swift end.[52]

The Obama administration similarly demonstrated a recognition of the critical importance of this form of interdependence between regional and global economies. It regularly acknowledged the importance of regional stability to its own economic health, as well as the economic health of its major allies such as Japan and the Republic of Korea. Many Obama administration speeches pointed to the Asia-Pacific region as the "home to some of the fastest growing economies in the world"; to the strong ties between the region and American society, including American companies; and the vital need for America to remain involved in this most prosperous part of the world.[53]

The economic consequences of conflict among countries that are bound together in complex ways has to be factored into the decision-making in Washington and Beijing, as well as elsewhere. This is especially so in states that are trying to enact a complex domestic reform agenda (as in China's case), or as with the United States seeking full recovery from the effects of the global financial crisis that began in 2008. This adds up to a varied set of US and Chinese domestic interests that will be intent on trying to ensure that the US and Chinese governments manage as well as possible a difficult, multifaceted, bilateral relationship.

DOMESTIC ECONOMIC AND POLITICAL PRIORITIES

That last point relates to the final section of this chapter: the understanding that economic performance offers a form of political legitimacy for many governments in the Asia-Pacific region, and is especially important in countries where democratic processes are weak or nonexistent.[54] This is a long-standing belief in the region and serves to link economics with security (regime and state) in ways that power transition theories tend to ignore. Of course, nationalism also can perform this legitimating function, but we have seen how often nationalist demonstrations over what are purportedly sovereignty questions (e.g. Vietnam as in May 2014) are at the root of a wider domestic dissatisfaction connected with the unfair and unjust distribution of the fruits of the economic boom that many Asia-Pacific states have been experiencing. For these reasons, governments will often attempt to curb nationalist protests in case they take on this wider significance.[55]

Thus, economic growth, even as that growth has dropped in 2016 to about 6.7 percent, remains a high priority for China, especially in 2017 when Xi hopes to cement his position as "core leader" at the Nineteenth Party Congress. China's reform agenda is huge and very costly, involving an extensive anticorruption campaign, attempts to reduce the vast inequalities in its society, provide better health care and social welfare to an ageing populace deal with environmental degradation, make growth more dependent on domestic rather than overseas consumption, break out of the middle-income trap, and suppress or contain the more violent forms of unrest among minorities in Tibet and Xinjiang.[56] No one should underestimate the importance of this reform agenda to the PRC leadership and the way these goals have to form a part of its calculations when it considers its economic and political ties with the United States as well as with its neighbors.

Similarly, for the United States, we saw under President Obama a stronger commitment to diplomacy (multilateral and unilateral) than in the recent past, and a skepticism about the value of overt uses of force. As his 2014 State of the Union address made clear, his administration wanted to maintain its domestic economic focus, it would not engage in open-ended conflicts overseas, and it would continue to stress the value of diplomacy, multilateral approaches, and negotiation.[57] Public sentiment, while generally critical of Obama's foreign policy, was in agreement with an approach that focused more on domestic problems. In 2013, for example, some 51 percent of Americans when polled stated that the United States was overextended abroad, and 47 percent maintained that problems at home, including the economy, should get more attention. Some 52 percent said that the United States "should mind its own business internationally and let other countries get along the best they can on their own."[58]

Notably, two of the 2016 presidential election candidates, Donald Trump for the Republican Party and Bernie Sanders for the Democrats, tapped into this sentiment, and once in office President Trump has continued to emphasize an "America First" approach. If this intention is approached strategically, it requires something close to the Obama administration's foreign policy approach. Even for the militarily powerful United States, it is not clear that upending the security and stability of the Asia-Pacific via a "shooting war with China" would be given preference over America's domestic economic priorities.

CONCLUSION

We cannot afford to be complacent. To get the policy right requires wisdom and subtlety, and we might see these attributes as being generally in short supply and particularly in 2017. Many policy elements have to be balanced in order to avoid being in tension with one another and to reinforce restraint rather than conflict. For the United States, it has been seeking a forward presence for deterrent and reassurance purposes in the Asia-Pacific, but not so forward that it exacerbates the security environment, disturbs regional governments, undermines their support for the US presence, and makes the ground infertile for opportunities for cooperation between the United States and China. On China's part, it has been active in seeking to protect its so-called core interests involving Taiwan and the sovereignty disputes in maritime areas. However, Beijing is also trying to balance these island claims with the provision of regional and global economic public goods, such as the much-welcomed AIIB and the "Belt and Road" initiative. It also continues to give regular attention to an agenda with the United States that reflects their interdependence in a number of policy areas, and in ways that allow for a continuing focus on its crucial domestic reform policies. We await a fully fleshed out Trump administration response and meanwhile reflect on the uncertainties introduced by the advent of a new leader in the White House.

Asia-Pacific states remain watchful, and some have articulated more clearly their policy preferences in an era of strategic change. They remain as committed as ever to protecting their space for policy maneuver. These processes, prevalent over the last few years, underline that the regional future is not about settlement or resolution of differences; more likely that future portends high levels of tension that require a continuing and complex series of negotiations among various affected parties. But neither do these processes suggest outright conflict. As has been argued here, war can be kept in check by an awareness of the stakes involved and of what can happen when we have shifts in relative power; the realization that turning power into real influence requires being attentive to the desires of others; and that there is still much to do to improve the well-being of one's own population, a primary source of legitimacy for many governments in the region and for the new US administration itself.

NOTES

1. For a particularly useful critique of power transition ideas, see Steve Chan, *China, the U.S., and the Power-Transition Theory* (London: Routledge, 2008). See also the chapters by G. John Ikenberry and William C. Wohlforth in this volume. The latter pointedly notes that China's "huge population dictates that its economy can match US output while still being dramatically poorer and less advanced."
2. Some parts of this argument are also explored in my "Constraints on Conflict in the Asia-Pacific: Balancing 'the War Ledger,'" *Political Science* 66, no. 2 (December 2014): 119–42.
3. For a more direct discussion of Sino-American cooperation at the global level, see my "U.S.-China Interactions in Global Governance and International Organizations," in *Tangled Titans: The United States and China*, ed. David Shambaugh (Lanham, MD: Rowman and Littlefield, 2013), 347–70.
4. A. F. K. Organski and Jacek Kugler, *The War Ledger* (Chicago: The University of Chicago Press, 1980); Robert Gilpin, *War and Change in World Politics* (Cambridge: Cambridge University Press, 1981); G. John Ikenberry, "A New Order of Things? China, the United States, and the Struggle over World Order," in this volume.

5. For one example of Allison's discussion of the "Thucydides Trap," see "Obama and Xi Must Think Broadly to Avoid a Classic Trap," *New York Times*, June 6, 2013. Joseph S. Nye Jr. challenges the relevance of Thucydides's insights. As he puts it, scholarship on that era shows that "Athenian power was in fact not growing." Moreover, the Spartans feared a slave revolt more than the rise of Athenian power. See Nye, "Inevitability and War," in *The Next Great War?*, ed. Richard N. Rosecrance and Steven E. Miller (Cambridge, MA: The MIT Press, 2015), 181.
6. Aaron L. Friedberg, *A Contest for Supremacy: China, America, and the Struggle for Mastery in Asia* (New York: Norton, 2011); John J. Mearsheimer, *The Tragedy of Great Power Politics*, 2nd ed. (New York: Norton, 2014), esp. chap. 9; Hugh White, *The China Choice: Why America Should Share Power* (Victoria, AU: Black Inc., 2012). For a valuable review of the Friedberg and White books, see Yuen Foong Khong, "Primacy or World Order? The United States and China's Rise—A Review Essay," *International Security* 38, no. 3 (Winter 2013–2014): 153–75.
7. Friedberg, *A Contest*, 2; John J. Mearsheimer, "Can China Rise Peacefully?," *The National Interest*, October 25 2014, http://nationalinterest.org/commentary/can-china-rise-peacefully-10204.
8. John J. Mearsheimer, "'Peaceful Rise' Will Meet US Containment," *Global Times*, November 6, 2013, http://www.globaltimes.cn.content/823045.shtml; "China's Unpeaceful Rise," *Current History* 105 (April 2006): 160–62; "The Gathering Storm: China's Challenge to US Power in Asia," *The Chinese Journal of International Politics* 3 (2010): 381–96.
9. Mearsheimer, "'Peaceful Rise.'"
10. Mearsheimer, "Can China Rise Peacefully."
11. Mearsheimer restates these assumptions in "Can China Rise Peacefully."
12. See, for example, Glenn H. Snyder, "Mearsheimer's World—Offensive Realism and the Struggle for Security: A Review Essay," *International Security* 27, no. 1 (Summer 2002): 149–73.
13. See Jonathan Kirshner, "The Tragedy of Offensive Realism: Classical Realism and the Rise of China," *European Journal of International Relations*, 18, no. 1: 53–75. See also the Ikenberry and Wohlforth chapters in this volume.
14. Kirshner, "The Tragedy," esp. 61–2. Emphasis in original quote at 61.
15. Kirshner, "The Tragedy," 61.
16. Chan, *China, the U.S., and the Power-Transition Theory*, p. 4.
17. See M. Taylor Fravel, "Territorial and Maritime Boundary Disputes in Asia," in *The Oxford Handbook of the International Relations of Asia*, ed. Saadia M. Pekkanen, John Ravenhill, and Rosemary Foot (New York: Oxford University Press, 2014), 524–46.
18. Mearsheimer, "Can China Rise Peacefully," 23.
19. G. John Ikenberry, "The Rise of China, the United States, and the Future of the Liberal International Order," in Shambaugh, *Tangled Titans*, 72.
20. Andrew Hurrell, *On Global Order* (Oxford: Oxford University Press, 2007), 9.
21. Andrew Hurrell, "Power Transitions, Global Justice, and the Virtues of Pluralism," *Ethics and International Affairs* 27, no. 2 (2013): 1–17.
22. Quoted in Robert B. Zoellick, "U.S., China and Thucydides," *The National Interest*, July/August 2013, http://nationalinterest.org/article/us-china-thucydides-8642.
23. Wang Yi, "Toward a New Model of Major-Country Relations between China and the United States," China.org.cn, September 20, 2013, http://www.china.org.cn/world/2013-09/21/content_30086631.htm.

24. "Foreign Minister Wang Yi's Exclusive Interview with the *Financial Times*," www.chinese-embassy.org.uk. January 29, 2014,
25. Wang Yi, "Toward a New Model."
26. Hillary Rodham Clinton, "Secretary Clinton on 40 Years of U.S.-China Relations" (Washington, DC, US Institute of Peace, March 7, 2012),U.S. Department of State's Bureau of International Information Programs. See too her similar statement in Beijing, September 2012, quoted in Christopher K. Johnson, Ernest Z. Bowere, Victor D. Cha, Michael J. Green, and Matthew P. Goodman., *Decoding China's Emerging 'Great Power' Strategy in Asia*, A report of the CSIS Freeman Chair in China Studies (Lanham, MD: Rowman and Littlefield, 2014), 19.
27. Campbell is quoted in Robert Haddick, "America Has No Answer to China's Salami Slicing," *War on the Rocks*, February 6, 2014, http://warontherocks.com/2014/02/america-has-no-answer-to-chinas-salami-slicing/.
28. Daniel R. Russel, "The Future of U.S.-China Relations," Testimony before the Senate Foreign Relations Committee, Washington, DC, June 25 2014, https://www.foreign.senate.gov/hearings/the-future-of-us_-china-relations-06-25-14.
29. Daniel R. Russel, "Remarks at 'China's Growing Pains' Conference," University of Southern California, Los Angeles, April 22, 2016.
30. "China Welcomes Mattis' Emphasis on South China Sea Diplomacy," *Reuters*, February 6, 2017, http://uk.reuters.com/article/us-usa-trump-southchinasea-china-idUSKBN15LOZS.
31. Xi signalled at this meeting a serious Chinese interest in membership of what has turned out to be an ill-fated Trans-Pacific Partnership agreement. National Security Adviser Susan Rice's Georgetown speech, "America's Future in Asia," given on November 20, 2013, included a passage welcoming China's membership.
32. "China-US Shared Interests Emphasized," *China Daily*, April 23, 2013, usa.chinadaily.com.cn/china/2013-04/23/content_16436026.htm; and discussed in Johnson, et al *Decoding China's Emerging 'Great Power' Strategy*, 20.
33. For an early discussion of this preference, see Evelyn Goh, *Meeting the China Challenge: The U.S. in Southeast Asian Regional Security Strategies* (Washington, DC: East West Center, 2005). See also Steve Chan, *Looking for Balance: China, the United States, and Power Balancing in East Asia* (Stanford, CA: Stanford University Press, 2012).
34. John Kerry, Secretary of State, "On the 70th Anniversary of the End of World War II in the Pacific" Press Statement, (Washington, DC, September 2, 2015).
35. Natasha Hamilton-Hart, *Hard Interests, Soft Illusions: Southeast Asia and American Power* (Ithaca, NY: Cornell University Press, 2013).
36. Andrew Chubb, "Can the US Tone Down to ASEAN's Tune?," *East Asia Forum*, May 26, 2014, http://www.eastasiaforum.org/2014/05/26/.
37. Yunling Zhang, "China's Neighbours and the Quest for Regional Community," *East Asia Forum*, February 3, 2017, http://www.eastasiaforum.org.
38. For a valuable discussion of this meeting, see Timothy R. Heath, "Diplomacy Work Forum: Xi Steps Up Efforts to Shape a China-Centered Regional Order," *ChinaBrief* 13, no. 22 (November 2013): 6–10.
39. See Wang Yi, "China Will Provide Three Important Opportunities for Neighbouring Countries," www.chinese-embassy.org.uk, January 16, 2014, http://www.fmprc.gov.cn/eng/zxxx/t1121116.shtml.
40. Heath, "Diplomacy Work Forum," 8.

41. Yang Jiechi, "Implementing the Chinese Dream," *The National Interest*, September 10, 2013, http://nationalinterest.org/commentary/implementing-the-chinese-dream-9026.
42. For a particularly powerful statement to this effect, see the remarks of China's Chief of the General Staff, General Fang Fenghui in Washington DC, May 15, 2014. "Presenters: Department of Defense Joint Press Conference by General Dempsey and General Fang, Pentagon Briefing Room," http://archive.defense.gov/Transcripts/Transcript.aspx?TranscriptID=5432.
43. Johnson, et al, *Decoding China's Emerging 'Great Power' Strategy in Asia*, 47.
44. "Understanding the US-China Trade Relationship," The US-China Business Council, January 10, 2017, https://www.uschina.org/reports. https://www.uschina.org/sites/default/filesOE%20US%20Jobs%20and%20China%20Trade%20Report.pdf This paper was prepared for the Business Council by Oxford Economics.
45. "Record Deal Making in 2016 Pushes Cumulative Chinese FDI in the US above $100 Billion," Rhodium Group, December 30, 2016, http://rhg.com/notes/record-deal-making-in-2016-pushes-cumulative-chinese-fdi-in-the-us-above-100-billion.
46. Charles W. Freeman III, "The Commercial and Economic Relationship" in Shambaugh, *Tangled Titans*, 181.
47. Prema-Chandra Athukorala, "Production Networks and Trade Patterns in East Asia: Regionalization or Globalization?" (Asian Development Bank Working Paper Series on Regional Economic Integration, no. 56, August 2010). See also Hyun-Hoon Lee, Donghyun Park, and Jing Wang, "The Role of the People's Republic of China in International Fragmentation and Production Networks: An Empirical Investigation" (ADP Working Paper Series, no. 87, September 2011).
48. Stephen Brooks, *Producing Security: Multinational Corporations, Globalization, and the Changing Calculus of Combat* (Princeton, NJ: Princeton University Press, 2005).
49. "Understanding the US-China Trade Relationship."
50. John Ravenhill, "Production Networks in Asia," in *The Oxford Handbook of the International Relations of Asia*, eds Saadia M. Pekkanen, John Ravenhill, and Rosemary Foot (New York: Oxford University Press, 2014), 358–59. See also his "Economics and Security in the Asia-Pacific Region," *The Pacific Review* 26, no. 1 (March 2013): 1–15.
51. Richard Katz, "Mutual Assured Production: Why Trade Will Limit Conflict Between China and Japan," *Foreign Affairs*, 92, no. 4: 18–24, July/August 2013. Quotations at pp. 18 and 21. See also Justin McCurry, "Why Will Japan and China Avoid Conflict? They Need Each Other," *The Christian Science Monitor*, February 5, 2014. In addition, there have been several meetings between Chinese and Japanese officials, visits by Japanese business delegations to Beijing and to major provinces, and meetings during the Boao Forum in southern China. Though relations are tense and difficult, there have also been three meetings between President Xi and Prime Minister Abe.
52. Michael Peel and Tom Mitchell, "Vietnam Urged to End Mob Violence," *Financial Times*, May 19, 2014. Of course, this international economic pressure may benefit China more than Vietnam even though its actions were the initial cause of the protests.
53. See, for example, "Maritime Disputes in East Asia," Daniel R. Russel, Assistant Secretary, Bureau of East Asian and Pacific Affairs, "Testimony Before the

House Committee on Foreign Affairs Subcommittee on Asia and the Pacific," Washington DC, February 5, 2014.
54. A point made strongly throughout Chan, in *Looking for Balance*.
55. And see, in this connection, Jessica Weiss, *Powerful Patriots: Nationalist Protest in China's Foreign Relations* (Oxford: Oxford University Press, 2014); and James Reilly, *Strong Society, Smart State: The Rise of Public Opinion in China's Japan Policy* (New York: Columbia University Press, 2012), both of whom argue that the Chinese government has managed to maintain controls over nationalist protest.
56. Minxin Pei's chapter in this volume goes further than this. He points to several reasons why this reform agenda is unlikely to be successful and indeed may lead to the collapse of the Chinese Communist regime. See too the chapter by Zhang Ruizhuang.
57. "President Barack Obama's State of the Union Address," January 28, 2014, http://www.whitehouse.gov/the-press-office/2014/01/28/president-barack-obamas-state-union-address.
58. Bruce Stokes, "Public Opinion May Restrict Obama's Second-Term Foreign Policy," Chatham House, Royal Institute of International Affairs: London, December 17, 2013.

PART II
Historical Perspectives

CHAPTER 5

The Rise and Fall of Great Powers

The Uses of History

GEIR LUNDESTAD

INTRODUCTION

Theory may have many different sources. History is definitely one of the major ones. You may come out of history's endlessly rich mine with gems of many different kinds. Thus, social scientists—realists, liberals, constructivists, anyone—wander into the annals of history. They produce the most different observations. Everything has happened in history. You can always find an example that would seem to indicate that what you have found is what history tells us. Except that history hardly ever tells us only one thing. It will almost always present us with many different stories.

As Ernest R. May argued in *"Lessons" of the Past*, there will always be many possible parallels.[1] It is difficult to find the right ones. Politicians, social scientists, even historians have their ideas in advance about what history tells us, and somewhere in history they are likely to find what they need to prove that their viewpoint is indeed the correct one. Thus, if after 1945 you favored a tough approach to the Soviet Union, you argued that Hitler's example most definitely told us that we had to stand up to the dictators of the world. If, on the other hand, you favored a softer approach, you pointed to those historians who had stressed that wars could actually arise through misunderstandings, as allegedly had been the case with the First World War.[2] As May argued, "During World War II had scholars been asked to re-examine Utrecht and Vienna as well as Versailles as possible parallels for the peacemaking to come, they might have worked out the implications of comparing Stalin not with Hitler but with Peter the Great or Alexander I or Lenin."[3]

As most historians know, the intellectually most satisfying accounts will almost always relate to a combination of possible parallels. No two events are exactly identical. There will always be some differences, larger or smaller, that make historical generalizations difficult, if not impossible.[4] As we have seen so often, there are indeed no experts on the future. The alleged laws of social science do not exist, as even the most cursory study of history will show. We historians have our problems too. Thus, we are quick to pronounce any development inevitable once it has happened, but we are not really much better than social scientists in predicting events before they have happened.

REALISM AND THE RISE OF CHINA

We are all familiar with the basic tenets of political science realism. The international system is anarchic. It consists of nation states that have it as their prime task to ensure, first, their own survival, then, their security and power. States can never be entirely certain about how other states will behave toward them. In this Hobbesian anarchy, competition inevitably prevails, and military power is the dominant instrument.

As Stephen Walt mentions in his chapter in the present book, the ancient Greek historian Thucydides is generally considered the common founder of realism, despite its many subschools. In his famous analysis of the Peloponnesian Wars, the Greek historian concluded, "The growth of the power of Athens, and the alarm which this inspired in Sparta, made war inevitable." Following upon this, a steady stream of realists have insisted that the constant rise and fall of great powers has always led to conflict and war. Most of their examples come from European history, and we are all familiar with them. In the words of Kenneth Waltz, the father of neorealism, "As nature abhors a vacuum, so international politics abhors unbalanced power. Faced by unbalanced power, states try to increase their own strength or they ally with others to bring the international distribution of power into balance. The reactions of other states to the drive for dominance of Charles I of Spain, of Louis XIV and Napoleon Bonaparte of France, of Wilhelm II and Adolph [sic] Hitler of Germany, illustrate the point."[5]

After 1945, the German problem was finally solved, first, through its unconditional surrender, then, by the country's division into two parts.

Again, the dreams of universal cooperation were soon replaced by the emerging conflict between East and West. In the West, the Soviet Union was seen as the big threat; in the East, the United States and its allies, although bound to face an economic depression, represented huge strength. The competition between East and West ended after a short half-century in the collapse of the Soviet Union. The United States reigned supreme, but only for a short period. It was bound to be challenged. Allegedly, China was the new challenger.

For John Mearsheimer, and many others for that matter, the answer to the question of whether China could rise peacefully was obvious. "My answer is no. If China continues its impressive economic growth over the next few decades, the United States and China are likely to engage in an intense security competition with considerable potential for war."[6] Since China was bound to seek regional hegemony and thereby challenge the United States, the United States should stop building up China in the many ways it was doing so, particularly economically. "Although it is certainly in China's interest to be the hegemon in Northeast Asia, it is clearly not in America's interest to have that happen."[7]

Many agree with Mearsheimer, although they may not see matters quite as starkly as he does. In the present collection, Stephen Walt, Christopher Layne, and Steven Lobell are clear-cut realists. In political science terms, Aaron Friedberg combines realism with liberalism, in his additional emphasis on the importance of the difference in political systems between the two countries. Friedberg still thinks China's ultimate goal is to "win without fighting," displacing the United States as the leading power definitely in East Asia, perhaps even in all of Asia, while avoiding a direct confrontation with the United States. To prevent such a development, the United States has to preserve "a favorable balance of power."[8] Henry Kissinger, that lingering realist, despite his elements of political pragmatism, believes that the competition between the United States and China "is more likely to be economic and social than military. A country with huge domestic tasks is not going to throw itself into a strategic confrontation or a quest for world domination."[9] Politicians naturally think that they personally can make a difference. Academics are less certain that they do, although in the present collection, William Wohlforth holds a position somewhat similar to Kissinger's.

RISE, DECLINE, AND WAR

The First World War led to the fall of four empires, those of Germany, Austria-Hungary, Russia, and the Ottoman Empire. The Second World

War led to the unconditional surrender of Germany and Japan, the decline of France and even the United Kingdom, and the rapid rise of the United States and the Soviet Union. While it is certainly true that wars have led to dramatic shifts in the distribution of power not only in Europe, but also in much of Asia and Africa as well, starting in 1945 the two new superpowers took charge even of Europe, the Soviet Union rather directly in the Eastern part and the United States more indirectly in the Western.

The reverse question—of whether the rise and fall of countries leads to conflict and war—is much more difficult to answer. Realists have provided a long list of examples of how the rise of one country—France, Germany, Japan, the Soviet Union—led to conflict and, in most cases, even war. States constantly seek security. Hegemons try to protect their leads. When one state is clearly stronger than the others, the weaker states will balance against the hegemon.[10]

For Waltz, "balances are produced whether or not intended." His theory predicts that "willy nilly, balances will form over time." This theory cannot be falsified by "a mélange of irrelevant diplomatic lore."[11] Yet, for the historian, the theory undoubtedly loses credibility as the historical examples pile up against it. And the historical mine does indeed provide some ambiguous and even some rather explicit examples directly contrary to the theory.

First, on the ambiguous side, as Paul Schroeder has instructed us, the main response to French efforts of European hegemony under Louis XIV and Napoleon was not really balancing but hiding and bandwagoning. These efforts largely failed because France would not let them succeed; in the end, the various powers "resisted because France kept on attacking them." After Russia's victory against Sweden at Poltava in 1709, most powers again bandwagoned against triumphant Russia in Eastern Europe. After Britain became dominant in the nineteenth century, it was much the same story. Most states wanted to maintain good relations with Britain. Bandwagoning was the rule. This was the case even with Bismarck's Germany.[12]

Britain and France had allegedly been hereditary enemies more or less since the Norman invasion. They had been at war many times, the last time in 1815. Although there was a slow improvement in relations after 1815, the dramatic turning point happened in the course of a few years, from the Fashoda Crisis of 1898 to, first, the British-French détente of 1904 and, then, to the First World War. Britain and France turned from enemies into allies. It might be argued that although Britain was struggling to maintain its former position, compared to France it was still rising, as evidenced by the outcome of the Fashoda Crisis and by Britain's increasing influence on the European continent where it had traditionally played a more limited role. Yet, while this proves that traditional enemies can become friends, and there were many reasons for the change, it has to be admitted that much of the explanation is provided by the rise of Germany.

Second, on the less ambiguous side, even Hitler's dramatic expansion from military rearmament and Rhineland to the Spanish Civil War, Anschluss, Munich, Prague, and Poland illustrated the difficulties of forming a coalition even against an aggressor so clearly bent on expansion. Cooperation between Britain and France was slow in forming; France was mired in internal conflict and changing governments; Britain pursued its appeasement policy to protect its worldwide interests as best it could. Cooperation with the Soviet Union took place only when the Soviet Union was directly attacked by Germany. The United States fully entered the war only after the attack on Pearl Harbor. This was not really realist history working more or less automatically against a rising state. Again, there was a lot of hiding and bandwagoning. Balancing is often the last resort. The realist history of balancing against the hegemon is a much simplified version of history, not to use stronger terms.[13]

Again, despite realism, the nature of the regimes involved is of course important. The rise of Germany after 1870 would have presented problems to the international system regardless, but the nature of the regime definitely enhanced these problems. Despite the early universal right for men to vote in Germany in 1871, the nature of the imperial-militaristic government was an extra dimension before the First World War. Naturally, the Nazi government from 1933 presented a much more dramatic challenge. Yet, again, even then the possible opponents hesitated to balance against Hitler. After the Second World War, the rise of a reformed Germany and also of a new Japan did not really present major challenges to the international system.

Third, the American-British rapprochement at the turn to the twentieth century is a clear-cut example of a peaceful rise without major conflict. Britain and the United States had quarreled since the days of American independence. There was the war of 1812, problems about the borders and the overall relationship between the United States and Canada, British sympathies for the American South during the American Civil War, and rivalry about their respective roles in Latin America. Following their bitter dispute of 1895–1896 over the Venezuelan boundary, the two countries were able to sort out many explosive issues and place their relationship on an entirely new footing.

In this case there could be no doubt, in relative terms the United States was clearly rising while Britain was declining. Britain could no longer pursue a policy of splendid isolation. A war with the United States was no longer possible; neither was a war with Japan. This was reflected in the British-Japanese alliance of 1902. Again, Japan was rising, Britain declining. A common enemy in Russia counted, although London entered into a détente with St. Petersburg in 1907. The two also had certain economic interests in common. Thus, one country's rise and another's decline did not prevent an improved relationship.[14] In fact, it has been argued that "when states fall in the hierarchy of great powers, peaceful retrenchment is the most common response, even over short time spans." Moreover, declining states may rebound, even then peacefully, as we have seen several times with the United Kingdom, Russia/the Soviet Union, and Germany.[15]

Fourth, the world's response to the rise of the United States after 1945 is also telling. After the Second World War, the United States was of course far stronger than the Soviet Union. I have argued elsewhere that the United States also expanded even more dramatically than did the Soviet Union.[16] As Stephen Walt has argued, the Europeans did not form a coalition against the strongest power; they balanced against what they saw as the greatest threat.[17] Again, threat was perceived primarily on the basis of geographical position and the nature of the regime. The Soviet Union was a communist dictatorship close at hand, while the United States was a democracy with considerable "soft power" far away from Europe. Despite the international anarchy, there was no war directly between the United States and the Soviet Union during the Cold War.

Again illustrating the special nature of the United States, the world showed few if any signs of balancing against the United States, even when in the 1990s, after the collapse of the Soviet Union, it was the only remaining superpower. In East Asia today, in the complex picture of cooperation and conflict, many governments have moved closer to the United States in security matters than they have to China, although there is no doubt that for the foreseeable future the United States will remain more powerful than China. Yet, in large part because of China's rising economic importance, few of these governments want to balance directly against China.

Finally, the geographical distance between the United States and China may also make this example different from the many European examples that dominate international theory, also in the present book. Chances of conflict would appear to increase dramatically if two states border on each other compared to if they are separated by vast stretches of water. The United States and the Soviet Union had had strained relations since the communist revolution in 1917. Yet, only when the two countries faced each other directly in the middle of Europe after 1945 did this have a dramatic impact on international relations. On the other hand, the United States is a global power with global interests. Any major power shift in any region of the world is bound to affect its role. The United States also has major allies in East Asia. Thus, while Washington may not take direct positions on the many island disputes in the region, it is bound by treaties to defend the territorial integrity of its allies. This reduces the geographical distance between the two counties a great deal.

THE UNITED STATES, CHINA, AND COOPERATION

In the liberal case, here most effectively presented by John Ikenberry, the effects of economic globalization are the most relevant part in analyzing American-Chinese relations. Realists tend to assume that states will work to increase their autonomy through autarkic policies designed to enhance self-sufficiency, and by extension security. Since 1978, China, however, has chosen to become integrated into a Western-dominated market structure. And its primary economic partners are its main political opponents, the United States, Japan, and Taiwan. To opt into the global commercial order was to derive huge material benefits in the form of foreign investment, market access, and foreign resources.[18] In fact, no country has ever risen so fast economically as China. Many have argued like Noah Feldman recently did that "[g]eostrategic conflict is inevitable. But mutual economic interdependence can help manage that conflict and keep it from spiraling out of control. And international institutions, much maligned but also underestimated, are part of the mechanism."[19]

While China was becoming the primary challenger to the leadership of the United States, the two were also cooperating in many different ways. While, in virtually all US campaigns since 1980, the new president criticized his predecessor for having been too friendly toward the Chinese, even the newcomers soon came to favor cooperation with China. There were strong forces pulling the two giants together; the United States and China were becoming increasingly interdependent. The United States had supported China's successful membership of the World Trade Organization (WTO) in 2001. The open American market had been crucial to China's growth, as it had been in Japan's case as well. Chinese exports to the United States amounted to around 8 percent of China's GNP and 18 percent of China's exports; a significant share of these exports came from American companies that had been established in China. Virtually all the major US companies were represented there. Foreign enterprises accounted for around 55 percent both of China's total exports and imports. What would happen to these numbers if American-Chinese relations seriously deteriorated?[20]

The United States was by far the world's largest importer, while China was surpassing Germany as the largest exporter. The huge surpluses China had in its foreign trade were then, to a large extent, invested in the United States, so China was actually financing parts of America's rapidly growing debt.[21] When demand in the United States collapsed during the economic crisis of 2008–2009, exports from China were badly hit too.

There is no doubt that US economic policies increasingly had to be carried out with an eye on the likely response from Beijing. As Hillary Clinton asked then Australian prime minister Kevin Rudd, "How do you deal toughly with your bank?"[22] China's position as the world's largest creditor strengthened its position tremendously. The US position as the world's largest debtor weakened its role, although it still had few problems in financing its debt. The world was awash in cheap money in 2010–2011, but that could easily change. International financial structures had to be adjusted, reflecting the rise of Asia, and especially China. And since China was also surpassing the United States as the world's greatest polluter, there could be no effective global environmental policy unless the two countries contributed.

It has to be remembered that while trade across the Pacific had surpassed that across the Atlantic in the late 1970s, and the gap has widened since, on the investment side, the story was a different one. American investment in Europe, and European investment in America, was much larger than in China and East Asia.[23] Americans and Europeans, despite the problems they were facing, were also ideologically and culturally much closer to each other than they were to the Japanese, not to mention the Chinese.

The Chinese had probably started investing sizeably in the United States in the 1990s because of rapid US economic growth. In many ways, the United States still had the most advanced economy in the world, and there was also much to learn. As growth began to falter, the Chinese may have emphasized the security of US Treasury bonds. In an uncertain world, when even the United States was hit, many still felt safest with America. There was also the problem of where else to go. As one Chinese official told an American audience in February 2009, "Except for US Treasuries, what can you hold? . . . US Treasuries are the safe haven. For everyone, including China, it is the only option . . . . We hate you guys. Once you start issuing 1–2 trillion dollars . . . we know that the dollar is going to depreciate, so we hate you guys, but there is nothing much we can do."[24] Finally, there was also the question of the political benefits for the Chinese in investing in the United States.

Many worried about what would happen if the Chinese stopped investing in the United States. This would harm America but would certainly also harm China, as it would have a negative impact on Chinese exports to the United States, and on the already huge Chinese investment in the United States. Dependency cut both ways. If China started to dump dollars, it would also hurt itself. To translate John Maynard Keynes's famous quote, "If I owe you a pound I have a problem; but if I owe you a million, the problem is yours." When the United States owes China billions, that is Washington's problem. When it owes China trillions, such amounts quickly become Beijing's problem. If China dumped dollars, the greenback would fall in value. That would have a negative side, but it would also make American goods more competitive. Some argued that this effect might actually be desirable for the American economy. Finally, there was an overriding political interest in maintaining good relations between what were more and more clearly becoming the two most important powers in the world.

INTERDEPENDENCE AND WAR

Mutual financial and economic dependence would seem to be a very strong argument indeed against going to war against each other. The trouble was that this argument had been made many times before and seemingly had been proven wrong, time and again. In 1910, Norman Angell published his famous book, *The Great Illusion*. The illusion was that nations gained by armed confrontation, war, or conquest. On the contrary, economic interdependence meant that war would be economically harmful to all the countries involved. Normal trade and investment patterns would be broken, and all would suffer. Even in the long run, conquest would not pay because the continued resistance to occupation would sap the local incentive to produce and thus make the conquered area worthless. Quite a few of Europe's leaders had actually read Angell's book.[25]

Angell did not maintain that war was impossible, only that it would be futile. Yet a few years later the First World War broke out among very close economic partners indeed. Great Britain was consistently Germany's most important trading partner; in 1910, Germany was Britain's second-most important partner, after the United States. Trade was also somewhat complementary, at least initially. The trouble was that increasingly the British and German economies were becoming more homogeneous; interdependence was replaced by trade rivalry. Emperor William II thus stated that "after the recognition of the superiority of German industry, England will soon set about its destruction, and will undoubtedly succeed if we do not energetically and quickly prevent this disaster with a vigorous naval buildup." Thus, economic and military rivalry soon came to flow together.

France imported almost as much from Germany as it did from Britain. And Germany depended on imports of French iron ore for its steel mills.[26]

The difference in Britain's trade with the United States and Germany was striking. Whereas Britain depended on the United States for foodstuffs and raw materials, her trade with Germany consisted mainly of manufactured articles. The notion soon developed that trade with Germany was harmful. The mutual benefits in American-British trade were widely recognized, while Germans increasingly feared closure of the British market as a result of the commercial competition.[27]

Similarly, by the turn of the century, Germany and the United States traded more with each other than with any other country save Britain. The trouble was that, again, the two economies were becoming increasingly homogeneous. Thus, the import of cheap American foodstuffs drove down German prices, benefiting consumers, but threatening the existence of the powerful Junkers. The United States similarly tried to restrict the flow of German sugar into the country. In the 1890s, rivalry spread to manufactured goods. More and more the two countries also competed against each other around the world. The "American menace" was accepted as real by most Germans. Many argued that the two countries were fighting for the commercial supremacy of the world. While financial connections developed between the United States and Britain, even this aspect was much less important in German-American relations.[28]

In general, trade and investment numbers before the First World War had been very high indeed. In relative terms, it took several decades after the Second World War before they became equally high. But starting in the late 1970 and then rapidly accelerating, trade relative to GDP exploded and became many times higher than it had ever been before 1914.[29] By the time China joined the WTO, the globalized economy was larger and more interdependent than almost anyone, certainly in China, had probably ever foreseen. International trade as a percentage of world GDP had gone from 38.5 percent in 1980 to 54 percent in 2005; international investment as a percentage of world GDP went from 0.5 percent to 2.3 percent. Globalization made the world increasingly interdependent. It linked job markets across borders. It increased mutual vulnerability in commodity markets and in the management of currency and foreign exchange. In addition, there were the many noneconomic dependencies, from the environment to health and information technology.[30] Globalization had become much wider and deeper than before the First World War.

In the American-Chinese relationship, the emphasis appears still to be on the mutual benefits of trade and investment, although the relevant numbers have declined somewhat after the 2008–2010 recession.

The Chinese exporter still needs the American importer; the American debtor needs the Chinese creditor; American capital needs China's labor. While there might be skepticism toward China among the US military and labor, American business has again and again underlined the need for good American-Chinese relations. China cannot keep up its high growth rate without access to the American market. This would augur well for the relationship, but, as we have seen, such relationships may change over time. There are certainly challenges to American-Chinese codependency. China needs to spend more; the United States to save and invest more. In history, nothing is guaranteed to last.[31]

THE UNITED STATES STILL FAR AHEAD

In the short run, the best guarantee against American-Chinese conflict is the simple fact that China quite simply is not strong enough to challenge the United States, at least not in the foreseeable future. The titles of some recent books would appear to tell you a different story: *The New Asian Hemisphere: The Inevitable Shift of Global Power to the East*; *When China Rules the World: The Rise of the Middle Kingdom and the End of the Western World*; *The Beijing Consensus: How China's Authoritarian Model Will Dominate the Twenty-First Century*. Growth curves are extended into the future, and depending on exactly what numbers you put in, China's GDP would surpass that of the United States sometime in the 2020s, if not earlier. If the GDP numbers are done in Purchasing Power Parity (PPP) instead of currency exchange rates, China's GDP actually surpassed that of the United States in October 2014.[32]

This is clearly an important development, since the United States has by far had the largest GDP since the 1870s. But the United States will still have a lead in GDP per capita, in military strength, and in the support of its allies. The rapid exploitation of shale oil and gas in the United States has changed not only America's energy picture, but also the country's economic outlook. The United States may already have become the world's largest producer of natural gas and may within a few years become the largest producer even of oil. In a slightly longer perspective, the United States could become largely self-sufficient in energy, whatever the meaning of that term. In the long run, China appears to have even larger such deposits than does the United States, but it is far behind in the exploitation of these resources.[33]

A more balanced approach has therefore received much recent support, most impressively from David Shambaugh in his *China Goes Global: The*

Partial Power, although I think Shambaugh goes too far in downplaying China's rise when he actually writes that China "is nowhere near being in the league of the United States . . . and therefore may better be thought as a middle power and regional power like Australia, Brazil, Britain, France, India, Japan, or Russia."[34] China is definitely becoming more important, particularly economically, than any of these powers.

The transfer of leadership from the United States to China is thus far from certain. China's GDP today, in market exchange terms, is still only 50 percent that of the United States. The high but still slowing growth rate in China is now putting the year when China will have the largest GDP in the world in market exchange terms back into the mid to late 2020s. Costs are rapidly rising in China. The gold rush of foreign investment is slowing. Some firms are leaving China entirely; others are struggling. It should be remembered that if and when China's GDP does surpass that of the United States in market terms, China will still be a relatively poor country. In fact, with a population more than four times that of the United States, per capita income would be only one-fourth of what it would be in the United States. Despite the tremendous progress made, China today is still relatively poor. On a list of countries ranked by GDP per capita, China comes in at around number ninety, roughly at the same level as Ecuador, Bosnia and Herzegovina, and Albania, even in PPP terms. A few of the contributions in the present volume even foresee the possible collapse of the Chinese economy and regime (particularly Minxin Pei, to some extent also David Shambaugh).

China has also been increasing its defense budget rapidly since the late 1990s. While the US defense budget had increased by 81.3 percent from 2001 to 2010, the Chinese budget had increased by 189 percent, faster than any other great power. China has the world's second-largest defense budget. It grows even more rapidly than the country's economy. China has a small, but modern, nuclear force. It has demonstrated its capacity to shoot down satellites in space. And its ambitious space program aims to put a man on the moon. Its navy is beginning to appear further and further out in the Pacific, even in waters it had not been in before, at least not for many centuries and in such numbers. China is trying, although with some difficulty, to develop a modern aircraft carrier. It launched its first one in 2011. Its armed forces are the largest in the world, with around two million men, although they are being reduced and modernized. While the role of its armed forces has long been to defend "Chinese territory," it is now, more broadly, to protect "Chinese interests."

Again, there was talk of China surpassing the United States in defense spending a few decades ahead in time, but the military gap is much larger in America's favor than the economic one. In 1990, the United States lead in spending had been around twenty-five to one. Today it is around three to one since the US defense budget has actually been declining due to America's budget problems. Still, China is still spending only about 2 percent of GDP on defense, more than the European average, but about the same as Britain and France, at least until now, and quite a bit less than the United States at around 4–5 percent.[35] China's nuclear force is probably too small to survive an American first strike. The United States still has eleven aircraft carrier groups and many other forms of offensive power. It can project its force virtually anywhere in the world. As Secretary of Defense Robert Gates stated in May 2010 when concern was expressed about the state of the US Navy: its displacement exceeds "at least the next 13 navies in the world combined, of which 11 are our allies or partners." In a serious conflict, with this strong navy the United States would, among other things, have a stranglehold on the crucial import of energy to China through the Hormuz and Malacca Straits.

While the United States has allies and bases all over the world, China has few, if any, traditional allies and true bases abroad—though it is developing port facilities in a few countries such as Pakistan, Burma, and Sri Lanka. China does not really have the capabilities for global power projection, at least not yet, as is seen in the problems it has developing its first aircraft carrier, and its lack of long-range bombers. In August 2010, even the Pentagon concluded that "China's ability to sustain military power at a distance, today, remains limited." It was, however, an increasingly important regional actor, also militarily. And the Pacific, particularly the Western part, could no longer simply be considered an American lake.

China also has a certain measure of "soft power." Still, Chinese culture is in many ways unique, and not as easily transferable as American culture and politics. Even nationalistic Chinese youth argue, with reference to the United States, "But we can't do what they do culturally: produce things like Tom and Jerry cartoons, 'Transformers,' 'Avatar,' 'Inception,' iPhones, Barbies. America has things we really, really like, on a cultural level." Most of the thousands of Chinese students who study abroad, particularly in the United States, do not return home. Beijing's insistence on nonintervention and national sovereignty might be attractive to many, but the question remains of how effective such an ideology will be in coping with the many challenges that can only be addressed at the global level, such as the environment, terrorism, disease, and even good governance.

The conclusion would appear obvious: China still has far to go before it can challenge the United States economically, militarily, and culturally. On this point, there would actually appear to be broad agreement among the contributors to this volume.

CONCLUSION

In history's incredibly rich mine, you can find anything you like. There are few, if any, laws in history. Realists, liberals, and others are both right and wrong. Some developments may under certain circumstances be more likely than others, but there will almost always be disagreements on what the circumstances are and what the outcome will then be. Even in the natural sciences, where the causes are often so much clearer, predictions are still difficult. One may, for instance, find that there is a close connection between smoking and cancer. The evidence in fact appears overwhelming on this point. Yet, it is still impossible to state with certainty what will happen in the individual case. Some who smoke will not get cancer; some who do not will.

While it is impossible to tell with any degree of certainty what will happen in the foreseeable future to the American-Chinese relationship, certain developments may still be more likely than others. On the pessimistic side, it is not difficult to sketch a scenario of conflict between China and its neighbors. It would focus on the territorial issue. For decades Taiwan was the primary issue, and that problem has far from been resolved, although the focus has recently moved elsewhere. China shares borders with fourteen countries. Historically there have been many border disputes. Now, however, most of these disputes have been sorted out, including the ones with Russia that led to such serious conflicts in the 1960s and 1970s. China acted quite reasonably in solving these disputes, getting only 6 percent of the disputed territory with Nepal, 8 percent with Burma, and 29 percent with Mongolia. It was showing a great deal of interest in promoting cross-border networks, although from a position of strength. The bitter conflict with India over substantial territories remains, however, preventing a rapprochement between the two countries.

More importantly, there is today the conflict over the Paracel Islands (with Taiwan and Vietnam), the Spratly Islands (with Vietnam, Taiwan, the Philippines, Malaysia, and Brunei) in the South China Sea, and the Senkaku or Diaoyu Islands (with Japan) in the East China Sea. In 2010, Chinese commentators began to describe the South China Sea as one of China's "core interests," on a par with Taiwan, Xinjiang, and Tibet. China was clearly on the offensive even in the East China and Yellow seas. Occasionally rather difficult incidents occurred that fired up public opinion in China, Japan, and the other countries involved. Defense forces were strengthened. The issues involved not only ownership of the islands, but also control over sea lanes and potentially large reserves of oil, natural gas, and fish. China showed little willingness to compromise on these issues; neither did most of the other states involved. The United States had no firm opinion on the territorial issues involved, but insisted on open shipping lanes, here as elsewhere. Confrontations can easily escalate. There is no guarantee that diplomatic solutions will be found. The military work out their contingency war plans, including the US Air-Sea Battle, which resemble all-or-nothing battle plans.[36]

At the moment, however, neither Beijing nor Washington have any interest in a major confrontation. China is pursuing an increasingly ambitious, but still rational foreign policy, so unlike the excesses of Mao Tse-Tung. Although the Chinese take considerable pleasure in moving up the power tables, references to the G-2 or to "Chinamerica" are to be avoided. In many different ways they actually admit that they are still far behind the United States.

The big evolution is that while China had earlier seen itself as an outsider in opposition to the dominant powers and institutions, it is now becoming more of an insider, though certainly one that is trying to reform many aspects of the international system. China has to be given its due influence in the UN and the entire UN system; the International Monetary Fund has to be reformed to reflect China's rise and not so much the fall of the United States as of Europe.

At the same time, China is creating its own institutions, such as its Development Fund or strengthening others such as the Shanghai Cooperation Organization. The G-20 was to be the new important forum at the expense of the dwindling G-7 (8); and trade rounds and environmental agreements had to reflect China's importance. China has not yet presented many concrete proposals to solve the world's problems; it still has left that largely to others. Yet, more and more, no overall agreements can be worked out without China on board.

The United States has had enough of war for now, even limited war. As Robert Gates stated, "Any future defense secretary who advises the president to again send a big American land army into Asia or into the Middle East or Africa should have 'his head examined,' as General MacArthur so delicately put it."[37] And not even MacArthur actually went to war against China itself, even in America's days of preponderance, when the Chinese intervened in the Korean War.

While military incidents cannot be excluded, for the foreseeable future China and the United States are unlikely to enter into a major war. While David Shambaugh expressed doubts on this point at the Nobel symposium, realists actually tended to agree. China is likely to continue to focus on its economic modernization. It has far to go to measure up to the Western world. The American-Chinese economies are still largely complementary.

A conflict with the United States or even with China's neighbors would have damaging repercussions for China's economic goals. The United States is so strong that it would make little or no sense for China to take it on in any military way. It cannot do so regionally, much less globally. There are also other deterrents against war, from nuclear weapons to emerging norms about international relations.

Thus, we should bet on peace. To do otherwise could rapidly become a self-fulfilling prophecy.

NOTES

1. Ernest R. May, *"Lessons" of the Past: The Use and Misuse of History in American Foreign Policy* (Oxford: Oxford University Press, 1973).
2. Barbara Tuchman, *The Guns of August* (New York: MacMillan, 1963), is often seen as a representative of the school of the First World War arising from a set of misunderstandings. See also Margaret MacMillan, "1914 and 2014: Should We Be Worried?," *International Affairs* 90, no. 1 (2014): 67–68.
3. May, *"Lessons" of the Past*, 178–79.
4. It is another matter that in their prize-winning volume *Thinking in Time: The Uses of History for Decision Makers* (New York: Free Press, 1986), Richard E. Neustadt and Ernest R. May offer "easily remembered rules that decision makers can follow to use history more extensively and to better effect. . . . And explain how it is possible to draw sound historical analogies—and how to spot false ones"—a claim hard to believe after having read May's earlier work.
5. Kenneth N. Waltz, "Evaluating Theories," *American Political Science Review* 91 (December 1997): 915.
6. John J. Mearsheimer, "China's Unpeaceful Rise," *Current History*, April 2006, 160–62. See also his *The Tragedy of Great Power Politics* (New York: Norton, 2001), particularly 401–2. In the new edition of *The Tragedy of Great Power Politics* (New York: Norton, 2014), the analysis is the same, although he also argues that it will actually take a long time before China can challenge the United States (380–83) and that because of nuclear weapons the conflict is "likely to be limited in terms of both goals and means" (410). He even ends the book by noting that "every theory confronts cases that contradict its main predictions" (411).
7. Mearsheimer, *The Tragedy of Great Power Politics*, 402.
8. Aaron Friedberg, *A Contest for Supremacy: China, America, and the Struggle for Mastery in Asia* (New York: Norton, 2011).
9. Henry Kissinger, *On China* (London: Allen Lane, 2011), 525–26.
10. In Waltz's opinion, states do not have to balance; it is only the best option. He thus writes that "because states coexist in a self-help system, they are free to do any fool thing they care to, but they are likely to be rewarded for behavior that is responsive to structural pressures and punished for behavior that is not." For this, see Kenneth N. Waltz, "Evaluating Theories," in *Realism and the Balance of Power: A New Debate*, ed. John A. Vasquez and Colin Elman (Upper Saddle River, NJ: Prentice Hall, 2003), 53.
11. Waltz, "Evaluating Theories," 51–53.

12. Paul Schroeder, "Historical Reality vs. Neo-Realist Theory," *International Security* 19, no. 1 (Summer 1994): 108–48; "Why Realism Does Not Work Well for International History (Whether or Not It Represents a Degenerate IR Research Strategy)," in Vasquez and Elman, *Realism and the Balancing of Power*, 114–27.
13. See the references to Schroeder in footnote 12. See also Steve Chan, *Looking for Balance: China, the United States, and Power Balancing in East Asia* (Stanford, CA: Stanford University Press, 2012), 119, 179; Steven E. Lobell, "Engaging the Enemy and the Lessons for the Obama Administration," *Political Science Quarterly* 128, no. 2 (2013).
14. Stephen R. Rock, *Why Peace Breaks Out: Great Power Rapprochment in Historical Perspective* (Chapel Hill: University of North Carolina Press, 1989).
15. Paul K. MacDonald and Joseph M. Parent, "Graceful Decline? The Surprising Success of Great Power Retrenchment," *International Security* 35, no. 4 (Spring 2011): 7–44.
16. The argument is most clearly spelled out in my "Empire by Invitation: The United States and Western Europe, 1945–1952," *Journal of Peace Research* 23 (1986): 263–77.
17. Stephen Walt, *The Origins of Alliances* (Ithaca, NY: Cornell University Press, 1987).
18. Quddus Z. Snyder, "Integrating Rising Powers: Liberal Systemic Theory and the Mechanism of Competition," *Review of International Studies* (2013): 39, 209–31. G. John Ikenberry is the main spokesman for the likelihood of China's integration with the rest of the world. For his most recent statement, see "The Illusion of Geopolitics: The Enduring Power of the Liberal Order," *Foreign Affairs*, May/June 2014, 80–90.
19. Noah Feldman, *Cool War: The Future of Global Competition* (New York: Random House, 2013), 165–66. See also Wendy Dobson, *Partners and Rivals: The Uneasy Future of China's Relationship with the United States* (Toronto: Toronto University Press, 2013). Joseph S. Nye often identifies the centrist position. In this case, he writes, "In the long term, there will always be elements of both competition and cooperation in the US-China relationship, but the two countries have more to gain from the cooperative element, and this can be strengthened by the rise in both countries' soft power. Prudent policies would aim to make that a trend in coming decades." See his "The Information Revolution and Power," *Current History*, January 2014, 22.
20. Most of these numbers are documented in my *The Rise & Decline of the American "Empire": Power and Its Limits in Comparative Perspective* (Oxford: Oxford University Press, 2012); see also Steve Chan, *Enduring Rivalries in the Asia-Pacific* (Cambridge: Cambridge University Press, 2013), 61–72.
21. About one-third of the US deficit was financed from other US government sources, primarily Social Security, one-third came from US pension funds, and one-third from abroad, with China as the major funder with 16 percent of the overall total. For this, see Niall Ferguson, "Debt Debate: China's View," *Newsweek*, August 7, 2011, Internet.
22. Elise Labott, "Analysis: Keeping a Check on America's Banker," CNN.com, January 18, 2011.
23. US Census Bureau, *Statistical Abstract of the United States: 2010* (Washington, DC: Government Printing Office, 2009), 782.
24. Daniel W. Drezner, "Bad Debts: Assessing China's Financial Influence in Great Power Politics," *International Security* 34, no. 2 (Fall 2009): 7–45, quote on 41.

See also Aaron L. Friedberg, "Implications of the Financial Crisis for the US-China Rivalry," *Survival* 52, no. 4 (August–September 2010): 31–54; Robert Skidelsky, "The World Finance Crisis & the American Mission," *New York Review of Books*, July 16, 2009, 31–33.

25. Margaret MacMillan, *The War That Ended Peace: How Europe Abandoned Peace for the First World War* (London: Profile Books, 2013), 273–74, 294.
26. In the end, the expected problems turned out to be smaller than expected. In the first days after the outbreak of war in August 1914, the City suffered some big blows, but remarkably quickly the stimulative effects of mobilization and war production took over. Therefore the financial crisis of 1914 was quickly forgotten. For this, see Richard Roberts, *Saving the City: The Great Financial Crisis of 1914* (Oxford: Oxford University Press, 2013).
27. Rock, *Why Peace Breaks Out*, 76–84; MacMillan, *The War that Ended Peace*, 256–57, 269–70; Christopher Clark, *The Sleepwalkers: How Europe Went to War in 1914* (London: Penguin, 2013), 164–67.
28. Rock, *Why Peace Breaks Out*, 134–41.
29. Russett and Oneal, *Triangulating Peace*, 125–55, 174–77; Pinker, *The Better Angels of our Nature*, 285–88.
30. Andrew J. Nathan and Andrew Scobell, "Globalization as a Security Strategy: Power and Vulnerability in the 'China Model,'" *Political Science Quarterly* 18, no. 3 (2013): 427–53. See also their *China's Search for Security* (New York: Columbia University Press, 2012).
31. For a sensible discussion of these complicated relationships, see Geoff Dyer, *The Contest of the Century: The New Era of Competition with China* (London: Penguin, 2014). For a more pessimistic approach, see Stephen Roach, *Unbalanced. The Codependency of America and China* (New Haven, CT: Yale University Press, 2014).
32. Yao Yang, "When Will China's Economy Overtake America's?," Yao Yang Project Syndicate, June 2, 2011; Economics focus, "The Celestial Economy," *Economist*, September 10, 2011, 78. For a debate about China's present and future role between Christopher Layne, Robert J. Lieber, James H. Lebovic, William Wohlforth, and myself, see H-Diplo, ISSF, Roundtable, vol. 6, no. 5 (2014), http://www.H-net.org/~diplo/ISSF. The debate is based on my book *The Rise & Decline of the American "Empire."* The following sections in the present account follow my book. The most recent numbers can be found by visiting the website of the International Comparisons Programme. See also *Economist*, October 11, 2014, 77.
33. For a good summing up of this situation, see David Hastings Dunn and Mark J. L. McClelland, "Shale Gas and the Revival of American Power: Debunking Decline?," *International Affairs* 89, no. 6 (2013): 1411–28; Robert A. Hefner III, "The United States of Gas: Why the Shale Revolution Could Have Happened Only in America," *Foreign Affairs*, May/June 2014, 9–14; Edward L. Morse, "Welcome to the Revolution: Why Shale Is the Next Shale," *Foreign Affairs*, May/June 2014, 3–7; Robert D. Blackwill and Meghan L. O'Sullivan, "America's Energy Edge," *Foreign Affairs*, March/April 2014.
34. David Shambaugh, *China Goes Global: The Partial Power* (Oxford: Oxford University Press, 2013), 310. See also Jonathan Fenby, *Will China Dominate the 21st Century?* (Cambridge: Polity, 2014); and the references in Shambaugh's chapter in the current volume, note 2. For a recent article by Shambaugh, with a slightly different approach, see his "The Illusion of Chinese Power," *The National Interest*, July/August 2014, 39–48.

35. SIPRI Yearbook 2015, *Armaments, Disarmament and International Security* (Oxford: Oxford University Press, 2015), 351–59.
36. Dyer, *The Contest of the Century*, 113–22; David W. Kearn Jr., "Air-Sea Battle and China's Anti-Access and Area Denial Challenge," *Orbis*, Winter 2014, 132–46; Evan Braden Montgomery, "Contested Primacy in the Western Pacific: China's Rise and the Future of U.S. Power Projection," *International Security*, Spring 2014, 115–49; Larry M. Wortzel, *The Dragon Extends Its Reach: Chinese Military Power Goes Global* (Washington, DC: Potomac Books, 2013).
37. Thom Shanker, "Warning against Wars Like Iraq and Afghanistan," *New York Times*, February 25, 2011, http://www.nytimes.com/2011/02/26/world/26gates.html?-.

CHAPTER 6

The Sound of Distant Thunder

The Pre-World War I Anglo-German Rivalry as a Model for Sino-American Relations in the Early Twenty-First Century

CHRISTOPHER LAYNE

INTRODUCTION

The rise of China has thrust great power politics back to its traditional place center stage in both the practice, and the study, of international politics.[1] At the same time—big historical anniversaries always seem to have this effect—the approach of the Great War's centenary produced a flood of commentary professing to see parallels between today's events in East Asia and those that led to the outbreak of World War I in Europe one hundred years ago. Just as the ascent of Wilhelmine Germany unsettled pre-1914 Europe, now it is a rising China that is roiling East Asia. Noting "the parallel between China's rise and that of imperial Germany over a century ago," the *Economist* also pithily observed that "even if history never repeats itself, the past likes to have a try."[2] In this chapter, I show that, like Britain and Germany before 1914, the United States and China are on a collision course.

Much has been written about China's "rise." But, from China's perspective, what is taking place is the *restoration*—not the rise—of Chinese power. In the seventeenth, eighteenth, and very early nineteenth centuries, China had the world's largest GDP. Indeed, even around 1800 its GDP exceeded the combined GDP's of all of Europe's great powers. As late as the end of the eighteenth century, China was still the "Middle Kingdom" that dominated East and Southeast Asia. The expansion of Western power—with Britain in the vanguard—began to challenge China's regional preeminence in the early nineteenth century.

The two Opium Wars with Britain, coupled with late Qing dynasty internal decay, opened the door for the Western powers to impose a series of "unequal" treaties upon China that gave them ports for trade, economic concessions, extraterritorial legal rights, and—eventually—supervision of China's finances. Much of China's history since the late nineteenth century—the Boxer Rebellion, the 1911 Revolution, the triumph of the Chinese Communist Party in the 1945–1949 Civil War, and the modernizing economic reforms initiated by Deng Xiaoping—was driven by the imperative of pushing back against Western (and Japanese) dominance.[3] Today, a rapidly ascending China is determined to reverse its "century of humiliation" and reclaim what it considers to be its rightful place at the apex of East and Southeast Asia's power hierarchy.

The question addressed by the contributions to this volume—does the rise and decline of great powers lead to conflict and war?—is not abstract. On the contrary, because of China's rise and the ongoing relative decline of American power, this is the central geopolitical question of our time, and it will remain so for decades to come. To be sure, there are analysts who are skeptical about China's future power trajectory, including Ruizhuang's Zhang's chapter in this volume. Those who are bearish about China's political and economic prospects argue that China's rise will stall out—or even be derailed—by an allegedly unsustainable economic growth model, or by domestic political instability, social unrest, demographics, and/or environmental degradation.[4] In this volume, however, there is broad agreement—including realist international relations (IR)scholars (Walt, Wohlforth), China experts (Shambaugh, Westad), and liberal IR scholars (Ikenberry, Foot) that in coming decades China's power will increase.[5]

The real battle line in this volume is about the geopolitical implications of China's rise, not its reality. Are the United States and China headed for conflict, or can the Sino-American relationship be managed peacefully? Will China embed itself in the extant international order—the Pax Americana—or will it seek to revise, or even overturn it? Some of the contributors to this volume (notably Lundestad, Foot, and Ikenberry) are optimistic. While acknowledging that the Sino-American relationship doubtless will become more competitive in coming years, they believe that countervailing imperatives for cooperation—the institutions of the prevailing liberal international order, economic interdependence, and domestic political and economic constraints—will enable Washington and Beijing to able to avoid conflict. John Ikenberry argues that, even as American power declines in coming decades, China will seek to integrate itself into the US-designed international order. William Wohlforth also offers a realist argument for why a Sino-American clash can be avoided: because it lags behind the United States in many power metrics—especially military capabilities—China will be dissuaded from mounting a head-on challenge to America's geopolitical dominance in East Asia.

Set against these (more or less) optimistic appraisals of where Sino-American relations are headed are the contributions of Stephen Walt and David Shambaugh. Invoking neorealist (Waltzian) international relations theory, Walt is pessimistic about the future of the Sino-American relationship. As the balance of power increasingly tilts in China's favor over the next several decades, he says, Beijing will move to reduce the US security presence in East and Southeast Asia, and there will be a real risk of armed conflict. Shambaugh argues that, over time, aggrieved Chinese nationalism coupled with unresolved regional territorial disputes—over Taiwan, the Senkaku/Diaoyuti Islands, and conflicting claims in the South China Sea—could draw the United States and China into a shooting war.

THE USES OF THEORY

In this chapter, I argue that like Britain and Germany a century ago, the United States and China are on a path that, sooner or later, is likely to eventuate in war. My argument draws upon neoclassical realist theory and on diplomatic history. Neoclassical realism rests on the foundation of Waltzian neorealist international relations theory.[6] Hence, its analytical starting point is the impact of international systemic constraints—the distribution of power (polarity) and the lack of a central authority to make and enforce rules ("anarchy")—on great powers' foreign policies. International politics is a "self-help" system in which great powers constantly fear—and must provide—for their own security. Consequently, they pay close attention to the distribution of relative power between themselves and actual or potential rivals. At the same time, neoclassical realists understand that it is necessary to "open the black box" and look inside the state, because domestic political factors also play a big role in shaping the grand strategies of great powers. Diplomatic history provides the evidence that international relations theorists use to test their theories.

In his contribution to this volume, Geir Lundestad disparages the utility of international relations theory and the manner in which IR theorists use history. According to him, IR theorists do not understand the complexity of the real world. Nothing ever happens exactly the same way, he says, which makes generalizing about international politics difficult—maybe even impossible. For this reason, he *claims* that theory and history cannot be used to make informed predictions about the future, or to divine recurrent patters of great power behavior and international outcomes. Of course, this does not prevent him from making his *own* prediction—based on "unspoken assumptions" about IR theory no less—about the future of Sino-American relations.

Lundestad notwithstanding, the history of international politics—especially that concerning the relations of great powers—has very definite patterns and regularities. Four of these have special salience to analyzing the future of the Sino-American relationship. First, great power politics is shaped fundamentally by the cyclical rise and decline of great powers. Invariably, the rise of new great powers is geopolitically destabilizing.[7] Second, rising great powers seek to dominate their regions (that is, they seek hegemony).[8] Third, rising challengers seek prestige equal to that of the incumbent hegemon, and they want their status acknowledged.[9] Fourth, when a rising challenger narrows the power gap separating itself from the incumbent hegemon, it will want to revise the prevailing international order to reflect its own interests, values, and norms rather than those of the declining incumbent.[10]

Mark Twain was correct when he said that while history does not repeat itself, it rhymes. Understanding the past can help us to think clearly about the future. "The present does not replicate the past," observe the diplomatic historians Michael Hunt and Steven I. Levine, "but historical parallels can provide fresh ways of understanding and dealing with current challenges."[11] To be sure, international relations theorists need to be meticulous in the use of sources, discriminating in their use of analogies, and careful in, the comparisons and conclusions they draw between past and present.[12] Nevertheless, the gap between international relations theorists and historians is much narrower than Lundestad would have us believe. Historians are as no less interested than IR theorists in testing propositions analytically and identifying chains of causality that connect explanatory variables.[13] Leading diplomatic historians—John Lewis Gaddis and Melvyn Leffler are notable examples—use IR theory in their own work while others—Marc Trachtenberg and Walter McDougall, for example—are equally at home teaching both history and international relations. In thinking about the future of Sino-American relations, the choice of appropriate methodology is not history *versus* theory. Rather it is using *both* history *and* theory to strike an appropriate balance between richness and rigor.

THE RETURN OF POWER POLITICS

Since the Cold War's end, American policy makers, pundits, IR scholars, and policy analysts have assured us that the Soviet Union's collapse meant both the end of history and the end of realpolitik (power politics). According to them (see the chapters in this volume by Foot, Lundestad, Ikenberry, and Wohlforth), globalization, the spread of democracy and liberal ideology, the (allegedly) emollient effects of international institutions, and the existence of nuclear weapons have made great power war a thing of the past.[14] Of course, this is pretty much what Europeans were told in the years before 1914.[15] The centenary commemoration of the Great War's outbreak is a stark reminder that European elites' hopes for peace were an illusion.[16] And, as Charles Emerson reminds us, the era leading up to the outbreak of World War I bears uncanny similarities to the present.[17] Most Europeans alive at the time, of course, had little inking of the catastrophe that lurked just around the corner. For them, Emerson notes, "1913 was a year of possibility not predestination."[18] 1913, of course, turned out to be the prelude to the deluge that swept away Europe's old order. That should be a warning to those who argue great power politics, and great power war, are relics of a past epoch of international affairs.

In fact, it sure looks as if the past is "having a try" in East Asia. There are two important—and unsettling—parallels between the Anglo-German relationship during the run-up to 1914 and the unfolding Sino-American relationship. First, both relationships involve power transition dynamics.[19] In itself, this is not news. But two dimensions of the Anglo-German power transition have not received the attention they deserve. One is that Britain and Germany were competing as much for status and prestige as for power and security. This made the competition between them intractable because Germany's rise posed a direct challenge to the then-extant international order, the Pax Britannica. Second, in Britain, liberal ideology contributed to what might be called a "perception spiral," which fostered in British policy makers, and the broader political nation, an image of Germany as an implacably hostile, and dangerous, rival.

THE DIFFICULTIES OF RISING PEACEFULLY

China's leaders talk of a "peaceful rise," and they have spent considerable time pondering the "lessons of the past" so that an ascending China can avoid the alleged foreign policy blunders of Wilhelmine Germany and Imperial Japan during their respective great power emergences. History, however, provides scant reason to believe that China's rise will be peaceful. Since the beginning of the modern international state system, there have been many examples of an ascending power challenging the position of the dominant power in the international system. These challenges usually have culminated in war.

The dynamics of the relationships between dominant powers in decline and the challengers that seek to displace them are defined by competition and instability, because they pose one of the foundational questions of great power relations: when the distribution of power is in flux, how can the aims of the status quo power(s) be reconciled with those of a revisionist power seeking to change the international order to reflect a balance of power that is tilting in its favor? Accommodation is difficult because the declining dominant power wants to preserve its leading place in the international system, while the rising challenger wants its growing power—and equal status—acknowledged. The historical example that offers the most insight into how the Sino-American relationship will be affected by power transition dynamics is the Anglo-German rivalry before World War I.

As the noted diplomatic historian Zara Steiner has observed, coupled with the existence of important factors that should have conduced to peace (dynastic ties, cultural and religious affinities, and economic interdependence), the absence of tangible territorial conflicts between Germany and Britain presents a puzzle for historians seeking to explain why Berlin and London found themselves at war in 1914. The Oxford historian Margaret Macmillan makes a similar point and asks, "[W]hy did Germany and Britain become such antagonists?"[20] Answering her own question, she explains,

> Political scientists might say the fact that Germany and Britain found themselves on opposite sides in the Great War was foreordained, the result of the clash between a major global power feeling its advantage slip away and a rising challenger. Such transitions are rarely managed peacefully. The established power is too often arrogant, lecturing the rest of the world about how to manage its affairs, and too often insensitive to the fears and concerns of lesser powers. Such a power, as Britain was then, and the United States is today, inevitably resists its own intimations of mortality and the rising one is impatient to get its fair share of whatever is on offer, whether colonies, trade, resources, or influence.[21]

In other words, power transition dynamics pushed Britain and Germany down the road to war.

In a power transition, both great powers are concerned about the shifting balance of power and what it means for their security. But what often tips the outcome to war is not the competition for power and security but rather the contest for status and prestige. The Anglo-German rivalry is illustrative. Most historians point to Germany's bid for world power status (*Weltpolitik*)—especially Berlin's decision to embark on a major program of naval expansion—as the primary driver of pre-1914 Anglo-German rivalry. But the naval race was at least as much a symptom as a cause of the Anglo-German antagonism. To be sure, as seen from London, the German naval build-up did pose a threat to core British interests. As an island nation completely dependent on overseas trade for its prosperity, Britain could not be indifferent to the rapid growth of German naval power just across the North Sea. Yet, it is also true that by 1912 the Anglo-German naval race was over, because Germany threw in the towel when it became clear that it could not afford to keep up its end of the battleship building competition. Measured by pure strategic logic, then, Germany's battleship building policy was a double blunder because it provoked Britain's hostility and failed to provide Germany with a fleet large enough to offset British naval superiority.

Strategic logic, however, was not the primary driver of German naval policy.[22] Great powers not only want security; they also want recognition of their role in the international system. That is, in addition to power and security, they also seek status and prestige.[23] Along with the acquisition of colonies, the construction of Germany's "luxury fleet" (as First Lord of the Admiralty Winston Churchill described it) was part of Berlin's strategy to gain equal status with London in the international system and to match Britain in prestige. As Bard College political scientist Michelle Murray says, Germany built battleships because they "were understood at the time to be emblematic of great power status."[24] German Chancellor Bethmann Hollweg asserted that to be a "really Great Power" Germany "*must* have a fleet, and a strong one . . . not merely for the purpose of defending her commerce but for the general purpose of her greatness."[25] It was Germany's desire to be recognized as Britain's equal that ramped up the intensity of the Anglo-German rivalry. This is because status and prestige are "positional goods," the competition for which tends to be zero-sum.[26] Status inconsistency—the disjuncture between the what Robert Gilpin calls the international system's hierarchy of prestige and the underlying distribution of power—is a potent generator of conflict as rising powers strive to reshape the international system to reflect—and gain recognition of—their rising power.

BILATERAL POWER RIVALRIES

In addition to the external dimension of the Anglo-German antagonism, there also was, on the British side, an important domestic dimension. Viewed through the lens of British liberalism, economic rivalry and ideological antipathy disposed British policy makers to regard Germany as a threat. Looking first at the economic aspect, although Britain and Germany were important trading partners, they also were economic competitors, and over time Britain came to regard Germany's economic growth as a dangerous *geopolitical* menace. Guided by the doctrine of economic nationalism, Germany prospered mightily during the 1880s and 1890s, and it narrowed the gap between itself and Britain in key metrics of national power.[27] This caused widespread apprehension among British elites, who blamed Britain's relative decline on "unfair" German trade and industrial policies: tariffs, state-sanctioned cartels, and state subsidies of export industries. Although the commercial competition between the two nations did not *cause* the rising enmity between Britain and Germany in the years preceding 1914, it colored British policy makers' perceptions of Germany, and, as Paul Kennedy observes, thereby spilled over into the geopolitical realm.[28]

In addition to economic rivalry, in the decades before 1914, ideology—reflecting the different political and social structures of Britain and Germany—became for the British an increasingly salient factor driving the Anglo-German antagonism. During the "long" nineteenth century (1815 to 1914), Britain was both the cradle and acme of liberalism both as a political philosophy and an economic doctrine. As Paul Kennedy has pointed out, British elites viewed Wilhelmine Germany's political culture—which privileged the military and its values, emphasized deference to authority, reserved for the state a large role in politics and economics, and subordinated the individual to the overarching interests of the national community—as fundamentally antithetical to their own liberal values.[29] The prewar Anglo-German ideological gap affected London's image of Germany and thus helped to fuel a perception spiral that solidified a hardening belief among the British political establishment that Germany was irredeemably hostile. Once the war began, the intensity of the ideological distaste for Germany harbored by British elites became glaringly obvious. Britain's wartime liberal crusade against Germany was simply the continuation of the prewar outlook of the British political class.

Like the Anglo-German antagonism, the deepening Sino-American rivalry is the product of both changes in the distribution of power and of economic and ideational factors. At the systemic level, just as their pre-1914

British counterparts worried about the dramatic shift in relative power between Germany and Britain, today's American policy elites are apprehensive about the changing distribution of relative power between the United States and China. And, as was true for British policy makers contemplating Germany's rise before 1914, American policy makers are unsettled not only by the fact of China's economic growth but also by its velocity. Since 2010, China has surpassed the United States as the world's leading manufacturing state, the leading trading state, and the leading exporter. According to the World Bank's International Comparison Program, measured by purchasing power parity (PPP), China *already* has overtaken the United States as the world's largest economy.[30] Although some economists question the validity of GDP calculations based on PPP, even using the market exchange rate metric, China is forecast to surpass the US in aggregate GDP by the early 2020s.[31]

As with the Anglo-German antagonism, economic rivalry and ideological antipathy are causing the perception of the "China threat" to congeal within the US foreign policy elite. In the United States—just as in pre-1914 Britain—many policy makers and political leaders believe that China's economic success is explained by the fact that it has adopted a range of neomercantilist—"unfair" and illiberal—policies. As reported by the *New York Times*, a big reason for President Obama's changing views about China's economic policy was his anger at "Beijing's refusal to play by the rules in trade" and his frustration over "the United States' lack of leverage to do anything about it."[32] The belief that China does not play by the rules in trade—and that it a "currency manipulator"—is widespread across the US political spectrum, and was in important factor in Donald Trump's victory in the 2016 U.S. presidential election. American policy makers also fear that China's trade and economic policies are intended to weaken the United States geopolitically as well as economically—a concern similar to that held about Germany by many in the British elite before 1914. The Obama administration's decision to indict five alleged Chinese military hackers for industrial espionage underscored these concerns.[33]

American apprehensions about rapid change in the balance of relative economic power with China reflects doubts—seldom acknowledged openly—about the relative decline of US power and, even more fundamentally, about whether America's economic and political development model remains superior to China's. As the Eurasia Group's Ian Bremmer and David Gordon have argued, "China's rise and state-capitalist model present the most significant commercial and geopolitical challenge that the U.S. has faced in two decades"; moreover, "China's state capitalism challenges the future of democratic capitalism."[34] In this regard, it appears that the *real* "China threat" perceived by US policy elites is to basic notions of American national identity. Indeed, "For Americans the success of a mainland [Chinese] regime that blends authoritarian rule with market-driven economics is an *affront*."[35] Here, in another echo of the Anglo-German antagonism, American self-doubt caused by China's economic rise blends into a deeper ideological antipathy toward China.

American leaders perceive China in the same way pre-1914 British policy makers thought of Germany: as a nation whose political system raises doubts about both the scope of its foreign policy ambitions and its trustworthiness as a diplomatic partner. The very fact that China is a one (communist) party state rather than a Western democracy "inherently creates misgivings among many Americans, including high-level officials."[36] In contrast to America's self-perception of itself as a nation built on classical liberal political and economic ideas, China is viewed as a nation that is collectivist, mercantilist, statist, lacking in representative government and rule of law, and a human rights violator. As Kenneth Lieberthal and Wang Jisi observe, "U.S. leaders believe that democracies are inherently more trustworthy than are authoritarian systems."[37] Just as liberal ideological antipathy colored British perceptions of Germany before 1914, America's liberal world view is contributing powerfully to policy makers' "enemy" image of China.

THE UNITED STATES AND STABILITY

As was true for Britain and Germany before World War I, powerful forces—both external and domestic—are pushing the United States and China down the road to confrontation. However, although the international system's structure constrains decision-makers and narrows the range of policy options from which they can choose, it does not foreclose the possibility of choice. Structure and agency always coexist uneasily side by side, which is why a Sino-American showdown in the years ahead, while probable, is not inevitable.

Whether a clash between the United States and China is avoidable hinges on what is at stake for both nations. For China, the answer is straightforward. China seeks to become the regional hegemon in East (and Southeast) Asia. This is what rising great powers *do*: they seek to establish geopolitical dominance in their own backyards. China seeks to dominate East Asia for both security reasons and to affirm its status and prestige as America's geopolitical equal. China's rise, however, poses the risk of conflict with the United States because China is rubbing up against entrenched

American power in East Asia. Indeed, since 1945, the United States has been the incumbent hegemon in East Asia.[38] There are two metaphors that explain why trouble is brewing between the United States and China. One is the "Dodge City" syndrome. Afficionados of American Westerns have all seen the movie where the two gunslingers confront each other in the town saloon and one says to the other, "This town ain't big enough for both of us." And we all know what happens next. A more intellectual perspective is the Newtonian Theory of Geopolitics: two hegemons cannot dominate the same region at the same time.

The United States will determine whether a Sino-American train wreck can be avoided. Today, America's predominance in East Asia contributes little, if anything, to US security (defined by the traditional geopolitical metrics of military power and geography). After all, in traditional geopolitical terms, the United States is the most secure great power in history. Its homeland is shielded from any kind of serious great power threat by geography and its overwhelming military capabilities—and nuclear deterrence. It is America's extraregional hegemony in East Asia, and the potential "entrapment" dynamics of US alliances in the region, that are the main cause of US *in*security. America's alliances and security guarantees in East Asia—especially with Japan—are potential transmission belts for war. This is a point underscored by the increasingly fraught Sino-Japanese conflict over the Diaoyuti/Senkaku Islands into which the United States has been injected because of its alliance with Tokyo.

So why does Washington remain committed to preserving its dominance in East Asia? The fundamental reason is ideational. The United States wants to dominate that region to ensure that its markets remain open to American economic penetration, and that it also remains open to penetration by America's liberal ideology. What American policy makers fear is the threat of *closure*, because that would undermine the extant international order—the Pax Americana—based on America's liberal beliefs about the virtues of economic openness and democracy. China is seen as a threat because its very existence challenges the idea of an "Open Door World" on which America's security is—wrongly—believed to depend. Aaron Friedberg concedes this point: "Ideology inclines the United States to be more suspicious and hostile toward China than it would be for strategic reasons alone."[39]

China's nondemocratic political system is also viewed as an ideational menace to the United States, because "if Asia comes to be dominated by an authoritarian China, the prospects for liberal reform in any of its nondemocratic neighbors will be greatly diminished. Even the region's established democracies could find themselves inhibited from pursuing policies, foreign and perhaps domestic as well, that might incur Beijing's wrath."[40] Its not stretching the point to suggest that the biggest threat to the United States in East Asia is not China but the liberal assumptions embedded in American foreign policy. America's ideological preferences have real-world consequences because they are powerful drivers of US grand strategy toward China. That grand strategy, however, not only puts the United States at odds with China, but also reinforces Beijing's insecurities and its deep-rooted fears of Washington's intentions and ambitions. It is *American* policy that generates the negative perception spiral that is pushing the United States and China down the road to confrontation.

Even before the Obama administration's strategic "pivot" to East Asia, Chinese policy makers perceived that the United States was engaged in a policy of encircling China strategically and thwarting its rise. At least as worrisome for Chinese leaders is the concern that the United States is trying to promote "regime change" by pressuring China to transform its political system into a liberal democracy. As seen in Beijing, the United States "uses ideas of democracy and human rights to de-legitimize and destabilize regimes that espouse alternative values" to American-style democratic free market capitalism.[41] Many in the US foreign policy establishment advocate policies that inevitably serve to heat up Sino-American tensions by reinforcing Beijing's preexisting fears of American intentions. A good example is Aaron Friedberg's 2011 book, *A Contest for Supremacy: China, America, and the Struggle for Mastery in Asia*, which calls for the United States to maintain its military superiority over China in East Asia, defend Taiwan's independence, create a powerful anti-Chinese alliance in East Asia and Southeast Asia, and work for regime change in China.

Another example is the very similar policy advocated by Andrew Nathan and Andrew Scobell in a 2012 *Foreign Affairs* article, in which there is a mind-boggling disconnect between the authors' analysis of Sino-American relations and their policy recommendations. The answer given by Nathan and Scobell to the question they raise—"how does China see the U.S.?"—is that Beijing is uncertain of US intentions, concerned about its security, resentful of American meddling in its domestic affairs, and determined to gain acknowledgment of its claims for status parity with the United States. All true. Instead of advocating policies that could ameliorate China's fears, however, they offer hard-line policy prescriptions that only can reinforce Beijing's distrust of US intentions. Two stand out. First, they flatly dismiss Beijing's claim to equal status and prestige with America. Second, they argue that the United States should stand its ground and rigidly uphold the geopolitical status quo in East Asia. Nathan and Scobell reflect a tendency among US foreign policy makers and analysts to act as if China is only entitled to assert interests that have been preapproved by the United States. That is not how great power politics works, however. By ignoring China's perception of its own interests, the United States is deliberately constructing a self-fulfilling prophecy of mistrust and rising hostility in Sino-American relations. If the United States really wants to avoid a train wreck with China, it will have to make difficult—even painful—adjustments and adopt a policy that accommodates China's rise. In this sense, the United States and China are rapidly approaching an "E. H. Carr Moment."

THE CARR MOMENT

In his classic study of international relations, *The Twenty Years' Crisis*, the British scholar E. H. Carr analyzed the political crisis of 1930s caused by the breakdown of the post-World War I order symbolized by the Versailles Treaty.[42] The Versailles system cracked, Carr argued, because of the growing gap between the order it represented and the actual distribution of power in Europe. Carr used the events of the 1930s to make a larger geopolitical point: international orders reflect the balance of power that existed at their creation. Over time, however, the relative power of states changes, and eventually the international order no longer reflects that actual distribution of power between (or among) the great powers. When that happens, the legitimacy of the prevailing order is put in question. As its power increases, the rising power becomes increasingly dissatisfied with the international order and seeks to revise it. The challenger wants to change the rules embodied in the existing international order—rules written, of course by the once-dominant but now declining great power that created the existing order. The incumbent hegemon, of course, wants to preserve the existing international order as it is—an order that it created to advance its interests. The Carr Moment presents the incumbent hegemon with a choice. It can dig in its heels and try to preserve the prevailing order—and its privileged position therein—or it can accede to the rising challenger's demands for revision. If it chooses the former course of action, it runs the risk of war with the dissatisfied challenger. If it chooses the later, it must come to terms with the reality of its decline and the end of its hegemonic position.

The Carr Moment is where the geopolitical rubber meets the road: the status quo power(s) must choose between accommodating or opposing the revisionist demands of the rising power(s). In his contribution to this volume (and elsewhere), John Ikenberry argues that China will not challenge the current international order, even as the distribution of power shifts in its favor over the next decade or two. This is a doubtful proposition, however. *The* geopolitical question—the Carr Moment—of our time is whether the declining hegmon in East Asia, the United States, will try to preserve a status quo that, over the next decade or two, increasingly no longer will reflect the prevailing distribution of power, or whether it can reconcile itself to the revisionist demands of a rising China that the international order in East Asia be aligned with the emerging power realities. Britain faced the same choice in the years leading up to World War I.

It is tempting to conclude that war between Britain and Germany a century ago was inevitable. Yet there was serious debate in London about whether to contain or conciliate Germany. In a January 1907 memorandum, Sir Eyre Crowe, a senior Foreign Office official, made the case for containment.[43] While allowing Germany its *present* place in the hierarchy of status and prestige, he argued, Britain should oppose Berlin if it sought more. Crowe argued that London should not accommodate Germany; doing so would only increase Berlin's expansionist appetite. Germany, he said, intended "ultimately to break up and supplant the British Empire." Crowe concluded that the Anglo-German rivalry resulted from a fundamental conflict of interests that could not be papered over by diplomatic fudging, the effect of which would be the sacrifice of British interests. War with Germany, Crowe argued, could be avoided only by submitting to Berlin's demands—which he believed would mean forfeiture of Britain's own great power status—or, as he counseled, by amassing enough power to deter Berlin.

Lord Thomas Sanderson—the recently retired Permanent Undersecretary of State in the Foreign Office—rebutted Crowe.[44] The key to understanding German diplomacy was the fact that a unified Germany was a latecomer on the world stage. "It was inevitable," he observed, that a rising power like Germany was "impatient to realize various long-suppressed aspirations, and to claim full recognition of its new position."[45] Sanderson understood that refusing to acknowledge Berlin's claims for status and prestige on par with Britain's was risky, because "a great and growing nation cannot be repressed." He understood the Carr Moment's logic: Britain's choice was either to accommodate or resist German aspirations—and resistance meant a high chance of war. For Sanderson, the choice was clear: "It would be a misfortune that [Germany] should be led to believe that in whatever direction she seeks to expand she will find the British lion in her path."[46] Rejecting Crowe's argument that Britain should uphold the status quo, Sanderson famously remarked that from Berlin's perspective "the British Empire must appear in the light of some huge giant sprawling over the globe, with gouty fingers and toes stretching in every direction, which cannot be approached without eliciting a scream."[47] As we know, Crowe's views prevailed over Sanderson's. In August 1914, Britain and Germany found themselves at war.

AFTER PAX AMERICANA

The international system is in the midst of a transition away from unipolarity, and, as US dominance wanes, Pax Americana will give way to a new but as yet undefined international order. Historically, transitional periods marked by hegemonic decline and the simultaneous emergence of new great powers have been unstable and war prone. It is hardly alarmist to say that today China and the United States are on a collision course. As was true for Britain and Germany before World War I, powerful forces—both external and domestic—are pushing the United States and China down the road to confrontation.

Whether Beijing and Washington will be able to bridge their differences through diplomacy in the coming years remains to be seen. However, avoiding Sino-American conflict will depend more—*much* more—on US policy than on China's. Here, the Crowe/Sanderson debate serves as an object lesson. Today, when it comes to China, the spirit of Sir Eyre Crowe pervades the American foreign policy community. The United States professes the benevolence of its intentions toward China, even as it refuses to make any significant concessions to what China views as its vital interests. Like Crowe, the US foreign policy establishment believes that Beijing should be satisfied with what it has—or more correctly, what Washington is willing to let China have—and not ask for more.

American foreign policy analysts correctly discern that Chinese leaders believe that the United States is determined to thwart China's rise. Nevertheless, they advocate the kind of hard-line policies that can only confirm Beijing's perceptions and reinforce its sense of insecurity. It is Washington that has the "last clear chance" to avoid the looming Sino-American conflict by undertaking a policy of strategic adjustment in East Asia. Such a policy would have to make real concessions to Beijing on issues that the Chinese consider to be of vital importance to them by doing the following:

- Halting arms sales to Taiwan, and making clear that the United States will not intervene in a conflict between Taiwan and China.
- Retracting the pledges made by President Obama, Defense Secretaries Robert Gates and Chuck Hegel, and then Secretary of State Hiliary

Clinton that the Senkaku (Diayouti) Islands are covered by the US-Japan Mutual Security Treaty.
- Showing flexibility with respect to China's territorial claims in the South China Sea.
- Withdrawing US forces from South Korea.
- Renouncing any US policy of regime change toward China, and adopting a policy of strict noninterference in China's internal affairs (including Tibet and Xinjiang).

America's political culture with its emphasis on exceptionalim, liberal ideology, and "openness" will make it difficult for the United States to adopt such policies.[48] So will American national identity, because, as William Wohlforth has commented, since the Cold War's end there is plenty of evidence that "U.S. decision-makers value their country's status of primacy."[49] Finally, history—or, more correctly, US policy makers' naive notions about it—will also get in the way of conciliating a rising China. When US policy makers look to history as a guide, the default option is to invoke the "lessons" of the 1930s, and to overlook the Great War's causes.[50] Such misuse of history could have tragic consequences for the Sino-American relationship in the future. "The proper lesson" to be drawn from the Great War's outbreak, Johns Hopkins scholar David Calleo observed, "is not so much the need for vigilance against aggressors, but the ruinous consequences of refusing reasonable accommodation to upstarts."[51] If the United States really wants to avoid a future head-on collision with China, it must eschew Crowe's counsel and embrace Sanderson's. For the evolving Sino-American relationship, that is the real lesson of 1914.

NOTES

1. For a counter-argument, see G. John Ikenberry, "The Illusion of Geopolitics: The Enduring Power of Liberal Order" *Foreign Affairs* 93:3 (May–June 2014): 80–90.
2. "Could Asia Really Go to War Over These?" *The Economist*, September 22, 2012, 13; "Chasing Ghosts," *The Economist*, June 11, 2009.
3. See Odd Arne Westad, *Restless Empire: China and the World Since 1750* (New York: Basic Books, 2012); Robert Bickers, *The Scramble for China: Foreign Devils in the Qing Empire, 1832–1914* (New York: Penguin, 2011).
4. For analysis of how China's rise could sidetracked, see Susan Shirk, *China: Fragile Superpower: How China's Internal Politics Could Derail Its Peaceful Rise* (Oxford: Oxford University Press, 2007).
5. Here, the chapter in this volume by William Wohlforth—the leading academic proponent of the view that the international system remains unipolar—is especially noteworthy. While affirming his conviction that the international

system still is unipolar, he concedes that China is about to pass the United States in one very important metric of power: aggregate GDP.

6. Kenneth N. Waltz, *Theory of International Politics* (Reading, MA: Addison-Wesley, 1979). On neoclassical realism, see Steven E. Lobell, Norrin M. Ripsman, and Jeffrey W. Taliaferro, *Neoclassical Realism, the State, and Foreign Policy* (Cambridge: Cambridge University Press, 2009).

7. See Christopher Layne, "The Unipolar Illusion: Why New Great Powers Will Rise," *International Security* 17:3 (Spring 1993): 5–51. Also, see Robert Gilpiin, *War and Change in World Politics* (Princeton: Princeton University Press, 1981); Fareed Zakaria, *From Wealth to Power: The Unusual Origins of America's World Role* (Princeton: Princeton University Press, 1998). Also relevant is the literature on "power transition" theory. For example, see A. F. K. Organski, *World Politics* (New York: Alfred A. Knopf, 1968); A. F. K. Organski and Jacek Kugler, *The War Ledger* (Chicago: University of Chicago Press, 1980); William R. Thompson, ed., *Systemic Transitions: Past, Present, and Future* (New York: Palgrave Macmillan, 2009).

8. John J. Mearsheimer, *The Tragedy of Great Power Politics* (New York, W. W. Norton, 2014, Updated Ed.); Christopher Layne, "China's Challenge to U.S. Hegemony," *Current History*, 107 (January 2008): 13–18.

9. Robert Gilpin, *War and Change in International Politics* (Cambridge: Cambridge University Press, 1981); T. V. Paul, Deborah Welch Larson, and William C. Wohlforth, eds., *Status in World Politics* (Cambridge: Cambridge University Press, 2014).

10. See E. H. Carr, *The Twenty Years' Crisis*, ed. Michael Cox (London: Palgrave Macmillan, 2001); Gilpin, *War and Change*; Christopher Layne, *After the Fall: International Politics, U.S. Grand Strategy, and the End of the Pax Americana* (New Haven, CT: Yale University Press, forthcoming).

11. Michael Hunt and Steven Levine, *Arc of Empire: America's Wars of Empire in Asia from the Philippines to Vietnam* (Chapel Hill, NC: University of North Carolina Press, 2012).

12. See Yuen Foong Khong, *Analogies at War: Korea, Munich, Dien Bien Phu, and the Vietnam Decisions of 1965* (Princeton: Princeton University Press, 1992).

13. On this point, see Gordon Craig, "The Historian and the Study of International Relations," *American Historical Review* 88:1 (February 1988): 9; Edward Ingram, "The Wonderland of the Political Scientist," *International Security* 22:1 (Fall 1997): 52; Melvyn P. Leffler, "Presidential Address: New Approaches, Old Interpretations, and Prospective Reconfigurations," *Diplomatic History* 19:2 (Spring 1995): 179.

14. For elaboration, see G. John Ikenberry, *Liberal Leviathan: The Origins, Crisis, and Transformation of the American World Order* (Princeton, NJ: Princeton University Press, 2011).

15. Obviously, nuclear weapons were not a factor in pre-1914 international politics. But in the years before the Great War, perceptive military observers argued that changes in military technology meant that any future great power war would be prolonged, costly, and ruinous to the states that fought it. Hence, they deduced that the great powers would not run the risk of a major war between (or among) them.

16. For a well-known articulation of the hopes for peace held by the European elite, see Norman Angell, *The Great Illusion: A Study of the Relation of Military Power to National Advantage* (New York: G. P. Putnam & Sons, 1913).

17. Charles Emerson, *1913: In Search of the World before the Great War* (New York: Public Affairs, 2013), xiv; emphasis in original.
18. Ibid., xiii.
19. In addition to Gilpin, *War and Change*, on power transitions, see A. F. K. Organski, *World Politics* (New York: Alfred A. Knopf, 1968); A. F. K. Organski and Jacek Kugler, *The War Ledger* (Chicago: University of Chicago Press, 1980); Jacek Kugler and Douglas Lemke, eds., *Parity and War: Evaluations and Extensions of the War Ledger* (Ann Arbor: University of Michigan Press, 1996); William R. Thompson, ed., *Systemic Transitions: Past, Present, and Future* (New York: Palgrave Macmillan, 2009); Jack Levy, "Power Transition Theory and the Rise of China," in *China's Ascent: Power, Security, and the Future of International Politics*, ed. Robert Ross and Zhu Feng (Ithaca, NY: Cornell University Press, 2008), 11–33. For the argument that, power transition dynamics notwithstanding, China will seek to avoid conflict with the United States, see Steve Chan, *China, the U.S., and Power Transition Theory: A Critique* (New York: Routledge, 2007).
20. Margaret Macmillan, *The War That Ended Peace: The Road to 1914* (New York: Random House, 2014), 63.
21. Ibid., 58
22. A strong case can be made that Tirptiz's battleship building was driven wholly by bureaucratic politics, and not a bit by strategy. On this, see Patrick J. Kelly, *Tirpitz and the Imperial German Navy* (Bloomington: Indiana University Press, 2011). On bureaucratic politics, see Graham Allison and Philip Zelikow, *Essence of Decision: Explaining the Cuban Missile Crisis*, 2nd ed. (New York: Longman, 1999). For a recent discussion about the strategic illogic of Tirpitz's "risk fleet" strategy, see Dirk Bonker, *Militarism in a Global Age: Naval Ambitions in Germany and the United States before World War I* (Ithaca, NY: Cornell University Press, 2012).
23. On the importance of status in international politics, see T. V. Paul, Deborah Welch Larson, and William C. Wohlforth, eds., *Status in World Politics* (Cambridge: Cambridge University Press, 2014).
24. Michelle Murray, "Identity, Insecurity, and Great Power Politics: The Tragedy of German Naval Ambition before the First World War," *Security Studies* 19:4 (Fall 2010): 665. Also see Jan Ruger, *The Great Naval Game: Britain and Germany in the Age of Empire* (Cambridge: Cambridge University Press, 2007).
25. James Joll and Gordon Martell, *The Origins of the First World War*, 3rd ed. (New York: Pearson Longman, 2007), 148.
26. Randall L. Schweller, "Realism and the Present Great Power System: Growth and Positional Conflict over Scarce Resources," in *Unipolar Politics: Realism and State Strategies after the Cold War*, ed. Ethan B. Kapstein and Michael Mastanduno (New York: Columbia University Press, 1999), 28–68.
27. Friederich List was the founding father of the German school of economic nationalism. In the latter half of the nineteenth century, this doctrine was advocated by the leading economists Gustav Schmoller and Adolph Wagner. On List's views, see E. M. Earle, "Adam Smith, Alexander Hamilton, and Friederich List," in *Makers of Modern Strategy: Military Thought from Machiavelli to the Nuclear Age*, ed. Peter Paret, with Gordon A, Craig and Felix Gilbert (Princeton, NJ: Princeton University Press, 1986), 217–61.
28. Paul Kennedy, *The Rise of the Anglo-German Antagonism, 1860–1914* (London: George Allen & Unwin, 1980), 305.
29. Ibid., 6.

30. Chris Giles, "China Poised to Overtake US as World's Leading Economic Power This Year," *Financial Times*, April 30, 2014.
31. "The Dating Game," *Economist*, December 27, 2011 http://www.economist.com/blogs/daily chart/2010/12/save_date.
32. Mark Landler, "Obama's Journey to Tougher Tack on a Rising China," *New York Times*, September 20, 2012.
33. Explaining the rationale behind the indictments, Attorney General Eric H. Holder Jr. said, "[W]hen a foreign nation uses military or intelligence resources as tools against an American executive or corporations to obtain trade secrets or sensitive business information for the benefit of its state-owned companies, we must say 'Enough is enough.'" Quoted in Michael S. Schmidt and David E. Sanger, "5 in China Army Face U.S. Charges of Cyberattacks," *New York Times*, May 19, 2004.
34. Ian Bremmer and David Gordon, "U.S. Needs Japan as Its Best Ally in Asia," *Financial Times*, September 9, 2012.
35. Aaron Friedberg, *A Contest for Supremacy: China, America, and the Struggle for Mastery in Asia* (New York, W. W. Norton, 2011), 44; emphasis added.
36. Kenneth Lieberthal and Wang Jisi, *Addressing U.S.-China Strategic Distrust*, John L. Thornton China Center Monograph Series, no. 4 (Washington, DC: Brookings Institution, 2012), 26.
37. Ibid., 24
38. John Mearsheimer argues that the "stopping power of water" prevents a great power from gaining hegemony outside its own region. This is not correct, however. Since the end of World War II, the United States has been an extraregional hegemon in the three areas of the world most important to it strategically: Western Europe, East Asia, and the Persian Gulf. See Christopher Layne, *The Peace of Illusions: American Grand Strategy from 1940 to the Present* (Ithaca, NY: Cornell University Press, 2006). For a critique of Mearsheimer, see Christopher Layne, "The 'Poster Child' for Offensive Realism: The United States as a Global Hegemon," *Security Studies* 12:2 (Winter 2002–2003): 120–64.
39. Friedberg, *A Contest for Supremacy*, 43–44.
40. Ibid., 8
41. Andrew Nathan and Andrew Scobell, "How China Sees America," *Foreign Affairs*, September/October 2012, 39.
42. Carr, *The Twenty Years' Crisis*.
43. Eyre Crowe, "Memorandum on the Present State of British Relations with France and Germany," in *British Documents on the Origins of the War, 1898–1914*, ed. G. P. Gooch and Harold Temperly (London: His Majesty's Stationery Office, 1928), 397–420.
44. Memorandum by Lord Sanderson, in Gooch and Temperly, *British Documents on the Origins of the War*, 420–31.
45. Ibid., 429.
46. Ibid., 431.
47. Ibid., 430.
48. See Louis Hartz, *The Liberal Tradition in America* (San Diego: Harcourt, Brace, and World, 1955); Michael Hunt, *Ideology and U.S. Foreign Policy* (New Haven, CT: Yale University Press, 1978); Layne, *Peace of Illusions*; William Appleman Williams, *The Tragedy of American Diplomacy* (New York: Delta, 1962); Michael C. Desch, "America's Liberal Illiberalism: 'The Ideological Origins of

Overreaction in U.S. Foreign Policy,'" *International Security* 32, no. 3 (Winter 2007–2008): 7–43.

49. William C. Wohlforth, "Unipolarity, Status Competition, and Great Power War," *World Politics* 61:1 (January 2009): 52.

50. The opening of the British archives in the 1970s produced a torrent of scholarship about London's diplomacy and grand strategy during the 1930s. The historical evidence refutes Winston Churchill's caricature of British policy makers in the 1930 as naïve appeasers. See David Reynolds, *In Command of History: Churchill Fighting and Writing the Second World War* (New York: Random House, 2005); Christopher Layne, "Security Studies and the Use of History: Neville Chamberlain's Grand Strategy Revisited," *Security Studies* 17:3 (Fall 2008): 397–437.

51. David Calleo, *The German Problem Reconsidered: Germany and the World Order, 1870 to the Present* (Cambridge: Cambridge University Press, 1978), 6.

CHAPTER 7

The Weight of the Past in China's Relations with Its Asian Neighbors

ODD ARNE WESTAD

INTRODUCTION

Historically, regional power shifts have tended to be messy affairs. Whether it was Germany and Britain in the twentieth century, Britain and Spain in the seventeenth century, or the Song and Liao states in the eleventh century, such changes often produced not only wars, but long, drawn-out forms of conflict that devastated the regions in which they occurred. With the exception of the Cold War between the United States and the Soviet Union, none of these power-shift conflicts have yet been truly global, and it is unlikely that the rivalry between the United States and China will spill over into a global confrontation any time soon.

The reason for this is that China will not be a global strategic power in this generation. Its capacities are simply too far behind those of the United States, not just in strictly military terms, but also in terms of what underpins strategic power: logistics, alliances, and the organization of society and state. Of course, many long-term economic trends are mainly (but not exclusively) stacked against the United States. But in terms of strategic power projection, China is very far behind, and it is not catching up quickly.[1] And, unlikely as it might seem at the moment, it is also possible that the Americans at some point may come to their senses and start consuming less, producing more, and investing in a twenty-first-century infrastructure.

Such a metamorphosis would of course change the strategic picture completely, though even with strong political leadership it would not happen overnight.[2] It is therefore likely that any confrontation between China and the United States would center on the eastern Asian region, which the Communist leadership in Beijing has made clear that it considers an area of Chinese predominance. In this chapter, I provide an overview of two of the key conflict areas within the region, Korea and Southeast Asia, mainly from a Chinese perspective, and indicate how a better understanding of the international history of the region can help with measuring the framework for current rivalries. I also suggest a few issues for consideration in terms of how the potential for great power conflict can be reduced.

THE UNITED STATES AND CHINA'S RELATIONS WITH ITS NEIGHBORS

First, though, it is important to note how strategic relations in eastern Asia have developed since the end of the Cold War. The collapse of the Soviet Union, much sought by both Washington and Beijing, fundamentally changed relations between China and the United States. Instead of viewing each other as real (or potential) allies against Moscow, without a common enemy the two rather quickly developed into rivals for influence in Asia. The power relationship was (and remains) profoundly uneven: the United States had capabilities that China did not possess in military terms, in terms of alliances, and, of course, in terms of soft power. The most fundamental aspect of the relationship was that China seemed fundamentally to accept a US-led and US-driven global economic system, based on the gradual opening of markets to trade and investments. Indeed, China—under a Communist leadership—was changing its own domestic economy to look like the American one, with market mechanisms driving economic change.[3]

Neither China nor the United States had much of a road map for this new era. The Chinese leadership under Jiang Zemin gave little thought to grand strategy, and the Clinton Administration even less. Still, both seem to have understood the domestic needs of their countries well within an international setting. Looking at their memoirs, it is interesting to see how both were eyeing the advantages that could be had by integrating China further into the global economic system. Chinese Communist leaders were concerned about how the end of the Cold War had led to an American global hegemony, and they wanted to raise their own influence in Asia in order to feel more secure. But the economic goals took precedence over everything else—both Jiang and Clinton think that facilitating

China's accession to the World Trade Organization was a major achievement of their careers.[4]

Looking back, US policies in the 1990s to integrate China further into the world economy were quite successful. In this regard, Clinton's policies created a lasting success, the long-term consequences of which we probably cannot yet fully see. The failure—a bit as with Russia in Europe—was not attempting to create a security framework that offered an opportunity for integrating China into its region. Would China have been open for such proposals? We do not know. But what is clear, in hindsight, is that Jiang's China—just like Yeltsin's Russia—was more geared toward cooperation with the United States than any of their successors had been.

George W. Bush's Middle Eastern adventures gave Chinese leaders an unprecedented and unexpected opportunity to expand their own position in eastern Asia. Hu Jintao—not the most inventive of foreign-policy makers—sensed that his country would benefit from being perceived regionally as a peaceful great power. China convinced South Korea that it was restraining and attempting to reform North Korea. It negotiated a free-trade agreement with Southeast Asia, whose large Muslim population was skeptical of US Middle Eastern policies. It built a stronger relationship with Russia and with the Central Asian states. Hu Jintao's first term in office may be seen as the apogee of Chinese influence in the eastern Asian region.

As with so many leaders before them, the Hu Jintao leadership's initial successes (which had been granted them in great part by US absenteeism) led to a degree of hubris that created China's first post-Cold War foreign-policy imbroglio. The combination of Bush's pivot to nowhere and the onset of the deepest global crisis of capitalism since the 1930s led Beijing to believe that it could force history's hand: that the "nice guy" approach to the region (which had brought slow but tangible results) could be replaced by a "tough guy" approach, which would bring China more of what it wanted faster.

It is clear that this approach did not work. While China (so far) has been shielded from the worst effects of the economic crisis itself, its overambitious regional strategy has turned much of the region against it and has allowed the United States to rebuild some of its links with China's eastern and southern neighbors. China's position today is therefore paradoxical. The Great Recession in the West has probably advanced China's relative economic position more than anything since the country's economic reforms began. But at the same time, the consequences of China's dependence on the global economic system and its diplomatic overreach with regard to most of its neighbors are clear for all to see. By looking at two key areas in its vicinity—Korea and Southeast Asia—we may be able to better understand some of the challenges China will be facing as its leaders attempt to deal with this new situation.[5]

CHINA AND THE KOREAN QUESTION

China's relationship with Korea needs to be understood in light of its deeper history. Although Korea was never integrated into China, for more than a millennium all Korean states recognized their subservience to a Chinese empire. While the Korean Choson state—a remarkably long-lasting entity that ruled most of the peninsula from 1392 to 1910—was almost completely autonomous in its internal affairs, its relations with other countries were always seen through the prism of its tributary relationship with China. China was also recognized by all Koreans as the center of cultural developments that encompassed Korea itself. The first Korean written language used Chinese characters, and the Korean civil service was patterned on China's experience under the Ming and Qing dynasties.

At the core of Korea's cultural or identity relationship with China stands neo-Confucian learning as it was first developed in the twelfth century AD. The teachings of Zhu Xi (朱熹, 1130–1200), central to Chinese Song dynasty neo-Confucianism, inspired a re-creation of the Korean state in China's image. Generations of Koreans were particularly preoccupied with Zhu's elucidation of the neo-Confucian principle *li* (理, often translated as "rational principle," "order," or even "hierarchy"). Zhu's teaching gave rise to a peculiar Korean emphasis on both meritocracy and family. Civil servants would have to have skills, but also lineage. The organization of Korean society was therefore centered on a small number of families who contributed scholars, officers, and bureaucrats to the state from one generation to the next. Their cultural and ideological dependence on China influenced the organization of Korean society, but also Korean views of the outside world.

The late nineteenth-century breakdown of the eastern Asian world order that put Qing China at the center was therefore a particular tragedy for Korean elites. They reacted to it in two different stages. The first, which lasted from mid-century up to the Sino-Japanese war of 1894–1895, was a period of denial, in which the majority of Confucian leaders in Korea insisted on China's continued centrality, even as Chinese leaders themselves seemed ready to cast it off. The second, which encompassed the first generation after the postwar Japanese occupation of Korea, was about creating very distinctive forms of Korean nationalism. China had failed as an example. Japanese ruthlessness and industrialization had proven itself to be superior, but also to be Korea's enemy. The only possible response, Korean elites thought, was to insist on Korean nationhood and on the exemplary significance of Korean society and thinking. Japan was rapacious. China had diverted from its principles. Only Korea—in spite of its enslavement—remained pure and true.[6]

The starting point for understanding the recurrent crises and states of war on the Korean peninsula since the 1890s is the strength and peculiar nature of Korean nationalism. Born just at the time when Korea fell under Japanese domination, Korean nationalist ideologies grew up in exile in the interwar period and took two distinctive paths, one traditionalist and one Communist. Though the modern states they wanted to build were different in nature, the two shared an uncommonly strong emphasis on their country as a victim of its neighbors (Japan mostly, but also China) and on the extraordinary strengths and abilities of the Korean people.

After a number of wars and rebellions (of which the so-called Korean War from 1950 to 1953 was only one), South Korea (the Republic of Korea) most unexpectedly grew into one of the world's economic powerhouses, while Communist North Korea (the Democratic People's Republic of Korea—DPRK) failed to provide even for its own people. But while interaction with the outside world tempered nationalism in South Korea into more of a normal set of strongly patriotic attitudes, North Korea's spectacular failure as a state did nothing to dampen the regime's nationalism or hinder its ability to inject it into a largely isolated population. North Korean nationalism is fervent, bellicose, and almost apocalyptic in nature. It sees no friends in the outside world and portrays South Koreans as deviants who have been contaminated by US and Japanese capitalism and consumerism.

North Korea's relationship with China is deeply influenced both by its deeper history and by events in the twentieth century. The Kim family's claim to having created a perfect Communist society is, at least in part, directed against China, which—as North Korean thinking goes—never managed such a feat. In the late twentieth century, as in the late nineteenth century, the Chinese deviated from the true path: their convictions were not powerful enough to produce the society that both they and the Koreans desired. The dependence that North Korea has on China both in security and economic terms fuels resentment in Pyongyang; stories that visiting high-ranking Chinese tell of petty slights at the hands of the Kim dynasty are legion. But the North Koreans have also learnt—in part from deeper history—to present just about the right amount of obsequiousness to Beijing to keep the relationship from collapsing.[7]

For China's leaders, North Korea is the problem from hell. Top policy makers in Beijing are worried about the effects of a collapse of Kim

Jong-un's government, which they fear could bring millions of refugees and, ultimately, place US troops on China's borders. But they are also alarmed by the pugnacity of the North Korean regime (and first and foremost by its acquisition of nuclear weapons) and dismayed by the way it treats China.[8] Of late, some influential Chinese foreign-policy advisers are worried about a spillover from the way the DPRK treats China to what others think they can get away with in their relations with Beijing. "Why on earth should a country like the Philippines treat us with respect when our next-door alliance partner treats us very badly?" one expert on Southeast Asia told me in Beijing in the autumn of 2013.

Xi Jinping's leadership group feels that North Korea is a problem inherited from its predecessors. But they also sense that it is an issue that probably will come to a head during their time in power. Like everyone else, they have difficulties timing the North Korean collapse. But most of them (or at least their advisors, whom I have spoken to) seem convinced that it will come, and that it will most likely be set off by some form of crisis inside North Korea itself. The reform Chinese leaders have called for in North Korea has not been implemented comprehensively enough to make a difference in economic terms. Indeed, it seems to have done little but stimulate the high levels of corruption that China's own reform era is known for. For Chinese leaders, as for many foreign observers, however little can be conjured about North Korea's future, it first and foremost seems to embody what is known as Stein's Law: "If something cannot go on forever, it will stop."

The North Korean issue is so intractable for Chinese leaders in part because it is a cause of conflict (or at least friction) among foreign-policy-making bureaucracies within Beijing. The Foreign Ministry struggles (and mostly fails) in putting forward proposals that generally emphasize international cooperation on the Korean nuclear issue. The International Department of the Central Committee of the Chinese Communist Party (CCP), which is generally considered to have the "leading role" on North Korea, seems deeply split in the matter—some of Pyongyang's sternest critics and foremost defenders are all found there. The Central Military Commission has in the past taken a benign view of North Korea (at least as compared to the threats it could see coming from other corners), but that seems to have changed since Kim Jong-un's dramatic December 2013 purge of his uncle Jang Song-thaek, who was close to some Chinese military leaders. The staffers of the "small leading groups" on national security and foreign affairs) within the top Party leadership attempt to coordinate different views and initiatives, but they often find themselves overwhelmed by the task or riven by factional conflict themselves. The new State Security

Commission has been set up to achieve better coordination but probably has too broad a mandate to succeed, and it has so far concentrated mainly on domestic security threats.[9]

China's disjointed foreign-policy process is not only a problem that ought to interest students of bureaucratic politics. It certainly does not only affect major issues in Chinese foreign affairs, such as Korea. First and foremost, it signals some of the deeper problems in China's policy making, most of which have historical roots. Different from what many in the West think, China does not have the advantage dictatorships sometimes are imagined to have, such as strong leadership or the ability to make decisions fast and act quickly. Instead, it seems to have all of the defects of a democracy but none of its advantages. Since the Cultural Revolution and even through the Deng Xiaoping era, there has been a continuous struggle for competencies within the Chinese leadership, resulting in overlapping authority and unclear policy processes. While all areas of Chinese politics suffer from these difficulties, foreign affairs suffer more than most because of the relatively few number of top leaders with any meaningful foreign-policy experience.

THE TROUBLESOME ALLY

Within foreign affairs—and shown most clearly by cases such as North Korea—there are specific difficulties with developing policy planning and strategies. There is sometimes a profound lack of coordination: on Korea, one often gets the impression that those working on North Korea have no idea what their colleagues handling South Korea are doing, and vice versa. One reason for this is the secrecy that is imposed in the relationship between different units. Another reason is the Communist principle of extreme centralization, which today does not work in practice because the top level is often reluctant to make strategic decisions. But at the individual advisory level, too, hesitancy and indecision proliferate. It is often seen as dangerous to make new and specific proposals, even internally. China, after all, is a political dictatorship in which any form of dissidence can be punished. In addition, as a reaction against the voluntarism and excesses of the Mao era, China today has a political system in which collectivism is highly valued. But the main explanation for China's foreign-policy inertia is probably similar to the experience of other countries at different stages of their own development: it is simply easier to attempt to hold firm to a few principles and react to whatever happens in the world, than it is to set out a more comprehensive approach.

On some issues, this could be seen as a rather sensible method for a developing great power to follow. It is not a given that China needs to have a comprehensive strategy on issues far away, such as Somalia or Sudan. But the problem is that there is little sense of direction in what is happening on China's own borders as well. Relations between China and the DPRK over the past ten years are a good example. China today supplies 90 percent of North Korea's energy imports, 80 percent of its consumer-goods imports, and 45 percent of its overall food supply.[10] Even so, the DPRK has carried out six nuclear tests, with China each time warning of serious consequences to the relationship if Pyongyang conducted tests again. Likewise, a number of visiting Chinese high-level delegations have recommended reforms in the North Korean economy, only to see the Kim-ists move in an opposite direction, torturing and executing Chinese-trained economic experts. The execution of Jang Song-thaek, with whom Chinese leaders (and its military leaders especially) had developed very close relations, was another low point in the relationship. Some of this seems to affect China's security and territoriality directly: there have been a number of reports of clashes between Chinese and North Korean border guards, and in the spring of 2013, North Korea hijacked three Chinese fishing boats in the Yellow Sea, demanding $100,000 in ransom for releasing them. None of these events bear witness to a comprehensive Chinese strategy for dealing with North Korea.

At the same time, the significance of the Republic of Korea for China is rapidly increasingly. China is currently South Korea's largest trading partner. And, more significantly, South Korea is China's third largest, facilitating much of the technology imports that China badly wants (and needs). The admiration for South Korea's industrial might and its approach to creating a flexible economy and a balanced social system (not to mention its music, film, and TV shows) is very high in Beijing. In both material and cultural terms, the ties between China and South Korea are many times stronger than those between the Chinese and the North, and they are getting stronger year by year, in spite of occasional diplomatic clashes.

If it had not been for the unfortunate existence of North Korea, relations between China and South Korea could come to approximate the nineteenth-century Sino-Korean ideals (if not always their practice). South Koreans of all generations are much more concerned about Japan, even today, than they are about China. During her visit to China in the summer of 2013, then South Korean president Park Geun-hye spoke convincingly, in Chinese, about the cultural ties that connect the two countries and about the unprecedented opportunities that open for both if they can cooperate politically and integrate further economically. But she also said that cooperation on matters regarding North Korea was a sine qua non for the further development of the relationship. Even though many see a strong signal in his visiting Seoul before ever going to Pyongyang, China's president Xi was more careful during his trip to the South Korean capital the following year. He did, however, speak of a "strategic partnership" between Beijing and Seoul, and called the South Korean government "a sincere friend and reliable partner."[11] The North Koreans, predictably, were furious. "Some spineless countries," said an official commentary, "are blindly following the stinking bottom of the U.S. by also struggling to embrace Park Geun-hye."[12]

Some observers argue that rather than seeing the current state of affairs in China's relations with the two Koreas as a problem, Chinese leaders may well see them as a plus. Being known as the only power that can keep an "irrational" DPRK regime in check can benefit China, this view holds. It enables Beijing to manipulate the whole security situation in Northeast Asia to its advantage. At the same time, Chinese leaders may be planning to very gradually integrate the DPRK into China, making it the de facto thirty-sixth Chinese province. But if this is the Chinese game, they are playing a bad hand very poorly at the moment. The DPRK seems to be drifting further away from China, rather than closer. And China seems less able to influence its decisions than before. At the same time, the South Korean public perception of China, even under the ROK's new liberal president Moon Jae-in, seems to be in decline, as one reputational risk the Chinese have to incur as a result of their steady sponsorship of one of the most unpalatable regimes on earth.[13]

The ultimate test of China's intentions will only be had when the North Korean regime goes. There are of course many scenarios for what could happen when the Kim regime collapses, and this is not the place to rehash them. What is clear today is that unless China and the United States, as well as South Korea and Japan, are able to improve their working relations overall, and especially on this issue, we could see a crisis of unprecedented proportions for all of eastern Asia. Both Washington and Beijing will have to show that the past can be avoided through wide-ranging consultations, which of course ought to start now, not when the crisis is already unfolding.

CHINA AND THE CHALLENGE OF SOUTHEAST ASIAN INTEGRATION

Modern China's relationship with its Southeast Asian neighbors was long an unmitigated disaster zone.[14] Even before the collapse of the Qing Empire,

Chinese immigrants to the region were seen by many locals as henchmen for China's interest or agents of European colonial powers. As has sometimes happened with European minorities, it did not matter much what kind of label was affixed to them: they were too Chinese one day, and too European the next, and their roles in business and industry were generally resented. From a Chinese mainland perspective, Southeast Asians were an unruly bunch, who far too easily had thrown their lot in with the European imperialists. China had fought two wars against Vietnam in the late eighteenth century—both unhappy and long-lasting affairs, as wars against Vietnam tend to be.

When Mao Zedong decided to offer assistance to the Vietnamese Communists in the mid-twentieth century, other Southeast Asians reacted by setting up the Association of Southeast Asian Nations (ASEAN) as an explicitly anti-Communist mutual aid organization and seeking assistance from the United States. Adding insult to injury, the Vietnamese Communists, whom Mao had so gladly supported, decided, after having won the civil war, to join the Soviets in an alliance directed against China. Beijing was provoked into attacking Vietnam in 1979. The Chinese People's Liberation Army lost almost half as many soldiers in less than an inglorious month as the United States lost in all of its war in Vietnam from 1964 to 1973.[15]

Deng Xiaoping's greatest feat in foreign affairs was turning around this sorry state of affairs. He did so by underlining historical ties that connected Southeast Asia, from Burma to Vietnam, with China. As Deng never tired of pointing out, with the exception of Vietnam, China's relations with its southern neighbors had been peaceful since the Ming dynasty. Chinese who had settled in Southeast Asia ought to be loyal citizens to their countries and not mingle unduly in politics. No longer did China fund rebel movements; on the contrary, Deng advised those over which China had influence to settle with their governments. His aims were economic as well as diplomatic: some of the biggest foreign investors in China between 1980 and 2000 came from the region, especially from Singapore and Thailand.[16]

Since Deng's time, China has therefore prided itself on the gradual improvement and solidification of its relations with the countries of ASEAN, mainly through economic means. Chinese leaders have emphasized the significance of shedding decades, if not centuries, of mistrust and confrontation and moving toward cooperation and integration. The China-ASEAN free-trade zone, which came into effect four years ago, was intended to be the symbol of this new relationship.

Over the last five years or so, however, many of the most promising aspects of this cooperation have come into doubt. There are several reasons for this. China has gone through a leadership transition, during which there has been no strong hand at the tiller in terms of foreign relations. There also have been uncertainties on the ASEAN side—in some countries more than others—over the prospect of being overwhelmed by a China that is rapidly expanding economically.

But most important, the relationship has increasingly been held hostage by the conflict over sovereignty in the South China Sea, where China has overlapping claims with the Philippines, Vietnam, Malaysia, and Brunei. China's insistence on full and exclusive control of small islands, islets, and shoals throughout this ocean area has poisoned the relationship between China and the other claimant countries, all of which are members of ASEAN. A number of ASEAN leaders have drawn historical parallels when worrying about the consequences of the conflict. "If we say yes to something we believe is wrong now, what guarantee is there that the wrong will not be further exacerbated down the line?" Philippine president Benigno Aquino asked in an interview in 2014. He added, "At what point do you say, 'Enough is enough'? Well, the world has to say it—remember that the Sudetenland was given in an attempt to appease Hitler to prevent World War II."[17] Even the new Philippine president, Rodrigo Duterte—ostensibly more friendly to China—has warned of war as possible outcome of tensions in the South China Sea.

Some of China's claims are obviously preposterous. Among them is the James Shoal, known as Zengmu in Chinese and Serupai in Malay, which is only about 50 miles from the Malaysian coast and 1,100 miles from China.[18] Beijing has left it unclear which of the South China Sea islands it claims a full exclusive economic zone around, but even if that only applies to a small number, the implications for access to resources in the region would be enormous. Some Southeast Asians (and Americans) also believe that China's ultimate aim is to control shipping lanes in a region through which more than half of the world's merchant-fleet tonnage passes every year.[19]

So far, neither side has managed to find a half-decent way of negotiating on the issue, but since 2008 China has become more assertive in furthering its claims. One reason, quite openly stated in Beijing in 2009 and 2010, was that the economic crisis in the West had made China's further rise almost unavoidable, and China needed to adjust the relationship between itself and "smaller countries" around it. Clashes between China and other claimants have since become ubiquitous: in May 2014, China moved an oil rig into disputed waters off Vietnam's coast, setting off a crisis that so far has seen a Vietnamese vessel sunk and at least four dead in anti-Chinese rioting in Vietnam. In Saigon, an elderly Vietnamese woman burned herself to death in order to protest China's policy—a scene reminiscent of similar self-immolations carried out against the US presence in Vietnam in the 1960s.

Some historians would say that the downward turn in the relationship is an unavoidable part of China's rise. Great powers, the theory goes, invariably throw their weight around and antagonize their neighbors. Look at the United States in the nineteenth century. How many Mexicans, or Caribbeans, or even Canadians would have seen the United States as a benign power then?[20] Ultimately, however, it is claimed, smaller nations make their peace with the great power, as they get used to its peculiar ways and the great power learns that more can be achieved through integration and interdependence than through land (or sea) grabs and military posturing.

But the China-ASEAN relationship is not necessarily moving in this direction. Chinese nationalism is more than matched by that of China's neighbors. The sheer unreasonableness of Beijing's position on how far its ownership extends in the South China Sea will feed long-term antagonism between the two sides. So too will the perceived Chinese intention to reduce or even break up ASEAN as part of its aspirations to instead deal with individual Southeast Asian countries. Bringing in the United States, Japan, or even India to counterbalance China is likely to lead to more conflict, not less. It is also uncertain to what degree the United States wants to increase its own presence in the region. In spite of the much-heralded US "pivot to Asia," President Obama's 2016 trip to the region seemed more like a royal visit to former colonies than a superpower imposing its will.[21] As for President Trump, a stepping up of the US presence in the region—whatever the circumstances—would square badly with his stated intention to have local allies take more responsibility for their own defense.

So the picture for the future is not rosy. The key is to increase the levels of interaction and trust between China and ASEAN. History shows that this can be done, even with a rising great power—think the United States versus Europe or Japan. But for it to happen, both sides must emphasize those aspects of interaction that bind them together rather than those that force them apart.

It is obvious that the main part of such an invigorated relationship would be economic. But there are other parts that need emphasis, too: cultural exchanges, educational ties, and security consultations all play a role in building long-term trust. The fact is that the lack of knowledge in China about Southeast Asia, and vice versa, is very profound. About twenty times as many ASEAN students go to study in the United States each year as come to China.[22] The Southeast Asian countries are gradually realizing that their substantial Chinese-origin minorities may be a benefit in relations with China rather than a security threat, but even this is a very slow process.[23]

For these deeper ties to take hold, however, the different sides need to negotiate effectively over issues that really matter in the relationship now. This is where South China Sea issues come into play. My guess is that, economically and strategically, resources and sea lanes in the South China Sea will be less important in the long term in the ASEAN-China relationship than the economic ties that connect their peoples. But for now, progress in these negotiations is essential to create trust on other matters.

THE PROMISE OF ASEAN

Is the South China Sea an issue for ASEAN as whole? Chinese leaders and some leaders in Southeast Asia would say no, or yes but only with great qualifications. Some would prefer to handle the issue country by country. They would quite obviously be wrong. Strategic cohesion on the issue of upholding the UN Convention on the Law of the Seas is a basic matter for the future of ASEAN, as is joint support and advice in terms of member states' negotiations with outside powers.

China's own long-term strategy with regard to ASEAN is hard to figure out. Beijing has always preferred to deal with individual states rather than with transnational organizations, believing the latter to be a distraction, or a nuisance, or both. It has had a particular dislike for integrationist organizations of states, be it the European Union or ASEAN. One explanation is that China prefers to deal with individual states because it is easier to prevail over them. In the continuation of this argument, some observers see China's ultimate aim simply as being the breakup of ASEAN. If so, China's current policy is contradictory—a bit like Britain in Europe, it is happy to deal with ASEAN as a whole when it is in China's interest to do so, but to fall back on abusing the institution when it does not do China's bidding.

China, in terms of its current approach, needs to rein in a self-centered and sometimes confrontational foreign policy, which is unlikely to succeed. Without a continuous, forward-looking process of negotiations, the ASEAN-China relationship will go nowhere. It is doubtful that President Xi Jinping seeks to fundamentally antagonize neighbors on whom China's continued rise to some extent depends.

CONCLUSION

More than forty years ago, in an off-the-record conclave of top Asianists discussing Southeast Asia and the US war in Vietnam, the eminent Malaysian historian Wang Gungwu warned the United States against becoming too involved in the relationship between China and its neighbors. The future relationship was not necessarily one-dimensional, Wang thought. Other states in eastern Asia would, over time, develop enough strength and cohesion to balance China's power. And even if China—because of its large population and territory—would emerge as the central state in the region, this was not necessarily a bad thing for eastern Asia or for the world. "China may only resume its traditional position of dominance in an even more nominal way than the largely nominal one it enjoyed in the past," Wang suggested.[24]

Wang Gungwu was right in 1972, at the height of China's Cultural Revolution and its assistance to Southeast Asian revolutionaries. He would be even more right today. If the past five years in eastern Asia has shown us anything, it is that it is more difficult for China to impose its will on others than most outside observers had believed at the beginning of the 2000s, when China's unavoidable rise to global superpower status was first mooted. China's power has grown, but so has that of its neighbors. Chinese nationalism has also grown, but so too has that of its neighbors.

History weighs on these relationships, but in ways that are not always easy to discern. China's traditional centrality has created links within the region that are sometimes nearly invisible for outsiders, but it has also created resentment and distrust. The idea, so often held by Westerners, that the region will necessarily gravitate toward China unless American power prevents it, is likely to be wrong. There is enough resistance against Chinese domination both in Northeast and Southeast Asia to frustrate any such schemes for the foreseeable future. Quite another matter is if the United States is seen by the Chinese as intervening to contain China's increasing interaction with its neighbors. Such a strategy could fuel unnecessary conflicts both with the larger region and globally. Ernest May and Zhou Hong had it about right when they wrote that "the long-term future of the United States and China will depend upon a bilateral ability to empathize with another primary party, to avoid pressing one's advantage, or to linger over imagined slights."[25]

The main change within the region over the past forty years is that China has already become infinitely more integrated with other Asian countries and with the rest of the world than it was forty years ago. Such integration does not rule out conflict, as the centennial year of the outbreak of World War I reminds us, but it does open up more avenues for cooperation. A lot of Chinese see these opportunities and want to develop them further. What stands in their way is a Chinese political system that simply does not serve its citizens well, domestically or internationally. Given time, it is much more likely that China's political system will change than that the present regime in Beijing will be able to bend other countries to its will.

US policy makers need to understand change on a broad scale. China is changing rapidly and becoming more powerful as a country, because it is a large nation with a big population. But trends over the past decade do not necessarily favor China over its neighbors, particularly not if China attempts to impose its will on many of them simultaneously. And while it may be true that eastern Asia has become more conflict-prone than it has been at any point since the end of the Cold War, present conflicts pale in comparison with what took place in the region during most of the twentieth century. It is therefore likely that the key US role in the immediate future will remain that of a balancer and integrator rather than as an active deterrent, although it will be prepared to play the latter role if large-scale conflict threatens to break out in the region.

The real challenge to outside powers—and first and foremost the United States—is to understand that China's rising supremacy within the region will be restricted by its internal difficulties and as well as by the profound skepticism its neighbors have toward working too closely with it. In the past, the United States has often been unable to develop an effective foreign policy in part because it has overestimated the strength of the forces ranged against it. The most important lesson for eastern Asia is probably not to repeat that mistake.

NOTES

1. There are, of course, enormous differences in projections of the growth of China's military power. Projecting from the latest IISS figures, it will still take about twenty years for China to catch up with the United States in terms of military spending even if current Chinese year-on-year budget increases continue. And as the IISS 2014 report notes, catching up in budget terms is not the same as catching up in overall strategic capabilities; International Institute of Strategic Studies, *The Military Balance 2014* (London: IISS, 2014). The best overview of China's international position overall is David L. Shambaugh, *China Goes Global: The Partial Power* (Oxford: Oxford University Press, 2013).
2. It could, of course, also be that other powers, including China, will attempt to control US foreign policy behavior—this, at the moment, seems more likely than a "unilateral" Chinese "rise"; see Stephen M. Walt, *Taming American Power: The Global Response to U.S. Primacy* (New York: Norton, 2005).
3. See my *Restless Empire: China and the World since 1750* (New York: Basic Books, 2012).
4. Jiang Zemin, 为了世界更美好：江泽民出访纪实 [For a better world: A record of Jiang Zemin's visits] (Beijing: Shijie zhishi, 2006); Bill Clinton, *My Life* (New York: Knopf, 2004).

5. I am avoiding dealing with other regions here, since they are well covered in other chapters of the book.
6. Key-Hiuk Kim's *The Last Phase of the East Asian World Order: Korea, Japan, and the Chinese Empire, 1860–1882* (Berkeley: University of California Press, 1980) is particularly good on the early phase of this process.
7. See, for instance, Charles K. Armstrong, "Familism, Socialism and Political Religion in North Korea," *Totalitarian Movements and Political Religions* 6, no. 3 (2005): 383.
8. There are several reports circulating in Beijing of veteran Chinese leaders having been made to wait outside Kim Jong-eun's door for an overly long time since he succeeded his father in 2011; some of them have found their way to the Chinese blogosphere: http://www.weibo.com/billupslee?_ga=1.205771795.1475870730.1402335693.
9. Also, it is still unclear where the National Security Commission (NSC) sits within the Chinese state and party structure: Imagine a US NSC as a kind of free-floating entity among the White House, State, the Pentagon, the FBI, and the CIA.
10. A good overview is Jayshree Bajoria and Beina Xu, "The China-North Korea Relationship," Council on Foreign Relations, February 2014, http://www.cfr.org/china/china-north-korea-relationship/p11097.
11. http://www.fmprc.gov.cn/mfa_eng/topics_665678/xjpzxdhgjxgsfw/t1172436.shtml.
12. "N. Korea Slams 'Spineless' China," *Chosun ilbo*, July 22, 2014, http://english.chosun.com/site/data/html_dir/2014/07/22/2014072201653.html.
13. Kate Whitehead, "Global Public Opinion Poll Reveals an Increasingly Negative View of China," *South China Morning Post*, October 14, 2013.
14. This section is based on my article "ASEAN's Challenge: A Swaggering China," in *Los Angeles Times*, April 7, 2014; reprinted with minor changes in *The Edge* (Malaysia), April 13, 2014, http://www.latimes.com/opinion/op-ed/la-oe-adv-westad-china-asean-south-china-sea-20140407-story.html.
15. Stein Tønnesson, *Vietnam 1946: How the War Began* (Berkeley: University of California Press, 2009), 2.
16. For a succinct overview, see Wang Gang, "邓小平睦邻外交思想与东亚区域合作" [Deng Xiaoping's good neighbor diplomacy and regional cooperation in Eastern Asia], *东南亚纵横* [Aspects of Southeast Asia] 5 (2007): 8–12.
17. Keith Bradsher, "Philippine Leader Sounds Alarm on China," *New York Times*, February 4, 2014.
18. China's is of course not the only preposterous claim in oceanic territorial terms; Norway's southernmost dependency is Bouvet Island in the south Atlantic, 8,000 miles from Norway, around which it claims an exclusive economic zone of 170,000 square miles.
19. See US Energy Information Administration, Analysis Briefs, *South China Sea*, February 7, 2013.
20. A celebration of the United States as a nineteenth-century nuisance is found in Robert Kagan, *Dangerous Nation* (New York: Knopf, 2006).
21. Jean-Pierre Lehmann, "President Obama's Pirouettes in Asia," *The Globalist*, May 1, 2014, http://www.theglobalist.com/president-obamas-pirouettes-in-asia/.
22. According to UNESCO figures, China receives about fifty thousand foreign students each year in all, slightly less than Austria.

23. People of Chinese ancestry serve in many key functions in Southeast Asia, including—in several cases—as their countries' ambassadors to China. President Aquino of the Philippines, quoted above, is mainly of Chinese descent. As in the United States, citizenship and personal origin increasingly count for more than ethnicity in Southeast Asia. We are still waiting to see a Chinese ambassador belonging to a domestic Southeast Asian minority, not to mention one born abroad (until very recently, even Chinese who were *educated* abroad could not serve in the Foreign Ministry).
24. Wang Gungwu, "Southeast Asia in the 1970s," paper presented at the Williamsburg Conference 1972, in Box 17, 10200-f, Hugh Scott Papers, University of Virginia Special Collections, Charlottesville, VA. I am grateful to Priscilla Roberts for this reference.
25. Ernest R. May and Zhou Hong, "A Power Transition and Its Effects," in *Power and Restraint: A Shared Vision for the U.S.-China Relationship*, ed. Richard N. Rosecrance and Guoliang Gu (New York: PublicAffairs, 2009), 23.

PART III
Domestic Dimensions

CHAPTER 8

The Rise and Fall of the China Model

Implications for World Peace

MINXIN PEI

INTRODUCTION

Among the most critical variables that will determine China's relationship with the West, one that deserves particular attention is the capacity of the ruing Chinese Communist Party (CCP) to sustain its political monopoly. Whether the CCP's one-party rule can continue is central to the question of war and peace among great powers in the twenty-first century. To most contributors of this volume, the nature of the Chinese political regime is viewed as either inconsequential or irrelevant in the discussion of the security, stability, and legitimacy of the current international system and the future of world peace. Stephen Walt identifies the growing Chinese power as the principal cause of conflict between the United States and China, and he does not consider whether the different regime types, a post-totalitarian autocracy and a liberal democracy, affect each other's threat perception. To the extent that political, not military, threat predominates the strategic thinking of China's authoritarian ruling elites, differences in regime types need to be considered in evaluating potential risks of a great power conflict between the United States and China. Rosemary Foot shares the realist's fear of a "Thucydides Trap" in Sino-US strategic competition, but she cautions that severe domestic constraints in both countries will likely limit the intensity and scope of US-China conflict. This insightful observation may overestimate the degree of control the CCP regime has over Chinese domestic developments. While difficult domestic challenges clearly will restrain Chinese leaders' ability to embark on a confrontational path abroad, these difficulties may also degrade the regime's capacity for survival and thus increase uncertainties. More worrisome are the increased risks of miscalculation by Chinese ruling elites, who may be tempted to exploit Chinese nationalism as a source of political support.

For a realist, William Wohlforth adopts a more nuanced view. While he believes the changing balance of power between the United States and China augurs a period of rising strategic competition, he rules out a doomsday scenario of outright war because China has closed its gap with the United States only in terms of the size of the economy but continues to lag significantly behind on other dimensions of power. More importantly, international politics today has been harnessed by a Western-dominated system of institutions. Wohlforth's confidence in the effectiveness of the existing international institutions in managing the growing strategic competition between China and the United States may be unwarranted. Whether these institutions operate effectively depends on how a rising power like China sees their legitimacy and whether it has the capability of challenging these institutions without paying a heavy price. From China's perspective, the current international institutions lack legitimacy since it played no role in setting them up. Thus, challenging is only a matter of time—China will do so when it has acquired the capability.[1] Like Wohlforth, John Ikenberry believes the existing international institutions can accommodate a rising power, albeit for different reasons. Ikenberry correctly argues that even though China was not an original architect of the existing world order, it has benefited hugely from its openness. China has no rational reason to challenge or replace an order that has made its rise possible. What Ikenberry has overlooked here is that gains, like power, are always relative. It is true that China has reaped enormous benefits from the existing order; Chinese elites continue to believe that the existing order still benefits their competitors, chiefly the United States, far more than it does China. Another overlooked source of Chinese dissatisfaction with the existing world order is that some critical parts of the world remain closed to China—the security alliances formed by democracies in particular.

The lack of consideration given to the nature of the Chinese regime unfortunately colors analysts' understanding of how the CCP views the security, stability, and legitimacy of the US-led international order and the future strategic intentions of the United States. Chinese leaders, as shown by their published speeches, consistently see the liberal democratic West as an existential political threat. Thus, Chinese security is primarily defined as regime security, not *national* security. As Lars Lagerkvist demonstrates in his chapter, the CCP devotes enormous resources to its efforts to control the flow of information and social protest. Seen from a regime obsessed with its internal security, stability does not mean a relatively stable distribution of power among great powers or compliance with international rules. It consists of the subjugation—if not absence—of forces hostile to its political monopoly. Legitimacy depends on mutual acceptance, not one-sided projection. More specifically, China does not believe that the existing US-led order has genuinely accepted its one-party dictatorship as a legitimate regime. This belief, in turn, leads China's rulers to reject the US-led order as illegitimate as well. If the nature of the Chinese regime is decisive in influencing Chinese perspectives on security, stability, and legitimacy, the implications are profoundly worrisome. The continuation of the CCP regime and expansion of its power will likely increase the probability of great power conflict, while the inability of the same regime in sustaining its acquisition of power will likely undercut its capacity to defend its rule at home and limit its ability to project power abroad. In judging their implications for world peace, we may view these two scenarios—a strong China under one-party rule or a declining China the CCP is struggling to govern—as fundamentally different. However, the danger to world peace posed by a declining China where one-party rule is under threat can also be substantial even though the nature of the danger is different. Briefly, the domestic woes of a weak China will produce spillover effects beyond Chinese borders (such as crime, migrants, and weapons). They will also undercut China's ability to contribute to international public goods, even though one may discount the danger of "lashing out" since an unstable regime is aware of the suicidal risks of seeking unwinnable military adventures abroad. By comparison, a strong, rising China poses traditional dangers to the existing international order, such as the expansion of its military capabilities, competition with the dominant power in the international system (the United States), temptations to use intimidation and force in the solution of disputes, establishment of its own spheres of influence, and perpetration of acts that undermine the rule of international law. Unfortunately, this point has not received sufficient attention in today's discussion on China's future mainly because of the international community's obsession with China's rise and overly optimistic projections about its future trajectory.

This chapter explores whether China will continue to expand its power through an examination of the durability of the survival strategy the CCP has adopted since its brush with collapse in the spring of 1989. Over the years, this strategy has been slapped with many labels, such as "resilient authoritarianism," "the Beijing Consensus," "Market Leninism," or "neoauthoritarianism." The most generic, and hence inclusive, label seems to be the "China Model," which has been used liberally (mostly by non-academics) to describe China's development success.[2] Most of the popular writings on the so-called China Model have focused on the CCP's record in delivering sustained rapid economic growth since 1989. This narrow focus overlooks other critical components of the CCP's survival strategy.

A more accurate definition of the "China Model" must take into account the other central elements of the CCP's survival strategy. In this chapter, we will examine all four elements of the CCP's survival strategy—economic growth, patronage and co-optation of social elites, selective repression, and manipulation of nationalism—and question the continuing viability of this strategy. Through an examination of the available evidence and recent trends, this chapter aims to demonstrate that the CCP's post-1989 survival strategy is reaching its limits. Specifically, China's investment-driven, export-led growth model has produced macroeconomic imbalances and slowing growth. Political patronage sustained by the regime's control of large segments of the economy has produced endemic corruption. Co-optation of social elites will likely yield diminishing returns due to growing alienation of the middle class and the regime's inherently exclusive nature. As a consequence, the regime will increasingly have to rely on repression and nationalism in maintaining power. The CCP's failure to continue a balanced survival strategy could produce different, albeit equally destabilizing, forces that threaten world peace. Internal weakness will increase the regime's sense of insecurity. Its views of the West are likely to be tinted even more with paranoia. Foreign decision-making will become more unpredictable as increasingly weak leaders must constantly resort to appeals to nationalism to maintain support. Risk-taking behavior and brinksmanship, rare during the heydays of China's rise, may become more frequent and even spark direct military conflicts with its neighbors and the United States. Due to the size of Chinese power, even a weakened giant can inflict considerable damage on peace and stability in Asia.

CHINESE ECONOMIC GROWTH

Sustained economic growth has been the primary driver of Chinese power. The country maintained double-digit growth between 1979 and 2010. Its gross domestic product (GDP) has risen, unadjusted for inflation, from $150 billion to $10.35 trillion from 1978 to 2014.[3] No doubt, this economic miracle has underwritten the CCP's rule by providing the party a source of political legitimacy and the means of supporting its repressive apparatus and military power. While opinions differ as to the causes of China's sustained rapid growth, most observers would agree that a combination of policy, favorable structural factors, and timing has contributed to the Chinese economic miracle.

Market-Oriented Reforms

China's economic rise would have been inconceivable had its leaders not rejected the disastrous Maoist ideology and economic policies at the end of the Cultural Revolution (1966–1976) and embraced a hybrid form of capitalism. Starting in the early 1980s, the Chinese government gradually dismantled some of the defining economic institutions of communism and liberalized the economy. The most important reforms adopted were decollectivized agriculture, opening to the West, legalization of private ownership of productive assets, and gradual privatization.[4] Taken together, these reforms have greatly raised the efficiency of the Chinese economy and unleashed productivity gains that have powered economic growth.

In addition, reforms generated a virtuous cycle at the crucial early stage, allowing private entrepreneurship to flourish without initially arousing political opposition.[5] In the rural areas, de-collectivizing agriculture raised productivity, freed up surplus labor, and encouraged private entrepreneurs to form businesses.[6] In the 1990s, economic reform accelerated after the Chinese leadership, shaken by the Tiananmen disaster and the disintegration of the Soviet Union, regarded economic growth as the sole source of legitimacy. Consequently, financial, fiscal, and state-owned enterprises (SOEs) reforms, and the accession to the World Trade Organization (WTO) generated enormous growth momentum.

Integration into the Global Economy

At the outset of his reform, Deng Xiaoping correctly identified the integration into the global economy as critical to the success of Chinese modernization. He and his successors consistently pursued the policy of "opening" by attracting foreign direct investment and promoting an export-led growth strategy. The data on foreign directive investment and foreign trade show that this strategy has been an unqualified success. Between 1979 and 2012, China attracted $2.16 trillion in foreign direct investment (FDI), which was critical in building China's export-oriented industrial base.[7] China's performance in foreign trade since 1979 has been extraordinary as well. In

1979, total Chinese foreign trade was $30 billion ($13.7 billion in exports and $15.7 billion in imports). In 2013, China's foreign trade was $4.2 trillion. With its $2.2 trillion in exports in 2013, China was the world's largest exporter by volume, with more than 11 percent of the world's market share.[8]

The positive effects of the inflow of capital and technology and the hundred-fold increase in foreign trade on China's economic growth cannot be overestimated. Net contribution from exports alone constituted a significant source of Chinese growth until after the global economic crisis of 2008. After China's accession to the WTO in 2001, Chinese export growth surged. Within twelve years, total export volume rose eight-fold, making a significant contribution to Chinese economic growth.[9]

The Demographic Dividend

When reform began, China was about to enjoy thirty years of favorable demographic conditions, with a declining fertility rate and dependency ratios and a rapid increase in young workers.[10] Like the East Asian dragons, this demographic dividend played an important role in China's economic ascendance. According to one study by demographers, the demographic dividend accounted for 15 percent of China's total economic growth between 1982 and 2000.[11] However, these favorable policy and structural factors have either disappeared or are disappearing. Sustained high growth in China in the coming decades will be constrained by systemic inefficiency due to rent-seeking in a hybrid economy in which the state continues to dominate the allocation of resources, calamitous environmental degradation, a less hospitable international environment, and demographic ageing.

Economic reform has not followed a linear trajectory in China. After a round of reforms spurred by the East Asian financial crisis (1997–1998) and the WTO entry, no further major institutional or structural reforms were adopted. Consequently, the economy developed severe macroimbalances, marked by excessively low consumption rates and unusually high investment rates. Monopolies by state-owned enterprises stifle competition in key sectors, such as finance, energy, natural resources, and telecom services. Local governments have become key players in infrastructure investments and other commercial developments, taking on large debts by relying on revenue from land sales and the real-estate sector. The fiscal structure has grown increasingly distorted as the central government receives the bulk of the tax income while local governments rely on informal revenues (primarily land-based revenues). Public spending on social services has failed to keep pace with either GDP growth or rising demand, resulting in an inadequate provision of public goods and a skimpy social safety net.

According to the World Bank, China's economic growth is unlikely to be sustained at around 7 percent a year in the period 2014–2020 and 5 percent in the period 2020–2030 if no significant reforms are undertaken.[12] To be sure, the Chinese government is aware of the dangers of stalled reform. In November 2013, the CCP's third plenum issued an ambitious blueprint of reform. The new party leader, Xi Jinping, has committed his political capital to the program by heading a special leading group that oversees the reform. Judging by the results since the reform plan was unveiled, only modest progress has occurred. The real difficulty in carrying out the reforms is not economic, but political. Xi will have to overcome the opposition within the party-state because the entrenched interest groups view radical economic reforms as threats to their privileges. Such opposition will remain deep and strong unless Xi decides to mobilize the Chinese public in response. So far, Xi has not shown that he is willing to take this risk because he fears this would threaten the party's rule. The prospects of real economic reform remain dim.

Environmental Degradation

China's growth since 1979 has been achieved at high social costs, one of which is environmental degradation. Various estimates suggest that environmental degradation costs China around 8 percent of GDP per year.[13] With two-thirds of its waterways polluted and 16 percent of its arable landed contaminated with harmful substances, China could face an environmental nightmare in the coming decades.[14] Combined with chronic water shortages and the effects of climate change, environmental degradation could contribute to a considerable fall in agricultural output and destabilizing internal migration driven by environmental refugees.

Mitigating environmental damage is still possible, although costly. It requires enforcing strict laws and regulations, phasing out heavy-polluting equipment and facilities, and adopting modern technologies. These efforts will incur significant one-time and ongoing expenditures. Evidently, although this step will improve the quality of life and economic growth, it will be costly and result in slower growth. Politically, environmental degradation has already become one of the most direct causes of social unrest.[15] Particularly noteworthy is the recent trend of environmental activism among urban middle-class elements, who have become increasingly vocal in their dissatisfaction with the government's poor record in environmental protection.

Less Accommodating External Environment

The favorable external environment that allowed China to take full advantage of globalization is unlikely to persist. The simplest explanation is that, as the world's largest exporter already, China has little room to increase its merchandise exports. Even without protectionism, it is virtually impossible to sustain the double-digit export growth that has powered Chinese growth in the past three decades.

There are other factors that will likely make China's external environment less accommodating. Three deserve special attention. The first one is the ongoing backlash against globalization and China's mercantilist trade policies in the West, the principal markets for Chinese exports. The second is China's growing strategic competition with the United States and, to a lesser extent, its assertive behavior in Asia. This trend could lead to protectionist measures taken by these countries to reduce their economic ties with China. Although this has yet to happen, the political logic for economic disengagement with China will become irresistible should China's geopolitical rivalry with the United States and its Asian allies escalate to the point of overt antagonism.

The third is competition for resources, in particular energy and commodities. Chinese economic development has followed a resource-intensive path. The country is already the world's largest consumer of energy, steel, cement, and nearly all the major commodities. Its insatiable demand for resources has already caused frictions with the West and unease in the developing world.[16] In the future, resource dependency and constraints could expose the Chinese economy to global political risks to an unprecedented degree.

Ageing Society

The one-time gain from the demographic dividend has all but disappeared. In the Chinese case, the disappearance of the demographic dividend is due to principally the declining fertility rate caused by growing affluence and the state's draconian one-child policy (imposed since the late 1970s). As a result, growth will fall through two channels.[17] One is reduced labor supply as fewer young workers enter the labor force. The youth population has already declined from 62.8 to 38.0 percent from 1982 to 2007.[18] The most obvious effect of declining labor supply is rising wages, which will reduce China's competitiveness. Indeed, in recent years, Chinese wages have been rising at a rapid pace, resulting in the erosion of its cost advantage in the global marketplace.

The other channel is ageing. The median age of the Chinese population will rise from 34.6 years to 42.1 years between 2010 and 2030; the old-age dependency ratio will increase from 11.4 to 23.8 percent during the same period.[19] For a middle-income country, addressing the needs of a fast-ageing society requires significant increases in healthcare and pension costs, thus reducing savings and the amount of capital available for investment. Lower growth is unavoidable.

Based on the above analysis, a significant slowdown in China's economic growth in the coming two decades is all but inevitable. Indeed, even without the adverse factors listed above, "reversion to the mean," a law of economic development resembling the law of gravity, will dictate that China's growth will fall significantly, perhaps well below the rate needed to sustain the party's political monopoly.[20]

PATRONAGE AND CO-OPTATION

As a posttotalitarian regime, the CCP relies also on patronage to secure the loyalty of its core supporters and social elites. There are two political imperatives for resorting to patronage and co-optation. The bankruptcy of the official ideology in the post-Mao era compels the CCP to offer tangible benefits to its closest followers in order to maintain their loyalty. With the increasing bureaucratization of the regime, the CCP risks basing its support on a narrow social base. It therefore must broaden its social base of support by co-opting emerging elites, mainly by recruiting a select minority from these new elites into the ruling party.

The maintenance of a patronage system designed to retain the loyalty of core members of the regime requires considerable economic resources and a system of promotion that can give these members realistic hopes of gaining access to the benefits provided by the patronage system. In the post-1989 era, the economic resources allocated by the state through multiple channels—primarily SOEs, massive fixed-asset investments, rights to land and mineral resources, and government contracts—allow the CCP to reward its core members with lucrative perks and financial gains. The political imperative of sustaining this patronage system is the most important reason why the CCP has retained privileges for SOEs and kept tight control over the economy. Even the ambitious reform plan unveiled at the third plenum of the Eighteenth Central Committee in November 2013 pledged to preserve the SOEs as a key pillar of the economy.

The institutionalization of this patronage system was achieved through the formalization of rules of recruitment and promotion that, at least on paper, provides a roadmap to aspiring members of the regime. Even though such formal rules are often violated in reality because of the intervention of powerful patrons intent upon promoting their personal protégés, the existence of such formal rules nevertheless serves a useful function: they allow the more junior members of the regime to keep alive their hopes of career advancement in the party's hierarchy.[21]

Parallel to this patronage system is a program of co-optation of social elites carried out by the CCP to broaden its social base and, in a subtle way, preempt the formation of counterelites in Chinese society. The initial steps taken to recruit emerging elites in Chinese society were aimed to attract highly educated college graduates to strengthen the regime's administrative capabilities.[22] The infusion of a younger and better-educated generation of members has indeed transformed the sociological profile of the CCP, turning it from a mass party based on workers and peasants into a technocratic party whose members are drawn mainly from college graduates or those with some college education.

Even with the recruitment of technocrats into the party, the CCP's leadership was under pressure to broaden the party's social base. As China's private entrepreneurs grew in size and economic power, the party took a significant step forward in 2001 by formally announcing that private entrepreneurs would be allowed to join the party. Since CCP members had already made up a large share of private entrepreneurs (as much as 40 percent), the practical impact in terms of recruiting new members among Chinese private entrepreneurs might be modest at best. However, the party's new efforts of co-optation were widely seen as successful because some research shows that private entrepreneurs have displayed more sympathetic attitudes toward one-party rule.[23]

While patronage and social co-optation undoubtedly have strengthened the CCP's rule, they are not without cost. Inside the regime, the prevalence of patronage will unavoidably result in corruption and competition for power. The attraction of material benefits also tends to lure opportunistic elements from Chinese society to join the party, further eroding the party's organizational integrity.

The patronage system inside the CCP regime produces several corrosive effects. Economically, corruption and cronyism are by far the most visible and damaging. In the post-1989 era, the exchange of political loyalty for corruption income has taken root inside the CCP and has resulted in ever-rising levels of corruption despite frequent crackdowns.[24] The costs of corruption in economic terms are considerable even though it is difficult to estimate with accuracy.[25]

It analyzing the damage of corruption, it is tempting to focus solely on its economic manifestations. However, the more insidious effect of corruption on a one-party regime is likely to be political in nature. In the Chinese context, corruption originating in the regime's patronage system has already gravely undermined the party's organizational integrity through the privatization of public authority, the encouragement of collusion, and the instigation of power struggles.

The privatization of public authority as a form of political corruption can be traced, theoretically, to the well-known agency problem. The delegation of authority by higher-level elites to lower-level ones invariably transfers considerable discretion to these agents, who are likely to exercise their power in pursuit of private objectives, not the institutional interests of the party.

More specifically, the power delegated to lower-level agents by the party in personnel matters can easily lead to misuse. Instead of seeking out the most qualified and capable individuals for recruitment and promotion, lower-level officials are likely to appoint their trusted loyalists to subordinate positions because they are bound to be beholden to them personally, not to the party. Over time, this practice has created local or bureaucratic networks centered on powerful patrons (such as local party chiefs). In addition to engaging in corrupt activities, these networks have effectively usurped the CCP's authority. The enormous patronage power delegated to local party bosses is also often abused to seek private monetary gains. The practice of "selling" executive positions in the government, exceedingly rare if not unheard of prior to the 1990s, has since become widespread throughout the country.[26] Another phenomenon related to the patronage system is widespread collusion among officials who engage in collective corruption and other criminal activities. Since collusion usually indicates late-stage institutional decay, the widespread collusion inside the Chinese party-state should be another red flag.[27]

If the patronage system inside the regime breeds corruption and organizational atrophy, the CCP's strategy of co-optation of social elites may provide only short-term relief. Social co-optation suffers from two inherent limits. The first one is the exclusive nature of the one-party state. Such a regime is, by definition, composed of a small elite (even with 86 million members, the CCP represents only 6.3 percent of the population). The exclusive nature of the regime dictates that it can only co-opt a limited number of new elites. This limit can be seen in the party's recruitment drive among college-educated individuals. Even though this has been an area where the party has made enormous progress, it is constrained by the fact that society produces candidates for co-optation at a much faster rate than the party can co-opt. For example, Chinese universities and colleges graduated 7 million bachelor's degree holders in 2013, but the CCP recruits only one million such individuals each year.[28]

The second limitation inherent in social co-optation is adverse selection. Individuals attracted to the party through co-optation are likely to be driven by desires for material gains, not enduring loyalty to the party. The adverse selection problem will lead to the recruitment of individuals with poor qualifications but opportunistic propensities. They may remain ostensibly loyal to the regime during good times but defect at the first sign of trouble.

SELECTIVE REPRESSION

For all the talk about "authoritarian resilience" in post-1989 China, the edifice of one-party rule rests firmly on the application of repression. In the discussion on the apparent success of the CCP since Tiananmen, an inordinate amount of attention has been given to the regime's adaptive tactics, but little attention is given to its use of repression.[29] The concept of authoritarian resilience tends to overlook the centrality of repression in sustaining dictatorships. Clearly, in post-Mao China, adaptive tactics allowed the one-party state to rule with more carrots and fewer sticks compared with the Maoist era. But the sticks—tools of repression—remain indispensable in fending off challenges to the party's authority.

What marks political repression in the post-1989 era is its sophistication, continuous refinement, and proven effectiveness. On the surface, the overall degree of repression in contemporary China is much lower than the Maoist era. The number of political prisoners is estimated to be slightly over a thousand (although hundreds of thousands are incarcerated through the government's use of "reform through education," a form of administrative detention).[30] Nevertheless, most of the key civil liberties, such as freedom of speech, association, and religion, are not protected.[31]

Because of the selective use of repression, most ordinary Chinese, who enjoy a degree of personal freedom unimaginable under Maoist rule, actually do not directly feel the heavy hand of the state. The targets of the CCP's repressive apparatus are those who threaten its survival—such as political dissidents, organizers of strikes and riots, human rights activists, and members of ethnic minorities in Tibet and Xinjiang.

In addition to the selective nature of repression, the CCP has significantly improved its repressive capabilities by making huge investments in manpower and technology and by resorting to unorthodox methods. The CCP's repressive capacity consists of several layers. Within Chinese society, the regime employs a vast network of informers who monitor the activities of their fellow citizens and provide intelligence to the government on a regular basis.[32] The second layer centers on the regular police force (which has specialized departments for domestic political security) and the secret police (part of the Ministry of State Security). A third layer, which was added in the late 1990s, is commonly known as the Internet police, which patrols Chinese cyberspace. The fourth layer is the People's Armed Police, a paramilitary force trained and equipped to quash riots and restore order on short notice (it is authorized to use lethal force). In addition to these networks and organizations, the CCP has also established, at each level of the state, special offices that coordinate activities related to internal security.

This vast apparatus of repression enables the regime not only to respond to and quash social protests instantly, but also to prevent small incidents from mushrooming into destabilizing events. Over the years, the party-state seems to have followed standard operating procedures that have proven their effectiveness. Typically, these procedures mix carrots and sticks. Local government officials, depending on circumstances, may choose concessions over repression when the latter might lead to escalations in violence. But on other occasions, local officials would resort to more brutal means of suppression. As a result, the regime has been able to cope with a rapid increase in social protest since Tiananmen (there are around two hundred thousand "mass incidents," or collective riots and protests, in the country each year, according to academic estimates).[33]

The most notable aspect of political repression in the post-Tiananmen era is the combination of overt repression (such as arrests and imprisonment) of dissent with the application of unorthodox methods. In some cases, such methods are nonviolent. For instance, dissidents and human rights activists would be invited to have "tea" with policemen and receive warnings about their activities. The government would also forcibly take them away from their homes for "vacations" in remote areas on sensitive anniversaries (such as June 4) or occasions (when key Western leaders visit China).

But more prevalent is the use of coercive and violent means. One trend in recent years is the use of criminal law against political dissidents, who are often charged with relatively minor criminal offenses (such as disturbing public order) and then locked up for several years as punishment. Another trend is the illegal house arrest of innocent people who have not been charged with any crime, such as Chen Guangcheng, a blind human rights activist, and Liu Xia, wife of jailed Nobel Peace Prize winner, Liu

Xiaobo. Perhaps the most disturbing trend in the use of unorthodox methods of repression is the employment of thugs by local authorities in harassing and beating political dissidents.[34]

If Chinese economic growth slows down significantly and, as a result, the CCP's performance-based legitimacy declines, it is likely that the regime will have to rely on this extensive, sophisticated, and highly effective apparatus of repression for survival. There are, however, two constraints on how repressive the CCP can be.

One obvious constraint is economic costs. China's domestic security spending has been rising at a rapid pace and recently surpassed its defense budget. Such expenditures might have been affordable while the economy was growing quickly and generating sufficient fiscal revenues for the state to finance a vast repressive apparatus. It is doubtful that the Chinese state will be able to sustain the same level and scope of repression during hard times.

Another constraint is political and moral. Escalation of repression can undermine the regime's international image, which the face-conscious Chinese leadership deeply cares about.[35] Even though China is unlikely to face economic sanctions from the West because of its human rights violations, Beijing's diplomatic ties with the West could suffer. Inside China, rising levels of repression can antagonize the moderate and open-minded elements of society who view such methods as morally repugnant and unacceptable. Inside the regime, the intensification of repression could also open up fissures among the elites. Softliners may view this step as unnecessary, counterproductive, and excessive.

MANIPULATION OF NATIONALISM

The fourth pillar of the CCP's post-1989 survival strategy is manipulation of nationalism as a source of legitimacy. In the 1980s, Chinese nationalism had a moderate orientation, largely due to the relatively liberal political environment and the policies of reform-minded top leadership.[36] This changed following the 1989 Tiananmen crackdown. The ruling elites identified nationalism as a critical source of legitimacy and subsequently implemented a systematic and highly effective program of reconstructing Chinese nationalism. The centerpiece of the post-1989 state-sponsored revival of Chinese nationalism was the so-called patriotic education campaign, a comprehensive program that revamped history textbooks, reconstructed national narratives, and renovated historical sites and symbols throughout China. The sole purpose of this program was to rekindle the

Chinese population's sense of national humiliation and, consequently, their antipathy toward the West.[37]

The "patriotic education campaign" achieved remarkable success in reawakening the most parochial and xenophobic strains in Chinese nationalism. Through official propaganda and a distorted historical narrative, the CCP was able to convince large segments of the Chinese population that the West would not want to see a powerful and prosperous China. Periodically, the official propaganda apparatus would go into overdrive whenever there were international incidents in which China was apparently disrespected or poorly treated. The first example was the US navy inspection of a Chinese cargo ship, *Yinhe*, in 1993 after the American government received erroneous intelligence suggesting that the ship was transporting materials that could be used for producing weapons of mass destruction bound for Iran. Other examples were the accidental bombing of the Chinese embassy in Belgrade by NATO during the Kosovo war in 1999, and the midair crash between a Chinese fighter jet and an American navy reconnaissance plane over the South China Sea in 2001.[38] Of course, American responsibility in some of these made it easier for the Chinese regime to convince their population that the United States harbored hostile intent toward China. For instance, Washington attributed intelligence failure to the Yinhe incident and the bombing of the Chinese embassy in Belgrade. This might be true, but it sounded unconvincing to the average Chinese, who firmly believed that the United States, the world's most advanced country, was incapable of making such dumb mistakes.

Besides the enormous investment of its resources in its nationalist project, the CCP was significantly aided by other factors. Externally, the 1990s was a decade during which the West made a moderate attempt to pressure China to improve its human rights record through the threat of sanctions. Despites its good intentions, this policy unfortunately backfired, because the CCP seized upon the West's threat of sanctions as evidence that the West, in particular the United States, wanted to prevent China from becoming a powerful country. Such propaganda resonated with the Chinese public. In the 1990s, the burgeoning pro-independence movement in Taiwan, championed by President Lee Teng-hui, also allowed the CCP to exploit Chinese nationalism because of the Chinese people's deep emotional attachment to Taiwan as "part of China." The collapse of the Soviet Union in 1991 was, in retrospect, a fortuitous event for the CCP, even though the Chinese ruling elites were initially shocked by the fall of the Soviet regime. The ensuing chaos in postcollapse Russia and some of the former Soviet republics was played up by the Chinese official media and cited as evidence of the dangers of democratic transition. The message the

Chinese authorities tried to convey was clear: only the CCP could protect China's national integrity and ensure its survival as a great power.

Despite its enormous success in exploiting Chinese nationalism to boost its rule, the CCP runs serious risks and faces uncertainties in the future if it continues to count on the manipulation of nationalism to sustain public support. The most obvious risk is that fueling nationalism at home could severely damage China's relations with the West, particularly the United States. Economically, xenophobia could antagonize the West, which is China's most important trading partner. The Western business community may be alienated as well. In the worst-case scenario, nationalism could escalate into protectionism and a trade war between China and its Western trading partners. In the realm of national security, jingoism is likely to lead to hardened public attitudes and domestic political pressures, which could back the Chinese government into a corner during crisis and make conflict more likely. The ongoing dispute between China and Japan over the Senkaku/Diaoyu Islands in the East China Sea is a disturbing illustration. Deliberate manipulation of public opinion, demonization of the Japanese leadership, and bombastic rhetoric by the Chinese government not only led to violent nationwide anti-Japanese riots in 2012 but also drove Beijing to adopt dangerous escalatory measures to demonstrate its resolve, thus creating conditions under which an accidental military clash has become a distinct possibility.[39]

The other overlooked risk to the CCP is domestic political instability. Overt manifestations of nationalism, such as the violent anti-Japanese riots throughout China in 2012, could undercut the regime's record as an effective enforcer of law and order. Such acts, if sustained, can easily lead to outbreaks of lawlessness. Another possibility is that, just as the CCP rode the wave of nationalism in the 1930s to discredit the Kuomintang government (which was portrayed as incapable of defending China against Japanese aggression), China's latent opposition may also exploit the small political opening created by rising Chinese nationalism to undermine the regime's credibility and test its capacity for social control. The CCP seems to be clearly cognizant of this risk and, as a result, has acted with some caution whenever incidents sparked by nationalism and xenophobia risk getting out of control.

The critical uncertainty in the future is the extent to which the CCP can continue to divert the Chinese people's attention away from its deteriorating governance performance (such as declining growth, rising corruption, and environmental degradation) through manipulation of Chinese nationalism. In all likelihood, this strategy will deliver diminishing returns because the macroenvironment is certain to be very different. Nationalism has become a substantial source of the CCP's legitimacy in the last quarter century because of China's apparent success in economic development. It is unlikely to provide the same level of support for the regime should China's economic performance falter and the reasons for such poor performance are seen by the public as domestic, not foreign.

CONCLUDING THOUGHTS

The analysis above paints a future in which the West could encounter a China that is very different from the China since Tiananmen. The CCP's survival strategy is reaching its limits. Maintaining one-party rule will become a more challenging task. In the coming decade, the CCP leadership faces two choices. First, it can adopt genuine radical reforms to sustain economic growth without political change. In other words, the CCP could emulate what the late leader Deng Xiaoping did in the early 1990s. As discussed above, such a course of action is unlikely to deliver another economic miracle because of the enormous opposition from the members of the regime who currently benefit from crony capitalism. Defeating the entrenched interest groups they represent will require the mobilization of groups currently excluded by the extractive state controlled by the CCP—this is a prospect, at least for now, the current CCP leadership has rejected.

Even if we concede that modest reforms may unlock some productivity, deteriorating structural conditions—demographic ageing, environmental degradation, high levels of inequality, and a less hospitable external environment—will impose hard limits on growth.

Although dissatisfaction with the CCP rule has been independent of the regime's economic performance, a significant deterioration in economic growth is likely to create several mutually reinforcing dynamics undermining the regime's survival. In addition to increasing social discontent due to rising unemployment and a falling standard of living, economic stagnation in the coming decade, should it come, will gravely undercut the regime's ability to sustain its patronage machine and strategy of social co-optation. Many of the CCP's opportunistic supporters will be less loyal. Competition for rent inside the regime will grow more ferocious, undercutting elite cohesion. Should such stagnation impose real financial constraints on the CCP, the party-state might not be able to continue to fund its immense repressive apparatus.

What makes this scenario all the more dangerous for the CCP is that economic stagnation could occur when China is entering the "democratic transition zone" as measured by per capita income. At around $10,000 per capita in PPP today, China will soon approach the level of Taiwan and South Korea in the mid-1980s, when both countries made the transition to democracy.[40] One can conceive of a scenario in which middle-class elements, disillusioned with one-party rule, join forces with other antiregime groups and challenge the CCP's authority in a manner that would be inconceivable today.

Under these circumstances, the CCP will have to resort to greater repression and manipulation of nationalism to maintain its power. Repression at home will likely further radicalize the opposition and alienate moderate social elements, thus creating a vicious cycle. Abroad, intensified repression will exacerbate tensions with the West as it worsens China's already-poor human rights record. Diplomatic tensions between China and the West could rise to record levels.

The most worrisome consequence would be from the CCP's manipulation of nationalism. If such manipulation is confined to rhetoric, the damage to China's relations with the West will be modest and largely atmospheric. However, as we have seen in recent developments in Sino-Japanese disputes, the one-party state could take on excessive risks and even lose control in a spiraling crisis. The incentive to divert domestic attention away from its own failings and the ever-present danger of strategic miscalculations and uncontrollable tactical escalations could lead to armed conflict between China and its neighbors, with a potential of involving the United States.

To some extent, this scenario—a weakening China whose legitimacy-challenged government is not fully in charge of its actions—is more dangerous than a strong China where a secure one-party state is in complete control. In recent years, as the result of the China rise hype, this scenario has not been given much thought. It is time to think through it seriously.

NOTES

1. One illustrative example is the maritime dispute in the South China Sea. China's position clearly challenges the existing international law. China used to be less assertive when it was weak, but it has become far more aggressive and confrontational in pressing its claims in recent years.
2. Joshua Cooper Ramo was the first to call attention to China's economic success under authoritarian rule. See Ramo, *The Beijing Consensus* (London: The Foreign Policy Centre, 2004). Many popular nonacademic writers have since come out with books on the same theme. See Martin Jacques, *When China Rules the World: The End of the Western World and the Birth of a New Global Order* (London: Penguin Books, 2012); Stefan Halper, *The Beijing Consensus: How China's Authoritarian Model Will Dominate the Twenty-First*

Century (New York: Basic Books, 2010). Academic researchers, while avoiding sensational titles, nevertheless share the same sentiments in praising China's economic progress. See Arvind Subramanian, *Eclipse: Living in the Shadow of China's Economic Dominance* (Washington, DC: The Petersen Institute for International Economics, 2011); and Justin Lin, *Demystifying the Chinese Economy* (New York: Cambridge University Press, 2012).

3. "China," The World Bank, 2017, http://data.worldbank.org/country/china.
4. For a discussion of the role of reform in China's growth, see Justin Yifu Lin, Fang Cai, and Zhou Li, *The China Miracle: Development Strategy and Economic Reform* (Hong Kong: The Chinese University Press, 2003).
5. China managed a difficult feat by adopting reforms that did not create losers right away, thus reducing opposition. See Lawrence J. Lau, Yingyi Qian, and Gerard Roland, "Reform without Losers: An Interpretation of China's Dual-Track Approach to Transition," *Journal of Political Economy* 108, no. 1 (February 2000): 120–43.
6. Yasheng Huang, *Capitalism with Chinese Characteristics: Entrepreneurship and the State* (New York: Cambridge University Press, 2008).
7. OECD, *FDI in Figures, February 2014*, http://www.oecd.org/investment/FDI-in-Figures-Feb-2014.pdf. Net inflow of foreign direct investment (FDI) was only $430 million in 1982; by 2012, net inflow of FDI reached $295 billion. See "Foreign Direct Investment, Net Inflows (BoP, Current US$)," The World Bank, 2017, http://data.worldbank.org/indicator/BX.KLT.DINV.CD.WD.
8. Data on foreign trade is from the Chinese Ministry of Commerce; data on the Chinese share of global exports are from the World Trade Organization website: http://stat.wto.org/CountryProfile/WSDBCountryPFView.aspx?Country=CN&.
9. "Export Value Index (2000 = 100)," The World Bank, 2017, http://data.worldbank.org/indicator/TX.VAL.MRCH.XD.WD/countries.
10. See Cai Fang, "Demographic Transition, Demographic Dividend, and Lewis Turning Point in China," *China Economic Journal* 3, no. 2 (2010): 107–19.
11. Wang Feng and Andrew Mason, "Demographic Dividend and Prospects for Economic Development in China" (paper prepared for UN Expert Group Meeting on Social and Economic Implications of Changing Population Age Structures, Mexico City, August 31–September 2, 2005).
12. The World Bank, *China 2030: Building a Modern, Harmonious and Creative Society* (Washington, DC: The World Bank, 2013).
13. For one of the most authoritative studies, see The World Bank, *Cost of Pollution in China: Economic Estimates of Physical Damages* (Washington, DC: The World Bank, 2007).
14. "Cost of Pollution; the Ministry of Environmental Protection and the Ministry of National Land Resources," The World Bank, http://www.mep.gov.cn/gkml/hbb/qt/201404/W020140417558995804588.pdf.
15. Yanhua Deng and Guobin Yang, "Pollution and Protest in China: Environmental Mobilization in Context," *The China Quarterly* 214 (June 2013): 321–36.
16. See Elizabeth Economy and Michael Levi, *By All Means Necessary: How China's Resource Quest Is Changing the World* (New York: Oxford University Press, 2014).
17. For an analysis of the effects on adverse demographic trends on Chinese growth, see Mitali Das and Papa N'Diaye, "Chronicle of a Decline Foretold: Has China Reached a Lewis Turning Point?" (IMF Working Paper WP/13/26, Washington, DC, International Monetary Fund, 2013).

18. Zhang Monan, "The Impact of Declining Demographic Dividend and Socioeconomic Transformation," *China-US Focus*, July 3, 2012, see http://www.chinausfocus.com/political-social-development/the-impact-of-declining-demographic-dividend-and-socioeconomic-transformation.
19. "World Population Prospects, the 2012 Revision," The United Nations, Population Division, https://esa.un.org/unpd/wpp/publications/Files/WPP2012_HIGHLIGHTS.pdf.
20. Lant Pritchett and Lawrence Summers, "Asiaphoria Meet Regression to the Mean" (Federal Reserve Bank of San Francisco Working Paper, November 2013).
21. Pierre F. Landr, *Decentralized Authoritarianism in China: The Communist Party's Control of Local Elites in the Post-Mao Era* (New York: Cambridge University Press, 2008).
22. Cheng Li, "The Chinese Communist Party: Recruiting and Controlling the New Elites," *Journal of Current Chinese Affairs* 3 (2009): 13–33.
23. Bruce Dickson, *Red Capitalism in China: The Party, Private Entrepreneurs and Prospects for Political Change* (New York: Cambridge University Press, 2003).
24. Andrew Wedeman, "Anti-Corruption Campaigns and the Intensification of Corruption in China," *Journal of Contemporary China* 14, no. 42 (2005): 93–116.
25. My own estimate is that the total cost of corruption in China is around 3 percent of GDP per year. See Minxin Pei, "Corruption Threatens China's Future," *Carnegie Endowment for International Peace Policy Brief No. 5* (2007), http://carnegieendowment.org/2007/10/09/corruption-threatens-china-s-future-pub-19628.
26. For an illuminating case study of this practice, see Jiangnan Zhu, "Why Are Offices for Sale in China? A Case Study of the Office-Selling Chain in Heilongjiang Province," *Asian Survey* 48, no. 4 (July/August 2008): 558–79.
27. Ting Gong, "Dangerous Collusion: Corruption as a Collective Venture in Contemporary China," *Communist and Post-Communist Studies* 35, no. 1 (2002): 85–103.
28. http://career.eol.cn/kuai_xun_4343/20131212/t20131212_1051646.shtml; http://news.sina.com.cn/c/2013-06-30/150627537053.shtml.
29. Sebastian Heilmann and Elizabeth Perry, eds., *Mao's Invisible Hand: The Political Foundations of Adaptive Governance in China* (Cambridge, MA: Harvard Contemporary China Series, 2011); Andrew Nathan, "Authoritarian Resilience," *Journal of Democracy* 14, no. 1 (2003): 6–17.
30. The Congressional-Executive Commission on China has a database of political prisoners on China. As of July 2014, it contains information on 1,216 political prisoners; see https://www.cecc.gov/publications/annual-reports/2014-annual-report. The number of people incarcerated in the Reform through Education system was sixty thousand as of 2012, according to a former official in the Chinese Ministry of Justice. The system imprisoned as many as three hundred thousand people at one point. http://news.china.com/domestic/945/20121019/17482216.html.
31. For a comprehensive survey of human rights conditions in China, see Congressional-Executive Commission on China, *Annual Report 2013* (Washington, DC: U.S. Congress, 2013).
32. The existence of networks of informers is kept secret and is poorly studied. Occasionally one comes across a reference to it. For instance, this network was mobilized during the Beijing Olympics to ensure security. Peter Coates, "Beijing

Spying Apparatus Gears Up for Olympics," *Newsweekly*, May 10, 2008, http://newsweekly.com.au/article.php?id=3535.
33. Yanqi Tong and Shaohua Lei, "Large-Scale Mass Incidents and Government Response in China," *International Journal of China Studies* 1, no. 2 (2010): 487–508. (October 2010); Christian Gobel and Lynette Ong, "Social Unrest in China," *European China Research and Advice Network Report* (2012).
34. See Xu Youyu and Hua Ze, eds., *In the Shadow of the Rising Dragon: Stories of Repression in the New China* (New York: Palgrave MacMillan, 2013).
35. This can be seen in Beijing's huge investments in projects to project its soft power abroad in recent years. See Katherine Bliss, *China's Projection of Soft Power in the Americas* (Washington, DC: CSIS, 2009).
36. Guoguang Wu provides an excellent analysis of the contrast between nationalism before 1990 and afterwards in Wu, "From Post-Imperial to Late-Communist Nationalism," *Third World Quarterly* 3 (2008): 467–82.
37. Zheng Wang, *Never Forget National Humiliation: Historical Memory in Chinese Politics and Foreign Relations* (New York: Columbia University Press, 2014).
38. Peter Hays Gries, *China's New Nationalism: Pride, Politics, and Diplomacy* (Berkeley: University of California Press, 2005).
39. Gregory J. Moore, "'In Your Face': Domestic Politics, Nationalism, and 'Face' in the Sino-Japanese Islands Dispute," *Asian Perspective* 38, no. 2 (April–June 2014): 219–40.
40. Yu Liu and Dingding Chen, "Why China Will Democratize?" *The Washington Quarterly* 35, no. 1 (2012): 41–63.

CHAPTER 9

Curtailing China's Rise before the Real Takeoff?

Censorship, Social Protests, and Political Legitimacy

JOHAN LAGERKVIST

INTRODUCTION

Assessing the further rise of the People's Republic of China (PRC) to global superpower status needs to begin with an investigation of the risks of contentious politics in the domestic arena and the measures taken by the party-state to keep them at bay. In discussions on current great power transition and the rise of China, there has been too little focus on domestic variables. China is a rapidly developing country bristling with social protests. The estimates diverge, but as many as 180,000 protests may take place yearly.[1] Such as huge amount of collective action indicates that severe challenges to the Chinese Communist Party (CCP) and its political legitimacy exist: in the form of socioeconomic inequality, environmental degradation, endemic corruption, and problems of accountability and abuse of power—especially at the lowest levels of the formal political system. Yet several studies speak of a confluence of interests between officially registered nongovernmental organizations (NGOs) and the party-state, either labeled as "dependent autonomy,"[2] "lack of antagonism between NGOs and the state,"[3] "contingent symbiosis,"[4] "consultative authoritarianism,"[5] or "co-dependent state–society relations,"[6] to capture the survival tactics of Chinese NGOs and clever co-optation by the state. Andrew Nathan has argued that "civil society is growing in scale and potential assertiveness, but remains under effective government surveillance and unable to form national linkages."[7] Even so, social protests are widespread, and the costs to check them increase annually in a context where civil society in China is said to have only potential assertiveness. So, who organizes the hundreds of thousands of social protests that occur in real-world China every single year, if not "assertive actors" in the civic domain? Beyond doubt, significant risks are embedded in the unstable relationship between state and society relations today. If emergent civil society is badly managed by the state party, most notably by overly relying on increasing the level of repression, China's further rise within the international system may be jeopardized. Could the marvelous trajectory of economic modernization that has expanded China's global profile over the last three decades even run off the rails due to internal conflict?

The answers to this question hinge on how state-society relations will evolve during the reign of General Secretary Xi Jinping. Since taking office in 2012, Xi has launched harsh campaigns against official corruption, dissent in society, journalists, and defense lawyers, and he has initiated drafts of new legislation such as the national security law, the law on cybersecurity, the foreign NGO management law, and a digital social credit system to register citizen behavior—all of which bear witness to a repressive tendency.[8] Moreover, the government has also established a new National Security Commission led by Xi himself.[9] Yet scholars have largely been unable to explain why these laws are forthcoming and why a "politics of securitization" is targeting cadres and officials as well as ordinary citizens. The consolidation of Xi Jinping's personal power and the intraparty struggle that preceded his rise to power do not suffice to explain such profound securitization. The party-state's nationalistic narrative that the country is well governed by the CCP and that the country is unfit to experiment with Western-style democracy permeates official discourse and the state-dominated media landscape. This is also a narrative that China strongly communicates in the global media landscape. Thus, while Beijing proclaims itself a responsible stakeholder in the liberal international system, the world is simultaneously told that authoritarian China is well governed and that Western-style democracy is not domestically suitable. It is worrisome that elites in the developed and democratic world have either been persuaded by, or have overlooked, the nature of this double-sided narrative. The optimistic perspective put forward by John Ikenberry in his chapter of this volume reflects the hopeful prognostication that Chinese leaders will come to realize how much is in it for them in the American-dominated liberal world order. As is illuminated in the chapter by Minxin Pei, however, different regime types and their worldviews matter. It is risky to downplay the fact that China may cooperate less with the current order even if domestic growth continues to benefit from open markets undergirded by economic liberalism. If the reforms under Premier Li Keqiang, who aims to make market mechanisms more decisive, help to sustain authoritarianism, an important question is whether the liberal international order may not be upset from within—with or without China's active assistance in multilateral institutions. How the liberal international order of the West and particularly the United States would respond to the growing clout of China is far from certain. Not just response in the form of containment, but also willing accommodation could lead to a creeping undoing of the current order. As argued in a report by the German Marshall Fund of the United States, the ZEIT-Stiftung, and the Bosch Stiftung, "Western democracies must recognize that their own liberal international order will not be universalized, and should seek to find common ground with emerging powers."[10] Although the report recognizes a tension between anchoring the liberal order and building a new rules-based post-Western world, its authors blatantly envisage that "cooperating more closely with illiberal emerging powers requires compromises that will fall short of Western aspirations."[11] Erosion of the liberal order may in fact emanate not just from a politically illiberal China, actively partaking and potentially changing this global arrangement from within, but also from accommodating Western elites. Arguably, Western democracies and citizenries worldwide have become more insecure about their basic values, which began eroding in the wake of the attacks of 9/11, most notably concerning individual privacy and mass surveillance—concerns that were vindicated by Edward Snowden's revelations in June 2013. Within-order change is not a foregone conclusion when the rise of China as an economic juggernaut yields respect, reluctantly or not, by Western elites who are willing to bargain with authoritarian technocracy.[12] Ikenberry holds the American-led liberal international order is at least loosely rules based, and he does not believe China has an alternative vision of order deep down its pocket. The latter belief is probably correct, but the crux is the adjective "loosely" in the former proposition. Herein, the remarks concerning the rationality and wisdom of policy makers in Stephen Walt's chapter warrants further pondering. History illustrates that the United States will not be inclined to comply with vague rules when its national interests are challenged. New assemblages in international relations consisting of nationalist and neoliberal ideologies may test the United States' commitment to the very order of its own making, and consequently also to its longevity. If China, under the continued conditions of global neoliberal capitalism, in the coming decades outgrows (in terms of GDP and influence) the United States, this transition could potentially unleash a domestic American process of nationalism and isolationism, in which public opinion and policy makers see defense of the open liberal order as no longer in their own national interest, but only in the interest of others.

However, before the above scenarios become real-world problems, Beijing will first have to successfully solve the near-term challenges to the domestic political order. Arguably, potential transformation and erosion of the sociopolitical landscape and polity inside China is a scenario that cannot be overlooked in analyses of China's rise. Governance in the People's Republic is beset by serious problems, the severity of which is too often neglected by Western elites. It is an understatement to say that all is not well in the state of China. Neither increasingly skillful internal and external propaganda work, nor the legacy of Leninist guardianship protecting the CCP from society alone can fully explain the draconian measures taken to counter challenges to political legitimacy. The measures can only be understood in a context of the current Chinese leadership's recognition that serious challenges to political legitimacy actually do exist: in the form of socioeconomic inequality, environmental degradation, endemic corruption and problems of accountability, and abuse of power at various administrative levels of the political system. Yet surveys indicate that the governing apparatus is generally regarded as legitimate by the public.[13] But why are social protests so widespread, costs for internal security so high, and information control so intense—if the government and ruling party score high marks on legitimacy? Continued repression of deviant intellectuals and ever-increasing costs attributed to system stability maintenance and social control point in another direction,[14] prompting a discussion of political legitimacy, that elusive but central term that Bernhard Crick called the "master question of politics" and Seymour Martin Lipset defined as "the capacity of the system to engender and maintain the belief that the existing political institutions are most appropriate ones for the society."[15]

Performance-related legitimacy derived from economic growth and jingoistic-related legitimacy originating in nationalism have boosted the marks of the party-state in the eyes of the citizenry. Holbig and Gilley point to other sources of legitimacy, such as defining values, culture, rights, and what amounts to good governance. In accordance with Lipset's definition of belief in the system, they argue that the key to understanding how the Communist Party employs these other kinds of legitimacy is "its ability to construct and influence the subjective values and meanings."[16]

To proactively propagate a selective but strong narrative about how indispensable the Party is to Chinese successes in the past, the present and the future are certainly important. However, with an increasingly restive society making use of digital communications, it is even more important for the party-state to constrain *alternative* narratives to fully secure domination of the party-state's version. Thus, battling challenges related to stability, regime change and political transition strongly depend on how stable the media control in China is. As argued by Zhao Yuezhi, the Chinese communication system is the central battlefield determining the country's future.[17] If we approach the puzzle of political legitimacy in China through Albert Hirschman's theory of loyalty,[18] it becomes possible to assess how loyal Internet companies are to the system of censorship, which is crucially important to maintain both legitimacy and stability.

This chapter focuses on the measures employed to ward off the myriad social challenges and the mobilization of people against the government. The first part analyzes an essential link in the censorship chain: social media companies that must monitor and delete citizens' communication, thus assisting in keeping a lid on social activism, its organization, and mobilization. The second part is an analysis of a well-known social protest that occurred in the village of Wukan in late 2011, which was a case of the ubiquitous grassroots phenomenon in China whereby citizens tried to lift the lid of censorship on communication. These two cases shed new light on the vulnerability of what is generally seen as a more tightly controlled media system and a polity enjoying robust legitimacy. First, the system of digital censorship is in itself a sign of lacking legitimacy. This is a dilemma shared between the state "principal" and the commercial company "agents" that have been given the task to police citizens' communication, which in itself is an indication that party policy is not entirely legitimate. Second, if loyalty to governing institutions on the fringes of the polity where social protests erupt is weak, it indicates problems of legitimacy outside the core information order at the end point of the administrative political system between local leaders and citizens. As a chain is only as strong as its weakest link, it is necessary to analyze what may be among the weakest links in the party-state's system of censorship: social media companies outside the traditional media and propaganda system, and the end point of the polity, that is, the local level, where the overwhelming majority of social protests in China take place.

In this chapter, it is argued that if the imperfect compliance or loyalty of these links is "thin," it indicates that the *legitimacy* of the crucial censorship system, media policy, and stability maintenance is unstable. As proposed by Hirschman, such unstable legitimacy may be offset by general appeals of the rulers to nationalistic sentiments, my country, right or wrong. As noted by both Odd Arne Westad and Minxin Pei in this volume, nationalistic maneuvering to counter the erosion of legitimacy has worked well so far. Erosion may also temporarily be offset by case-by-case policy rewards or other tactical concessions by the state, after either informal or formal negotiations. Nonetheless, concession can only go so far, until the repression that underpins party rule is still at hand. However, as Pei argues, more overt repression is also likely to alienate the citizenry and further erode political legitimacy. Likewise, use of nationalism for the purposes of mass distraction, as in the island disputes with Japan, is also a double-edged sword, which can also be wielded by ultranationalists against the Communist Party.

TIGHTENING ONLINE CENSORSHIP

By applying economic incentives and appealing to nationalism to legitimize media policy and governance, the party-state has—hitherto but not indefinitely—been able to mitigate challenges to political stability. Outsourcing surveillance and censorship aspects of the propaganda system to commercial companies, and the construction of a convincing narrative that views China's rise and domestic and foreign challenges has the potential to curtail nationalism. Use of social media, like the digital communications practices that preceded it on the Chinese Internet, has challenged the Leninist political system and state-controlled mass media. Leaks of political scandals, social protests, and other contested issues travel fast through the networked world of social media. China has the world's largest Internet population, standing at 721 million.[19]

Of these, the majority are mobile Internet users, of whom a majority are active on social networking sites. Displaying how central media control had become for the party-state, the CCP decided at its third plenum in November 2013 that a new domestic security organization—the "State Security Committee"—would be headed by General Secretary Xi Jinping. Under the committee's framework is another new task force: The Internet Security and Information Leading Group. Its creation shows that the leadership is cognizant of possible crises related to social protests enabled by social media. At the first meeting of the group, Xi Jinping called for the Party to continue to mold online public opinion. He said that it was integral to the process of "making cyberspace clean and bright."[20]

Efforts to maintain media control and stability entail different practices of social control. A specific practice is the division of labor between social media businesses and party-state officials to censor media consumers in an emergent civil society amid increasing marketization. Since the early 1990s, Chinese entrepreneurs in the Information and communications technology (ICT) sector have faced a conundrum of being pulled in different directions by consumerism, social norms, and state control. Serving two masters, with diverging interests in open networks and the flow of information, is both a financial and a strategic burden for these companies. The enterprises' endurance hinges on the complex interplay between outside and transnational norms on the one hand, and domestic norms and other broader structural transformations in Chinese society, such as generational and ideational change, administrative reform inside the Chinese Communist Party (CCP), and growing class divides, on the other. Societal anxiety and state attempts to defuse it often gain visibility via channels to the world of bits and bytes.

This world also amplifies a tension of a normative and moral nature between social control and the need and preference for raw and undiluted information throughout China's civil society and business world. The uneasy coexistence between potentially destabilizing discussions on Chinese social networking sites, such as Sina Weibo and Tencent's WeChat, and the party-state's fixation on social stability is a social fact today. Many media companies, both new and traditional, have set up social networking services, but Sina and Tencent are the biggest players in this segment of the social media world. On August 14, 2009, Sina announced that registration on Sina's microblog service, Weibo, its equivalent of the Twitter microblog, was open to Chinese netizens.

The first part of this chapter offers an analysis of the extent to which social media companies are "in agreement" with and how they "negotiate" party directives to uphold the information order of the PRC. It is based on ethnographic fieldwork, conducted in Beijing from 2011 through 2013, devoted to understanding the strategies of the two major microblogging media companies, Sina and Tencent. Interviews were carried out with fourteen informants: twelve social media professionals and executives, as well as two journalists employed by traditional media organizations in Beijing.

What are the perspectives of professionals and business leaders in the social media sector on their paradoxical role of both facilitating and containing freer speech? The question speaks to the dilemma of principal-agent relations, which arises in the biggest Chinese microblogging companies' dealings with real-name registration and real-time censorship of microblogs under conditions of state-delegated responsibility for censoring of users' content. Internet businesses in China are especially interesting to investigate because they fall outside the conventional lines of the party-state bureaucracy's direct control over traditional mass media—making them an important factor in the movement toward political accountability and participation, and perhaps more inclusive politics.

CLIMATE OF COMPLIANCE

The obedient posture of Chinese media entrepreneurs has been a longstanding theme, becoming more pronounced in 1999. Regulations to prohibit new media organizations were implemented to prevent media startups from running wild in the new territory of online journalism. By and large, a general climate of serving political masters permeates the business world, and a political scene of rampant corruption has existed for decades despite recurring official rhetoric about the vice of embezzlement. Nonetheless, Chinese business leaders do not unconditionally accept the authoritarian information order, nor are they willing to support political liberties "only when they do not perceive such a transformation as a threat to their material well-being."[21] It is more probable that many pragmatically tolerate current arrangements because they bring more benefits than costs. Yet, as Chen and Dickson note, the "continuation of regime support is contingent on the government's policy performance."[22] Therefore, allegiance to the actually existing information order, and by extension, the legitimacy of the party-state's authoritarian politics, may be quite "thin."

Business executives very rarely oppose government policies publicly. However, they do convey concerns about how state censorship and surveillance negatively impact profits off-screen. Since the broad social demonstrations of the Tiananmen movement of 1989, many domestic entrepreneurs have been socialized to kowtow to an authoritarian developmental ethos, whose guiding principle upholds that social and political stability benefit Chinese society as a whole, including business, because stability is a prerequisite for sustained economic growth, which in turn generates order and a more harmonious society.

However, despite its shiny façade, minor cracks may be emerging in relations between government officials and "red capitalists" in the Internet and communications sector. Two examples of vocal resistance in the recent past are conspicuous. First, strong opposition was mounted to "Green Dam youth escort software," a decision by the Ministry of Information Industry to have all domestic producers of laptop computers install software called Green Dam to stop access to online pornography. The government's failure to implement Green Dam suggests that there was a limit to industry passivity. Second, when Google decided to move its search engine from mainland China to freer Hong Kong, several business executives voiced concern that the American company's departure would be problematic for innovation in China's information industry. At the China IT Leader Summit in Shenzhen on March 28, 2010, Tian Suning of Media China Corporation said it was unwise to turn Google into an enemy of China, and Ding Jian of AsiaInfo even questioned the short- and long-term wisdom of the Chinese government's censorship policy. However, not all Chinese Internet entrepreneurs and businesses were openly supportive of Google.[23] Thus, there have emerged indications that some business leaders in the new media sector are worried that China's information flows may have long-term negative consequences for the economy, even if some media companies benefit from short-term economic benefits when foreign companies exit the Chinese market.

This concern is more prevalent among social media companies than among those providing general Internet services or hardware. The larger of the former companies, such as Sina and Renren, were drawn to social media by through their established roles as news aggregators in the form of Web. The friend-sharing, and service portal *Tencent* differs from this model, as it started out as a peer-to-peer communication platform. Of all businesses in the Chinese Internet industry, Tencent and Sina are among the companies that are closest to the public, providing it with a plethora of news and interacting with it through their microblogging services every day. Because these two companies must cultivate an awareness of local trends and sentiments lest the networking public abandon them, the hitherto servile attitude of the information industry sector is, to some extent, conditional. However, divergence from business as usual is discernible mostly when it concerns industry strategy and fiscal costs of surveillance rather than individual or societal freedom.

The tactics, beliefs, and ideas of professionals in information businesses are as important to study as are the implications of the services that these businesses introduce to society. This is especially so in China, where cadre-capitalist interest alliances crisscross the terrain of the national economy. An important research problem concerns the perceptions of those who are trusted with rolling out this new infrastructure, setting up new, seemingly modern, and unfettered communicative platforms, and who are yet mandated to supervise citizen-clients' use of them. The questions that follow on are these: How do private social media businesses deal with the state's delegation of control of social media services? How does the dilemma of principal-agent relations manifest itself in a real-world case of state-private business relations in China?

Since the late 1990s, responsibility for patrolling deviant voices has been delegated to lower-level state entities and commercial companies in the long chain of command that begins with the Politburo Standing Committee. Since the deadly Wenzhou high-speed train crash in 2011, which was followed by fierce commentary about the corruption-infested Ministry of Railways' lack of attention to public safety, the delegation of control and the censorship of microblog providers further increased.[24] This delegation of control highlights a dilemma of principal-agency, whereby original tasks and intentions may be compromised down the line of a bureaucracy.[25] In the Chinese context, this dilemma has been studied from various political economy angles. Studies focusing on this problematic against the backdrop of a fragmented authoritarian state range in topic from local communist cadres' actions to pacify social protest in rural areas of the Chinese hinterland,[26] to delegation of control in the industrial and fiscal sectors,[27] to bureaucratic struggles that led to a competitive system of sovereign wealth funds.[28]

China's sphere of digital communications, especially microblogs, has been hailed as China's first free speech arena. Early on, international media argued that the impact of Chinese microblogs "cannot be overestimated," and their progression as vehicles for public opinion formation even prompted some observers of Chinese politics to claim that the Internet has become a "virtual political system."[29] Although the above statements underestimated the resilience of the Chinese state, for a couple of years—2009–2012, before the rise to power of Xi Jinping as general secretary—microblogging did pressure the government to pay more attention to public opinion. Precisely for that reason, microblogs were targeted as the number-one digital threat by the state policy since many incidents went viral and were picked up by mainstream media because of huge information cascades triggered by them, particularly Sina Weibo. In 2011, researchers at Shanghai's Jiaotong University reported that social media such as Weibo were the first reporters of 65 percent of the 138 nationwide public opinion "hot events" that made headlines during 2010.[30] Most of these incidents were spurred by frustrations over local corruption, land grabs, and environmental degradation.

Interviews conducted with young software developers and mid-level managers indicate a more liberal attitude to free speech than the generally more pragmatic values of older professionals. This incipient generational gap may grow and already lead to complaints and internal debates about government policies. As a manager of a social media division at Tencent in Beijing argued, "Regarding the stance on free flow of information, I think that all companies that are in this line of business want more, not less freedom and narrower information flow. That is only natural."[31] This statement indicates that if industry sectors in China may find authoritarianism acceptable, parts of the ICT sector have other ideals and merely tolerate authoritarianism for now. This points to a transformation in outlook over the past decade, given that in 2004 and 2005, when the author interviewed Internet industry professionals in Beijing and Shanghai, they were more prone to accept state control as a given good for both society and business.[32] Today, however, with younger professionals entering the workforce, they seem to expect policy outcomes to favor them as a quid pro quo for their commitment to upholding the social order. This change of perspective points to a difference between front-stage and back-stage rhetoric akin to the description of "feigned compliance" in Chinese political culture.[33] Repeating the words of government leaders is thus an act of verbal conformity that reveals nothing about individual deviancy. Translated to the empirical landscape of the social media sector, it entails that compliance can be pretended and that allegiance to Party norms regarding media control may be thin and legitimacy for government policies weak.

However, due to feigned public compliance, there exist few overt signs of tension between social media entrepreneurs and the authoritarian capitalism that upholds the legitimacy of the Communist Party. Besides Ding Jian of AsiaInfo, no senior business leader has problematized state regulations policy on the grounds that limiting free information flow is detrimental to both the economy and society.[34] Therefore, the consensus between top managers in the dominant social media companies and the government seems to hold. China's police and security organs are confident they can handle the challenges presented by the new communications technology and social media used by different actors in society. And apart from the professed normative consensus on "keeping the lid" on media-enabled collective action, increasing resources from the national budget go to upholding domestic security, augmented by the delegation of censorship and surveillance practices to Internet companies that add to stability enhancement from their own budgets. Nonetheless, new strategies and resources channeled to stability maintenance over the past five years indicate how serious the party-state is about media-enabled social protest.

REVISITING THE PRINCIPAL-AGENT DILEMMA

How can an authoritarian state such as China dare to trust business enterprises outside the state system to implement costly policies, using tens of thousands of their own workers to monitor social media? Steven Solnick's early study of the Soviet Union and China during the 1980s sheds light on the basis of the Chinese state's confidence. Solnick showed how the central government in Beijing managed to retain significant power over lower levels of the bureaucracy despite decentralization of decision-making. Since China maintained a "reputation" of implementing severe sanctions if disobeyed, outsourcing of sensitive management responsibility was not as risky as in Russia. This experience may explain why, since the end of the 1990s, the once-centralized guardianship of the media system gradually dispersed to commercial Internet service providers and social media services such as Sina and Tencent.

Thus, the Chinese government's positive track record of handling principal-agent dilemmas in general, and successful control over media companies in particular, explains why control of even sensitive matters such as preventing the mobilization of social protests can be outsourced. Compared to Solnick's bureaucratic study, however, the social media industry in China is a particularly interesting case, since these companies are located *outside* the traditional lines of direct control by the party-state bureaucracy. Studies of the principal-agent dilemma have mostly concerned situations *inside* state bureaucracies and private firms. Implementation of policy and law in China is already cumbersome within layered officialdom. Adding one more, and outer, layer of policing is a risk. Delegating surveillance to private companies could lead to potential foot-dragging, as it confers an extra cost for the industry. So far, however, the scheme to let companies do frontline spying on users of social media has been a cost-effective strategy of monitoring mobilizers of dissent in civil society.

Regular leaks from Internet businesses of sensitive keywords to monitor on behalf of the state point to a principal-agent dilemma in the social media sector. News items in the immediate aftermath of the implementation of the real-name system for Weibo users in March 2012 indicated that Sina's design and operation were flawed, making possible the use of false identities.[35] The system's failure was an example of foot-dragging between the agent (social media business) and the principal (party-state), which was also indicated by Sina's leader Zhao's signals about how negative the new regulations were for shareholders. Foot-dragging was later balanced by the forthcoming behavior of Chen Tong, Sina's vice president responsible for all content posted on its Weibo service. At a conference in Beijing, Chen made a show of Sina's progovernment credentials by inviting officials and promoting their use of government Weibo accounts.

Organizing conferences about government Weibo makes for an opportunity to showcase loyalist attitudes while also helping to directly lobby for the company's views on policy issues.[36] Clearly, complaints about the delegation of social control may generate policy rewards for hard surveillance work. As one leader of the organization the Internet Society of China (ISOC) argued, "If the ICT capitalists want to stay in operation, they must obey the laws; in return, they also get service and support from the government."[37] Careful observation of the chain of command in the arena of media control shows that companies, which monitor deviant behavior on social media, may receive policy benefits as a reward. For instance, as a top executive of Sina argued, "Meeting with government leaders means there is an opportunity for us to present our industry concerns—about working permits and household registration for our workers, as well as concerns about taxes."[38]

The stick is the hovering presence of arbitrary sanctions imposed by a state that only selectively adheres to constitutionalism and the rule of law, especially with regard to issues of social and political stability. The principal-agent dilemma is ongoing between state regulators and entrepreneurs in the social media sector. It is a delicate balancing act alongside generational and ideational changes in a pluralizing society with thin and potentially shifting allegiances.

SOCIAL PROTESTS IN RURAL AREAS: THE WUKAN INCIDENT

As many as 180,000 popular protests may take place across the People's Republic of China (PRC) every year.[39] By the fall of 2011, one of these local and mostly isolated conflicts made world headlines. A protest that had started in September in the large village of Wukan, Guangdong Province, peaked in December. Street-level demonstrations there were prompted by a drawn-out struggle that had been brewing for years regarding a dispute over compensation for collectively used land that had been sold to real-estate developers. On December 11, the conflict escalated when the 10,000 villagers pillorized the responsible party secretary. Taken from old-style social movement repertoire, locals erected barricades and occupied the small public square.

During the stalemate that followed, with the Communist Party leaders and police of the nearby city of Lufeng on one side and the Wukan villagers on the other, domestic and foreign reporters slipped into the village's hastily organized media center. An analysis of what took place in Wukan yields a nuanced picture of media strategies of social activists at the local level. It concretely illuminates how social organization was carried out, and how it was possible for the villagers to "lift the lid" on information diffusion about the conflict. The final outcome also indicates how legitimate the censorship system, stability maintenance, and governance are in rural areas. The following analysis is based on fieldwork interviews in Wukan,[40] interpretations of media discourses, and readings of some influential Chinese scholars' commentary on Wukan's role as a potential "pointer" about trends of accountability, security-stability, and legitimacy in rural China.

Central and provincial leaders like to portray themselves as benign, and in many countryside localities, this image remains intact. When a cycle of contention starts, accusations are directed at the local officials, and hopes are placed on higher administrative levels. To a certain extent, such a blame game of corrupt locals and "honest outsiders" played out also in Wukan, when the governor and party secretary of Guangdong Province, Wang Yang, decided to intervene in December 2011. His deputy, Zhu Mingguo, was ordered to initiate a dialogue with the Wukan protestors, effectively bypassing county-level officials whom the villagers did not trust. The ousted village leaders, who were accused of illegally selling villagers' land, had colluded with higher administrative officials at the township level to be able to stay in power through rigged elections to the village committee for over forty years.

On December 20, the leader of the ad hoc village committee, Lin Zulian, met with Zhu Mingguo and the Shanwei party secretary Zheng Yanxiong. At the meeting, Lin put forward three concrete demands. First, he insisted on the immediate release of three detained villagers and the return of the body of Xue Jinbo, another village leader who had died in police custody. Second, he wanted the Provincial government to accept the authority of his ad hoc committee. Third, regarding the origin of the whole conflict, he demanded that the land dispute be resolved as stipulated by law.[41] It did not take long for Zhu Mingguo to agree to Lin's demands, and the Wukan stalemate was ended. It was also decided that a new village election should be held, something the previous corrupt leadership never had organized. For the first time ever, Wukan would implement the election practices stipulated in the Organic Law of the Villagers Committees of the People's Republic of China. A new election had to reinstate correct practices and secure voting according to the organic law on village committee elections.[42] In March 2012, the voting in Wukan resulted in the leader of the ad hoc negotiating committee, Lin Zulian, being elected as new chairman of the village committee. The stepping in of the provincial government and especially of Party Secretary Wang Yang to resolve the crisis peacefully by sending his deputy, Zhu Mingguo, to Wukan was important. The reasons were twofold. First, it had become a global media event. Second, Wang wanted to send a message that he was able to handle rural issues competently in the run-up to the Eighteenth Party Congress in October 2012. After the Party Congress, however, the consolidation of General Secretary Xi Jinping's rule and implementation of more repressive politics have led to much harder pressure on the elected the Wukan village committee from the local government in Lufeng, which has delayed negotiations on the settlement of financial compensation for the illegal land sales. Between villagers' demands, foot-dragging, and accusations of corruption from the authorities, the work of the elected village leaders was hamstrung.

THE WUKAN VILLAGERS' EFFECTIVE MEDIA STRATEGY

Despite the party-state's tighter control of digital communications in recent years, governments at different administrative levels and their attempts to censor information about social protests and discontent continue to be challenged by citizens. Due to the widespread use of handheld communications devices and increasing social activism, governance, censorship, and the rose-tinted party-state narrative are all questioned. Some of the most spectacular viral leaks during the last five years have concerned protests against land grabs in the countryside. This is not surprising, as more and more rural Chinese can afford to buy smartphones. Technological changes and new social agency make possible dissemination of information that before the Internet was easily controlled by the state. These changes have transformed the Chinese public from being standby citizens to actually "do[ing] citizenship."[43]

Crucial for the involvement of provincial cadres was the setting up of a media center that catered to foreign, Hong Kong, and Taiwanese journalists. This made possible the real-time diffusion of information about the conflict to the outside world. Wukan's youth, many of them migrant workers arriving from urban centers such as Shenzhen and very skilled in the arts of digital media communication, set up a Wukan media presence on Tencent's QQ messaging service and a microblog account with both Tencent and Sina. As argued by a Mainland Chinese informant with the nongovernmental organization China Labour Bulletin in Hong Kong, "This new young generation of migrant-workers cannot go back and cultivate the land. They do not possess that knowledge. But they are very skilled in the use of new media technologies, and far more demanding regarding wages and working conditions."[44]

The way young Wukan villagers managed to harness social media platform discussions on Sina Weibo and on Tencent Weibo strongly impacted the outcome of what could been a violent crackdown. Arguably, the decision of the party secretary, Wang Yang, to resolve the crisis peacefully by sending his deputy to Wukan for negotiations had to do with its meteoric rise to the headlines of both national and global media. The vast volume of Weibo postings quickly brought the incident from being one of many social protests in rural China to an exceptionally iconic event. Thus, the authorities could not cover up what happened in Wukan. Images of the villagers occupying the main square, overturning police vehicles, and giving fiery speeches were quickly forwarded throughout millions of Weibo accounts. Officials at both the Provincial and Central level were forced to discuss rural discontent after information about the incident had gone viral on both the firewalled Chinese Internet and the global networks outside the "Great Firewall."

Censors at Sina Weibo found it very difficult, or unnecessary, to censor relevant keywords. The Wukan villagers' use of their Weibo accounts, other social media, and real-time dissemination of the conflict was certainly significant. It was Wukan's media center that made this specific protest stand out as successful and set it apart from other popular protest in rural China. In the nearby village of Panhe, a similar protest took place one month later but received only scant foreign or domestic media attention—either online or offline. No media center was set up there, and the lack of attention given to the Panhe protests, despite heavy use of police violence to disperse the protesters, explains why demonstrations there did not result in a negotiated solution on equally illegal behavior concerning corrupt land deals.[45] Thus, to reach out to policymakers above the local administrative level in today's China, every social protest mobilization has to have an effective media strategy.

After a peaceful outcome of the immediate conflict had been negotiated in Wukan, the process of normalizing and stabilizing the conflict entered a new phase. Through a reading of Sina Weibo postings from January through May 2012, the immediate solution to the Wukan crisis—the holding of a truly democratic election to the village committee—can be understood. Because the election to the village committee in Wukan, contrary to the majority of elections in rural China, was organized according to the Communist Party rulebook, the conflict and its outcome continued to be discussed on Weibo. For example, the many popular tweets by outspoken lawyer Yuan Yulai regarding the long-term consequences of the Wukan incident were deleted.[46] Nonetheless, some statements about China's prospects for democracy and the maturity of citizens continued to circulate, and these were widely read by many users of social media. In contrast to the peak of protests in December, Sina censors now deleted the most controversial postings on the long-term and broader implications of rural democracy for Chinese politics. Yet from the undeleted tweets it was possible to capture how people across the country perceived the incident's origins as similar to corrupt practices elsewhere, and how they believed that free elections—if properly conducted—could serve as a cure and increase transparency and legitimacy.

According to some observers, Wukan was more than just an iconic media event. It showed how "the Guangdong government moved beyond its habitual fixation with 'maintaining stability' to recognize that the appeals of the Wukan villagers arose out of concern for their livelihoods, rather than out of some animus against the Party or China's political system." It was a significant turning point. However, the reason for avoidance of bloodshed had less to do with the lack of an open "animus against the Party" than the villagers' effective media strategy.[47] The positive statements by the new village leadership displaying its loyalty by acknowledging the party-state hierarchy as legitimate also served to dampen suspicion about deep-seated hostility toward the political system in general. The former protest leader Lin Zulian, in his new capacity as elected leader of Wukan's legitimate village committee, wished to display continued loyalty toward the party in March 2012: "As a party secretary, I understand our country's policies for rural areas and at the same time support the work of village committee. Self-government can be realized when the village committee plays its own role and the party branch provides policy support."[48]

After new pressure from the provincial and local governments in 2014 and after the village committee elections of March 2014, Lin declared, "I will give the village party committee a bigger role in village affairs. We should not kick them out just because they are former officials."[49] The Wukan case offers a glimpse into how rural society in China has become more active in a realm of shadows outside the purview of the state and on social media. Simultaneously, Wukan illustrates how crucial it is for democratically elected village leaders to profess loyalty to the authoritarian party-state. However, under circumstances of increasing repression in Xi Jinping's China, this loyalty cannot be taken for granted, and legitimacy to the political system may be much thinner than it seems.

CONCLUSIONS AND IMPLICATIONS

The first part of the chapter analyzed social media businesses' compliance with the party-state's control policies in light of an evolving principal-agent dilemma embedded in the law and policy implementation chain of social control. The findings on how commercial social media businesses deal with the burden of delegated control of users show that the party-state has temporarily solved the dilemma by maintaining the risk of sanctions for the industry while rewarding compliant businesses with policy rewards. Equilibrium and continued compliance, however, are contingent on the state's continued reward of policy kickbacks. The not-so-diligent implementation of a real-name registration system for microblogs by the media giant Sina, during the politically turbulent spring of 2012, pointed to growing friction in the relations between business and government.

This situation suggests potentially more far-reaching consequences for principal-agent relations between party-state cadres and commercial agents. Those ICT entrepreneurs who pragmatically accept that "this is China's political system and the country does need stability"[50] may say this to protect themselves from the authorities. For the Chinese party-state, the likelihood that the next generation of social media entrepreneurs will contribute to the erosion of the media system and political legitimacy is a serious challenge, notwithstanding the harsher political climate ushered in under General Secretary Xi Jinping.

The outcome of the negotiations at Wukan suggests that the protestors sought resolution to an economic conflict that had its origins in local misconduct by political leaders. Displaying loyalty to the existing polity, they wished to see proper institutionalization of democratic village elections as outlined in the Organic Law of the Villagers Committees of the People's Republic of China. Their wish corresponded well also with how the Governor of Guangdong, Wang Yang, publically pronounced on Wukan's significance. At the annual session of the National People's Congress in March 2012, Wang said there was nothing special about the village elections in Wukan: "[T]he elections were held according to the organization rules of the village and the election regulations of Guangdong province. There was nothing new about this."[51] But such exemplary uncorrupt model elections did not spread to nearby villages outside Wukan, such as Longtou and Panhe.[52] Tellingly, since 2012, democratic governance in Wukan has also been sabotaged by the local and provincial government.[53] Therefore, what the provincial government sought to achieve was the containment of the spread of social protests to other parts of Guangdong Province. To that end, it deployed different tactics for different locales.

The findings in this chapter on loyalty to government policy and institutions inside the system of censorship and at the lowest rung of the administrative level in the Chinese countryside can be theorized in line with Albert Hirschman's strategies of "voice," "exit," and "loyalty."[54] Conceptualizing the choice between these strategies by within-system agents or outside actors helps us to understand responses to the decline in legitimacy of various principal-organizations, including the national bureaucracy or the state. "Exit" from the nation-state, as when seeking affiliation with underground secret societies or even exile, is a radical route chosen by a minority. As pointed out by David Shambaugh in his chapter of this volume, however, if these few are the nation's economic elite, their lack of confidence and loyalty to the existing polity should worry the party leadership. This observation corresponds also to the insight of Minxin Pei's chapter: a part of this elite, who are "opportunistic supporters" and have exchanged loyalty for corrupt exploitation, may remain loyal only as long as economic growth rates are high.

"Voice," or speaking truth to power, is possible within limits, but only if discontent trumps both individual and broader concerns about social stability, or if policy rewards or tactical shifts in exchange for loyalty can be negotiated. If "voice" goes further than mere vocal opposition to include also mobilization of collective action, such behavior needs to be carefully dressed in words and deeds showcasing both patriotism and "loyalty." The notion of a loyal Chinese society as highlighted by the Wukan case corresponds to the Western, originally British, idea of a loyal opposition, whereby opponents of a particular policy and governance do not seek the overthrow of the political system, yet are able to criticize and oppose government policies. The transition theorist Juan Linz also used this term to describe reform-minded elements of the Spanish nomenklatura and opposition under General Franco's rule. Linz made the case that a semiopposition, that is, elements that are not dominant in the political system, may yet choose to "participate in power without fundamentally challenging the regime."[55]

The Wukan incident cannot be regarded as a turning point in either state-society or rural-central relations, as no outright antigovernment slogans were used or views of a semiopposition expressed. Both "voice" and "loyalty" were expressed in what was an economic conflict, underpinned by bad and corrupt governance by former leaders of the existing village committee and county-level government, that mobilized villagers to occupy the town square. Yet if loyalty is no more than feigned compliance, it has further implications. This indicates that political legitimacy for rural governance, including stability maintenance and censorship of communication about systemic problems, may also be thin, contrary to the robustness suggested by both quantitative and qualitative studies. The debate on China's emerging civil society has stagnated around a consensus appraisal of dependent and submissive registered social organizations.[56] That body of research disregards on the one hand the existence of nonregistered social organizations and on the other the fragility of state-society relations characterized by codependency and the semiautonomous existence of registered social organizations based on feigned loyalty and sinister co-optation in order to gain resources in the form of grants, unpaid labor, public support, and access to information.

Secondly, the construction of a plausible propagandistic narrative around these deliverables and the censorship or alternative narratives secure high scores on legitimacy among respondents. That is if we accept that political legitimacy is understood as Juan Linz: "the belief that in spite of shortcomings and failures, the existing political institutions are better than any others that might be established and that they therefore can demand obedience." In the absence of other competing visions, narratives, and political parties, the high scores on political legitimacy in the PRC prove how respondents' answers depend on the continued censorship of such alternatives. But as this kind of legitimacy is indeed thin, the party-state has further intensified the censoring of digital communications and traditional mass media. Yet despite continued effective control over all media forms, inherent risks to China's authoritarian system of censorship exist at both its top and bottom.

The party-state may only temporarily have solved the principal-agent dilemma at the top of the censorship system, as norms among young urban managers of social networking companies are at odds with the directives of the Communist Party. Moreover, as a much younger cohort of technocrats enter the state bureaucracy, they are likely to carry the more liberal norms with them.[57] In the years ahead, given a serious economic or political crisis in which "thin legitimacy" at both the top of the censorship system and at the bottom of society plays out in a way detrimental to the party-state, potentially large-scale unrest could still be fueled by the use of social media, which despite pervasive control could mobilize people into "connective action."[58] If China's system of censorship would crumble, then all the challenges and tensions in society and the late Leninist party-state could come into full play. This would be the nightmare scenario of the Communist Party, destabilizing its rule at home while also derailing its further rise to preeminence on the global stage.

NOTES

1. See Bloomberg. (2011, June 13). China cracks down in wake of riots, Bombings.
2. Yiyi. Lu, *Non-Governmental Organisations in China* (London: Routledge, 2009).
3. Carolyn. Hsu, "Beyond Civil Society: An Organizational Perspective on State-NGO Relations in the People's Republic of China," *Journal of Civil Society* 6, no. 3 (2010): 259–77, quote on 260.

4. Anthony. Spires, "Contingent Symbiosis and Civil Society in an Authoritarian State: Understanding the Survival of China's Grassroots NGOs," *American Journal of Sociology* 117, no. 1 (2011): 1–45.
5. Jessica. Teets, *Civil Society under Authoritarianism: The China Model* (Cambridge: Cambridge University Press, 2014).
6. Timothy. Hildebrandt, *Social Organizations and the Authoritarian State in China* (Cambridge: Cambridge University Press, 2013).
7. Andrew. Nathan, "China at the Tipping Point? Foreseeing the Unforseeable," *Journal of Democracy* 24, no. 1 (2013): 20–25.
8. The National People's Congress passed the National Security Law on July 1, 2015. See http://www.chinadaily.com.cn/hqcj/zgjj/2015-07-01/content_13912103.html.
9. David. Lampton, "Xi Jinping and the National Security Commission: Policy Coordination and Political Power," *Journal of Contemporary China* 24, no. 95 (2015): 759–77; Yiqin Fu, "What Will China's National Security Commission Actually Do?: The Four Functions of China's Top National Security Body," *Foreign Policy*, August 5, 2014, http://foreignpolicy.com/2014/05/08/what-will-chinas-national-security-commission-actually-do/.
10. Trine Flockhart, Charles Kupchan, Christina Lin, Bartlomiej Nowak, Patrick Quirk, and Lanxin Xiang, *Liberal Order in a Post-Western World* (Washington, DC: Transatlantic Academy, 2014), ix.
11. See note 2, above.
12. For a longer argument see Johan Lagerkvist, Lagerkvist, J. (2014). The legacy of the 1989 Beijing massacre: Establishing neo-authoritarian rule, silencing civil society. *International Journal of China Studies*, 5(2), 349–369. "Legacy," 364–65.
13. See www.asiabarometer.org; Bruce Gilley, "The Meaning of State Legitimacy: Results for 72 Countries," *European Journal of Political Research* 45 (2006): 499–525; Martin King Whyte, *Myth of the Social Volcano: Perceptions of Inequality and Distributive Injustice in Contemporary China* (Stanford, CA: Stanford University Press, 2012); Yang Dali, Jiang Junyan, and Chen Lijun, "Mandate without Elections: Performance, Dependence, and Popular Approval of Subnational Governments in China," published online, http://www.junyanjiang.com/uploads/5/8/1/9/58193547/mandate_without_elections.pdf.
14. See https://freedomhouse.org/sites/default/files/FIW%202013%20Booklet.pdf. In the global ranking by Freedom House in 2013, China was placed as low as 179 of 191 countries, and in terms of Internet freedom the People's Republic of China (PRC) was ranked as 86 of 91 countries.
15. Bernard Crick, *In Defense of Politics* (Chicago: Chicago University Press, 1962), 150–51; Seymour Martin Lipset, *Political Man: The Social Bases of Politics* (New York: Doubleday, 1960), 64–65.
16. Heike Holbig and Bruce Gilley, "In Search of Legitimacy in Post-Revolutionary China: Bringing Ideology and Governance Back In" (GIGA Working Paper, no. 127, March, Hamburg, GIGA, 2010, 6).
17. Zhao Yuezhi, *Communication in China: Political Economy, Power, and Conflict* (Lanham: Rowman & Littlefield, 2008).
18. Albert. O. Hirschman, *Exit, Voice, and Loyalty: Responses to Decline in Firms, Organizations, and States* (Cambridge, MA: Harvard University Press, 1970), 75–76.
19. See "CNNIC Released its 34th Statistical Report on Internet Development in China," http://www.reuters.com/article/us-china-internet-idUSPEK34240620080424.

20. Shannon Tiezzi, "The War Over China's Internet," *The Diplomat*, April 28, 2014, http://thediplomat.com/2014/04/the-war-over-chinas-internet/.
21. Teresa Wright, *Accepting Authoritarianism: State-Society Relations in China's Reform Era* (Stanford, CA: Stanford University Press, 2010), 56–57.
22. Bruce Dickson and Chen Jie, *Allies of the State: China's Private Entrepreneurs and Democratic Change* (Cambridge, MA: Harvard University Press, 2010), 16–17.
23. See "China's Top IT Entrepreneurs Call for Internet Special Zone," *China Digital Times*, 2010, http://www.szpost.com/2010/03/china-shenzhen-it-leader-summit-2010-to-be-held-in-shenzhen.html.
24. Johan Lagerkvist, "New Media Entrepreneurs in China: Allies of the Party-State or Civil Society" *Columbia Journal of International Affairs* 65, no. 1 (2011): 169–82.
25. A. Niskanen William, "The Peculiar Economics of Bureaucracy," *American Economic Review* 58, no. 2 (1968): 293–305.
26. Maria Edin, "State Capacity and Local Agent Control in China: CCP Cadre Management from a Township Perspective," *China Quarterly* 173 (2003): 35–52.
27. Stephen Solnick, "The Breakdown of Hierarchies in the Soviet Union and China: A Neoinstitutional Perspective," *World Politics* 48 (1996): 209–38.
28. Sarah Eaton and Zhang Ming, "A Principal-Agent Analysis of China's Sovereign Wealth System: Byzantine by Design," *Review of International Political Economy* 17, no. 3 (2010): 481–506.
29. Elizabeth Economy and Jared Mondschein, "China: The New Virtual Political System," Council on Foreign Relations, April 27, 2011, http://www.cfr.org/china/china-new-virtual-political-system/p24805.
30. *Chinese Society Public Opinion and Crisis Management Report 2011*, 2011, http://china-media-news.org/2011/07/18/new-chinese-society-public-opinion-and-crisis-management-report-2011-65-of-hot-events-first-on-new-media; accessed on February 12, 2011.
31. Interview with mid-level program manager of Tencent's microblog division at the company's Beijing office, September 6, 2011.
32. Lagerkvist, "Media," 175.
33. Lucian Pye, *The Spirit of Chinese Politics: A Psychocultural Study of the Authority Crisis in Political Development* (Cambridge: MIT Press, 1968).
34. Ding Jian actually ventured to talk about a noncensored Internet in the southern experimental city of Shenzhen at the IT Leaders Summit in 2010.
35. Christina Larson, "The New Epicenter of China's Discontent: Dispatch from a City That Wasn't Supposed to Be on the Brink," *Foreign Policy*, August 23, 2011, http://www.foreignpolicy.com/articles/2011/08/23/the_new_epicenter_of-china_s_discontent.
36. Sina and Chen Tong organized a conference on this theme in November 2011 in Beijing.
37. Interview with senior company executive in Beijing, September 27, 2011.
38. Interview with Sina manager in Beijing, September 21, 2012.
39. See Sun Liping, "Social Disorder Is a Present and Serious Challenge" [in Chinese] *Economic Observer*, February 28, 2011, http://www.eeo.com.cn/Politics/by_region/2011/02/28/194539.shtml.
40. This part of the chapter is based on fieldwork conducted in Hong Kong and Wukan from August 20 through August 28, 2012. In Hong Kong, two informants at the China Labour Bulletin were interviewed. In Wukan, five

people were interviewed, including the newly elected village leader Lin Zulian. All interviews were conducted in Chinese and lasted for about sixty minutes and were semistructured.

41. Qu Yunxu, "An Insider's Account of the Wukan Protest," *Caixin*, March 19, 2012, http://www.chinafile.com/reporting-opinion/caixin-media/insiders-account-wukan-protest.
42. See Organic Law of the Villagers Committees of the People's Republic of China, http://www.china.org.cn/english/government/207279.htm.
43. Peter Dahlgren, *Media and Political Engagement: Citizens, Communication and Democracy* (Cambridge: Cambridge University Press, 2009).
44. Interview with representative of China Labour Bulletin on the rise of a "new generation of migrant workers" having better education and communication skills needed to quickly establishing all-important media visibility. In Hong Kong, August 27, 2012.
45. Xu Wen, "Panhe Land Protests Halted after Villagers Detained by Security Forces," *Global Times*, February 17, 2012, http://www.globaltimes.cn/content/696284.shtml.
46. See David Bandurski, "The Legacy of Wukan," China Media Project, uploaded January 30, 2012, http://cmp.hku.hk/2012/01/30/18237/.
47. Ou Ning, "What Wukan Means," *China File*, April 18, 2012, http://www.chinafile.com/what-wukan-means.
48. See Qu Yunxu, "An Insider's Account of the Wukan Protest."
49. Echo Hui, "Wukan Elects Village Chief, but Not All Are Happy," *South China Morning Post*, March 31, 2014, http://www.scmp.com/news/china/article/1461639/china-rebel-village-votes-hopes-fade-fair-poll.
50. Interview with manager at Sina Headquarters in Beijing, September 14, 2011.
51. See Zachary Wei, "Rebel Village Vote: No Big Deal?," *Wall Street Journal*, March 5, 2012, http://blogs.wsj.com/chinarealtime/2012/03/05/wukan-rebel-village-vote-no-big-deal/?mod=WSJBlog&mod=chinablog.
52. Louisa Lim, "Voting Is Victory, at Least for Rebel Chinese Village," National Public Radio, March 4, 2012, http://www.npr.org/2012/03/04/147888068/vote-in-small-chinese-village-holds-big-meaning. In nearby Longtou, also in Governor Wang Yang's Province, Guangdong Province, villagers were not optimistic about the future: "Now we don't think Wukan will influence us that much . . . . The government has dealt with Wukan, but our situation is still messy, and they're not dealing with us."
53. Echo Hui, "Chinese Authorities Just Won't Give Up, Says Wukan Protest Leader Who Fled to US," *South China Morning Post*, March 26, 2014, http://china.timesofnews.com/wukan-protest-leader-fled-to-us-fearing-for-safety.
54. Albert O. Hirschman, *Exit, Voice, and Loyalty: Responses to Decline in Firms, Organizations, and States* (Cambridge, MA: Harvard University Press, 2007).
55. Juan Linz, "Opposition in and under an Authoritarian Regime: The Case of Spain," in *Regimes and Oppositions*, ed. Robert Dahl (New Haven, CT: Yale University Press, 1973), 192.
56. Johan Lagerkvist, "The Unknown Terrain of Social Protests in China: 'Exit,' 'Voice,' 'Loyalty,' and 'Shadow,'" *Journal of Civil Society* 11, no. 2 (2015): 137–53.
57. Johan Lagerkvist, *After the Internet, Before Democracy: Competing Norms in Chinese Media and Society* (Bern: Peter Lang, 2010), 285. Cf. the German

film *The Lives of Others* (2006), showing how censors of the secret police, the Stasi, became uneasy over their task to spy on their fellow citizens' lives and communication. I am grateful to David Shambaugh for pointing out this movie to me.
58. Lance Bennett and Alexandra Segerberg, "Social Media and the Organization of Collective Action: Using Twitter to Explore the Ecologies of Two Climate Change Protests," *The Communication Review* 14 (2011): 197–215.

PART IV
Domestic Politics—International Policies

CHAPTER 10

Is China a Global Power?

DAVID SHAMBAUGH

INTRODUCTION

The question of whether the United States and China are predestined to repeat the traditional pattern of great power competition and conflict rests on several suppositions—which are based on historical, structural, institutional, perceptual, global, regional, and domestic precedents and factors. While the other chapters in this volume focus on the first six of these, this chapter joins those of Minxin Pei and Johan Lagerkvist to examine the domestic dimension. The domestic dimension is particularly relevant to the question of potential rising power/established power conflict because power transition theory is premised primarily on the relative domestic capabilities of powers.[1] Specifically, power transition theory holds that the period when a rising power *approaches parity* with the established power is *the most* unstable time and when the two powers are most prone to conflict—which Kenneth Organski and Jacek Kugler identified as the "crossover" point.[2] In this transitional period, either the predominant power is likely to launch a preemptive war to stave off the challenge of the rising power, *or*, more commonly, the challenger may strike first. This is what Harvard political scientist Graham Allison more recently describes as "Thucydides's Trap."[3]

Thus, in order to ascertain the applicability of power transition theory to the case of the United States and China (presently and in the future), it is essential to objectively assess the *relative capabilities* of the two powers. This chapter attempts to do so by carefully examining the Chinese side of the equation—and it finds that China's comprehensive power remains *far behind* that of the United States on a *global* basis. Within Asia, however, the power gap is narrower, and thus the dangers of great power conflict in a *regional* context are far greater. But, on a global basis, China still lags considerably behind the United States—and will continue to do so for decades into the future. Thus I conclude that a *global* conflict between the United States and China is unlikely—but that a regional one is increasingly possible. In Tom Christensen's well-chosen words, China can still "pose problems without catching up."[4]

My judgment about China's relative weakness is at substantial variance with the conventional wisdom of many other observers and public opinion surveys that perceive the China juggernaut as unstoppable and that the United States and the world must therefore adjust to the reality of the Asian giant as a—perhaps *the*—major global power in the years to come. A mini-industry of "China rise" prognosticators has emerged over the past decade—all painting a picture of the twenty-first-century world in which China is a dominant actor.[5] But more recently, since 2013, a newer genre of books has appeared which questions the core strengths of China and the supposed inevitability of its rise to great power status.[6]

Such skepticism is warranted. Recall that not so long ago, in the 1980s, similar forecasts were made about Japan being "No. 1" and joining the elite club of great powers—before it sank into a three decade long stagnation and was shown to be a largely single-dimensional power (economic) that did not have a broader foundation to fall back on. Before that, it was the Soviet Union that was said to be a global superpower—over which a half-century Cold War was waged—only for it to collapse almost overnight in 1991. The post-mortem on the USSR similarly revealed a largely single-dimensional power (military) and a system that had corroded from within for decades. In the wake of the Cold War, for a while, some observers posited that the expanded and strengthened European Union would emerge as a new global power and pole in the international system—only for the EU to prove itself impotent and incompetent on a range of global challenges. Europe, too, was exposed as a largely single-dimensional power (economic).

So, when it comes to China today, a little sobriety and skepticism would seem justified. At a minimum, it behooves analysts to carefully examine the bases on which such bold prognostications are made.

It is true that China is the world's most important rising power—far exceeding the capacities of Indonesia, India, Brazil, and South Africa—and in some categories, it has already surpassed the capabilities of other "middle powers" like Russia, Japan, Britain, Germany, and France. By many measures, it seems that China is now the world's undisputed second leading power after the United States, and in some categories it has already overtaken the United States. China certainly possesses many of the trappings of a global power: the world's largest population, a large continental land mass, the world's second-largest economy, the world's largest trading nation, the world's largest consumer of energy, the world's largest greenhouse gas emitter, the world's largest foreign exchange reserves, the world's second-largest recipient and third-largest originator of foreign direct investment, the world's second-largest military budget and largest standing armed forces, a manned space program, an aircraft carrier, the world's largest museum, the world's largest hydroelectric dam, the world's largest national highway network, the world's best high-speed rail system, the world's largest number of millionaires and billionaires, the world's largest producer of many goods, and many other impressive statistics.

By these and many other measures of *capabilities*, China is seemingly a leading global power. It is certainly more than a single-dimensional power. When scrutinized carefully, though, I argue in this chapter that China's intrinsic strengths and aspirations to great power status exhibit multiple and significant weaknesses. Moreover, capabilities are but only *one* measure of national and international power—and not the most important one. Generations of social scientists have determined that a more significant indicator of power is *influence*—the ability to shape events and the actions of others. As the late political scientist Robert Dahl famously observed, "A has power over B to the extent that A can get B to do something that B would not otherwise do." Capabilities that are not converted into actions toward achieving certain ends are not worth much. Their existence may have an impressive or deterrent effect, but it is the ability to influence the action of another or the outcome of an event that matters. There are, of course, various means by which nations use their capabilities to influence the actions of others and the course of events: attraction, persuasion, co-optation, coercion, remuneration, inducement, or the threat or use of force. Power, and the exercise of it, is therefore intrinsically *relational*—the use of these and other instruments toward others in order to influence a situation to one's own benefit.

Thus, when we look at China's presence and behavior on the world stage today, we need to look beyond its superficially impressive capabilities and ask whether China is, in fact, *influencing* the actions of others, the train of events, and the trajectory of international affairs in various domains? The short answer is: not much. In very few—if any—domains can it be concluded that China is actually influencing other nations, setting global standards, or shaping global trends. While Beijing has recently stepped up its contributions to global governance in several domains since Xi Jinping came to power, it still remains a generally passive power, whose reflex action is to shy away from challenges and hide when international crises erupt. It may go along with other nations in addressing global challenges or crises, but Beijing never leads, never assembles coalitions, and never acts unilaterally. China is also a "partial power" in that it does not possess a comprehensive toolbox of capabilities to project on the world stage. To be sure, it is more than a single-dimensional power (unlike the EU, Japan, or the former Soviet Union), but it is still not yet a comprehensive power—as it lacks soft power, international diplomatic influence, and global military reach.

Moreover, when China's capabilities are carefully examined, they are actually not as strong as they may seem on first glance. Many indicators are quantitatively impressive, but they are not qualitatively so. It is the lack of *qualitative* power that translates into China's lack of real influence. The Chinese have the proverb *waiying, neiruan* (外硬 内软): strong on the outside, soft on the inside. This is an apt characterization of China today. When one scratches beneath the surface of the many impressive statistics about China, one finds pervasive weaknesses, important impediments, and a soft foundation on which to become a global power. China may turn out to be a twenty-first-century paper tiger.

China's global power position can be evaluated in five broad areas: China's international diplomacy, military capabilities, cultural and soft power, economic power, and a number of social factors. Let us examine each in turn.

CHINA'S DIPLOMATIC POWER

In formal respects, China's diplomacy has truly gone global. Over the past forty years, China has traveled a path from a nation isolated from the international community to one integrated into it. Today the People's Republic enjoys diplomatic relations with 175 countries, is a member of more than 150 international organizations, and is party to more than 300 multilateral treaties. It receives far more visiting foreign dignitaries every year than any other nation, and its own leaders travel the world regularly.

Despite this integration into the international community and Beijing's active diplomacy, the diplomatic sphere is a realm where China's position as a partial power is apparent. On the one hand, it enjoys the symbols of being a major world power (being a permanent member of the UN Security Council, a member of the G-20 and other key global bodies, and a participant in all major international summits); but, on the other hand, Chinese officials still remain remarkably reactive and passive in these venues and on many global challenges. China does not *lead*. It does not shape international diplomacy, drive other nations' policies, forge global consensus, put together coalitions, or take initiative to solve global problems. This is not to say that Beijing does not participate in multilateral efforts organized by others (usually the United States), but it never takes the initiative to lead an effort or build an international coalition. Being a global power requires getting in the middle of disputes, bringing parties together, forging coalitions and consensus, and—yes—using pressure when necessary. Beijing often prefers to sit on the sidelines and simply call for nations to solve their problems through "peaceful means" and find "win-win solutions." Such hollow invocations are hardly conducive to problem solving. Beijing is also completely allergic to coercive measures and only goes along with UN Security Council sanctions when it is clear that not doing so would leave Beijing isolated and negatively impact China's international image. This is not the behavior of a global power or leader.

Beijing's high-level diplomacy is really a kind of theatrical show, more symbolism than substance. It is intended primarily to enhance the Communist Party's legitimacy among domestic audiences by showing Chinese leaders hobnobbing with the world's elite, while signaling to the international community that it has returned to global power status after several centuries of impotence. As such, the Chinese government goes to extraordinary lengths to meticulously stage-manage its leaders' interactions with their foreign counterparts. Substantively, though, Chinese diplomacy remains remarkably risk-averse and guided by narrow national interests. Chinese diplomacy takes a kind of lowest-common-denominator approach, usually adopting the safest and least controversial position, usually waiting to see the positions of other governments before revealing its own. The notable exception to this general passivity concerns China's reflexive reactions to protect its own narrow and neuralgic self-interests: Taiwan, Tibet, Xinjiang, human rights, and its contested territorial claims. On these issues, Beijing is hypervigilant and diplomatically forceful, but its attempts to defend these interests are often clumsy and wind up being counterproductive to its international image and goals. Other than seeking to protect these narrow national interests, though, Chinese diplomacy remains extremely passive for a state of its size and importance.

When it comes to global governance—which entails contributing to the common global good proportionate to a nation's aggregate capabilities—Beijing's behavior conveys a mixed picture. On the one hand, China does contribute to various aspects of global governance: climate change, UN peacekeeping operations (UNPKO), antipiracy operations in the Gulf of Aden, counterterrorism, overseas development assistance (ODA), nonproliferation of nuclear materials, public health, disaster relief, and combatting international crime. In these areas, Beijing deserves credit. Moreover, it is apparent that since Xi Jinping came to power in 2012, China has noticeably *increased* its contributions to global governace. However, China could and *should* still do more. One obvious area is the instability in the Middle East and combatting the threats that the Islamic State (ISIS or ISIL) presents to the world. Many nations are involved in the multinational military coalition to degrade and destroy ISIS/ISIL, but China is nowhere to be seen.

Why is China's global governance diplomacy so constrained for a power of its size and capabilities? There are five main reasons. First, because China has an extremely narrow definition of its national interests that generally does not include activities outside China's sovereign borders. Second, because there exists deep skepticism inside of China about the liberal premises and basic concept of global governance, seeing it as the latest "trap" laid by the West (primarily the United States) to "bleed" China by getting it involved in crises and places where it does not have a direct national interest—thus diverting its resources and restraining its rise. Third, Chinese citizens often criticize the government for allocating resources abroad when poverty and other pressing challenges still exist at home. Fourth, because Chinese have a kind of "transactional" approach to expending effort, especially when it involves money. This grows out of Chinese commercial culture but extends into many other realms of Chinese behavior. That is, the Chinese want to know exactly what they will get back from a certain investment and when. Fifth, and finally, I do not find China to be as tied into the liberal international institutional infrastructure as John Ikenberry argues in his chapter in this volume (and elsewhere); rather, while China is institutionally embedded in the liberal institutional architecture, it clearly chafes at several of its restrictions and thus opts (like the United States) for an *à la carte* approach to global governance. China's involvement in multilateral global governance is what is known as "shallow integration"—being a formal member without necessarily accepting the underlying premises, norms, and attendant responsibilities of membership.

Thus, in the realm of diplomacy—bilateral, multilateral, and global governance—Beijing still demonstrates a distinct passivity and reluctance to get involved. It is far from being the "responsible international stakeholder" that Robert Zoellick called for in his famous 2005 speech.[7] Chinese diplomacy remains narrowly self-interested, and its involvement in global governance, while growing under Xi Jinping, is still not commensurate with being the world's No. 2 power. The real business of Chinese diplomacy is, in fact, business. Examine the composition of the Chinese president's or premier's delegations abroad and one finds large numbers of corporate CEOs—in search of energy supplies, natural resources, and trade and investment opportunities. Such mercantilist diplomacy does not earn Beijing international respect—and is, in fact, beginning to generate increasing criticisms and blowback around the world (most notably in Africa and Latin America).

CHINA'S MILITARY POWER

China's military capabilities are another area where it is a partial power: certainly a regional power, but not yet a global military power. China is not able to project conventional military power outside of its Asian neighbourhood—notwithstanding its intercontinental ballistic missiles, space program, and cyber warfare capacities. Even within Asia its military power projection capacities remain limited (although growing rapidly). It is not at all certain that China could project air and naval power on its periphery out to 2,500 nautical miles (such as in its East or South China Sea disputes) and *sustain* it long enough to wage and prevail in a conflict. Its military forces are not battle-tested, having not fought a war since 1979.

To be certain, China's military modernization has been growing steadily for twenty-five years. It now has the world's second-largest military budget ($146 billion in the 2016 official budget), the largest standing armed forces, scores of new advanced weapons, a navy that is sailing further and further out into the western Pacific Ocean and occasionally into the Indian Ocean, has rotated ships to the Gulf of Aden for several years as part of the multinational task force, and it now possesses a modest aircraft carrier. So China's military is no pushover. It is certainly capable of defending its homeland, and has likely gained the capacity to wage a successful conflict over Taiwan (absent a fast and full American intervention). China certainly is perceived to be a regional military power in Asia and thus is altering the balance of power in the region, but Chinese military forces still possess *no* global conventional power projection capabilities. China has no bases abroad (this could be changing with the establishment of some kind of military facility in Djoubuti), no long-range logistics or communications lines, and rudimentary global satellite coverage; the navy is still primarily a coastal littoral force; the air force has no long-range strike or proven stealth capacity; and the ground forces are not configured for rapid long-range deployment. While still overwhelmingly focused on its own immediate periphery, Chinese military writings do discuss developing more global capabilities over time. Beijing's "One Belt, One Road" economic initiative to connect China to Europe via the Indian Ocean and Central Asia also has military potential.

Moreover, strategically, I find China to be a "lonely power"—lacking close friends and possessing *no allies* (save a formal security treaty with North Korea). Even in China's closest relationship (Russia), elements of distrust and historical suspicions percolate beneath the surface of seemingly harmonious state-to-state relations. Not a single other nation looks to Beijing for its security and protection (except perhaps Pakistan)—thus demonstrating a distinct lack of strategic influence as a major power. This said, Beijing is beginning to develop closer military ties with several Southeast Asian countries—primarily Thailand, Cambodia, and Myanmar. It trains officers from these countries in China and sells some weapons to them. Nonetheless, most countries in Asia maintain their defense ties with the United States and improve their coordination with each other—precisely because of the uncertainty and possible threat they perceive from China. Beijing has certainly been very proactive over the past decade in establishing "strategic partnerships" with nations all around the world, but these are more rhetoric than reality and, in any event, are not very strategic in nature. They are more framework agreements for guiding bilateral relations. Beijing has also been quite proactive in creating regional dialogue groupings that also facilitate a variety of exchanges between China and the various regions, for example, the Shanghai Cooperation Organization (Eurasia), China-Arab Cooperation Forum, Forum of China-Africa Cooperation, China-Community of Latin American and Caribbean States Forum.

While these groupings are mainly to facilitate China's entry into these regions and build a variety of commercial and other exchanges, some of these organizations have military/security dimensions. While not a Chinese initiative, the Conference on Interaction and Confidence Building Measures in Asia (CICA) is another alternative security organization in which China is very active. At its 2014 annual meeting in Shanghai, Chinese President Xi Jinping outlined China's vision for the future security architecture in Asia that would include "common security, universal security, equal security, inclusive security, and comprehensive security."[8] Xi specifically rejected an alliance-based approach favored by the United States: "To beef up and entrench a military alliance targeted at a third party is not conducive to maintaining common security," and Xi implicitly made very clear that the United States should have no role in Asian security: "In the final analysis, it is for the people of Asia to run the affairs of Asia, solve the problems of Asia and uphold the security of Asia. The people of Asia have the capability and wisdom to achieve peace and stability in the region through enhanced cooperation."[9] By using the term "Asia" and not "Asia-Pacific," Xi was also implicitly excluding the United States (and presumably Australia and New Zealand) from any role in his vision for regional security.

Thus, in the security realm, China is clearly pushing back against the longstanding American-led "hub and spokes" alliance architecture in Asia and the world. This is actually not new, but rather dates to former President Jiang Zemin's 1996 enunciation of China's "New Security Concept" and the subsequent publication of a government document on the subject.[10] Since then, China has frequently attacked bilateral and multilateral alliances as "relics of the Cold War" while pushing its alternative vision for "cooperative security." To the extent that China is a *revisionist* actor in international affairs, it is in this sphere of institutionalized alliance-based security.

CHINA'S SEARCH FOR SOFT POWER

Turning from hard power to soft power, how does China stack up as a global cultural power?[11] Not very well. No other societies are taking their cultural cues from China, no other countries are seeking to copy the Chinese political system, nor is its economic system replicable elsewhere. China is not a model many other nations seek to emulate. To be certain, China's 3000+ years of civilization is much respected around the world, and everyone is impressed by the extraordinary socio-economic development of the past four decades. But admiration is much different than emulation.

The problem for China in all four realms is that it is *sui generis*, unique rather than possessing universal appeal beyond its borders or ethnic Chinese communities (the essence of soft power). Largely because of China's cultural, economic, social, and political uniqueness, its global soft power appeal remains weak. China's cultural products—art, film, literature, music, design, architecture, education—are still relatively unknown outside of China and do not (yet) set global cultural trends. As admirable as China's economic development is, it is the product of a unique combination of features that cannot be replicated in other countries (competitive economies of scale, Soviet-style state planning and industrial policy, individual entrepreneurship, a large and disciplined workforce, a large R & D establishment, and massive foreign investment). Even if a "China Model" exists (which is debatable), it is not exportable, as this combination of growth factors exists nowhere else. China's political system is similarly an eclectic amalgam of Leninist communism, Asian authoritarianism, Confucian traditionalism, and a strong internal security state. Its political distinctiveness cannot be replicated—one does not see other states trying to do so.

Despite the enormous efforts and resources the Chinese government is pouring into trying to build its soft power and improve its international image since 2008, China continues to have a mixed-to-negative global reputation. Public opinion surveys reveal that everywhere in the world perceptions of China are mixed, declining, and increasingly fraught with problems.[12] The Pew Global Attitudes Survey of 2013 (table 10.1) clearly shows that Chinese ideas and customs do not resonate well in either Latin America or Africa—precisely the regions where one would assume they would be most popular.

The same is true in Asia, according to an extensive survey conducted by the Chicago Council on Global Affairs.[13] China certainly has its work cut out for it in explaining itself better to the world. Many of its policies rub up against basic foreign (especially Western) sensitivities—particularly concerning its political system, treatment of human rights, minority policies, and "legal" practices. Detaining and imprisoning high-profile dissidents and artists like Liu Xiaobo and Ai Weiwei hardly helps China's international image. Moreover, China's government policy making remains opaque (despite improvements). Its society is complex and difficult for foreigners to access. Restrictions on foreign news reporting in China are severe,

Table 10.1 SPREAD OF CHINESE IDEAS AND CUSTOMS

	Chinese music, movies, and television			Chinese ideas and customs are spreading here		
	Like	Dislike	DK	Good	Bad	DK
	%	%	%	%	%	%
Argentina	11	68	21	28	55	17
Bolivia	37	44	19	30	51	19
Brazil	19	75	6	36	58	6
Chile	25	50	25	27	57	16
El Salvador	28	61	11	37	50	13
Mexico	19	56	25	27	55	18
Venezuela	38	58	4	37	51	12
Ghana	42	51	6	31	60	9
Kenya	36	45	19	54	34	11
Nigeria	54	32	14	58	24	18
Senegal	32	54	14	62	25	14
S. Africa	22	60	19	37	46	17
Uganda	28	46	26	31	46	23

Source: Pew Research Center (2013).

and make China more rather than less difficult to comprehend. The language of China's officialdom often does not translate well across national boundaries, coming across as hollow slogans with unintelligible content. Ultimately, there is not much—if anything—the Chinese government can do about this soft power deficit. Soft power appeal, as noted above, comes primarily and intrinsically from *society*—not from government. Moreover, China's public diplomacy (or "external propaganda work") remains clumsy, rhetorical, propagandistic, and relatively unsophisticated. One might say that China's public diplomacy actually *hinders* China's soft power.

CHINA'S ECONOMIC POWER

What about China's global economic power? This is the one area where one would expect China to be a global power and trendsetter—yet again I find that its impact is much more shallow than anticipated. As in other areas, it is quantitatively impressive but qualitatively weak. When evaluated qualitatively instead of quantitatively, China's global economic profile is not very impressive. It remains a processing and assembly economy—*not* a creative and inventive one. Most of the goods that are assembled or produced in China for export are intellectually created elsewhere. China's rampant theft of intellectual property and its government programs to spur "indigenous innovation" (which pour billions into domestic R & D every year) are clear admissions of its failure to create. This may—and likely will—change over time, but to date China is not setting global standards in hardly any technology or product line (or, for that matter, in the natural sciences, medical sciences, social sciences, or humanities).

If China is to spur innovation, it will, of course, have to invest more in research and development funding. In 2009 China spent only 1.7 percent of its GDP on R & D, compared with 2.9 percent in the United States and 2.8 percent in Germany, and over 3.3 percent in Japan.[14] The "research intensity" of China's R & D spending does not even rank it in the top twenty nations globally, as an estimated 80 percent is spent on product development and only 5 percent on basic research.[15] China's lack of Nobel Prizes is also a telling indication. Between 1949 and 2010, 584 Nobel Prizes were awarded. Ethnic Chinese won ten of these (eight in the sciences), but eight of the ten worked outside of China.[16] The two exceptions were the Liu Xiaobo's 2010 Peace Prize and Mo Yan's 2011 prize for literature. Citations in professional journals are another indicator. In the world's most-cited articles (across all academic disciplines), Chinese scholars account for only 4 percent—whereas Americans account for 49 percent.[17]

China's economy is now mired in the infamous "middle income trap." The only way out of the trap is through innovation—as Japan, South Korea, Singapore, and Taiwan previously proved.[18] And this requires much more than government investment in R & D—it fundamentally requires an educational system premised on critical thinking and freedom of exploration. This, in turn, requires a political system that is relatively open, democratic, and does not permit censorship or "no go zones" in research. Students and intellectuals must be rewarded—not persecuted or penalized—for challenging conventional wisdom and making mistakes. Until this occurs, China will be forever caught in the middle income trap—assembling and producing but not creating and inventing.

Seen in this light, China's economic power is much weaker than it appears on the surface. When examining China's overseas direct investment (ODI), similar weaknesses are evident. Despite the high government priority for Chinese firms to "go out" into the world, so far China's foreign investment remains quite small. Its total stock of ODI barely places China in the top twenty globally, although its annual outflows are growing rapidly and now ranks number three in the world ($112 billion in 2014). Yet, this remains one-fourth of American ODI in the same year.

More significantly, as in other areas of China's global profile, one needs to delve beyond and behind the quantitative statistics to ask qualitative questions: where does it go, and is it real investment? Scratch beneath the surface of China's ODI figures, and they are not all that they are cracked up to be. The top four destinations of China's ODI (2011) reveals that it is capital flowing into tax havens (British Virgin Islands, Grand Cayman Islands, Luxembourg) or into Hong Kong. Thus, this is not foreign investment per se—it is money being parked abroad in safe havens. This is not only true for Chinese government and companies, but also for individual assets. The 2014 annual *Blue Book on Chinese International Migration*, compiled by the Center for China & Globalization, recently reported that since 1990 a total of 9,343,000 Chinese had emigrated abroad, taking 2.8 trillion *renminbi* (US $46 billion) with them![19] This is not a new development, but has been a growing trend over the past decade. When a nation's economic elite leave in such large numbers and are so anxious to secure their personal financial savings abroad, it speaks volumes about their (lack of) confidence in their own domestic political and economic systems.

Recently, though, China's ODI profile and geographic footprint have been changing. China is ramping up its investments and purchases across Asia, in Europe, and the United States. Chinese buyers are snatching up all kinds of assets—residential and commercial properties, factories, industrial parks, R & D facilities, farms, forests, mines, oil and gas fields, and various other resources. Chinese corporations are aggressively snatching up foreign companies through mergers and acquisitions (M & As). Individual Chinese have also been buying large amounts of valuable art on the international auction market.[20] Thus, the profile of Chinese outbound investment is rapidly changing, but its impact and receptivity abroad remains uncertain.

What about Chinese multinational corporations? How competitive are they abroad? As in other categories, there is much more weakness than strength. On the surface, judging from the Global Fortune 500 rankings, Chinese companies now rank second only to American multinationals (50 vs. 120 in 2013). But the Fortune 500 rankings are calculated on the basis of total revenue and profit—not *where* a company makes its money. When examining the fifty Chinese companies on the 2013 list (well down from 76 in 2012), it is quickly apparent that relatively few even operate abroad, and only a handful earn more than half their revenues overseas. So these are not truly *multinational* corporations, but are really domestic corporate actors.

Many Chinese firms may aspire to go global, but thus far those that have tried have not fared very well. To date, there have been many more failures than success stories among aspiring Chinese multinationals. Many Chinese M & As have stumbled because they did not do their due diligence beforehand or because of the clash of corporate cultures. By all accounts, the major weakness of Chinese multinationals is human resources—particularly management. Multilingual and multicultural managers are scarce. Chinese companies and their management have displayed an inability to escape their own national corporate culture and business practices. Because of their preference for hierarchy and clearly defined workplace roles, the Chinese tend not to adapt well to "flatter" management structures that prize decentralization and individual initiative. These proclivities have resulted in repeated culture clashes in Chinese mergers with Western companies. Chinese companies have also demonstrated difficulties adapting to foreign legal, regulatory, tax, and political environments. Transparency and corporate governance are not attributes normally associated with Chinese companies—whose decision-making processes are usually opaque, whose business practices are frequently corrupt, and whose accounting procedures are often fraudulent. Not only have these tendencies negatively impacted business operations abroad, but also Chinese companies trying to list on foreign stock markets. Many Chinese companies have been found to have filed fraudulent information with securities regulators in the United States prior to their Initial Public Offerings (IPOs).

The lack of Chinese corporate competitiveness is also evident when it comes to international brands. Only a handful of Chinese companies have been able to establish a brand presence abroad: Alibaba, Tencent, Tsingtao Beer, Haier white goods, Huawei telecoms, Air China, Geely automobiles, and a handful of others. But not a single Chinese company ranks among the *Business Week/Interbrand* Top 100 global brands! The popularity and presence of Chinese multinational corporations and brands will surely improve over time, but so far most Chinese companies have struggled in the global environment. Thus even in the economic sphere, where we would expect China to exhibit real international strength and power, qualitative weaknesses again underlie the impressive quantitative statistics.

STILL A DEVELOPING COUNTRY

Other measures of China's domestic capacities also do not indicate very high or positive global rankings. In 2013, Freedom House ranked China 179 out of 191 countries for freedom of the press and 86 out of 91 for internet freedom. Since 2002, the World Bank's composite Worldwide Governance Indicators have consistently ranked China in the 30th percentile for political stability, 50th percentile for government effectiveness, 40th percentile for regulatory quality, 30th percentile for control of corruption and rule of law, and 10th percentile for accountability. The World Economic Forum ranked China only 29th globally on its composite Global Competitiveness Index in 2013, 68th for corruption, 54th for business ethics, and 82nd for accountability. Transparency International ranks China even lower (80th) in its 2013 international corruption index. In virtually all these estimates and categories, China has *deteriorated* over the past decade.

By these and other measures, it is clear that China's global presence and reputation is mixed at best. In many categories China finds itself clustered together with the least well-performing and least respected countries in the world.

The United Nations 2013 Human Development Report further illustrates that despite the considerable and admirable socioeconomic progress that China has made since the 1980s, the nation remains very much a developing country. The PRC ranks 101st in the overall human development index (out of 187 countries surveyed). The average per capita income is now nearly $9,000, yet 13.1 percent of the population still live on under $1.25 per day. In life expectancy, infant mortality, health care provision, educational quality, and inequality, China still lags well behind industrialized nations. Its environmental contamination and pollution (air, ground, and water) is the worst in the world and is contributing to rapidly rising cancer rates. Despite recent government efforts to expand primary and catastrophic healthcare delivery and insurance, most Chinese still face great uncertainties when illness strikes. The Gini coefficient (measuring income inequality) is now nearly .5, among the highest in the world. China's primary and secondary schools are producing world-class test results, but the university system still lags well behind global leaders. These observations are not meant to belittle China's miraculous developmental accomplishments over the past three decades, but they are simply further reminders that China is nowhere near the top of the global tables in many categories of development.

CONCLUSION AND OUTLOOK

Taken together, these domestic and global indicators make abundantly clear that China remains far from being a global power—and lags well behind the United States in virtually every category of power and influence. Whether measuring by capability or influence, China still has a very long way to go before it can be considered a global power.

What does this argument and evidence presented in this chapter mean for the subject of this volume—will China's rise result in conflict and war (with the United States)? My main argument that China remains a very long way from becoming a global power on par with the United States (in all the categories explored above) suggests that *on a global structural basis* conflict and war are not at all likely. This is simply because China is not yet a comprehensive and influential global power and thus is not yet challenging the United States globally. To be certain, China's global *footprint* is growing, and China now has a diplomatic, economic, and cultural (but not security) presence on every continent—and is the only other nation aside from the United States to possess such global presence. However, this presence has yet to be translated into *influence* (except in the economic-energy spheres), and until it does so, China will not be a frontal challenge to American interests. While China *is* promoting an alternative set of regional institutions and they *are* being promoted as a distinct alternative to US-led alliances and liberal norms, these efforts have so far not seemingly gained much traction and thus cannot be said to be a successful challenge to the United States. This was certainly the case prior to the Trump administration in 2017—which has precipitated a dramatic decline in America's global standing and influence.[21] Whether China can take advantage of this precipitous decline in American standing in the world remains to be seen.[22]

Thus, on a global structural basis, I do not yet see power transition theorists being proven correct.[23] To be sure, the two titans remain "tangled" (as described in my earlier edited volume[24]), and the competitive dimension of the Sino-American relationship is steadily rising and has now become *the* dominant feature in the US-China relationship, eclipsing the cooperative element, but it has not yet crossed the threshold into an adversarial relationship.[25] Over time this could well occur as the result of one or two developments.

First, a global US-China clash could occur if China (like the former Soviet Union) began to aggressively push an alternative global order based on illiberal principles and Beijing begins to intervene in other countries around the world to establish and expand its influence. This would necessarily involve promoting alternative norms and institutional arrangements (bilateral and multilateral) that were explicitly aimed against the United States and its allies. To some extent we already see China doing this (in tandem with Russia) through the Shanghai Cooperation Organization (SCO), the Asian Infrastructure Investment Bank (AIIB), CICA, and "New Security Concept." But, thus far, other than the BRICS nations (Brazil, Russia, India, China, South Africa) and the Central Asian states, Beijing's campaign is not gaining much global traction. China is a "partial revisionist" but still, on the whole, remains a participaint in and an upholder of the post-World War II institutional order. Thus, with respect to the first integrating theme of the volume, it cannot be said that the US and China will clash over competing global systems.

The second way in which a US-China clash could occur is the much more likely scenario of the two powers being drawn into a military conflict in Asia—affecting the US-led regional *security order* (the second integrating theme of the volume). If this occurred, it is very likely that such a conflict could not be contained within Asia—but would very likely lead to direct attacks on each nation's homelands as well as their assets around the world. Even a military accident (like the EP-3 crisis of 2001), a skirmish over disputed islands, or freedom of navigation in the East or South China Seas could easily escalate quickly. Third-party states could also trigger a confrontation between the two powers. Moreover, for decades the very real possibility of a conflict over Taiwan has also existed—and that possibility will always remain as long as the island resists absorption into a unitary political state with the mainland. The dramatic amelioration of cross-strait tensions in recent years has been a welcome development and has removed much of the security anxiety that has long existed, but tensions over Taiwan could always flare up again in the future.

More likely than a conflict over Taiwan is one involving America's allies Japan and the Philippines. In both cases President Barack Obama made it explicitly clear during his April 2014 visit to both countries that the United States would honor its bilateral security treaty (alliance) commitments in the case of armed conflict with China over their disputed maritime claims in the East and South China Seas respectively.[26] The very real danger of a US-China military clash triggered by China seeking to assert its claims in the East or South China Seas cannot to be easily dismissed. Most worrisome is that should a limited (air or naval) military engagement occur, it would not be easily controlled or contained. Horizontal and vertical escalation could rapidly take place, including US military strikes against mainland Chinese targets and Chinese reprisals against the American homeland. History is filled with examples of major wars being triggered by seemingly minor incidents—China's territorial claims in Asia could be just such a time bomb waiting to detonate. History is also filled with examples of major wars being fueled by aggrieved nationalism—which Chinese society and government today have in spades. Any of these possible conflict scenarios would necessary disrupt the stability of the Asian and international order (the third integrating theme of this volume).

This is a toxic cocktail—China's aggrieved nationalism combined with minor territorial disputes juxtaposed against a superpower's commitments to its allies and maintaining its primacy in Asia and the world. While China remains nowhere near to challenging the United States' primacy on a global basis, this combination of factors close to China's borders are potentially incendiary. Hopefully, Washington and Beijing will have the good sense to avoid being drawn into direct conflict initiated by such indirect factors. But this is not at all a certainty. All sides (Washington, Beijing, and regional actors) seem to be hardening their positions.

The only way to ameliorate this increasing security dilemma is, perhaps, as Australian strategist Hugh White has suggested—for the United States to unilaterally forgo its claim to regional primacy in Asia and to share power and responsibility for regional security with China and other regional powers (White envisions a concert of powers).[27] But for America to pull back from its half-century-long primacy in Asia is akin to Britain's "East of Suez" strategic retreat. This is hardly likely to occur. To the contrary, the Obama administration's "pivot" to Asia strategic reorientation is evidence of just the opposite—the United States is *increasing* its presence, influence, and commitments in the region.[28] The Trump administration has reiterated America's security commitments in Asia.

This suggests the future of international relations in Asia will be characterized by US-China strategic competition rather than strategic cooperation. Managing and containing the strategic competition, so that it does not bleed into a full adversarial relationship or that a minor incident triggers a broader conflict, will be *the priority* challenge for both governments in the future.

NOTES

This chapter draws in places from my article "The Illusion of Chinese Power" that originally appeared in *The National Interest*, No. 132, July/August 2014, pp. 39–48.

1. See Robert S. Ross and Zhu Feng, eds., *China's Ascent: Power, Security, and the Future of International Politics* (Ithaca, NY: Cornell University Press, 2008), 314. In particular, see the chapter by Jack Levy, "Power Transition Theory and the Rise of China." Also relevant are Steve Chan, *China, The U.S., and the Power Transition Theory: A Critique* (London: Routledge, 2008); David Lai, *The United States and China in Power Transition* (Carlisle Barracks, PA: U.S. Army War College Strategic Studies Institute, 2011).
2. A. F. K. Organski and Jacek Kugler, *The War Ledger* (Chicago: University of Chicago Press, 1980).
3. Graham Allison, *Destined for War: Can America and China Escape Thucydides's Trap* (Boston and New York: Houghton Mifflin Harcourt, 2017).
4. Thomas C. Christensen, "Posing Problems without Catching Up: China's Rise and Challenges for U.S. Security Policy," *International Security* 25, no. 4 (2001):5–44.
5. See Martin Jacques, *When China Rules the World: The Rise of the Middle Kingdom and the End of the Western World*, 2nd ed. (London: Allen Lane, 2012); Arvind Subramanian, *Eclipse: Living in the Shadow of China's Economic Dominance* (Washington, DC: Petersen Institute of International Economics, 2011); James Kynge, *China Shakes the World: A Titan's Rise and Troubled Future* (London: Mariner Books, 2007); Aaron Friedberg, *A Contest for Supremacy: China, America, and the Struggle for Mastery in Asia* (New York: W. W. Norton, 2011); Ted Fishman, *China Inc.: How the Rise of the Next Superpower Challenges America and the World* (New York: Scribner, 2006); Juan Pablo Cardinal and Heriberto Araujo, *China's Silent Army: The Pioneers, Traders, Fixers and Workers Who are Remaking the World in China's Image* (New York: Crown Books, 2013); Larry M. Wortzel, *The Dragon Extends Its Reach: Chinese Military Power Goes Global* (Dulles, VA: Potomac Books, 2013); David Kang, *China Rising* (New York: Columbia University Press, 2007); Bates Gill, *Rising Star* (Washington, DC: Brookings, 2007).
6. See David Shambaugh, *China Goes Global: The Partial Power* (Oxford: Oxford University Press, 2013); Jonathan Fenby, *Will China Dominate the 21st Century?* (Cambridge: Polity, 2014); Jonathan Fenby, *Tiger Head, Snake Tail: China Today* (New York: Simon & Schuster, 2013); Mel Gurtov, *Will This Be China's Century? A Skeptic's View* (Boulder, CO: Lynne Reinner, 2013); Regina M. Abrami, William C. Kirby, and F. Warren McFarlan, *Can China Lead? Reaching the Limits of Power and Growth* (Cambridge, MA: Harvard Business Review Press, 2014); Geoff Dyer, *The Contest of the Century: The New of Competition with China—And How America Can Win* (New York: Knopf, 2014); Josef Joffe, *The Myth of America's Decline* (New York: W. W. Norton, 2014); Timothy Beardson,

Stumbling Giant: The Threats to China's Future (New Haven, CT: Yale University Press, 2013); David Shambaugh, *China's Future* (Cambridge: Polity, 2016); Orville Schell and John DeLury, *Wealth and Power: China's Long March to the 21st Century* (New York: Random House, 2013). This new wave of skepticism about China's rise was presaged much earlier in provocative and prescient articles by Avery Goldstein and the late Gerald Segal. See Avery Goldstein, "Great Expectations: Interpreting China's Arrival," *International Security* 22, no. 3 (Winter 1997–1998): 36–73; Gerald Segal, "Does China Matter?," *Foreign Affairs*, September/October 1999, 24–36. For further discussion of Segal's article and thesis, see Barry Buzan and Rosemary Foot, eds., *Does China Matter? A Reassessment* (London: Routledge, 2004).

7. Robert B. Zoellick, "Whither China: From Membership to Responsibility" (speech at the National Committee on U.S.-China Relations, September 21, 2005, http://2001-2009.state.gov/s/d/former/zoellick/rem/53682.htm).
8. His Excellency Xi Jinping, "Remarks at the Fourth Summit of Conference on Interaction and Confidence Building Measures in Asia," Shanghai, May 21, 2014, available at: http://www.china.org.cn/world/2014-05/28/content_32511846.htm.
9. Ibid.
10. "China's Position Paper on the New Security Concept," August 6, 2002, available at: http://www.china-un.org/eng/xw/t27742.htm.
11. For further analysis, see David Shambaugh, "China's Soft Power Push: The Search for Respect," *Foreign Affairs*, July/August 2015, pp. 99–107.
12. "Global Image of the United States and China," Pew Research Center, July 18, 2013, available at: http://www.pewglobal.org/2013/07/18/global-image-of-the-united-states-and-china/.
13. Chicago Council on Global Affairs, *Soft Power in Asia Survey*, available at: https://www.brookings.edu/wp-content/uploads/2012/04/0617_east_asia_report.pdf.
14. "International Comparisons of Gross Domestic Expenditures on R&D, and R&D Share of Gross Domestic Product," National Science Foundation, available at: https://www.nsf.gov/statistics/seind14/index.cfm/chapter-4/tt04-04.htm.
15. As noted in Beardson, *Stumbling Giant*, 90.
16. Ibid., 104.
17. "Outputs of S&E Research: Articles and Patents," National Science Foundation, http://www.nsf.gov/statistics/seind12/c5/c5s4.htm#s4.
18. The World Bank and Development Research Council of the State Council, *China 2030: Building a Modern, Harmonious, and Creative Society* (Washington, DC: The International Bank for Reconstruction and Development and Development Research Center of the State Council, 2013), 12.
19. No Author, "Outflow of Wealth Accelerates as More Chinese Emigrate," *Xinhua News Agency*, February 7, 2014.
20. See Shambaugh, *China Goes Global*, 248–52.
21. Pew Research Center, "U.S. Image Suffers as Publics Around World Question Trump's Leadership," June 26, 2017, available at: http://www.pewglobal.org/2017/06/26/u-s-image-suffers-as-publics-around-world-question-trumps-leadership/.
22. See David Shambaugh, "China Rethinks its Global Role in the Age of Trump," Bloomberg View, June 13, 2017, available at: https://www.bloomberg.com/view/articles/2017-06-13/china-rethinks-its-global-role-in-the-age-of-trump.

23. See Zbigniew Brzezinski and John Mearsheimer, "Clash of the Titans," *Foreign Policy*, January 5, 2005, pp. 46-48.
24. David Shambaugh, *Tangled Titans: The United States & China* (Lanham, MD: Rowman & Littlefield, 2013).
25. See David Shambaugh, "Tangled Titans: Conceptualizing the U.S.-China Relationship," ibid, pp. 3-26
26. See David Shambaugh, "America Reengages Asia," *The Asan Forum*, May 23, 2014, available at: http://www.theasanforum.org/america-reengages-asia/.
27. Hugh White, *The China Choice: Why We Should Share Power* (Oxford: Oxford University Press, 2013).
28. See David Shambaugh, "Assessing the American 'Pivot' to Asia," *Strategic Studies Quarterly* (Summer 2013), pp. 10–18; "President Obama's Asia Scorecard," *The Wilson Quarterly*, Winter 2016, http://wilsonquarterly.com/quarterly/the-post-obama-world/president-obamas-asia-scorecard/.

CHAPTER 11

Despite the "New Assertiveness," China Is Not Up for Challenging the Global Order

ZHANG RUIZHUANG

INTRODUCTION: IS THE WOLF REALLY COMING THIS TIME?

Ever since China set out its new long march of "peaceful development" (aka "peaceful rise" in later years) in 1978, especially after the world had witnessed its shocking growth rate in the first three decades, people started to ask, what would a rising China mean for the rest of the world? Would it contribute to the international community positively or negatively? Would it play a constructive or destructive role in the existing world order? Quite often since the 1990s we have heard the "China threat thesis" asserting that a grown China could be nothing but a troublemaker for the world. For too many times people heard the cry "wolf!" but never saw it coming. This time, however, is said to be different: the wolf is coming indeed!

Two major developments in world affairs since 2007 caused dramatic changes in many Chinese attitudes toward their own country and the world. On the one hand, the Western World suffered a series of economic setbacks culminating in a world financial crisis. On the other, China overtook Japan in GDP in 2010 to become the second-largest economy in the world. Moreover, statistics show that China surpassed Germany to become the top exporting country in 2009, while it overtook the United States to become number one in merchandise trade in 2012.

While many Chinese were still doubtful about the newly acquired number-two status of their own country (judged against their own living standard), tides of enthusiastic applause from the West helped convince some to accept this new title. Fred Bergsten, a distinguished American economist, invented the term "G2," suggesting that G8 might be replaced by G2 (Group of Two, i.e., US and China) in managing the word affairs.[1] As if the expression was not sensational enough, another neologism was coined by a Harvard professor Naill Ferguson —"Chimerica."[2] Few Chinese had read Ferguson's essay and no one cared about what he really meant by the term; they (misled by Chinese media and so-called experts) simply took the liberty to interpret it as the symbol of China's new pride: Americans need us and want us so much that they wish to join us!

THE CHINA MODEL

Beginning in 1840 China suffered aggression, defeat, plunder, exploitation, and humiliation at the hand of Western powers for over a century. In 1958, Mao Zedong promised to lead China to catch up with the United Kingdom in economic terms within fifteen years, but his Great Leap Forward failed miserably. After the opening up in the 1980s, Chinese people were stunned by the gap they found between China and the developed West. For too long, Chinese national pride had been suppressed and the pressure of self-abasement had accumulated so much so that a release was in desperate need. Now that the marvel of "catching up" had appeared before the eyes of the world, some leading Chinese scholars could not wait to jump on the bandwagon to declare that China had become a superpower.

Yan Xuetong, for one, argued that the current international structure was changing from "unipolarity plus" (one superpower plus several great powers) to "bipolarity plus" (two superpowers plus several great powers), suggesting China was turning into the second superpower.[3] Even more sensationally, he published an essay "How China Can Defeat America" in the *New York Times*,[4] leaving readers with the impression that China had already become a rival on par with the United States. Another professor from Tsinghua University, Hu Angang, was a little more cautious in his new book[5] in predicting that China was to become a "new type of superpower" in 2020—that is only a few years down the road.

For some Chinese scholars, the success of China's economic development is beyond doubt and not worth arguing any more. What is worth doing now is to sum up and generalize China's successful experience. Inspired by Joshua Cooper Ramo's monograph *The Beijing Consensus*,[6] Beijing

University professor Pan Wei has been busy since 2008 writing essays and making speeches on the subject of the "China Model" (aka "China Path"), which culminated in a book coedited with Maya: *Sixty Years of the People's Republic and the China Model* (Triad Press, 2010). Later on, Pan collaborated with Maya again to produce a collection of essays by fifteen prominent authors in a variety of fields entitled *Self-Confidence in Path: How China Made It—Brand New Model of Great Power Rising in Human History* (Beijing United Press, 2013). For people like Pan Wei and Ma Ya, China has shown the world a great success not only in its economic development, but also in its sociopolitical institutions and values system. For the first time in modern history, China no longer needs to feel inferior to Western civilization. Such theses play right into the hands of the official propaganda apparatus, which has been advocating "three self-confidences" put forward by Xi Jinping: self-confidence in (Deng Xiaoping's) theory, in (China's developmental) path, and in (China's socio-political) system.

As early as 2006, people in the West started talking about the upcoming "Chinese Century"[7] and then about "When China rules the world."[8] Emboldened by such imported exaggerations, a group of so-called angry youth (愤青) tending toward radical nationalism followed suit with their own book, bellowing, "China Is Unhappy!"[9] Wang Xiaodong, a core figure among the authors, made clear his points of view in a series of interviews and newspaper essays: China is the most successful country in today's world; therefore we should present to the world the China Model. We Chinese should crush evil and maintain peace for the good people of the world (除暴安良), and we should manage for the whole world more resources far beyond our border, because history has proven that we can do a better job than any other nation or people in this regard. In other words, we are fully capable of maintaining order and managing resources for the world, and we should make greater contributions to the welfare of the world.[10] This time, he continued, the financial crisis shows an overall decay from the top down to the bottom in American society, suggesting the end of an era, and not just for Wall Street.[11]

Upon reading the triumphalist lines cited above, one cannot but question what the Chinese are up to. Are they ready to take over the world or at least remodel the world order? In the past thirty years of China's rise, many people in the West have been highly alerted by the rapid growth of China's economic strength and are very suspicious about China's intentions with its newly acquired power. In the West, and especially in the United States, the 1990s witnessed volley after volley of uproars about the "China threat." In the first decade of this century, one heated debate about China centered on whether it was a revisionist or status quo state. Now the new catchword for the latest round of alarm is the "new assertiveness."[12] With the impressive growth of China's national power, people wonder if this time the wolf is truly coming.

While it is legitimate and understandable to be concerned with the triumphalist attitude within China toward itself and the world, it is important to distinguish between the popular mood and the government stance. And when it comes to the official position, it is important to distinguish between the rhetoric and the policies, between the deviation and the well established stance. For instance, even though many pundits are boastful about China's "economic marvel," the Chinese government has nonetheless remained low-key about its self-identity. Yang Jiechi, a member of the State Council and the former foreign minister, made it clear that "China's fundamental identity as a developing country has not changed."[13] He moreover stated, "There is indeed such a point of view in the international public opinion claiming the gravity of world power is shifting from the West to the East. I don't concur with such a view."[14]

True, in China's official foreign policy jargon, there are indeed slogans such as "promoting the New International Political and Economic Order (NIPEO),"[15] indicating a desire to reshape the current global order. Yet upon careful examination, one may find it is nothing more than rhetoric posing no threat at all to the international status quo. There are three reasons for this assessment. First, most contents of NIPEO fall within the bounds of United Nation Charter and hence are compliant with the current global order. Second, even with the full text of the Chinese version of New International Political Order (NIPO), one can only find highly abstract principles with no operational directives. In other words, NIPO is not meant for practical implementation but only for propaganda consumption. Third, New International Economic Order (NIEO) has come into being since 1970s whereas NIPO since 2002, yet the Chinese government has done nothing so far in promoting them in terms of modifying the existing rules and norms.

It is certainly an understatement, however, to say that assertiveness in Chinese foreign relations behavior has not increased at all. One prominent change can be found in Chinese leaders' self-confidence in justifying Chinese policies both at home and abroad, which is obviously enhanced by the economic achievements in the past thirty years. In 2009, for instance, then Vice President Xi Jinping declared to the world when he paid a visit to Mexico, "There are some foreigners who had eaten their fill and had nothing better to do, pointing their fingers at our affairs. China does not, first, export revolution; second, export poverty and hunger; or third, cause unnecessary trouble for you. What else is there to say?"[16] His remark was not prompted by any particular incident but was meant to be a preemptive warning against any kind of foreign intervention, including critical lecturing.

As if this line were not tough enough, there has been indeed some hawkishness in the discourse of the Chinese military leaders as of late. One example is that when American Secretary of Defense Chuck Hagel visited China in May 2014, the Vice Chairman of the Chinese Central Military Committee, General Fan Changlong, told him straightforwardly, "Mr. Secretary has made some remarks recently with which the Chinese people are dissatisfied.... The US House passed a bill with regard to arms sale to Taiwan, and it was completely wrong."[17] Also in talks with Hagel, Chinese Defense Minister General Chang Wanquan asked the US to "correct" a series of "wrong words and deeds" delivered recently by "high ranking officials in American government and the military."[18] One month later, the Chinese General Chief of Staff and his American counterpart had a heated exchange of complaints and accusations when the Chinese general Fang Fenghui visited the United States. Fang criticized the US rebalancing strategy in the West Pacific, blaming it for instigating Japan and other neighbors of China in the South China Sea to maneuver against China. He declared, "We are not stirring up trouble, nor are we afraid of trouble; we have been steadfast in safeguarding our sovereignty, security and territorial integrity. We would never yield a single inch of land we inherited from our ancestors."[19]

These are clearly signs pointing to China's so-called new assertiveness, since it was very rare for military leaders to air their viewpoints openly and publicly, let alone critically with such controversial "in your face" comments. But do these signs suggest that China is out to change course in dealing with the outside world? Not likely, and the reason lies in the fact that these tough words are not followed by any tough deeds. Yes, China did suspend a Sino-US joint working group on cyber-hacking after five of its military officers were charged by the United States for cyber-theft, but similar suspensions of various programs of bilateral cooperation used as weapon of protest and pressure can be traced back to early 1980s and have always been used intermittently. Then what about the escalated tensions in the East China Sea and South China Sea? China's territorial claims in those areas are decades, if not centuries old; there is nothing new about them.

To sum up, the phenomenal growth of Chinese economy accompanied with triumphalist discourses from within China have made the rest of the world wonder if China is out to reshape the world, as all great powers have tended to do when their power grew rapidly. Upon careful examination of the current situation in China, we may find that this is not the case if only we distinguish between popular mood and governmental stance, between official rhetoric and policies, and between new changes and old patterns. Why is it not so? Let me examine some of the most substantial determinants of China's position toward the current global order in the next section.

NATIONAL POWER: THE KEY DETERMINANT

One of the most important, if not *the* most important, determinant is the country's power position in the world. And the reason is simple: only the most powerful countries can afford to be revisionist, as it takes power to challenge and reform the existing world order. This is a question of capability: whether one can or cannot possibly mess with the world affairs. Since World War II, only the United States (with its Western allies, which are great strategic assets, part of its global power) has had the power to establish the world order. While China appears to be powerful enough to play a revisionist role, it is not actually as strong as it appears to be. Do not be fooled by some false impressions, as the saying goes in Chinese: there is a lot of water in it!

Take GDP, the index everyone is talking about nowadays regarding China, the reason for which people label China as the second-largest economy in the world. But how reliable is this indicator? The official GDP is published by the Chinese State Bureau of Statistics each year, yet in the past ten years, the national figures were at odds with the sum of all provinces added up by a difference of 4–20 percent![20] And this is not the only source for statistical error: a HSBC/PKU economist found up to 10 percent error in official Chinese figures due to miscalculation of the inflation factor.[21]

The unreliability of GDP lies not only in the inaccuracy of the figure, but also in its implication for the national economy. The problem is, how much Chinese GDP is really Chinese? And how much does it have to do with Chinese interests? The *People's Daily* once ran a story disclosing that China earns only thirty-five cents for a Barbie doll assembled in China that is sold in the United States for twenty dollars.[22] If this is truly the case, then the Chinese GDP generated by the so-called export processing industry does not much benefit the Chinese. And the problem is not limited to the "export processing" industry. According to official statistics, among the twenty-eight main industries that China has opened up, foreign capital has controlled twenty-one industries as a whole, with foreign shares at more than 70 percent, and controls the top five enterprises in each of the twenty-eight industries.[23] China meant to achieve national industrialization or industrial upgrading through globalization but ended up with its national industries mostly falling under foreign control instead.[24]

In order to get a true and accurate picture of the Chinese economy, we should not focus only on a few selected indices such as GDP or the total amount of industrial production or foreign trade. To be sure, with the largest population and the third- or fourth-largest territory in the world, China's economy is easy to stand out by sheer size. No doubt: it is huge—but is it strong? We may see quite a different picture if we check out more metrics of the economy. First, big is not always good. In his recent visit to Europe, Chinese President Xi Jinping told his audience in a speech that more than 200 million Chinese are still living under the poverty line set by the World Bank—that is roughly the population of France, Germany, and the United Kingdom combined.[25] China's population in poverty is still the second-largest in the world, although nobody would deny China's great achievement in lifting about a half-billion people out of poverty in three decades. Second, anything measured in "per capita" terms regarding China would appear humble, such as GDP per capita: China's ranking is only 97 out of 187 economies, at about the same level as Thailand and Turkmenistan.[26]

The Chinese economy's low efficiency, high consumption of resources, severe environmental pollution, and its labor-intensive/low-tech industrial structure aggravated by the lack of innovation, have all made its development hard to sustain. The efficiency of the Chinese economy is extremely low, with its overall labor productivity being only 5.9 percent of the United States, 7.7 percent of Japan, and 24.8 percent of Russia.[27] In 2009, China's and Japan's share of world GDP was about the same (8.6 percent vs. 8.7 percent), but China's share of world consumption of coal and petroleum were 46.9 percent and 10.4 percent respectively, compared with Japan's 3.3 percent and 5.1 percent.[28] Accordingly, China's carbon dioxide emission for each million-dollar-GDP was 12 times higher than Japan and 5 times higher than the US, and was ranked 57 out of 60 countries.[29] Among the 10 worst polluted cities worldwide, 7 are in China, whereas among 500 Chinese cities, only 5 reached the air quality recommended by WHO.[30] In the meanwhile, a government report disclosed that 70 percent of the nation's rivers are classified in the "Hazardous 5" category—they are so badly polluted that their water quality is too poor not only for drinking but even for industrial usage.[31]

THE CHALLENGE OF DOMESTIC STABILITY

Other than pure economic factors that are major roadblocks for China's sustainable development, there are problems of social equality and political stability too. In the last three decades, China's national wealth and average personal income have increased twelve-fold. Unfortunately, instead of making everyone better off and happier, a significant portion of the populace has been more or less left out in the cold and become increasingly resentful against the highly lopsided distribution of the newly acquired national wealth. According to the official statistics, China's Gini coefficient rose from 0.16 in 1978 to 0.412 in 2000, already exceeding the international alarm line of 0.4. It went on growing to reach its height at 0.491 in 2008 and started to move downward year by year to 0.473 in 2013.[32] This figure is substantially lower than the nongovernmental figure of 0.61 but still much higher than most countries in the world. According to World Bank, in China, 1 percent of families owns 41.4 percent of national wealth.[33] Even the official Xinhua News Agency warned that China's wealth gap has approached the "red line" of social tolerance.[34]

The extreme rich-poor polarization of the society has caused widespread resentment of social injustice and rampant official corruption. Together with disturbing incidents of forceful dismantling of peoples' residences for the sake of property development that have become common and frequent everywhere in China, such moods have led to two spectacular and destabilizing phenomena in Chinese society: one is the so-called *shangfang* (上访, visiting the higher authority for complaint and appeal), and the other *qunti shijian* (群体事件, massive unrest). *Shangfang* refers to a form of administrative appeal process where people take their grievances against lower-level government officials to the higher authority for a correction. A Xinhua news dispatch reported that since 1992, the cases of *shangfang* increased for twelve years in a row but started to decrease since 2005,[35] although it did not mention the reason for fewer cases is probably the deployment of the huge *jiefang* (截访, cutting off visits) force consisting of policemen and parapolicemen whose mission is to stop the visitors by "any means" before they reach the higher authority. "Any means," from bribing, intimidating, beating, kidnapping to illegal imprisonment, are rampant in *jiefang* practice, and they in turn caused more *shangfang*. The dispatch did not expose the exact number of cases there have been, but only mentioned that just in half a year in 2008, the leaders above the county level received 3.87 million visits, and this is only the tip of the iceberg. One major reason that China's stability-maintenance expenditure exceeds its national defense expenditure lies in the maintenance of this force of *jiefang*, from which one can speculate how big and severe a problem it poses for the Chinese government.

The other big problem that gives Beijing a headache is, of course, the so-called *qunti shijian*, which in fact refers to mass turmoil, including but not limited to demonstration (parade or assembly), strike, barricades, confrontation, and physical conflict between protesters and law enforcement officials. It is also a relatively new phenomenon growing along with the economic takeoff. Between 1993 and 2003, the number of the *qunti shijian* increased from 10,000 to 60,000, and the people involved increased from 730,000 to 3 million. The number of the incidents grew year by year at an increasing pace, reaching 100,000 in 2009 and 180,000 in 2010.[36] As Yu Jianrong, a renowned sociologist at CASS, pointed out, the crux of the *qunti shijian* lies in the conflict of interest between the people and the government, which is also the main source of all sorts of social problems in China today.[37]

As though these troubles are not enough, China suffered a series of terrorist attacks recently in many cities launched by the Uighur separatists. The Chinese authorities are so concerned that they have taken a series of extraordinary security measures: at first, people had to show their identification to buy a mobile phone chip; then it was needed for a train ticket, then a kitchen knife, and lately, in some cities, a box of matches! Not long ago, the Beijing municipality mobilized and put a quarter million "volunteers" (retired men and women with red armbands) on its streets to monitor the "suspicious" activities. If the Chinese government has so much to worry about its domestic order, then how much time and energy is left for caring about the global order?

As the American experience makes abundantly clear, any great power must have extremely strong economic power in order to provide public goods for the world community, which is a necessary requirement for setting up and maintaining global order. It must be able to afford to keep its market open, to fund international institutions (as the main donor) and to provide generous aid to countries in need. Although the United States has withdrawn significantly from its superpower role and the incurred international obligations for years now, it did once live up to that standard in the wake of the Second World War. But China is in no way comparable with the US, even after the latter's alleged decline. China's share of the UN membership is a good illustration of China's international commitment in comparison with other major powers: It was at its lowest at 0.72 percent in 1995, when the US and Japan's were 25 percent and 20 percent respectively. From then on, China's has increased step by step and eventually to 5.15 percent currently, whereas the US and Japans' decreased to 22 percent and 10.8 percent respectively, where the difference is still clear to see.[38] Some may argue that China can afford a larger share now that its GDP has grown so big, but the UN bases its membership distribution on GDP per capita, and that makes more sense. Indeed, with the size of the Chinese economy, China can afford more international financial responsibilities, but it will appear strikingly incommensurate with ordinary Chinese peoples' living standard. Charity starts at home. When China has such a low national income per capita and so many problems to be solved domestically, it is hard to expect it to play a significant role in world affairs.

Now we know some truth behind the glorious façade of Chinese power, and we know that China's economic power has increased dramatically but not to the point where China can mess with the international affairs at will, if it had such a will at all.

But does China have the will to challenge or change the current global order? My answer to the question is "no," or at least "not yet." First of all, one's will is a function of one's ability to a significant extent. Generally a rational actor does not have the will to do something beyond his or her capability. But whether one's ability is enough for doing something is not always certain and definite, and this is when other factors cut in to play a role. In the next section, I support my argument by looking at some other determinants of China's will regarding the world order.

CHANGING THE WORLD ORDER FROM WITHIN

Among other factors that determine China's attitude toward the world order, the first and foremost is China's perception of the nature of the current world order, be it political or economic. The backbone of the international political order is the principles, norms, and rules of international relations stipulated in the United Nations Charter, supplemented by some international regimes established later on, such as the nuclear nonproliferation regime, the humanitarian intervention regime (aka "responsibility to protect," or R2P), the environmental regime, and so forth. China's assessment of these principles and norms is based on a dual standard—nominally they are judged against their normative value: whether they are legitimate, just and reasonable; but in actuality, the bottom line is China's own national interests: if such interests are well served, the Chinese will abide by and uphold them; otherwise Beijing will choose to avoid and elude the stipulations, sometimes complain about them, but only in very few cases will it take the path of challenge and straightforward confrontation.

The United Nations and the international norms it embodies are something that China embraces wholeheartedly, not only because China has a huge vested interest in the Organization—it became one of the five permanent members of its Security Council in 1971—but also because the UN Charter conforms completely with China's official position on the principles of international relations. In 2003, China formally put forward the "Propositions on the Establishment of New International Political and Economic Order (NIPEO)."[39] Among the five propositions, three are almost identical with the relevant articles of the UN Charter.[40]

As to those additional regimes that came to be part of the international order later on, China found some acceptable and even beneficial, such as the nuclear nonproliferation regime, since China had already been one of the five members of the original "nuclear club" by the time the regime was set up (NPT [Non-Proliferation Treaty], 1968). On the issue of human rights and humanitarian intervention, China's attitude has been ambiguous and its approach ambivalent. Among the rights advocated by UN human rights institutions, China found some acceptable and some not. As result, China signed (1997) and ratified (2001) the International Covenant on Economic, Social, and Cultural Rights but not the International Covenant on Civil and Political Rights. (Interestingly, the US did the opposite, ratifying the latter but not the former.) Although many Western countries have tried to use the UN human rights institution to pressure China, China did not challenge the authority of the UN Commission on Human Rights (UNCHR), nor did it withdraw from that institution. Instead it has engaged in diplomatic battles in Geneva with the Western countries led by the United States in every annual meeting of UNCHR since 1991. China had successfully mobilized majority votes to frustrate Western motions criticizing China's human rights conditions for eleven years in a row until the Commission was replaced by the UN Human Rights Council in 2006.[41]

The Responsibility to Protect (R2P) is a relatively new principle first raised in a report by the International Commission on Intervention and State Sovereignty (ICISS) in 2001, and it was adopted by the United Nations 2005 World Summit, and then was confirmed in the UN Secretary General's report *Implementing the Responsibility to Protect* and in a general assembly resolution in 2009. Since the very beginning of its existence, the Chinese government has been highly alert to its implications, especially to its prospect of replacing the longstanding UN norm of nonintervention, so as to serve as a legal loophole for the Western powers to militarily intervene against small or weak states. Yet again, China did not make outright opposition to the new R2P principle but instead used its influence in the United Nations to neutralize its effect by putting it under strict constraints such as "actions to be taken through Security Council," which brings back the old "collective action based on consensus" framework. Moreover, its application is also put under strictly limited scenarios: only in cases of genocide, war crimes, ethnic cleansing, and crimes against humanity could it be initiated. In its propositions for NIPEO, China put its position on this issue this way: There should be respect for national idiosyncrasy and a nation's rights to choose its own social system and developmental path; differences in social systems and values should not be an excuse to interfere with internal affairs of other nations (the fourth point of the Proposition).[42] While striving to safeguard its interests and principles, China has tried its best to avoid head-on confrontation with the current global order and the modifications made by the United States and its Western allies in all these years. Basically China has fared quite well in this regard.

China's attitude toward the international economic order is even more positive. The bulk of the current international economic order is still the Bretton Woods System, which consists of three pillar regimes: World Trade Organization (WTO, formerly General Agreement on Tariffs and Trade—GATT), the International Monetary Fund (IMF), and the World Bank (WB). Although some argue that the Bretton Woods System ended after the US economic hegemony declined in the 1970s, most of the world still consider the System alive and well, even though the United States influence has somewhat weakened. Recall that when China started to embark on its economic takeoff in late 1970s, its catchword consisted of two parts: reform (改革) and opening up（开放）. The former referred to the overhaul of its domestic system, whereas the latter to merging into the international economic system. Deng Xiaoping knew very well that China's economic development would be just a bubble without a true integration with the international economy. This mindset determined from the very beginning China's positive attitude toward the existing international economic order.

China took the three pillar regimes of the Bretton Woods System as the bridge for its integration with the world economy. Moreover, it took WTO as its major pursuit, as advancing China's foreign trade has been a priority since the opening up of China to international economy. China started negotiations with the United States on the "recovery of its seat" in the GATT (Nationalist China was a founding member of the Organization since 1947 but withdrew from it later) in 1986 and almost succeeded in gaining approval in 1989. Unfortunately, that process was disrupted by the June 4th tragedy, which touched off the Western sanction led by the United States. Then the Organization became the WTO in 1995, and the negotiation on China's membership had to start all over again. The following years were extremely hard for the Chinese government because it was ruthlessly pressed by the United States, who held the key to China's admission and played tough to squeeze the maximal concession from China, and it was under huge domestic pressure of public opinion from both ends of the political spectrum: on the pro-side, people questioned the government's competence in international negotiations; on the con-side, the government was accused of being too submissive and imploring to Americans! Finally, in 1999, the United States opened the door (Who said the System is not American?), and China completed its twelve years of hard bargaining that eventually earned China an entrance ticket to the WTO.

From then on, the WTO has played a critical role in changing China dramatically, making China a highly globalized economy. China has benefited greatly from access to the world market, and it has fulfilled its obligation of opening its own economy to global competition to an extent beyond imagination fifteen years ago. It is now a completely indivisible part of the world economy, the advantage of which it enjoys very much. Now, why should China, having gained so much from integration with the world, turn against it and abandon its hard-earned membership in the international system?

China's relationship with the IMF and World Bank has been even smoother and more constructive. China joined the IMF in 1980, and in the thirty years since, China has turned itself from a borrower to a loaner. After the IMF's latest round of reforms in 2010, China has become its third-largest shareholder with a voting power of 6.07 percent, trailing only Japan and the United States (16.67 percent share with veto power).[43] The greatest advantage China got from IMF was not the money it borrowed but in two other senses: first, the IMF provides channels for China to connect with the outside world; and second, through numerous training programs and personnel exchanges, China has learnt from the IMF a great deal about international finance and management, of which the expertise was nearly zero in China beforehand.

The story with the World Bank is rather similar, with only one difference: China has benefited greatly in monetary terms from its various aid programs (soft loans, technology transfers, and donations). Up to 2010, the World Bank (including International Bank for Reconstruction and Development [IBRD] and the International Development Association [IDA]) has provided China with loans of $47.8 billion in total, in support of 326 projects, making China the fourth-largest borrower from World Bank.[44] Since 2007, China has started to turn itself from beneficiary to benefactor, with its first donation to the IDA of $30 million, making it one of very few donors from developing countries. As with the IMF, World Bank reform has recently lifted China's holding share and voting power to the third place (4.42 percent), again trailing Japan and the US (15.85 percent, with veto power).[45]

The fifth and last point of China's Proposition on NIPEO is about the international economic order. Regardless of the cliché such as "mutual benefit and cooperation to promote common development," this entry does maintain an old slogan that was quite popular back in the 1970s: "to reform the old and unjust international economic order so as to benefit the vast number of developing countries." Long-lasting as it is, the slogan is as toothless as it has been all these years. Why? Because it is too abstract to be put in practice. "To reform the old order": fine, but how? The Southern countries have failed to put forward any practical and feasible proposal to specifically modify the rules and norms of the current order, leaving their demand for improving the plight of Southern countries a pile of empty words. China is still upholding the slogan because it wants to conform with its identity as a developing country and to show solidarity with other developing countries. In fact, however, China has been co-opted into the current order irreversibly. Even if China had any idea of reforming the current regimes, it would try to work it out from within and not from without, as it already has huge vested interests in the system. The fact that China has provided a large amount of economic aid through the World Bank system to many developing countries suggests that China has found the system a useful channel for South-to-South cooperation and will stick to it.

Other than China's perception of the nature of the current global order, there are two more factors carrying their respective weight on China's attitude toward the order. One is China's relationship with the United States, and the other is Chinese leaders' predisposition therein. Why are Sino-US relations important in this matter? Simply because the current international order is American. Recall that Sino-US relations started back in the 1970s on the basis of a common cause: balancing the Soviet threat for both countries. This common cause turned the two deadly enemies into quasi-allies, which configured the mindset of China toward world affairs for the next half century: it is better to accept the US hegemony (and its order) rather than to be rolled over by the Soviet tanks (or by other security threats). Such a position was set up by two all-time heavyweights in the Chinese political arena, Mao Zedong and Zhou Enlai, and it was reconfirmed by another heavyweight, Deng Xiaoping, so as to have become the very premise and guideline of foreign affairs for the Chinese Communist Party and the State. In all the years since, although anti-hegemonism has been a recurrent theme in China's foreign policy rhetoric, the real motto has been that Sino-US relations are "the priority among all priorities" (重中之重) for China's foreign relations. Even today, Xi Jinping expresses his intention to maintain good relations with the United States by attempting a "new type of major power relationship."[46] The policy orientation is so deeply embedded in China's foreign policy establishment that it has been taken for granted and beyond challenge. So long as the status quo in the

Chinese officialdom persists, it is highly unlikely for China to turn around and try to upset the international status quo.

One more factor can serve as a reassurance of China's position toward American hegemony and its world order, and that is the predisposition of a succession of Chinese leaders in regard to the United States. This factor is important because China's foreign policy making has been a top-down process all the time, and it is the top leaders who dictate foreign policies to the foreign affairs functionaries and pundits, not the other way around. It is a reassurance because, among all else, almost every Chinese leader at the top level has at least one child or grandchild sent to the United States for education or immigration. Although some of them started to recall their young ones back home out of political considerations since Xi took power, the initial attitude toward America cannot be changed so easily and quickly. It is well known how much significance Chinese parents attach to the education and career of their children, so where they send them says a lot about the parents' preferences.

CONCLUSION

As if the news stories about China's economic myth are not sensational enough, the World Bank published its ICP (International Comparison Program) Report in April, 2014 which estimates that China will pass the United States as world's leading economic power that year.[47] Bear in mind, though, that the same Program lowered its estimate of China's GDP of 2005 by 40 percent(!) in revision only one year after its initial publication in 2006![48] The fact of the matter is, with all its weakness and problems, China still has a long way to go to become a superpower in its true and full sense. Overestimating China's power is harmful indeed: inside the country, it fans false national pride and blind euphoria, encouraging baseless ambition and assertiveness; outside the country, it sounds a premature alarm on China's power and intentions as to what role China will play for the world order.

A country's power position can be measured by numerous statistics and from a variety of aspects, but the most critical one should be how united and coherent it is, or it may fall apart one day no matter how strong and wealthy it may have been. Such unity and coherence can be measured in turn by how much centripetal force the country can generate for its people and how much confidence its people have in the country's future. Unfortunately, China does not fare well in this regard. According to a report by the China and Globalization Think Tank, China's immigrants to foreign lands have increased by 129 percent since 1990 to a total of 9.34 million by 2012.[49] This may be taken as what some call a "voting with feet."[50] What makes it a serious problem is that most of them belong to the upper layers of the society.

First, we have the officials. According to a source from the Central Party School, there are 1.18 million so-called naked officials at various levels of government in China.[51] "Naked official" means that only the official himself remains in China while all his family members have moved and now live abroad. The ensuing complications are so detrimental to the national interest that the Chinese government started crackdowns recently, forcing its officials to bring their families back or leave the government. And there are illegal fugitives too: In what the *International Business Times* called the "Great Escape," more than 16,000 corrupt officials have fled from China with 1 trillion RMB ($158 billion) in stolen money in the past two decades, while 18,000-plus were captured when trying to leave China during the past ten years.[52] According to another source, in the decade up to 2011, the total amount of money that has been illegally transferred abroad reached $3.8 trillion, plus $1 trillion and 1.5 trillion in 2012 and 2013 respectively.[53]

Then we have the outflow of the rich or superrich. Take Chinese immigrants to the US via investment (EB-5), for example. The 2012 figure is 2.5 times that of 2011, and 7.9 times that of 2010. Among all the EB-5 visas the US issued in 2013, 75 percent were for Chinese. In 2011, the investment capital transferred from China to foreign countries amounted to $2.8 trillion, about 3 percent of Chinese GDP that year.[54] According to a joint report by Hoogewerf Institute and Bank of China, 14 percent of the Chinese rich have immigrated or are in the process of immigrating; 46 percent are considering doing so. *Forbes* has also reported that among the superrich Chinese (with more than 10 million yuan of assets), 74 percent want to move abroad.[55]

And then we have the outflow of the celebrities. Among the thirty-some famed actors and actresses in the cast of the movie *The Founding Ceremony* celebrating the sixtieth anniversary of the People's Republic, some twenty-plus have obtained foreign nationality through naturalization. People teased that this birthday gift to the PRC was made by the Joint Force of Eight Nations (the expedition that invaded China and plundered Beijing in 1900).

And then we have the outflow of the best and brightest. Every year, tens of thousands of the best college or high-school graduates, the cream of the crop, go abroad to study. According to the Report on Chinese Students Abroad (2012), 2.24 million Chinese students went abroad for education between 1978 and 2011, but only 36 percent of them have come back to China (mostly government sent), whereas in sciences and technology the proportion that chose to stay abroad reached 87 percent. This means China suffers from the worst brain drain in the world.[56]

The Chinese are known for their reluctance to leave home and their enduring attachment to their native land. But why are so many Chinese eager to leave China, the great booming land, when they are not just the rank and file of the society but elites who have already had power, wealth, fame, or talent? Are they not supposed to be the core of the vested interests and the strongest backbone for the country? Why are they fleeing, and what are they fleeing from? This may serve as a caveat for all optimists for China's power and a pacifier for all alarmists about China's revisionist role for world order.

It is good that China as a whole has not gotten lost in the chorus chanting its marvelous achievements, at least not yet so far. So long as it knows where it stands exactly in the global distribution of power, it will unwaveringly stick to its chosen trajectory. But there is one premise for this: the United States has to keep the nature of the current global order as inclusive, accommodating, and fair as possible. If the United States changes the rules of the game and stacks the deck to hinder China's rise, then the whole game may change.

NOTES

1. Fred Bergsten, "A Partnership of Equals: How Should Washington Respond to China's Economic Challenge?," *Foreign Affairs*, July/August 2008, 57–69.
2. Naill Ferguson, "Not Two Countries, but One: Chimerica," *Telegraph*, May 4, 2007.
3. Yan Xuetong, "Uni-Superpower Plus Multi-Powers Is Heading to China-US Bi-Superpowers Plus Multi-Powers," *Global Times*, December 30, 2011.
4. Yan Xuetong, "How China Can Defeat America," *New York Times*, November 20, 2011.
5. Hu Angang, *China in 2020: A New Type of Superpower* (Hangzhou: Zhejiang People's Press, 2012).
6. Joshua Cooper Ramo, The Beijing Consensus, London: the Foreign Policy Center, 2004.
7. Oded Shenkar, *The Chinese Century: The Rising Chinese Economy and Its Impact on the Global Economy* (London: FT Press, 2006).
8. Martin Jacques, *When China Rules the World: The End of the Western World and the Birth of a New Global Order* (London: Penguin, 2009).
9. Song Xiaojun, Wang Xiaodong, Huang Jisu, Song Qiang and Liu Yang;, *zhongguo bu gaoxin g* (Nanjing: Jiangsu People's Press, 2009).
10. Interview with Wang Xiaodong, Douban Books: Introduction to *China Is Unhappy*, http://book.douban.com/reading/10576131/.

11. Wang Xiaodong, "Not Just an End for the Wall Street," *Chinese Youth*, October 17, 2008.
12. See, for example, Michael Swaine, "Perceptions of an Assertive China," *China Leadership Monitor* 32 (2010); "China's Assertive Behavior Part II: The Maritime Periphery," *China Leadership Monitor* 35 (2011); Alastair Iain Johnston, "How New and Assertive Is China's New Assertiveness?," *International Security* 37, no. 4, 2013, pp 7–48; Dingding Chen, Xiaoyu Pu, and Alastair Iain Johnston, "Debating China's Assertiveness," *International Security* 38, no.3 2013/14, pp 176–83.
13. Yang Jiechi, speech at press conference, March 6, 2012, news.sohu.com/20120306/n336839600.shtml.
14. Yang Jiechi, speech at press conference, July 30, 2010, news.163.com/10/0731/09/6CTLB35100014AEE.html.
15. According to the Chinese Foreign Ministry, NIPEO includes five major aspects: (1) Mutual respect of sovereignty and territorial integration; (2) peaceful solution of international disputes; (3) sovereign equality; (4) respecting national idiosyncrasy, seeking common ground while tolerating difference; and (5) mutual benefit and cooperation. news.xinhuanet.com/ziliao/2003-01/19/content_696057.htm
16. Xi Jinping on Foreigners "pointing fingers" at China, *Chinese Digital Times*, February 11, 2009, chinadigitaltimes.net/2009/02/xi-jinping-习近平-on-foreigners-pointing-fingers-at-china-with-video/.
17. "Fan Changlong: 'Dissatisfied' with Remarks by Chuck Hagel" CCTV News, April 9, 2014, http://english.cntv.cn/2014/04/09/VIDE1397012766823388.shtml.
18. Ibid.
19. Xiao Qiang, Zhao Qiang and Liu Yupeng "Fang Fenghui's criticism against "rebalancing" angered Dempsey". See *Global Times*, May 17, 2014, news.sohu.com/20140517/n399676294.shtml.
20. "Central vs. Local GDP: 3 Trillion Difference" [in Chinese], [中央地方GDP统计相差3万亿] *Chinese Business Management*, August 3, 2013, money.163.com/13/0803/00/95AHQEAD00253B0H.html; "What Does 2 Trillion Difference in GDP Reflect?" [in Chinese], [GDP 两万亿元误差折射了什么？] *Guangmin Daily*, January 24, 2014, http://epaper.gmw.cn/gmrb/html/2014-01/24/nbs.D110000gmrb_10.htm.
21. Christopher Balding, "How Badly Flawed Is Chinese Economic Data?," SSRN, revised August 14, 2013, http://papers.ssrn.com/sol3/papers.cfm?abstract_id=2307054
22. "Chinese Firm Earns 35 Cents while Foreign Boss Gains 20 USD" [in Chinese], [加工一个芭比娃娃中国企业挣35美分外企赚20美元] *People's Daily*, May 28, 2012, http://news.xinhuanet.com/fortune/2012-05/28/c_123200455.htm.
23. Center of Global Merger and Acquisition, *Map of Chinese Industries*, Chinese Economy Press, 2007, http://wenku.baidu.com/view/9e1bb40d4a7302768e9939e9.html; Anon., *Map of Chinese Industries 2010–2011* (Beijing: Social Sciences Literature Press, 2011); Zuo Pengfei, "Chinese Industries under Foreign Control" [in Chinese][中国产业外资控制情况], Doc88 website May 31, 2012, http://www.doc88.com/p-303517065175.html.
24. Yue Jianyong, *China's Rise in the Age of Globalization: Myth or Reality?* Palgrave Studies in Economic History (London: Springer, 2017), 5–16.
25. "Xi's Trip Builds Bridge to Europe," *China Daily*, April 1, 2014, http://www.chinadaily.com.cn/world/2014xivisiteu/2014-04/01/content_17398123.htm.

26. IMF Economic Outlook, April 2014, http://www.chinadaily.com.cn/world/2014xivisiteu/201404/01/content_17398123.htm.
27. Wu Ming, "Head of State Bureau of Statistics Blasts True National Situation: 100 Years behind the US!," *Chinese Economy Weekly*, March 29, 2011, 4.
28. Ibid.
29. Duan Xiaohua and Liu Yuling, "Assessment of China's International Competitiveness 2004" [in Chinese], [2004中国国际竞争力评价] Chinese Science and Technology Statistics Net, August 22, 2005, www.sts.org.cn/fxyj/zcfx/documents/20050822.htm.
30. Liang Jialin, "China Has Seven of Ten Worst Polluted Cities of the World" [in Chinese], Tengxun News, January 15, 2013 http://news.qq.com/a/20130115/000007.htm.
31. State Bureau of Sea and Ocean, "70% of Chinese Rivers Classified as Hazardous Fifth at Entrance to Sea" [in Chinese], [中国七成河流入海水质为劣五类] Caixin News Net, November 22, 2013, http://china.caixin.com/2013-11-22/100608228.html.
32. "Gini Coefficient Still High, Rich-Poor Gap Still Huge" [in Chinese], [基尼系数仍居高位，贫富差距悬殊依旧] *New Observer*, January 21, 2014, http://news.sina.com.cn/newobserv/pass/.
33. Ibid.
34. "The Rich-Poor Gap in China Has Approached the 'Red Line' of Social Tolerance", [in Chinese] [我国贫富差距正在逼近社会容忍"红线"] *Xinhua News Agency*, May 10, 2010, http://jjckb.xinhuanet.com/sdbd/2010-05/10/content_220612.htm.
35. "*Xinfang* Went Down Continuously since 2005" [in Chinese] [中国信访量2005年以来连续下降], *Xinhua News Agency*, July 13, 2012, http://china.caixin.com/2012-07-13/100410743.html.
36. "Conservative Estimate of the Number of China's Qunti Shijian Cases" [in Chinese], [中国群体性事件保守数量统计] *Tianya Community*, August 23, 2012, http://bbs.tianya.cn/post-develop-1066439-1.shtml.
37. Yu Jianrong, "The Crux of *quanti shijian* Lies in Interest Conflict between Government-People" [in Chinese], [群体性事件症结在于官民矛盾] *China Net*, January 13, 2010, http://www.china.com.cn/book/zhuanti/qkjc/txt/2010-01/13/content_19228539.htm.
38. Lu Yao, "Revealing China's Share of UN Membership" [in Chinese],[揭秘联合国会费里的中国份额] *Modern Express*, June 20, 2012, http://news.sina.com.cn/c/2010-06-25/051817705970s.shtml; "UN Membership" [in Chinese],[联合国会费] in *360 Encyclopedia*, http://baike.so.com/doc/5766057.html#5766057-5978825-3.
39. Chinese Foreign Ministry, "Propositions on the Establishment of the New International Political and Economic Order" [in Chinese], [中国对建立国际政治经济新秩序的主张] Chinese Ambassy in France Website, http://www.amb-chine.fr/chn/zgyw/t152172.htm.
40. For example, the first three items of the Chinese propositions can be summarized as follows: (1) Mutual respect of sovereignty and territorial integrity, nonaggression, noninterference of internal affairs; (2) peaceful resolution of international disputes, opposing the use of force and threat of force; (3) sovereign equality and equal consultation on world affairs. In comparison, it is not hard to find that they are in the same spirit as some relevant UN Charter provisions—Articles 2(1), 2(4), and 2(7).

41. "Background Data: The Abolished UNCHR" [in Chinese],[背景资料：被取消的联合国人权委员会] *Xinhua News Agency*, October 7, 2009, http://www.360doc.com/content/09/1007/19/59889_6927681.shtml.
42. Same as note 39.
43. "What Benefit Can China Get from IMF?" [in Chinese] [中国能从国际货币基金组织得到什么好处？], *Baidu Zhidao*, April 12，2012, http://zhidao.baidu.com/question/409445579.html.
44. "Survey of Cooperation between China and the World Bank Group" [in Chinese][中国与世界银行集团合作概况], Finance Ministry, PRC, http://www.mof.gov.cn/zhuantihuigu/cw30/bjzlC/201009/t20100903_337285.html; "Chinese Aid Going Abroad: China and Foreign Aid in 60 Years" [in Chinese] [中国援助开始走向世界：中国与对外援助60年], China Net, September 30, 2009, http://www.china.com.cn/international/txt/2009-09/30/content_18634014_3.htm.
45. "China Became the Third Largest Shareholder of the World Bank" [in Chinese] [中国成为世界银行第三大股东国], Sina News, April 26, 2010, http://finance.sina.com.cn/focus/shgdg_2010/.
46. Cheng Li, "A New Type of Major Power Relationship? Brookings Foundation, September 26, 2014, https://www.brookings.edu/on-the-record/a-new-type-of-major-power-relationship/.
47. "China Poised to Pass US as World's Leading Economic Power this Year," *Financial Times*, April 29, 2014, http://www.ft.com/cms/s/0/d79ffff8-cfb7-11e3-9b2b-00144feabdc0.html#axzz347sHp7L1.
48. World Bank, *2005 International Comparison Program Preliminary Results, December 2007*, siteresources.worldbank.org/ICPINT/Resources/ICPreportprelim.pdf.
49. *Observer*, "Report Claims Near 10 million Immigrants and 2.8 Trillion US Going Abroad", [报道称中国海外移民总数近千万，2.8万亿资产转移] *Observer*，January 22，2014，http://www.guancha.cn/society/2014_01_22_201351.shtml.
50. Albert O Hirschman, *Exit, Voice, and Loyalty: Responses to Decline in Firms, Organizations, and States* (Cambridge, MA: Harvard University Press, 2007), 21–30.
51. "Expert Claims There are 1.18 Million 'Naked Officials'" *Netease New Media*, February 23, 2013, http://news.163.com/13/0226/17/8OLH3P7I0001124J.html.
52. "The Great Escape: Suspected Corrupt Bureaucrats (and Their Billions) Flee China in Droves," *International Business Times*, June 6, 2012, www.ibtimes.com/great-escape-suspected-corrupt-bureaucrats-and-their-billions-flee-china-droves-701746.
53. "Last Year 714 Public Servants Fled with 1 Trillion US" [in Chinese], [去年中国公职人员外逃714人，卷走1万亿美元] big5.soundofhope.org/node/315399. Radio Free Asia, January 20, 2013, http://www.rfa.org/mandarin/Xinwen/xin2-01202013111413.html.
54. Same as note 49.
55. Yan Changhai, "China Becomes No. One Immigration Source" [in Chinese], [中国成为移民人数最多d国家] *Tianya Community*，December 23, 2012 http://bbs.tianya.cn/post-free-2968825-1.shtml.
56. "More than 60% of Chinese Students Remain Abroad" [in Chinese],[超六成中国留学生滞留海外] *Shenzhen Business Daily*, September 18, 2012, http://finance.ifeng.com/roll/20120918/7048047.shtml; "In Science and Technology, Chinese Students Retaining Rate Reached 87%" [in Chinese], [在科学和工程领域，中国海外留学生滞留率达87%] *Huxiu Net*, June 6, 2013, http://www.huxiu.com/article/15509/1.html.

PART V
China and Its Rivals

CHAPTER 12

Coexistence in China's Regional and Global Maritime Security Strategies

Revisionism by Defensive Means

LISELOTTE ODGAARD

INTRODUCTION

The chapter argues that China's pursuit of a coexistence policy is intended to protect its core security interests of preserving communist party rule, protecting China's sovereignty and territorial integrity, and securing China's economic and social development by convincing the international community of the legitimacy of coexistence.[1] China's coexistence policy encompasses the attempt to position China as a mediator rather than a leader, to insist on regime consent as a basis for interference in domestic policies, to promote the non-use of force for purposes of conflict resolution, and to embed its policies in the UN system. I argue that China has only obtained some reciprocal legitimacy in the sense of recognition that China contributes to international peace and stability far from China's shores. In contrast to the United States, China is not seeking a community type of value-based legitimacy. China has embedded its coexistence strategy in the UN system to present an alternative to the liberal global institutions initiated by the United States after the Second World War. China's post-Cold War program of coexistence is designed as a platform for enhancing and consolidating its position as a rising power leading the developing world. Coexistence allows states to focus on pursuing national interests on the basis of their particular historical and local conditions because it is not based on values. The procedural character of China's strategy also entails that it does not facilitate extensive international integration in the sense that liberal institutions require commitment to basic values of free trade and representative democracy. Instead, China's strategy relies predominantly on policy coordination with a view to unilateral interest pursuits. Moreover, China has only demonstrated limited reciprocal legitimacy, and this impedes the prospects of a common framework of world order between Beijing and Washington because it implies mistrust in Beijing's willingness to protect the common interest in peace and stability. China's defiance of pursuing a Sino-centric, value-based order lowers the level of cooperation and institutionalization in the international system, but it also minimizes the prospects of a Cold War type of ideological rift between China and the United States.

The coexistence argument suggests that China is not engaged in a zero-sum game or pursuing a hierarchical order where China lays down the law to other states. Instead, China seeks to promote a world order that can accommodate different understandings of legitimate state conduct on the basis of an agree-to-disagree approach to international interaction and a concern for focusing on the right to noninterference and to pursue national interests and individual development models. This approach contrasts with US liberal internationalist aspirations. Washington and its key partners pursue an extensive agenda of international cooperation and reform of domestic state-society relations on the basis of liberal market economic and political democratic values.

The coexistence argument focuses on the intermediate (i.e., decade-long) time horizon in China's strategic planning. This focus differs from many widely held perceptions in the policy-making community and in academia. These usually argue that China pursues some form of long-term regional hegemony or dominance. Realists argue that China will opt for regional hegemony due to shifts in the balance of power in China's favor. These will lead to greater security competition between Washington and Beijing. In this volume, Stephen Walt explains that China will try to reduce the US security presence in Asia, leading to an intense competition for allies and influence.[2] William Wohlforth argues that China's rise has facilitated a more pugnacious policy of pushback against US preeminence in Asia, giving the United States strong incentives to double down on most of its current security commitments, which makes it harder to adjust the status quo in tandem with shifting power balances.[3] In the liberal understanding of China's rise, Beijing's hegemonic aspirations will likely be shaped by the existing liberal order even as China seeks greater authority and voice to match its newfound economic strength. For example, Ikenberry argues that China increasingly engages in security competition and balance of power politics in East Asia. However, the resilience of liberal order encourages China to revise the political hierarchy and enhance its position and status within the global system rather than engaging in world-scale revisionist struggles over rival models of modernity or divergent ideologies of international order.[4] Constructivist arguments gravitate toward the position that the jury is still out, with the possibility of a Sino-centric order emerging out of China's evolving national identity that accompanies its economic and military rise. An example is William Callahan, who explores the possibility of a Chinese utopia defined by order rather than freedom, which is ultimately a new kind of hegemony where imperial China's hierarchical governance is updated for the twenty-first century.[5] Rosemary Foot argues that in a world where power is diffused and the collective action challenges are hugely demanding, China will keep pressing and protecting its territorial core interests, and the best we can hope for is that US-Chinese interdependence facilitates continued regional peace and stability.[6]

These readings of China's regional hegemonic aspirations have some merit in highlighting the tension between balancing and accommodation dynamics between the United States and China, in particular with regards to China's near abroad. However, this chapter takes issue with the long time horizon that is often applied in analyses of China's security outlook and performance and in the tendency to interpret China's motives and behavior on the basis of Beijing's long-term aspirations rather than its immediate security concerns. The problem with the long-term view is that too many unforeseen developments are likely to interfere with the conclusions before they come to fruition. The coexistence argument rests on the assumption that China's intermediate strategic planning will have determinant consequences for its long-term role in the world order and hence the prospects of balancing versus accommodation winning out in US-China relations.

To substantiate this argument, I investigate two cases: the Diaoyu/Senkakus as a regional security issue that constitutes a threat to state sovereignty and territorial integrity, and China's contribution to antipiracy operations in the Gulf of Aden as a global security issue that poses threats to China's social and economic development. These issues reflect the principal aspects of Chinese external security concerns: regional and global security and China's core security interests—regime survival, Chinese territorial sovereignty, and socioeconomic development. In addition, these issues are hard cases for China's coexistence policy, since they involve some use of hard power and are often analyzed from the perspective of China's hegemonic aspirations. China's Diaoyu/Senkaku policy is usually portrayed as the hegemonic expansion of China's territorial and maritime space at the expense of the security of neighboring states by using force and by promoting Sino-centric interpretations of international law.[7] China's antipiracy policy in the Gulf of Aden is viewed through a hegemonic lens, where China is seen to perform as a responsible great power, using force to secure merchant shipping to protect the economic order preconditioning China's development against barbarian pirates.[8] In these cases, China is depicted as using hard power to protect its national interests, enabling it to realize its long-term regional hegemonic aspirations.

This chapter uses the coexistence concept to provide a different perspective on China's approach to protecting core security interests. First, I discuss coexistence theoretically in the context of strategic studies, defining it as a defensive revisionist strategy. Second, I examine the Diaoyu/Senkaku dispute and China's participation in antipiracy operations in the Gulf of Aden, arguing that although China applies coexistence, it has only obtained some reciprocal legitimacy for this policy in the Gulf of Aden. Third, I conclude by addressing the consequences of China's coexistence approach for international peace and stability.

COEXISTENCE AND LEGITIMACY IN INTERNATIONAL POLITICAL CHANGE

Coexistence is a defensive strategy for managing existing or emerging great power status that rests on the assumption that the legitimacy of a state's international actions has determining influence on its foreign policy choices. Coexistence aims at establishing a world order with a limited international agenda that focuses on policy coordination to avoid great power conflict that might jeopardize international peace and stability and allows states to concentrate on national development and security.

Historically, coexistence has been employed by great powers that struggled to enter or stay in the club of great powers due to relative economic and/or military weakness.[9] Coexistence rarely appears in Western literature on international relations, one reason being that the concept is seen as a brainchild of the communist Eastern Bloc. It emerged with Lenin's need to explain how the Soviet state emerging in 1917 could survive without successful revolutions in neighboring countries. The Soviet version of peaceful coexistence can be seen as an attempt to ameliorate the competitive dynamics between communism and capitalism by facilitating diplomatic and trade relations between these two blocs. In this broad sense, it resembles Chinese coexistence policies that are also designed to ameliorate tensions between China's communist political system and the dominant liberal world order by means of diplomatic and economic interaction. However, in Soviet policies, "world revolution" was always a theme alongside peaceful coexistence. This led to the inherently contradictory and duplicitous foreign policy, whereby the Soviet regime preached and practiced coexistence with Western countries while at the same time actively supporting the overthrow of their governments.[10] By contrast, China is not a revolutionary power in the sense that it seeks to overthrow the existing world order or the liberal governments that heavily influence the current world order. Instead, I argue that China is a revisionist state attempting to revise or reform the existing world order in a way that better accommodates China's interests.

The literature on strategy usually describes defensive strategies as status quo oriented. By contrast, China's coexistence policy entails combining defensive strategies with revisionist objectives. China uses coexistence as a defensive strategy for the management of its growing power and influence vis-à-vis other international actors. Compared to offensive strategies that meet aggression with aggression, defensive strategies rely less on military capabilities and more on political will. Since their purpose is to deny external aggression, they also draw more heavily on civilian than on military organizations. Moreover, a defensive strategy implies never striking the first blow.[11] Deterrence, which is about discouraging external aggression, can be seen as a subset of defensive strategies. States, great and small powers alike, who find themselves short on economic and military resources, often make recourse to deterrence strategies to add political will to the balance. Will is as much a product of political cohesion as of any material source, and political cohesion may make up for resource deficiencies.[12]

This chapter argues that coexistence is used by China as a kind of defensive strategy that includes elements of deterrence with the objective of orchestrating endogenous systemic change. Coexistence relies on the establishment of a political framework founded in the common interests of states in preserving peace and stability. The pursuit of this type of world order requires more in terms of political and diplomatic influence and less in terms of superior economic and military capabilities to establish an order where some basic level of reciprocal legitimacy is the main mechanism ensuring a stable world order. Without reciprocity, there is not much faith that coexistence serves to protect the common interest in peace and stability.

Legitimacy is not to be confused with justice, because it means no more than international agreement on the nature of workable policy coordination arrangements and the permissible aims and methods of foreign policy.[13] Legitimacy serves to limit the scope of international conflict, but it does not necessarily lead to a value-based international community. Legitimacy can be based on reciprocity. A state's goodwill, or reputation, vis-à-vis other states, and its status as a reliable partner are the bases for its successful interaction with others. These are assets that states cannot afford to take lightly.[14] As a consequence, states put a high premium on showing their commitment to the collectivity of states by observing the rules of international conduct, or at least claiming to do so. Moreover, legitimacy can be based on values. In this case, the set-up for world order becomes an end in itself. Consequently, its usefulness is not questioned, or at least it is seen as a means to preserve some wider set of values.[15]

As pointed out by Barry Posen, both great powers and small powers that suffer geographical, technological, economic, and military constraints gravitate toward defensive and deterrence strategies that involve a relatively high element of political will. Coexistence is one such strategy. Coexistence is characterized by an inherent element of revisionist activism, which stems from a perceived need to fortify the international structures that are seen as providing security. Coexistence entails a revisionist response by means of defensive strategies in the sense of stopping assaults, whether they be of an economic, military, or political nature, on the capabilities and institutions of the world order that are seen as essential to state survival. The revisionist response consists of what Robert Gilpin called "systemic change." It is an internal system change concerning governance. It involves reinterpreting the fundamental institutions dynamics of the existing system, thereby changing how it works without changing the whole set-up or the actors that make up the system.[16]

Coexistence as a defensive revisionist strategy becomes legitimate through reciprocal legitimacy achieved by using security management, diplomacy, and international law to facilitate international acceptance of the central aspects of a revised version of the international order. In the following section, I address to what extent China can be said to pursue coexistence in its maritime policy with regards to the Diaoyu/Senkaku Islands.

THE DIAOYU/SENKAKU DISPUTE

The Diaoyu/Senkaku[17] dispute between China and Japan dates back to 1895, when Japan, following its victory in the Sino-Japanese war, erected a sovereignty marker on one of more than eight features in the East China

Sea to lay claim to the islands in accordance with the principles for acquiring sovereignty applied by Western powers. Despite its long history, the dispute did not turn into a security issue until 1970, when mainland China issued its first claim to the Diaoyu/Senkakus following Japanese protests against Taiwanese oil concessions in the East China Sea.[18] In 2002, the Japanese government leased three islands from descendants of the Japanese who claimed to have first discovered the islands.[19] In 2005, the Japanese Coast Guard took control of these contested features together with the lighthouse built on them, a measure that would give Tokyo a freer hand to exercise effective control.[20]

China's sovereignty, territorial integrity, and national unity are core national security interests. China's 2015 white paper states that China has an arduous task to safeguard its national unification, territorial integrity, and development interests. It alludes to the activities of the United States and neighboring states such as Japan by stating that some of China's offshore neighbors take provocative actions and reinforce their military presence on China's reefs and islands that they have illegally occupied, and a tiny few external countries maintain constant close air-and-sea surveillance and reconnaissance against China.[21]

Since 1972, China's recommended method for lowering tensions in the dispute is to shelve the sovereignty issue so as to allow both sides to proceed with making use of the area without fear of violent conflict ensuing.[22] This method does not entail a leading role for China, but rather an attempt to mediate between different outlooks by "agreeing to disagree" on who has sovereignty rights over the Diaoyu/Senkakus. The shelving option is a defensive strategy, since it avoids pronouncing a winner and a loser or designating a wrong and a right position on the sovereignty issue. It also indicates a defensive approach to nationalism, which arguably reflects China's modern history of vulnerability to threats against China's sovereignty, territorial integrity, and national unity and the Chinese Communist Party (CCP) leadership's fear of domestic instability. The method was first used in 1978 as an innovative effort at dispute management. The dispute had flared when Japan, in response to conservative nationalist factions, had included the Diaoyu/Senkaku Islands on the agenda of the normalization talks in 1978, and China responded by dispatching a flotilla of fishing vessels to the islands to demonstrate China's claim. Deng Xiaoping's shelving proposal became the fallback option for Beijing and Tokyo when nationalist actors continued to be a nuisance. It was a point of consensus to reassure each other that policy makers did not seek to alter the territorial status quo.[23]

From 2010 onward, nationalism seems to be a greater concern for China in how to handle the dispute. This was reflected in China's rupture with Japan in 2012 over Tokyo's purchase of three of the Diaoyu/Senkaku Islands. Finding itself caught between popular nationalism and preserving diplomatic relations with Japan, the official newspaper, the *People's Daily*, published an editorial that several times referred to "irrational conduct," and pointed out that wild anti-Japanese actions would be no more logical than Japan's actions. China would act in accordance with international norms, the editorial said. Yet it took issue with Deng's guideline on keeping a low profile, stating that a "bloodied people is destined to be bullied, and a country that always maintains a low profile will inevitably be defeated."[24] The reaction illustrates that while the defensive strategy still dominates the thinking of the Chinese leadership, populist nationalist voices emerging in social media in China and abroad increasingly demand a departure from the unwillingness to appoint winners and losers, recommending that China stands up for its rights and treat the island dispute as a zero-sum game.

China's proposal for dual use of the area where the Diaoyu/Senkakus are located is to jointly develop the resources around the islands on the basis of mutual governmental consent and national development priorities. The last time China and Japan announced a mutual commitment to shelve the sovereignty dispute, the two countries agreed that they "[were] committed to making the East China Sea a sea of peace, cooperation and friendship" and "to carry out joint development based on the principle of mutual benefit as a temporary arrangement pending the final demarcation and without prejudice to the positions of either side on matters concerning the law of the sea."[25] The exchanges on joint development came on the heels of the Japanese Coast Guard's initiation of a continuous presence around the contested islands in 2002 and Chinese and Japanese engagement in competitive energy exploration, fishing, and patrolling of the area.[26] However, Tokyo does not recognize being party to a dispute with China over the Diaoyu/Senkakus.[27] Without this recognition, the Chinese proposal of agreeing to disagree and proceed with joint development is not feasible. At the same time, nationalist voices in China has become ever more concerned about China's perceived softness toward Japan. To ameliorate these concerns, China has established a presence in the area to improve its bargaining position vis-à-vis Japan.

China has established a semipermanent presence in the vicinity of the islands by means of a growing civilian and paramilitary maritime force to demonstrate Beijing's commitment to the non-use of force in the Diaoyu/Senkaku dispute. People's Liberation Army (PLA) Navy ships and aircraft have been deployed to the area. However, their presence has been much less frequent than that of the civilian law enforcement agencies. The display of strength exhibited by the presence of the PLA Navy is seen by the

Chinese authorities as a means to deter Japanese escalation and further militarization of the situation. This display of strength is emphasized by China's decision to publicize instances of Chinese government vessels in the area, aiming to show that it can assert administrative control at the same level as Japan. In May 2014, China increased the momentum of deterrence by conducting its annual joint naval exercises with Russia in the East China Sea off Shanghai.[28] The joint exercises came on the heels of US President Obama's confirmation of Japan's administrative control of the islands in April 2014. Beijing intends to increase its civilian law enforcement force, intending to build thirty-six additional coast guard vessels over the next five years and incorporate another eleven retired PLA Navy ships after modification by removing their heavy armament.[29] In October 2013, China began flying drones in the area.[30] Following Japan's announcement that it would shoot down drones that allegedly infringed into its airspace, in November 2013 China announced the establishment of an Air Defense Identification Zone (ADIZ). The Chinese ADIZ overlaps with the Japanese ADIZ, both of which include the Diaoyu/Senkakus.[31] Dialogue between China and Japan has been scant since September 2012, when, in Beijing's view, the latest round of escalation in the dispute started. The gradual resumption of diplomatic ties from late 2014 has not led to optimism about the long-term trend in Chinese-Japanese relations. In 2016, Chinese foreign minister Wang Yi described relations as having been greatly harmed due to Japanese leaders' mistaken approach to historical issues. Consequently, future prospects do not allow for optimism in China's view.[32]

China's sovereignty claim is founded in an essentially historical interpretation of international law according to which China never lost sovereignty over the Diaoyu/Senkakus. In 1895, when Japan set up sovereignty markers to claim the Diaoyu/Senkakus, Japan had accepted Western international law, whereas China had not, adhering to the Chinese understanding of sovereignty. According to this interpretation, effective control is only applied as a reaction to foreign threats against Chinese territorial and maritime boundaries and not as a necessary day-to-day practice with regard to all areas over which China claims sovereignty.[33] Arguably, China was not aware of the Japanese marker, and also the Japanese action did not constitute a threat to use force.

China's historical interpretation is not recognized as a legitimate basis for sovereignty claims in modern international law and is therefore at odds with the majority view on how to interpret the UN system's rules on sovereignty. Recognizing the lack of legitimacy, China has increased its ability to assert its claim by means of effective control, which is the modern post-World War II definition of how sovereignty is acquired. To substantiate that other states have acknowledged China's claim, China refers to the Cairo Declaration of December 1943. On this occasion, the United States and Britain declared that all Chinese territories occupied by Japan must be returned to China.[34] In China's view, this encompasses returning the Diaoyu/Senkakus.

The frequency of patrolling may be adjusted as part of Beijing's political signaling or in response to actions taken by Japan or the United States.[35] However, China is likely to maintain a semipermanent presence, which it has established in the sea and airspace in the vicinity of the Diaoyu/Senkakus since 2012. Over time, this will make it difficult to argue that China is not entitled to a presence. The establishment of a predominantly civilian presence signals that China does not have hegemonic intentions of throwing Japan out of the area or using aggressive means. Instead, Beijing's objective is for Japan to acknowledge being party to a sovereignty dispute and to establish a modus vivendi that accommodates the de facto presence of both states.

For Japan, the alleged coexistence policy of Chinese authorities is interpreted as an aggressive land grab of territory over which Japan has exercised effective control for more than a century.[36] Japan has responded by taking further steps to consolidate administrative control over the Diaoyu/Senkakus.[37] The United States acknowledges Japan's administrative control but takes no position on the sovereignty issue.[38] In April 2014, US President Obama explicitly confirmed that the Japan-US Security Treaty's Article 5, obliging Washington to defend Japan, encompasses the Diaoyu/Senkakus.[39] This is the first time a US president has extended this confirmation in public. The move can be interpreted as solid US support for Japan's attempt to defend itself against what Tokyo sees as China's unlawful encroachment on its sovereign rights.

In July 2016, the tribunal constituted under the UN Convention of the Law of the Sea in the arbitration instituted by the Philippines against China issued its award on the South China Sea. China has historical claims in this part of Asia as well. Prior to the award, China had made clear that it will neither accept nor participate in the arbitration on the grounds that the Philippines had agreed to negotiate their dispute bilaterally and that in China's view, the tribunal lacks jurisdiction in the matter. The tribunal concluded that there was no legal basis for China to claim historic rights, and that none of the Spratly Islands in the central part of the South China Sea are capable of generating extended maritime zones.[40] Immediately after the ruling, Japanese foreign minister Fumio Kishida advocated the importance of the rule of law, stating that the tribunal's ruling was legally binding and hence that the parties, hinting at China, were required to comply.[41] Moreover, the Japanese and Philippine Coast Guard held joint military exercises on July 13, 2017 in an effort to further boost their defense partnership formalized in 2016.[42]

China responded by signaling that it maintains its claims in the South China Sea, conducting air patrols over contested areas in the South China Sea. In the East China Sea, China increased patrolling near the Diaoyu/Senkaku islands, even temporarily sailing with fishing and coast guard vessels within the contiguous twenty-four-nautical-mile zone and on August 5, 2016, within the territorial sea of the islands.[43] Beijing's escalation of its activities in the East China Sea arguably is a strong signal that it intends to maintain its historic claim to the islands and reinforce its semipermanent presence.

China's coexistence strategy to meet the security challenges against China's alleged sovereignty over the Diaoyu/Senkaku islands involves combining a defensive strategy with major deterrence aspects and active elements, which are intended to strengthen the application of the strategy used to protect China's sovereignty, territorial integrity, and national unity. The central part of the strategy is to deter Japanese attempts at challenging Chinese sovereignty over the Diaoyu/Senkakus combined with an active fortification of China's claim by means of a semipermanent civilian and paramilitary presence. This presence signals China's defensive objectives of extracting Japanese recognition of a sovereignty dispute and acceptance of a modus vivendi whereby Beijing and Tokyo agree to disagree on the legal basis of their presence, shelve the sovereignty issue, and reopen dialogue on how to jointly develop the area's resources. Japan is responding by trying to redress the change in status quo by fortifying its administrative control, strengthening its presence against a background of continued US recognition of Tokyo's administrative control. As a result, China's coexistence strategy rests solely on power. Reciprocal legitimacy is absent, since Japan responds by stepping up its presence and strengthening its deterrence capabilities rather than resuming political dialogue on the basis of acknowledgement of the presence of China in the disputed area. Consequently, tensions in the area are continuing to rise and are producing risks of accidental violent conflict. Value-based legitimacy is not in the cards. Japan subscribes to the liberal values of the US alliance system and bases its claim on the post-World War II interpretation of sovereign rights as derived from effective control by one state. Tokyo refuses to acknowledge the possibility of a cosharing arrangement without a clarification of whose claim is recognized in modern international law.

ANTIPIRACY OPERATIONS IN THE GULF OF ADEN

China sees piracy as a threat to economic and social development in China. This global security issue has become increasingly prominent with the gradual integration of China's economy into the world economic system since 1978. Overseas interests have become an integral component of China's national interests. The Gulf of Aden, which has been the main focus of China's antipiracy missions, accounts for $3 trillion of foreign trade and nearly $1 trillion of marine logistics, and it carries more than 50 percent of the total oil and energy imports.[44] Security issues arising from China's global economic engagement involve protecting merchant vessels at sea, evacuating Chinese nationals, and performing emergency rescues. These tasks have become important for China to safeguard its national interests and fulfill China's international obligations.[45] The deployment of two Chinese destroyers and a support vessel in December 2008 to join international fleets of warships to protect civilian ships off the Somali coast marks the first time Chinese warships have patrolled outside of Chinese waters.[46] NATO's contribution to anti-piracy in the area, Operation Ocean Shield, was closed December 15, 2016, due to a significant decrease in the number of piracy attacks in the Gulf of Aden. The decrease was, at least partly, a result of the international antipiracy missions. However, as of 2017 most contributing countries, including the United States and China, continue to participate in anti-piracy efforts in the Gulf of Aden. The US-led Operation Enduring Freedom, of which Operation Ocean Shield formed part, is ongoing. On December 17, 2016, China sent its twenty-fifth convoy fleet composed of two missile frigates, a supply ship, two ship-bourne helicopters, special combat soldiers, and more than 700 seamen and officers to the Gulf of Aden.[47]

China demonstrates a preference for mediation rather than leadership in how it approaches antipiracy in the Gulf of Aden. China defies extensive cooperation that involves integration with the armed forces of other countries and submission to one-country leadership on a rotating basis. China's participation in NATO's "Shared Awareness and Deconfliction" (SHADE) from 2009 to 2016 reflects Beijing's limited agenda for international joint action in antipiracy operations. SHADE's mission was to ensure effective coordination and to avoid conflict between the military resources and operations of different states participating in combating piracy. For China, SHADE was a means of validating its antipiracy efforts in a forum where participation is voluntary and does not place any navy under the authority of another. According to US naval officials, China has defied opting for chairmanship in the forum in line with its concern to avoid international cooperation based on leadership and extensive cooperation.[48] Similarly, China's defiance of membership of the thirty-nation naval partnership Combined Maritime Forces (CMF) implies that China is not looking for a leadership position in the antipiracy operations in the Gulf of Aden.[49]

Indeed, China's distributed unilateral approach contrasts with the antipiracy efforts of naval forces of multilateral organizations such as NATO, the EU, and CMF, which has jointly performed defensive and offensive antipiracy operations in the international transit corridor and on Somali territory.[50] China's mandate is to provide independent escorts for merchant ships only. China has focused on increased coordination to improve efficiency through SHADE. Since January 2012, independent deployments like those carried out by China, India, Japan, and South Korea have strengthened their convoy coordination by adjusting their escort schedules and optimizing available assets.[51] These actions establish a practice for managing international antipiracy operations on the basis of a unilateral approach without designated state leadership.

China emphasizes capacity-building of countries and regional organizations in fighting piracy, and the necessity of fighting poverty and economic and social underdevelopment in the countries hosting pirates to address the root causes of piracy.[52] This reflects a concern for regime consent regarding antipiracy efforts and for facilitating countries' pursuit of their national and regional development models. China provides financial and capacity-oriented support for countries and regions hosting pirates to "help Africans help themselves." An important part of China's capacity-building efforts focuses on the transport sector. In Somalia itself, China has undertaken infrastructure projects in the southern part, with approval from the government in Mogadishu. China's two-pronged antipiracy contribution of military action and development aid is an attempt to counter accusations that China's contributions are only motivated by a concern for protecting Chinese nationals, energy supplies, and investments.[53]

China has a preference for the non-use of force, which entails that China's military actions focus on a combination of defensive and deterrence measures at sea and support for the peacekeeping and stabilization efforts of UN-sponsored regional organizations. NATO forces' erosion of pirates' logistics and support base by disabling pirate vessels, attaching tracking beacons to mother ships, and allowing the use of force to disable or destroy pirate vessels is beyond the mandate of the Chinese forces.[54] The Chinese task forces are mainly charged with safeguarding the security of Chinese ships and personnel and ships delivering humanitarian supplies for the World Food Programme (WFP) and other international organizations, and sheltering passing foreign vessels. By December 2012, the task force had rescued 2 Chinese ships from pirates who had boarded them and 22 that were being chased by pirates. The Chinese Navy task force had provided protection for 4 WFP ships and 2,455 foreign ships, accounting for 49 percent of the total escorted ships. They helped 4 foreign ships, recovered 4 ships released from captivity, and saved 20 foreign ships from pursuit by pirates.[55]

The equipment of the Chinese task force is highly modern, but a lot of it appears to sit idle most of the time, implying that China uses the task force for posture, to show off how modernized its navy is to deter other countries from challenging core Chinese interests. This posturing is targeted at the other states contributing to antipiracy operations. China's posturing also means that they have been slow to accept any other tasks than merely escorting designated ships. Since 2008, China has gradually moved toward providing security in a wider sense, so that by 2013, China was willing to help other escorts than their own if they asked for assistance.[56]

On land, China does not contribute to offensive military operations to prevent pirates from venturing offshore. Instead, China supports antiterror operations conducted by local countries and UN-based organizations with the argument that terrorism and piracy are interlinked.[57] To address the immediate security concerns on land, China has supported the African Union Mission in Somalia (AMISOM), which is targeting the Somali-based Al-Qaeda Islamist militant group Al-Shabaab with support from the Somalia National Army. By 2011, China had provided $2.2 million to the African Union (AU) peacekeeping operations in Somalia, and $780,000 to Uganda and Burundi, respectively, to be used for purchasing logistical supplies to support the two countries' participation in AMISOM.[58] In addition, China engages in military cooperation with countries such as Ethiopia, Kenya, and Djibouti due to their considerable contributions to AMISOM and to enable them to protect themselves against spillover from Somalia's security issues. In addition, China has agreed with Djibouti on establishing logistical facilities for the use of China's military. Beijing states that this will enable Chinese troops to better fulfill escort missions and make contributions to regional peace and stability.[59] China is concerned to demonstrate that its on-land support for antiterror activities is endorsed by the Somali government, firmly based in the UN Charter, and carried out by regional organizations such as the AU, which subscribes to the UN Charter.

China is concerned to keep its antipiracy efforts within the confines of the UN Charter. This puts some restrictions on China's willingness to engage. China supported all four UNSC resolutions passed in 2008 that established a mandate for the Somali antipiracy effort. The antipiracy operations in the Gulf of Aden have highlighted two issues not adequately addressed in international law. These are, first, the use of force against pirates and armed robbers at sea for any other purpose than self-defense, and second, the actions taken by states capturing pirates and armed robbers.[60] China refrains from using offensive force, staying in line with its principles of defensive and deterrence uses of force and at the same time avoiding entanglement in legal issues that could question its commitment to coexistence. Identifying and confirming pirate targets at sea accurately is problematic, as is collecting evidence. With regard to the seizure of pirates, China has not kept a single pirate in detention on its own soil.[61] China only performs "catch-and-release" operations, at most stopping pirates attacking vessels and destroying their equipment and then letting them go.[62] The legal issues are complex and include how to produce evidence in proceedings taking place far away from the scene of an alleged crime if pirates are prosecuted on the seizing state's territory. Moreover, surrendering pirates to the authorities of the host country, which may violate national laws of the seizing country or international laws in their prosecution, makes this option problematic.[63]

China's coexistence strategy to meet the security challenges of piracy in the Gulf of Aden combines defensive and deterrence strategies with active elements so as to strengthen the foundations of China's social and economic development. The central part of the strategy is to deny and deter attempts at violating the free movement of merchant ships in the Gulf of Aden by actions that are in line with China's national laws and respects the sovereignty of the Somali government. This strategy translates into China's pursuit of a unilateral approach to antipiracy operations focusing on international coordination and escorting ships without Chinese engagement in offensive uses of force targeting pirates. The active elements of the strategy are China's extensive involvement in coordinating activities with other antipiracy fighting countries, its contributions to social and economic development and to UN-endorsed regional counter-terrorist operations undertaken by regional states, and China's support for UN-sponsored frameworks that focus on long-term capacity-building measures to eradicate piracy. China's coexistence strategy in the Gulf of Aden has obtained some reciprocal legitimacy, but relative power also goes some way toward explaining the general acceptance of China's efforts. Relative power explanations mainly emerge in China's wider antipiracy efforts, which involve a wide range of social, economic, and military assistance to states that host pirates or are subject to the consequences of the impoverished conditions that engender piracy. The weak states in the Horn of Africa would not be able to undertake peacekeeping operations or establish infrastructure without overseas development assistance. Their need for assistance is allowing China to shape the future development on the Horn of Africa in accordance with the Chinese approach to principles of security management. Moreover, China has used the antipiracy efforts as a stepping stone for justifying a larger strategic engagement on the Horn of Africa, most significantly with its port facility in Djibouti which is akin to a military base and which can be used to protect Chinese economic and strategic interests. Finally, China obtains much-needed training and valuable information about the military capabilities of other countries by participating in the anti-piracy operations. However, reciprocal legitimacy still dominates China's role in antipiracy. Indeed, Beijing goes to great lengths to ensure that its contribution is within its coexistence interpretation of the UN Charter without opposing the Western-dominated NATO and US contributions that encompass the application of more offensive strategic elements. Value-based legitimacy is absent, since China does not promote a Sino-centric approach. Instead, Beijing advocates accommodating different approaches to antipiracy by means of coordination.

CONCLUSION

The chapter has argued that China pursues a coexistence strategy of mediation, regime consent, and the non-use of force embedded in the UN system to protect its core interests of regime survival, sovereignty and territorial integrity, and continuous socioeconomic development. Legitimacy for China's version of coexistence is limited to modest levels of reciprocal legitimacy far from China's shores. The strategy combines active defense and deterrence so as to achieve revisionist intrasystem change through a reinterpretation of the principles of global security management.

Coexistence means that Beijing offers a different kind of strategy for how to bring security to the table compared to Washington. China's attempt to change the status quo by active defense means that China prioritizes coordination on the basis of unilateral contributions rather than integration on the basis of multilateral cooperation. It also means that China attaches value to freedom of action to pursue national interests, as opposed to the burdens of responsibility that come with international leadership. Beijing does not have a pariah-state policy whereby some states are excluded. On the contrary, China argues that economic engagement with regimes irrespective of their ideological preferences is more likely to engender compliance with legitimate principles of behavior than exclusion. China is against the use of force as a standard means of conflict resolution, although it maintains it may be used temporarily for purposes of stability. Of course, one reason for this preference is that Beijing's military capabilities are weak compared to those of Washington, as pointed out by Shambaugh.[64] However, it is not the only reason.

China's rising power and influence are based on a worldwide economic engagement that is translated into political-strategic influence such as that exercised by Beijing in the Horn of Africa. China has benefited greatly from going about its rise without resorting to actual force. The costs for the United States and states targeted by force for the purposes of conflict resolution, such as Iraq, Afghanistan, and Libya, have helped confirm that the use of force is a difficult instrument to use to provide security management. Finally, China has hooked up with the UN system in its pursuit of a gradual change of the status quo. This way of going about exercising influence has several advantages. If China embedded its overseas activities in Sino-centric concepts of world order, Beijing would meet immediate resistance to principles of conduct that have no a priori legitimacy with other states. By contrast, the UN system has universal legitimacy, so China only has to persuade the international community that its interpretation of right and wrong conduct is in compliance with the UN Charter. On this basis, China has successfully defended the fundamental status of absolute sovereignty and introduced its coexistence strategy for global security management as a legitimate way of pursuing security in the Gulf of Aden. Regionally, China has not demonstrated sufficient concern for the interests of other states to allow for reciprocal legitimacy.

What are the consequences of China's coexistence-style world order for US-China relations? In contrast to Washington, Beijing is not looking for value-based legitimacy and the obligations that accompany this type of influence. China's security management is based on a revised version of procedural universal rules that may have elements of Chinese values, such as avoiding the loss of face by preferring to shelve disputes rather than pronouncing a winner and a loser. However, coexistence is not embedded in a Sino-centric world order concept. Instead, it is based on value pluralism and principles of conduct that already have international legitimacy because they are an inherent part of the UN system.

China does not want to be drawn into the protracted conflicts that often come with disagreements founded in ideological belief systems. Value-based standards often lead to the formulation of ambitious objectives that are difficult to realize, such as intervening in other states to facilitate domestic political reform. China prioritizes its domestic development to consolidate the Chinese nation-state and regime and China's continued rise. Beijing is not ready to have its performance measured according to a value-based standard that would be difficult to meet with its additional demands for putting state interests aside to defend values. In contrast to the liberal world order, China's coexistence pursuit does not establish a hierarchy of states with those subscribing to the values at the center of the order.

China's attempt to gradually change the existing world order from within without a revolutionary objective of overthrowing the order emerges from the absence of a value-based concept of world order that could offer alternative long-term visions to those inherent in the liberal version of world order. China has thrived on this low-key manner of managing its rise, and so we should not expect China to pursue Sino-centric versions of world order for the foreseeable future. As a consequence, China and the United States do not end up in protracted ideological conflicts that make it difficult to maintain a minimal kind of world order. They can manage relations on a pragmatic basis because of the absence of ideological hostility. On the other hand, their versions of world order are fundamentally different interpretations of how to go about managing global security issues. Therefore, permanent conflict resolution mechanisms are difficult to establish. As a result, ad hoc conflict resolution and trial-and-error dynamics are common features of the post-Cold War world order. This allows for swift adjustments to change. However, it also requires that states be flexible in their responses because of the lack of universal agreement on how to solve security issues that threaten international peace and stability. This system is easier for Beijing to navigate than for Washington because China is not tied down by value-based commitments.

The two competing interpretations of world order exist side by side across different issue areas and geographical regions. Both Washington and Beijing are looking to attract partners willing to support their version of world order. This gives secondary and small powers considerable leverage because they do not have to choose between the two. Instead, they can side with Washington on some issues and with Beijing on others. The central role of secondary and small powers keeps China's version of world order alive. The absence of community-based principles from China's international agenda and Beijing's modest levels of reciprocal legitimacy means that most states prefer siding with Washington if forced to choose. China remains vulnerable to fluctuating economic trends that may weaken its ability to continue to keep a constituency of partial supporters happy. If China's economy takes a significant downward turn, Beijing's efforts at consolidating its version of world order is likely to come to an end.[65]

Modest levels of reciprocal legitimacy explain why China's international behavior gives rise to conflict and tension in the international system.

Reciprocity means that the international community trusts that a particular state will respect the principles of its version of world order and that it pursues these not only for its own benefit, but also to protect common interests in peace and stability. China has limited reciprocal legitimacy because its behavior, especially in its neighborhood, calls into question if China is sufficiently committed to coexistence as a recipe for world order. In particular, China's adherence to a historical understanding of legitimacy that deviates from modern universal interpretations of how sovereignty is acquired gives rise to suspicions as regards China's long-term intentions. Insufficient trust in China's willingness to be a responsible great power that looks after the common interests of states and not just its own national interests means that as China exercises more and more influence at the international level, other countries will interpret China's intentions as threatening their security. The resentment and pushback against China's growing influence that ensues create conflict and tension.

If China is to reach its "Teddy Roosevelt Moment" in the sense of taking on a visible and active role on the world stage that involves major responsibility for global security management, Beijing needs to leave behind ambitions to rectify century-old violations of China's alleged territorial and maritime space, even if it weakens China's geostrategic position in Asia in the interim. At issue is not so much China's growing strategic presence in its neighborhood; indeed, that is to be expected from a rising power. Instead, it is China's insistence to correct historic wrongs that gives rise to concerns that restoration of the Chinese motherland is accompanied by resurrection of a Chinese hierarchical hegemonic regional order that is ill-suited to the modern international system of sovereign states. For the majority of small and secondary powers, independence is an asset they do not want to lose even if they have to trade some of it in for US security guarantees. A minority of radical but influential nationalist voices has pushed the moderate mainstream in a Sino-centric value-based direction regarding Beijing's neighborhood policy.[66] It remains to be seen if China increases the elements of reciprocity in its pursuit of global security management, or if, by contrast, the Sino-centric tendencies become more pronounced.

In the meantime, international peace and stability mainly rests on the ability of Washington and Beijing to manage conflict and tension by applying pragmatic ad hoc conflict management. Drawing on the lessons from antipiracy operations in the Gulf of Aden, this requires that both the United States and China make room for their different versions of security management in the same theater. When they succeed in accommodating each other, success in terms of defusing conflict and increasing international peace and stability seems possible.

NOTES

1. The author would like to thank Nicolai Christoffersen, Christian Rune, Richard J. Samuels and the other participants at the Nobel symposium in June 2014 for comments and suggestions for draft chapters. Any errors and omissions remain the responsibility of the author.
2. Stephen M. Walt, "Rising Powers and the Risks of War: A Realist View of Sino-American Relations," this volume.
3. William C. Wohlforth, "Not Quite the Same as It Ever Was: Power Shifts and Contestation over the American-Led World Order," this volume.
4. G. John Ikenberry, "A New Order of Things? China, America, and the Struggle over World Order," this volume.
5. William A. Callahan, "Chinese Visions of World Order: Post-Hegemonic or a New Hegemony?," *International Studies Review* 10, no. 4 (2008): 749–61.
6. Rosemary Foot, "Restraints on Conflict in the China-US Relationship: Contesting Power Transition Theory," this volume.
7. International Crisis Group, "Dangerous Waters: China-Japan Relations on the Rocks," *Asia Report* no. 45, April 8, 2013, https://www.crisisgroup.org/asia/north-east-asia/china/dangerous-waters-china-japan-relations-rocks.
8. Lindsay Black and Yih-Jye Hwang, "China and Japan's Quest for Great Power Status: Norm Entrepreneurship in Antipiracy Responses," *International Relations* 26, no. 4 (2012): 431–51.
9. For a detailed account, see Liselotte Odgaard, *Beijing and Coexistence: Beijing's National Security Strategy for the Twenty-First Century* (Washington, DC: Woodrow Wilson Center Press / Baltimore: Johns Hopkins University Press, 2012), 35–40.
10. Warren Lerner, "The Historical Origins of the Soviet Doctrine of Peaceful Coexistence," *Law and Contemporary Problems* 29, no. 4 (Autumn 1964): 865–70.
11. Barry Posen, "Explaining Military Doctrine," in *The Use of Force: Military Power and International Politics*, 5th ed., ed. Robert J. Art and Kenneth N. Waltz (Lanham, MD: Rowman and Littlefield, 1999), 23–43, reference to 25.
12. Ibid., 36–37.
13. Henry Kissinger, *A World Restored: Metternich, Castlereagh and the Problems of Peace 1812–1822* (London: Phoenix Press, 1957), 1.
14. F. S. Northedge, *The International Political System* (London: Faber & Faber, 1976), 112–13, 150–51.
15. Hedley Bull, *The Anarchical Society: A Study of Order in World Politics*, 2nd ed. (1977; Houndmills: MacMillan, 1995), 133–34.
16. Robert Gilpin, *War and Change in World Politics* (Cambridge: Cambridge University Press, 1981), 41–47.
17. China calls the islands Diaoyu; Japan calls them the Senkakus.
18. Unryu Suganuma, *Sovereign Rights and Territorial Space in Sino-Japanese Relations: Irredentism, and the Diaoyu/Senkaku Islands* (Honolulu: University of Hawaii Press, 2000), 134; Greg Austin, *China's Ocean Frontier: International Law, Military Force and National Development* (Canberra: Allen & Unwin, 1998), 49; M. Taylor Fravel, *Strong Borders, Secure Nation: Cooperation and Conflict in China's Territorial Disputes* (Princeton, NJ: Princeton University Press, 2008), 334.
19. "China Lodges Protest Over Senkaku Lease," *The Japan Times*, January 6, 2003, http://www.japantimes.co.jp/news/2003/01/06/national/china-lodges-protest-over-senkaku-lease/#.WWM6Lojyhdg.

20. Yong Deng, *China's Struggle for Status: The Realignment of International Relations* (Cambridge: Cambridge University Press, 2008), 182.
21. "China's Military Strategy," The State Council Information Office of the People's Republic of China, May 2015, http://eng.mod.gov.cn/Press/2015-05/26/content_4586805.htm.
22. James Manicom, *Bridging Troubled Waters: China, Japan, and Maritime Order in the East China Sea* (Washington, DC: Georgetown University Press, 2014), 46.
23. Ibid., 46–47.
24. *People's Daily* editorial, quoted in Mel Gurtov, *Will This Be China's Century? A Skeptic's View* (Boulder, CO: Lynne Rienner, 2013), 21.
25. "China-Japan Joint Press Communiqué," Ministry of Foreign Affairs of the People's Republic of China, April 11, 2007, http://www.fmprc.gov.cn/mfa_eng/wjdt_665385/2649_665393/t311005.shtml.
26. Yong, *China's Struggle for Status*, 183.
27. Taiwan is also party to the dispute.
28. "China, Russia to Hold Joint Military Exercises in May," *Xinhua*, May 1, 2014, http://news.xinhuanet.com/english/china/2014-05/01/c_133303158.htm.
29. "China Plans to Build 36 Marine Law Enforcement Vessels in Next Five Years," *People's Daily*, January 25, 2013, http://english.people.com.cn/90786/8107265.html.
30. Japan's Defense Ministry To Develop Protocol Over Trespassing Drones," *Japan Daily Press*, October 2, 2013, http://japandailypress.com/japans-defense-ministry-to-develop-protocol-over-trespassing-drones-0237048/.
31. Ministry of Foreign Affairs of the People's Republic of China, "Statement by Defense Ministry Spokesman Geng Yansheng on China's Air Defense Identification Zone (ADIZ)", December 3, 2013, http://www.fmprc.gov.cn/ce/cebe/eng/zt/dhfksbq13/t1109762.htm.
32. Shannon Tiezzi, "China's Foreign Minister: No Cause for Optimism in China-Japan Relations," *The Diplomat*, March 9, 2016, http://thediplomat.com/2016/03/chinas-foreign-minister-no-cause-for-optimism-in-china-japan-relations/.
33. Jonathan Spence, "The Once and Future China," *Foreign Policy*, January/February 2005, 44–46.
34. "Japan/U.S. Double Dealing on Diaoyu Islands Is a Betrayal of History," *People's Daily*, May 6, 2014, http://english.people.com.cn/98649/8618292.html.
35. M. Taylor Fravel and Alastair Iain Johnston, "Chinese Signaling in the East China Sea?," *Washington Post*, April 12, 2014, http://www.washingtonpost.com/blogs/monkey-cage/wp/2014/04/12/chinese-signaling-in-the-east-china-sea//?print=1.
36. Yoshihide Soeya, "The Rise of China in Asia: Japan at the Nexus," this volume.
37. Austin, *China's Ocean Frontier*, 162–76.
38. "Press Briefing by Press Secretary Robert Gibbs, Special Assistant to the President and Senior Director for Asian Affairs Jeff Bader, and Deputy National Security Advisor for Strategic Communications Ben Rhodes," Washington, DC, The White House Office of the Press Secretary, http://www.whitehouse.gov/the-press-office/2010/09/23/press-briefing-press-secretary-robert-gibbs-special-assistant-president-.
39. "Q&A: Japan's Yomiuri Shimbun Interviews President Obama," *Washington Post*, April 23, 2014, http://www.washingtonpost.com/world/qanda-japans-yomiuri-shimbun-interviews-president-obama/2014/04/23/d01bb5fc-cae3-11e3-95f7-7ecdde72d2ea_story.html.

40. "The South China Sea Arbitration (The Republic of the Philippines v. The People's Republic of China)," Permanent Court of Arbitration, press release, The Hague, July 12, 2016, https://pcacases.com/web/sendAttach/1801.
41. "Arbitration between the Republic of the Philippines and the People's Republic of China Regarding the South China Sea (Final Award by the Tribunal) (Statement by Foreign Minister Fumio Kishida)," Ministry of Foreign Affairs of Japan, press release, July 12, 2016, http://www.mofa.go.jp/press/release/press4e_001204.html.
42. Prashanth Parameswaran, "Japan, Philippines to Launch Maritime Exercise Amid South China Sea Uncertainty," *The Diplomat*, July 11, 2016, http://thediplomat.com/2016/07/japan-philippines-to-launch-maritime-exercise-amid-south-china-sea-uncertainty/.
43. Jeremy Page, "Beijing's South China Sea Moves Vex U.S. Pacific Fleet Chief," *Wall Street Journal*, August 9, 2016, http://www.wsj.com/articles/chinas-south-china-sea-moves-draw-ire-of-u-s-pacific-fleet-chief-1470762489.
44. Li Yancheng, "Chinese Navy Escorted over 3,000 Merchant Vessels in Gulf of Aden," *People's Daily*, March 10, 2011, http://english.peopledaily.com.cn/98666/101812/101886/7314838.html.
45. Information Office of the State Council, *The Diversified Employment of China's Armed Forces*, April 16, 2013, http://www.china.org.cn/government/whitepaper/node_7181425.htm.
46. "Chinese Naval Fleet Carries Out First Escort Mission Off Somalia," *People's Daily/Xinhua*, January 6, 2009, http://english.people.com.cn/90001/90776/90883/6568232.html.
47. "China Sends Escort Fleet to Gulf of Aden," *Xinhua*, December, 17, 2016, http://english.chinamil.com.cn/view/2016-12/17/content_7412333.htm.
48. Andrew S. Erickson and Austin M. Strange, "No Substitute for Experience: Chinese Antipiracy Operations in the Gulf of Aden," *China Maritime Studies*, no. 10, (Newport: U.S. Naval War College, November 2013), 60–63.
49. Commodore Henning Amundsen, Commander Standing NATO Maritime Group ONE June 7 to December 7, 2013, and staff at Navy HQ Bergen, Norway, author's interview, May 16, 2014.
50. Erickson and Strange, "No Substitute for Experience," 65–67.
51. The Information Office of the State Council, *The Diversified Employment of China's Armed Forces*.
52. "Statement by Ambassador Wang Min at the Security Council Open Debate on Piracy," Permanent Mission of the People's Republic of China to the UN, November 19, 2012, http://www.china-un.org/eng/chinaandun/securitycouncil/thematicissues/piracy/t993262.htm.
53. Commodore Henning Amundsen staff at Navy HQ Bergen, author's interview; regarding China's motives for development assistance, see for example "Between Extremes: China and Africa," Briefing Note 1202, London, Africa Research Institute, October 2012, http://africaresearchinstitute.org/newsite/wp-content/uploads/2013/03/Briefing-Note-1202-pdf.pdf.
54. Commodore Henning Amundsen staff at Navy HQ Bergen, author's interview.
55. The Information Office of the State Council, *The Diversified Employment of China's Armed Forces*.
56. Commodore Henning Amundsen staff at Navy HQ Bergen, author's interview.
57. Most likely, in some areas of Somalia, piracy is used to finance terrorist activities, whereas in other areas there is no link. Ibid.

58. "China Says Military Action Not Final Solution to Somali Piracy," *People's Daily/Xinhua*, November 18, 2011, http://english.peopledaily.com.cn/90883/7649776.html.
59. Yan Meng and Yao Chun, "Djibouti Wants to Reinforce Military Cooperation with China," *People's Daily/Xinhua*, February 27, 2014, http://english.people.com.cn/90883/8549361.html; Shannon Tiezzi, "China Has 'Reached Consensus' with Djibouti on Military Base," *The Diplomat*, January 23, 2016, http://thediplomat.com/2016/01/china-has-reached-consensus-with-djibouti-on-military-base/.
60. Tullio Treves, "Piracy, Law of the Sea, and Use of Force: Developments off the Coast of Somalia," *European Journal of International Law* 20, no. 2 (2009): 399–414.
61. Erickson and Strange, "No Substitute for Experience," 71–73.
62. Commodore Henning Amundsen staff at Navy HQ Bergen, author's interview.
63. Treves, "Piracy, Law of the Sea, and Use of Force."
64. David Shambaugh, "Is China a Global Power?," this volume.
65. Zhang Ruizhuang, "Despite the 'New Assertiveness,' China Is Not Up for Challenging the Global Order," this volume, provides arguments as to why China is not able to suggest a different type of world order.
66. Liselotte Odgaard, "Maritime Security in East Asia: Peaceful Coexistence and Active Defense in China's Diaoyu/Senkaku Policy," *Journal of Contemporary China* 26, no. 103 (January 2017): 118–133.

CHAPTER 13

The Rise of China in Asia

Japan at the Nexus

YOSHIHIDE SOEYA

INTRODUCTION

Will China rise peacefully? The question is a complex one for the neighbors of China, who cannot avoid the direct and tangible impact of the rise of China regardless of the answer. Even if China rises peacefully, this would not guarantee that China would be nice to its neighbors. For major external actors such as the United States and the European Union (EU), accommodating the peaceful rise of China would mean acquiescing to Chinese power and/or peaceful coexistence with China on the global stage. Would this, however, be the same for its Asian neighbors? If not, how different would it be, and what are the implications of the differences for a shifting order in Asia? Finally, what is the place of Japan in this transforming Asian order, how is it responding to the rise of China, and how should it in coming years?

In attempting to answer these questions, this chapter will be divided into three parts. The first part will examine the dual and divergent implications of the rise of China for the world and for Asia. This dualism was most succinctly and vividly expressed by a Southeast Asian official attending the Shangri-La dialogue in Singapore in May-June 2014, who said, "We do not think China wants to rule the world. China just wants to rule us."[1] Then, what China wants on the global stage, on the one hand, and in Asia, on the other, may not be the same. We will look into this difference, by deciphering the concept of "a new model of major power relations," for which the current leadership of the Chinese Communist Party (CCP) under Xi Jinping appears to be aspiring as a long-term goal.

The chapter will then see, in the second part, how the dual aspects of the rise of China manifest themselves in the relationship between China and Japan. Japan is indeed situated at the nexus of Asia and the world, as a neighbor of China, an ally of the United States, and a leading member of the global liberal international order. Japan's peculiar experiences with China since the late 1970s are particularly relevant in addressing three critical issue areas concerning the dual nature of the rise of China.

Firstly, Japan was a primary supporter of the rapid economic growth of China since Deng Xiaoping's open-door and reform policies. The Japanese government justified its massive economic assistance to China by arguing that the economic development of China would be important for the social and political stability of China, which then was intended to foster stable relations between Japan and China, and also the stability of Asia and the world.[2] In a nutshell, the Japanese intention was to bring China into the postwar liberal international order.

Secondly, however, on the flip side of Deng Xiaoping's strategy was the redefinition of the "one-hundred year history of humiliation" as a new source of legitimacy of the CCP's rule and the unity of the Chinese people and society.[3] Originally, the intention was not to single out Japan as a target, but, if only inadvertently, it was to be expected that Japan would eventually find itself in the spotlight, complicating Sino-Japanese relations by involving public sentiments and domestic politics of both countries in an ever-growing vicious cycle as the years went by.

Thirdly, as the Chinese economy has continued to grow, which ironically enough was indeed the objective of Japan's China policy for more than three decades, China has become increasingly assertive in "reclaiming" what, they believe, used to be their territories "since ancient times." Over the "Senkaku/Diaoyu" islands dispute, we argue, there is a virtual clash of paradigms regarding preferred international orders, between the Chinese faith in the legitimacy of a Sino-centric order in Asia, on the one hand, and the Japanese emphasis on the legitimacy of the modern international relations and laws, on the other.

In the third part, we will see how Japan has coped with the rise of China in recent years amid the phenomenon of a "normalizing" Japan. Confusion about the concept of a "normal" Japan and the dual nature of the rise of China simply add to the complexity of Japan-China relations in the regional context. We will then assess the most recent diplomacy under the leadership of Shinzo Abe, to be followed by the discussion of an alternative, "middle power" strategy.

The key implication of the analysis presented in this chapter is that whether a strong China will be able to coexist with its Asian neighbors in a peaceful and benign manner is critical, not only in an Asian context, but also for the stable transition of shfting international orders where the rise of China is a central transforming element, a key assumption of this book project. The worst case scenario is, as the chapter by Stephen Walt in this volume amply demonstrates, a strategic clash between the United States and China, one that might be accelerated if China keeps pushing the margins of its sphere of influence into the South China Sea and the East China Sea, and eventually more toward the Western Pacific.

Hugh White recently presented a prescription to avoid this ultimate strategic clash, arguing for power-sharing between the United States and China across the Pacific.[4] The premise of the argument is concerned with Chinese nationalism: China no longer accepts US primacy as the basis of an Asian order. This is an understandable urge of a rising China, whose status should be accepted and respected for the stability of the Asia-Pacific. One conundrum arising from this thesis, however, particularly for China's immediate neighbors, is whether a strong China rejecting US primacy can be a benign hegemon in Asia. Many Chinese appear to believe so or at least like to argue that it could, but their behavior particularly with regards to territorial disputes toward some of their neighbors tends to convince their neighbors otherwise.

In this decidedly realist exposition of the strategic relationship between the United States and China, what is often missing is the examination of the place and role of Chinese neighbors in Asia in the transformation of an Asia order. Obviously, Asian countries stand to be directly impacted by the behaviors of a powerful China, and their coping strategies, or the lack of them, should affect the shape of an Asia order in a significant way.

Such a strategy cannot be effectively constructed by any single country, including Japan, and it should be clear, at least conceptually, that the truly equal partnership is the key to building cooperation among Chinese neighbors, with a view to consolidating the effective infrastructure of a transforming regional order. We call such an approach a "middle power" strategy (to be elaborated below), and argue that applying such perspective to cooperation between Japan and other Asian countries has become increasingly important at a time when the rise of China has become an organizing principle in the transformation of an Asian order and the role of the United States therein is being re-examined.

THE RISE OF CHINA IN GLOBAL AND ASIAN CONTEXTS

As the chapters by Stephen Walt and John Ikenberry in this volume explicitly demonstrate, there has been a grand debate in Western academia regarding the theoretical implications of the rise of China. The debate is essentially about the major themes and trends in the transformation of the world order, that is, between realism anticipating a geopolitical clash between a declining hegemon and an ascending power,[5] and liberalism emphasizing the durability of the US-led liberal international order and the likelihood of China to be accommodated in it.[6]

In addressing the question of the rise of China in the policy area, however, the discussions tend to fluctuate between the realist prognosis and the liberal theorization. For instance, it has become a cliché to say that the Chinese ascendance has dual and contradictory aspects, that is, sources of security instability and economic prosperity. The role of the United States is also characterized by dualism, that is, as being the most powerful superpower in the world and yet also a declining power in relative terms. The strategic relationship between China and the United States, therefore, has been complex, fluctuating between hopes and despairs, cooperation and conflict.

In retrospect, the first explicit manifestation of the US approach after the end of the Cold War was the US definition of China as a stakeholder in the future international system.[7] This was a step forward from the previous discourse on the US China policy, which had tended to be preoccupied with the dichotomy between engagement and containment.[8] These approaches had one thing in common: both treated China as an outsider of the US-led international system. By contrast, the stakeholder argument assumed that China was already integrated into the system. Then came Fred Bergsten's argument of G-2, recognizing both the fundamental differences with China and the necessity to work with China in managing the global agenda.[9]

There is also evidence to suggest that liberal internationalists in China prefer to tread the course toward becoming a responsible member of the international community. After all, today's spectacular rise of China is a result of China fully taking advantage of the liberal international order led by the United States and other industrialized democracies, particularly since Deng Xiaoping's open-door and reform policies initiated in the late 1970s. This implies that in order for China to continue to rise and tackle associated problems both domestically and internationally, it will continue to have to live under the existing liberal international order, and even craft its grand strategy according to these global imperatives.[10] The chapter by

Zhang Ruizhuang in this volume also affirms the likelihood of China engaging in the liberal international order in a constructive way.

In the realm of security in the Asia-Pacific, however, the picture is starkly different. A case in point is the position expressed by the 2010 Quadrennial Defense Review (QDR) of the United States, where the Pentagon expressed concerns about China's expanding military capabilities that might deny US forces' access to East Asia. Specifically, the QDR stated, "Anti-access strategies seek to deny outside countries the ability to project power into a region, thereby allowing aggression or other destabilizing actions to be conducted by the anti-access power."[11]

In more recent years, President Barack Obama's strategy of "pivoting" to Asia has also highlighted the aspect of strategic competition between the United States and China. In response to aggressive Chinese behavior in the South China Sea and the East China Sea, the United States expanded joint naval exercises with Japan, reached new agreements to sell arms to the Philippines, agreed to send US marines to Australia, and restored defense cooperation with Indonesia and New Zealand. Robert Ross calls these developments "the end of engagement."[12]

In the eyes of the Chinese, however, there is perhaps no contradiction in the seemingly dichotomous choice between engaging in the liberal international order and geopolitical rivalry. In order to understand this perception of the Chinese, it should be important to decipher peculiar Chinese nationalism into two critical sentiments dominant among the Chinese. One is a strong awareness of perceived victimization and humiliation in the modern history of China since the 1840–1842 Opium War. The other is a growing sense of confidence and pride among the Chinese, emanating from the recent spectacular rise to a great power status. These sentiments combine to make up unique nationalism among the Chinese people.[13] As a result, many Chinese believe today that Asia with China as the strong center is the natural state of Asia, and that the time has come to bring Asia back to such "normalcy." For the Chinese, a strong China "reclaiming" their core interests in Asia should be compatible with a China engaging in the liberal international order at the global level.

This unique role and status of a strong China is amply demonstrated by the idea of a "new model of major power relations" (新型大国关系, xinxing daguo guanxi) between the United States and China. One of the earlier articulations of the concept, originally phrased as "a new type of relationship between major countries in the 21st century," was made by then vice president Xi Jinping in Washington, DC on February 15, 2012.[14] Xi said that such a relationship would be characterized by (1) "mutual understanding and strategic trust," (2) "respecting each other's 'core interests,'"

(3) "mutually beneficial cooperation," and (4) "enhancing cooperation and coordination in international affairs and on global issues."[15] On June 7, 2013, Xi Jingpin, now the general secretary of the CCP, reaffirmed the same four key elements at the occasion of the summit meeting with President Barack Obama in California.

Analytically, the four elements in Xi Jinping's formula of "a new model of major power relations" could be grouped into two categories; (1) strategic trust and (2) "core interests" are more relevant in the Asia-Pacific context, whereas (3) mutual benefits and (4) coordination on global issues are important for the US-China relationship at the global level. Put simply, China wants to coexist with the United States peacefully in the Asia-Pacific region as well as at the global level, but one critical condition is for the United States to respect an Asian order with China as the primary architect. Initially, the Obama administration's response to this Chinese overture was not necessarily negative. In November 2013, for instance, National Security Advisor Susan Rice stated the following:

> When it comes to China, we seek to operationalize a new model of major power relations. That means managing inevitable competition while forging deeper cooperation on issues where our interests converge—in Asia and beyond. We both seek the denuclearization of the Korean Peninsula, a peaceful resolution to the Iranian nuclear issue, a stable and secure Afghanistan, and an end to conflict in Sudan. There are opportunities for us to take concerted action to bolster peace and development in places like sub-Saharan Africa, where sustainable growth would deliver lasting benefit to the peoples of Africa as well as to both our countries.[16]

Arguably, the context in which Susan Rice referred to "a new model of major power relations" is primarily, if not exclusively, a global one, where China is regarded as an insider of the global system, and the United States is ready to coexist and work with such a China. Rice's reference to the United States seeking "to operationalize" such relations, however, were received with some alarm in some corners in Asia, precisely because, in the Asian context, the Chinese emphasis on "a new model of major power relations" connotes the Chinese desire to see a gradual decrease in US presence and influence in the region. Understandably, in order for China to continue to push for the realization of a China-centered Asia, the presence of the United States is the biggest obstacle.

This was made explicit in the statements made by Xi Jinping on both of the occasions in the United States mentioned above (in February 2012 and in June 2013), that "the Pacific Ocean is wide enough to incorporate [the interests of] both China and the U.S."[17] In his meeting with US Secretary of Defense Chuck Hagel in August 2013 in Washington, DC, China's minister of national defense, General Chang Wanquan, also repeated Xi's words by saying that "President Xi used to say that the Pacific is wide enough to accommodate both two great countries, China and United States."[18] Now, we will turn to the examination of the role of Japan in standing at the nexus of this dichotomy between a rising China on the global stage and an assertive China in the Asian context.

THE ORIGIN OF THE HISTORY PROBLEM

In the late 1970s, upon returning to power, Deng Xiaoping started courageous open-door and reform policies and turned to Japan as a primary provider of official development assistance (ODA) and foreign direct investment. His trip to Japan in October 1978, prior to the visit to the United States in January the following year, was successful in impressing the Japanese with an image of a new China under Deng's leadership.

In response, Japan became a leading developed country supporting the Chinese modernization through massive ODA and foreign direct investment. In 1982, China caught up with Indonesia as the leading recipient of Japanese ODA. The official slogan by the Japanese government was that the economic development of China was essential for the stability of Chinese politics and society, which would be the basis of stable bilateral relations between Japan and China, and by extension of regional and global stability.

As Michael Yahuda analyzes, however, Deng Xiaping's open-door and reform policies inevitably shook the foundation of Mao's ideology as a source of legitimacy of the CCP. Deng Xiaoping thus started to emphasize patriotism by using modern history as a new source of unity of the Chinese people. Unwittingly, therefore, "Japan came to be embroiled in China's new quest to promote patriotism amid the struggles for economic reform."[19] Thus, Yahuda argues that the structural origin of the history problem between Japan and China lies in "changes in the domestic politics of identity within China."[20]

Significantly, the Nanjing Memorial, officially named the "Memorial Hall of the Victims in Nanjing Massacre by Japanese Invaders," was opened on August 15, 1985. This was followed by the opening of the "Museum of the War of Chinese People's Resistance against Japanese Aggression" on July 7, 1987, commemorating the fiftieth anniversary of the Marco Polo Bridge Incident. Since the erection of these two major museums, the CCP "began to downplay the civil war in favor of a national war against Japan."[21]

The message of these museums is that of victimization by the Japanese aggressors, which is connected to the overall emphasis on Chinese history of humiliation since the Opium War of 1840–1842, which resulted in the loss of Hong Kong to the British.[22]

On the diplomatic front, China seized the occasion of the Japanese mass media report in June 1982 that the Ministry of Education of Japan instructed a history textbook draft expression of "aggression toward Northeast China" to be changed to "advance toward Northeast China," in describing the nature of Japanese actions in the 1910s and the 1920s, prior to the establishment of Manchukuo in 1932. After some delay, the Chinese government started extensive campaigns to criticize Japan in Chinese media. The textbook issue had thus become the very first case of the history controversy between Japan and China in the postwar years. In response, the Kiichi Miyazawa cabinet decided to add a "neighborly country clause" to the textbook inspection criteria. In early September, the Chinese government accepted these efforts by Japan, and the issue subsided.[23]

Then came the controversy over the Yasukuni Shrine in the summer of 1985. Until then, almost all prime ministers of postwar Japan had visited the Yasukuni Shrine annually during their tenures. It had never been raised as a diplomatic issue until August 1985, when China, having said nothing about the previous nine visits by Yasuhiro Nakaosne to the Yasukuni Shrine as prime minister, suddenly made a diplomatic issue of his tenth visit, with the logic that this visit was made as an official one. Nakasone compromised diplomatically, and Tokyo and Beijing struck a deal, agreeing to the gentlemen's agreement that prime minister, foreign minister, and cabinet secretary would not visit the Yasukuni Shrine while in office, but that China would condone the visits by other officials and politicians.[24]

The Japanese government thus attempted to deal with the new "history problem" in a conciliatory manner. Perhaps the Chinese leadership was confident that they should be able to control the dual aspects of Deng Xiaoping's strategy, that is, implanting history as a new source of unity of the Chinese people, underpinning the legitimacy of the CCP rule, and gaining the upper hand against Japan in a moral sense, while advancing cooperation with Japan as an important supporter of Chinese economic modernization and development.

In the 1990s, however, Japan started to adjust its security policies to changing security environments in the post-Cold War era in the direction of becoming a "normal" country, as seen below. This phenomenon of "normalizing" Japan then became entangled with the history problem, creating a typical vicious cycle between Japan and China involving popular emotions and domestic politics of both nations. The territorial disputes over the Senkaku (which China calls Diaoyu) Islands became a symbolic issue aggravating the vicious cycle.

THE "SENKAKU/DIAOYU" DISPUTE AS A PARADIGM CLASH

When China was in the throes of revolution of the Chinese model under Mao Zedong, the "Senkaku/Diaoyu" issue was nonexistent. The *People's Daily* dated January 8 1953, in its support for the people in Okinawa fighting against the American occupation, defined the Okinawa Archipelago as consisting of seven groups of islands including the Senkaku.[25]

Against these backgrounds, for Tokyo, it came entirely out of the blue that China contested the Japanese ownership in December 1971 (Taiwan did so a bit earlier in the late 1960s). Chinese Foreign Ministry's statement said that the "Diaoyu" islands had been part of Taiwan since "ancient times," thus claiming the Chinese sovereignty for the first time in history.[26] In the meantime, Deng Xiaoping said in 1978 that he would wish the future generation to handle the issue wisely, but in 1992, China announced the territorial law designating "Diaoyu" as Chinese territory. This was an attempt at virtually changing the status quo, but Japan did not respond with any countermeasures, and China did not take any further actions.

Since then, there have been occasional incidents where Chinese fishing boats entered into the Senkaku waters, but in December 2008 official Chinese vessels intruded into the territorial waters of the Senkaku for the first time. Presumably, since around that time, the Chinese definition and handling of the "Senkaku/Diaoyu" dispute has become identical with those of the islands in the South China Sea. The firm position of China on the South China Sea dispute has manifested itself explicitly in the speech by the deputy chief of the General Staff of Chinese People's Liberation Army (PLA) Wang Guanzhong at the Shangri-La Dialogue held in Singapore on May 30–June 1, 2014.

In response to Shinzo Abe's keynote speech, touched on below, Wang Guanzhong rebuffed Abe's exposition of the importance of rule of law as ill intentioned reagainst China,[27] and asserted the Chinese understanding of its nine-dashed line claim to the South China Sea. China, he said, discovered the islands in the South China Sea as early as the Han Dynasty, that is, more than two thousand years ago; the nine-dashed line was drawn and declared in 1948; this was forty-six years before 1994, when the United Nations Convention on the Law of the Sea (UNCLOS) was ratified, which should not have retroactive effect; Japan had taken these "Chinese" islands in the South China Sea by force during World War II, which were returned to China on the basis of the Cairo Declaration and the Potsdam Declaration; Chinese neighbors began to claim these islands in the late 1960s and the 1970s when they found out that there were reserves of natural resources.

As amply demonstrated here, the historical context is of central importance in the eyes of the Chinese. Modern history since the 1840–1842 Opium War is, in Chinese eyes, a history of humiliation, where China suffered continuous aggressions at the hands of the Western powers, including Japan.[28] For the Chinese, therefore, "restoration" of the ownership of the islands of in the South China Sea is to do justice to history, and the same is now true as to the "Diaoyu" islands.

When seen from a Japanese perspective, the Japanese assertion about the legality and legitimacy of the possession of the Senkaku islands dates back to January 1895, when the Meji government had made a cabinet decision to include the islands into Japanese territories. This was three months before the singing of the Shimonoseki Treaty in April of the same year, the Japanese argument goes, which ended the Sino-Japanese War and made Taiwan a colony of Japan. The Senkaku islands, therefore, were legally not part of the territories that Japan agreed to give up by accepting the Potsdam Declaration in 1945, according to the Japanese government.[29]

All the more, these islands have been the private property of Japanese citizens for more than a century, with an interruption of twenty-six years from 1945 to 1971 when the United States occupied the Senkaku as part of the Okinawa Archipelago. At one point, there were as many as two hundred residents on the islands, engaging in fishing and working for canning factories.[30] After the end of the Cold War, mutual relations between Japan and China started to follow a rapid downward spiral. In September 2012, amid quickly worsening relations with China over the islands dispute, the Japanese government decided to terminate the lease agreement of the Senkaku Islands that had been in effect since 2002, purchasing them from the Japanese owner. The purpose was to prevent Shintaro Ishihara, then governor of Tokyo, from buying the islands. The government did so in the hope of maintaining the status quo, by continuing to control the islands and Japan's relationship with China in a restrained manner.[31]

Initially, Tokyo was optimistic and believed that Beijing would correctly assess the spirit of its gesture. But this assumption turned out to be seriously wrong. China started to propagate the Japanese "nationalization" of the islands as a grave breach of the status quo. Although the decision-making process of the Chinese move is opaque, its meanings and implications are clear. Now, the "Senkaku/Diaoyu" dispute is not only a bilateral problem between Japan and China, but is indicative of a paradigm clash over preferred regional orders. In the eyes of the Japanese, if China were to succeed in grabbing the islands, it would be tantamount to the realization of the new model of major power relations with the United States, since such an eventuality would mean that the United States should stay away from the conflict and Japan should give in to China.

CHINA POLICY OF A "NORMAL" JAPAN

Changes in Japanese security policies after the end of the Cold War, in general, and Japan's response to the rise of China, in particular, are often depicted as Japan's moves toward a "normal" Japan. Typically, holders of these views tend to argue that Japan aspires to play a "normal military role" in the game of power politics, and would finally cast off the postwar constraints on its security policy deriving from the postwar "Peace Constitution." There was even a neo-realist prediction that the structural pressure created by the demise of the Cold War would inevitably force Japan to acquire a nuclear deterrent.[32] Many observers interpreted any aspect of Japan's move, including the increasing debate, toward changing the war-renouncing Article 9 of the Constitution as indicating such an overall trend.

During the last two decades, however, the US-Japan alliance has been strengthened rather than weakened, increasing Japan's dependence on the United States, rendering Japan's military independence virtually meaningless at the time of the rise of China. Japan's efforts in the domain of national defense have in fact been upgraded, but, equally or more importantly, the constitutional constraints remain intact, and many of these military efforts remain closely institutionalized in the US-Japan alliance.

True, after the end of the Cold War, open debate about revising the Peace Constitution gradually emerged in Japanese society. However, the dominant argument for the constitutional revision in Japan regards Article 9 as an obstacle to Japan's "international contributions."[33] Aptly enough, Japan's failure to be part of multinational coalition efforts in the 1991 Gulf War, which resulted in a "checkbook diplomacy" of contributing only financially, gave rise to a sense of trauma in Tokyo, which provided the central impetus for Japanese participation in United Nations Peace Keeping Operations (PKO) in the mid-1990s for the first time in the post-World War II era. Significantly, the driver behind the participation of Japanese Self Defense Forces (SDF) in the PKO has been internationalism rather than nationalism.

Significantly, as internationalism inspired the new Japanese debate on security policies in the 1990s, the Japanese government simultaneously engaged in serious attempts to mitigate the burden of history with its neighbors, including the statement by Chief Cabinet Secretary Yohei Kono on the issue of "comfort women",[34] and the statement by Prime Minister Tomiichi Murayama on the fiftieth anniversary of the end of World War II.[35] It was not a coincidence that Tokyo pursued internationalism-inspired changes in security policies and reconciliation on the history problem simultaneously in the 1990s, as it struggled to cope with the end of the Cold War in search of a new foreign policy.

From the end of the 1990s, however, nationalist elements in Japanese society and politics have virtually hijacked the internationalist trend. Particularly during the first administration of Prime Minister Shinzo Abe (September 2006–September 2007), nationalist voices became bigger in the debate about constitutional revision. Likewise, the strengthening of the US-Japan alliance became part of the nationalist agenda on security policy. Closely associated with this phenomenon was the challenge by nationalists of the internationalists' interpretation and handling of the history issue as being overly self-degrading. As a result, Japanese debates and politics have begun to assume a nationalistic tone and have become increasingly detached from a strategic debate on security and defense policies.

In tandem with the nationalist "hijacking" of the internationalist agenda of security policy, Sino-Japanese relations have continued on a downward spiral. The crisis in the Taiwan Strait in 1995 encouraged Japan's nationalist politicians to talk about the importance of democracy in an attempt to legitimize the US-Japan alliance in the post-Cold War context, as well as to highlight the difference between Taiwan and China. This gave rise to the so-called value-based diplomacy articulated by the first Abe administration and intended to put implicit pressure on China.

At about the same time, anti-Japanese sentiments in China continued to be aggravated, as seen in a series of massive anti-Japanese demonstrations in many cities across the country, particularly those in the spring of 2005. This vicious cycle produced an atmosphere in which much of the Japanese public has become sympathetic with the nationalist argument, stressing that Japan's efforts to help China modernize and its conciliatory approaches toward the history issue have not paid off.

Amid this obvious vicious cycle of emotionalism, in December 2012, Japanese voters once again gave power to the Liberal Democratic Party (LDP) under the leadership of Shinzo Abe. Lacking any real ability to deal with China's rise unilaterally, strengthening Japan's alliance with the United States was once again a natural response for Abe. In his trip to Washington soon after inauguration for a summit meeting with President Barack Obama, Abe said on February 22, 2013: "We simply cannot tolerate any challenge [against the Senkaku] now, and in the future. No nation should make any miscalculation about the firmness of our resolve. No one should ever doubt the robustness of the Japan-U.S. alliance." Abe continued, "In order for us, Japan and the United States, to jointly provide the region and the world with more rule of law, more democracy, more security and less poverty, Japan must stay strong."[36] The intensifying territorial dispute with China is another case of nationalists regaining control. The value system of Japanese civil society is still virtually postmodern, where territorial integrity is of secondary importance for the majority of people.[37] This is why the Japanese government has exercised much restraint toward the territorial disputes throughout much of the postwar years, including the one on the Senkaku islands as discussed above. Now, regressive nationalists have begun to attack these traditional policies of self-restraint openly, confusing both external perceptions and the Japanese decision-making process.

This trend reached a peak at the 2014 Shangri-La Dialogue held in Singapore. In the keynote address on May 30, 2014, Abe, without mentioning but clearly targeting China, said the following:

Now, when we say "the rule of law at sea"—what exactly do we mean in concrete terms? If we take the fundamental spirit that we have infused into international law over the ages and reformulate it into three principles, we find the rule of law at sea is actually a matter of common sense. The first principle is that states shall make their claims based on international law. The second is that states shall not use force or coercion in trying to drive their claims. The third principle is that states shall seek to settle disputes by peaceful means. So to reiterate this, it means making claims that are faithful in light of international law, not resorting to force or coercion, and resolving all disputes through peaceful means.[38]

On the surface, Abe's words are general and internationalist, but the nationalist urge of competing with or even challenging the aggressive Chinese moves is also obvious between the lines.

As a result, while there has been general support for Abe's policy from many governments in the region, there has been less willingness to actually work with and take joint actions with Tokyo. This has given rise to a situation where the rivalry between Tokyo and Beijing stands out, whereas regional cooperation does not materialize easily. This situation would perhaps be welcome for Beijing, but it should also mean that each East Asian country is left alone at the time the rise of China does require a regional approach.

This leads us to the discussion of an alternative approach, by Japan as well as other countries in the region, as a prescription for the future.

THE CASE FOR AN ALTERNATIVE STRATEGY

Insofar as security policies of Shinzo Abe are concerned, there is a contradiction between Abe's somewhat regressive nationalism as his central motivating factor for removing postwar constraints on its security policy, on the one hand, and the substance and implications of changing policies that still remain within the postwar parameters of the Peace Constitution and the US-Japan alliance, on the other. The "legislation for peace and security," passed in the Japanese National Diet in September 2015, is exactly a case in point.

Japan's new security legislation covers three areas of Japanese security and defense policies: (1) situations threatening Japan's survival, (2) situations of important influence, and (3) international peace cooperation. Categories (2) and (3) involve changes from the previous typical Japanese self-restraints in the management of the US-Japan alliance (Guidelines of Defense Cooperation between Japan and the United States), and participation in international peacekeeping operations, and thus signify an internationalist evolution of Japan's security policy.

Category (1), however, pertains to the issue of the right to the collective self-defense, and gives rise to a question as to the balance between nationalism and internationalism. As a result of the legislation for peace and security, the revised "three conditions for the use of force for self-defense" now states as follows:

(1) When an armed attack against Japan occurs *or when an armed attack against a foreign country that is in a close relationship with Japan occurs and as a result threatens Japan's survival and poses a clear danger to fundamentally overturn people's right to life, liberty, and pursuit of happiness.*
(2) When there are no other appropriate means available to repel the attack, ensure Japan's survival and protect its people.
(3) Use of force should be limited to the minimum extent.[39]

The section in italics gives room for the exercise of the right to collective self-defense, which successive Japanese governments have previously rejected due to the limitations arising from Article 9 of the Japanese Constitution. Now, under condition (1), the new addition makes collective self-defense part of self-defense in a broader sense of the term, which thus is interpreted as not violating Article 9.

An interesting fact is that, while the right to collective self-defense is a legitimate one for all sovereign states, which is justified by Article 51 of the UN Charter, the revised interpretation in the new legislation allows the exercise of the right for Japan basically only at 50 percent of what is allowed by the UN Charter, that is, only in situations where Japan's survival is directly threatened. In other words, the new legislation would not allow Japan to engage in military operations with the United States and other friendly nations if the case has no direct bearing on Japan's security. This is what I mean by 50 percent (at most, and perhaps even less in reality) of the stipulation of the UN Charter, which is in principle for the sake of international peace and order rather than a single country's security.

Legally, the incomplete nature of the new legislation is because of Article 9: as long as the Japanese government has to justify the right to collective self-defense without changing the Constitution, this is perhaps the maximum interpretation possible within the confines of Article 9. A twist, however, is that the right to the collective self-defense was originally brought up as an extension of Shinzo Abe's aspiration to change the Constitution, but the new interpretation was made in the name of defending Article 9. Also, the United States does welcome this new legislation, because it will clearly strengthen the alliance mechanism. All this was as if an invisible hand pushed the "Abe agenda" back into the box of the "postwar regime," from which he wanted to escape.

Prime Minister Abe has repeatedly mentioned "the worsening security environment surrounding Japan" and "deterrence" as the justifications of the new security legislation. It was obvious that in mentioning these two reasons he has had China in mind. Virtually, the China factor played an important role in selling the "Abe agenda" (the right to the collective self-defense) to the Japanese public. Its substantial implications for Japan's China policy, however, remain quite vague other than therhetorical ones.

Moreover, Japan's somewhat excessive preoccupation with the "China threat" tends to discourage other East Asian nations from moving into effective security cooperation with Japan. After all, many East Asian nations in the vicinity of China share concerns about China, but they do not believe they have an option of directly confronting, let alone containing, China. I also believe that Japan, even with the new security legislation, does not have such an option either, and that building effective security cooperation among East Asian countries should be the first priority of its alternative strategy.

It should naturally follow from the above discussion that an alternative, regional approach does not imply ganging up on China nor containing it by any means. The ultimate purpose should be to coexist with a strong China in peace and prosperity. In short, China is a small universe in its own right, and this alternative strategic approach should be regarded, first and foremost, as a survival strategy of Asian nations. The nations in Asia are facing a common historic challenge presented by the rise of China, and they must find a way to survive and eventually to coexist with a strong China. This requires a "middle power" strategy on the part of Asian countries, including Japan. If Tokyo is able to synthesize its security policy pronouncements and overtures with the actual substance of Japan's regional engagement in cultural, social, economic, political, and even security domains of relations with Asian neighbors, Japan's strength and national power would be utilized most effectively in advancing "middle power" cooperation in the region.

As such, the concept of "middle power" is not about the size of a nation nor its national power. It is a strategic concept, implying particular characteristics of a strategy backed by commitment to liberal values and multilateral cooperation. First and foremost, a "middle power" strategy is characterized by the absence of unilateralism. As such, a "middle power" strategy does not have the option of directly and unilaterally engaging in the balance of power game among great powers, and its strengths are to be exerted most effectively in the middle grounds, primarily in the domain of nontraditional and soft security through multilateral cooperation.[40]

It then follows that the critical task for Japan now and ahead is to match its strategy explicitly with "middle power internationalism,"[41] amply demonstrated by its actual behaviors and rooted in its societal values. In fact, prior to the return of Shinzo Abe as the Prime Minister in late 2012, the recognition was growing in the Japanese debate that, on top of the alliance with the United States, security cooperation with the Asian neighbors should be equally important as a central component of Japanese strategy in a new era. Conceptually, it was assumed that the integration of the alliance with the United States, on the one hand, and security cooperation with regional countries, on the other, should be critical in Japan's response to the rise of China and shifting US-China strategic relations.[42]

As a recent case, the Japan-Australia Joint Declaration on Security Cooperation signed in March 2007 was indeed an embodiment of such a development of Japanese security policy and thinking. The agreed areas of security cooperation in the declaration are relevant primarily for human security, including law enforcement on combating transnational crime, counterterrorism, disarmament and non-proliferation, peace operations, humanitarian relief operations, and contingency planning for pandemics.[43]

On the basis of this joint security declaration, Japan and Australia signed the Japan-Australia Acquisition and Cross-Servicing Agreement (ACSA)[44] on May 15, 2010, enabling the militaries of both countries to mutually cooperate by reciprocally providing supplies and services. This was indeed a historic achievement in the postwar history of Japanese security policy, setting the legal framework for the Japanese SDF to cooperate with a foreign country other than the United States for the first time. There is no reason to believe that a similar agreement cannot be emulated between Tokyo and Seoul. In fact, at the end of the Lee Myungbak government in the first half of 2012, Tokyo and Seoul actually completed the negotiations of the General Security of Military Information Act (GSOMIA), whose signing was postponed due to political reasons, and the bilateral ACSA was also under consideration.

South Korea and Australia had signed a comprehensive agreement in 2009, entitled "Joint Statement on Enhanced Global and Security Cooperation between Australia and the Republic of Korea."[45] Thus, one can reasonably argue that there is already a foundation upon which to begin to design security cooperation among Japan, Australia, and South Korea. Trilateralizing nontraditional security cooperation among the three countries would signify an important step toward multilateral security cooperation in the region that would not exclude China, but rather would provide an effective platform for China to associate itself with the region in a constructive way on the basis of liberal internationalism.

CONCLUSION

In retrospect, the confusion in the security profile of Japan has long been a source of confusion in the discussions of East Asian security, not least because some expect Japan to play the role of a great power for better or worse. Japan's actual security profile is much closer to that of a "middle power," which makes the choice of the alliance with the United States a must as the foundation of its security policy. Seeking strategic independence, let alone "remilitalization," is totally off the radar of Japanese strategic debates and actual policies, and Japan has invested its resources in typical areas of "middle power" diplomacy including nonproliferation of WMDs, arms control at international institutions, economic assistance to facilitate regional integration, and human security.[46]

In this connection, the conventional wisdom to look to Japan as one of the "great powers" including China and the United States in East Asia has blinded many observers to a more relevant perspective to the regional role of Japan and by extension East Asian security. The prevailing views about a "normal" Japan also suffers from the same problem, an important source of a myth about the strategic rivalry between Japan and China. Politically, Japan and China are engaging in competition on a regional scale, but there are no serious strategic, let alone military, implications there.

As discussed in this chapter, however, Japan stands at the nexus of the dualism associated with the rise of China in two fundamental ways. Firstly, Japan used to be, and arguably still is, a major facilitator of China's continuous engagement in the liberal international order, and simultaneously on the forefront of the geopolitical challenge by China over the "Senkaku/Diaoyu" dispute. Secondly, the outcome of this geopolitical challenge will have a decisive impact on the future of a security order in the Asia-Pacific. Indeed, as an ultimate scenario, if China succeeds in getting the Senkaku Islands without US involvement, this would virtually mean the realization of the Chinese dream of establishing "a new model of major power relations" across the Pacific.

Of course, this is a conceptual and hypothetical argument, and this scenario may not be realized easily or anytime soon. The chapter by Rosemary Foot in this volume appropriately portrays factors that would restrain the escalation of conflict between the United States and China. The chapter by Odd Arne Westad rightly points out limitations to the Chinese desire to influence regional affairs in the Korean Peninsula and Southeast Asia. In her recent study, Evelyn Goh also argues that the United States will remain a dominant power in East Asia in the foreseeable future, and what is happening in the region is not a power transition but "an order transition," where the US hegemonic order is being renegotiated.[47] Indeed, "middle power" cooperation among the China's neighbors may not be sustainable without the continuous role of the United States as the backbone of stability in the Asia-Pacific region.

Under these premises, this chapter focused on the undercurrent of long-term implications arising from and sustained by the Chinese nationalism aspiring for a new order in Asia, which will not disappear easily and will continue to affect various contemporary issues within the parameters of the international order supported by the US presence and power. Equally long-term and strategic thinking is very much needed on the part of China's neighbors including Japan, the ultimate goal of which, as repeatedly mentioned above, should be to coexist with a strong China in peace and prosperity. Japan, standing at the nexus of the historic challenges from the rise of China, might also be an effective nexus of "middle power" cooperation in the region.

NOTES

1. Daniel Twining, "Is the 'Chinese Dream' Asia's Nightmare?," *Nikkei Asia Review*, June 11, 2014, http://asia.nikkei.com/Viewpoints/Geopolitico/Daniel-Twining-Is-the-Chinese-Dream-Asia-s-nightmare.
2. Ryosei Kokubun, Yoshihide Soeya, Akio Takahara, and Shin Kawashima, *Nitchu Kankei-shi* [Modern history of Japan-China relations] (Tokyo: Yuhikaku, 2013). Its English translation as been published as Ryosei Kokubun, Yoshihide Soeya, Akio Takahara, and Shin Kawashima (translated by Keith Krulak), *Japan–China Relations in the Moder Era* (London: Routledge, 2017). Citations here are based on the original Japanese version.
3. Michael Yhuda, *Sino-Japanese Relations after the Cold War: Two Tigers Sharing a Mountain* (London: Routledge, 2013).
4. Hugh White, *The China Choice: Why We Should Share Power* (Oxford: Oxford University Press, 2013).
5. John J. Mearsheimer, *The Tragedy of Great Power Politics* (New York: W. W. Norton, 2001).
6. G. John Ikenberry, *Liberal Leviathan: The Origins, Crisis, and Transformation of the American World Order* (Princeton, NJ: Princeton University Press, 2011).
7. Robert Zoellick, "Whither China: From Membership to Responsibility?" (remarks to the National Committee on U.S.-China Relations, September 21, 2005, http://www.kas.de/wf/doc/kas_7358-544-1-30.pdf).
8. The so-called the Cox report of 1999 is an example of the swing from the China policy of the Clinton administration that had tended to emphasize engagement. *Report of the Select Committee on U.S. National Security and Military/Commercial Concerns with the People's Republic of China, Submitted by Mr. Cox of California, Chairman* (Washington, DC: U.S. Government Printing Office, May 25, 1999).
9. C. Fred Bergsten, "A Partnership of Equals," *Foreign Affairs*, July/August, 2008, 57–69.
10. Wang Jisi, "China's Search for a Grand Strategy," *Foreign Affairs*, March/April 2011, 68–79.
11. The United States Department of Defense, *Quadrennial Defense Review Report* (Washington, D.C.: US Government Printing Office, 2010), 31.
12. Robert S. Ross, "The Problem with the Pivot," *Foreign Affairs*, November–December 2012, 70–82.
13. Zhao Suisheng, *A Nation-State by Construction: Dynamics of Modern Chinese Nationalism* (Palo Alto, CA: Stanford University Press, 2004).
14. "Luncheon in Honor of Vice President Xi Jinping," National Committee on U.S.-China Relations, http://www.ncuscr.org/programs/luncheon-honor-vice-president-xi-jinping.
15. David M. Lampton, "A New Type of Major-Power Relationship: Seeking a Durable Foundation for US-China Ties," *Asia Policy* 16 (July 2013): 51–68.
16. Susan E. Rice, "America's Future in Asia" (Georgetown University, Washington, DC, November 20, 2013, http://www.whitehouse.gov/the-press-office/2013/11/21/remarks-prepared-delivery-national-security-advisor-susan-e-rice).
17. Willy Lam, "Beijing's Aggressive New Foreign Policy and Implications for the South China Sea," *China Brief* 13, no. 13 (June 21, 2013), https://jamestown.org/wp-content/uploads/2013/06/cb_08_09.pdf.
18. "Department of Defense Press Briefing with Secretary Hagel and Gen. Chang from the Pentagon, Presenters: Secretary of Defense Chuck Hagel and China's

Minister of National Defence General Chang Wanquan," August 19, 2013, http://archive.defense.gov/transcripts/transcript.aspx?transcriptid=5289
19. Yahuda, *Sino-Japanese Relations after the Cold War*, 15.
20. Ibid., 8.
21. Daniel Sneider, "Interrupted Memories: The Debate over Wartime Memory in Northeast Asia," in *Confronting Memories of World War II*, ed. Daniel Chirot, Gi-Wook Shin, and Daniel Sneider (Seattle: University of Washington Press, 2014), 54.
22. Ibid., 50–54.
23. Kokubun, Soeya, Takahara, and Kawashima, *Nitchu Kankei-shi* [Modern History of Japan-China Relations], 150–52.
24. After Nakasona, from Noboru Takeshita to Shinzo Abe, there have been seventeen prime ministers of Japan, and only three of them visited the Yasukini Shrine while in office, i.e., Ryutaro Hashimono in 1996, Junichiro Koizumi annually in 2001–2006, and Shinzo Abe in 2013. There has never been a case of a foreign minister's visit, while Shinzo Abe's visit in 2006 is the only exception as cabinet secretary.
25. 人民日報＜People's Daily＞, January 8, 1953. The article is uploaded at: http://www.mofa.go.jp/mofaj/area/senkaku/images/qa/img03_l.jpg.
26. The Japanese government did not protest this Chinese announcement explicitly, by giving priority to the overall relationship with Beijing, with which diplomatic normalization was achieved in September 1972. An internal Foreign Ministry document, however, had already stated in July 1972, anticipating diplomatic normalization with China, that "the Japanese government is in no position to negotiate the sovereignty issue of the Senkaku islands with any other government, since it is the unequivocal fact that these islands are Japanese territories." Ministry of Foreign Affairs of Japan, "Nitchukan-no Kenan Jiko" [Pending issues between Japan and China], July 10, 1972) disclosed by the freedom of information act of Japan; Kokubun, Soeya, Takahara, and Kawashima, *Nitchu Kankei-shi* [Modern history of Japan-China relations], 128.
27. Wang Guanzhong, "Major Power Perspectives on Peace and Security in the Asia Pacific" (The 13th IISS Asia Securtiy Summit, The Shangri-La Dialogue, Fourth Plenary Session, June 1, 2014, http://www.iiss.org/-/media/Documents/Events/Shangri-La%20Dialogue/SLD%2014/Wang.pdf).
28. Zheng Wang, *Never Forget National Humiliation: Historical Memory in Chinese Politics and Foreign Relations* (New York: Columbia University Press, 2012).
29. "Japanese Territory: Senkaku Islands," Ministry of Foreign Affairs Japan, April 13, 2016, http://www.mofa.go.jp/region/asia-paci/senkaku/.
30. Ibid.
31. Tsuyoshi Sunohara, *Anto: Senkaku Kokuyu-ka* [Secret battle: Nationalization of the Senkakus] (Tokyo: Shincho-sha, 2013).
32. Kenneth N. Waltz, "The Emerging Structure of International Politics," *International Security* 18, no. 2 (Autumn 1993): 44–79.
33. Yoshihide Soeya, "A 'Normal' Middle Power: Interpreting Changes in Japanese Security Policy in the 1990s and After," in *Japan as a 'Normal Country'?: A Country in Search of Its Place in the World*, ed. Yoshihide Soeya, Masayuki Tadokoro, David Welch (Toronto: University of Toronto Press, 2011), 72–97.
34. "Statement by the Chief Cabinet Secretary Yohei Kono on the result of the study on the issue of 'comfort women'," August 4, 1993, http://www.mofa.go.jp/policy/women/fund/state9308.html.

35. "Statement by Prime Minister Tomiichi Murayama 'On the occasion of the 50th anniversary of the war's end'," August 15, 1995, http://www.mofa.go.jp/announce/press/pm/murayama/9508.html.
36. Shinzo Abe, "Japan Is Back," (policy speech, Center for Strategic and International Studies, February 22, 2013, http://www.kantei.go.jp/foreign/96_abe/statement/201302/22speech_e.html).
37. Masayuki Tadokoro, "Change and Continuity in Japan's 'Abnormalcy': An Emerging External Attitude of the Japanese Public," in Soeya, Tadokoro, and Welch, *Japan as a 'Normal Country'?: A Country in Search of its Place in the World*, 38–71.
38. Shinzo Abe, "Shangri-La Dialogue 2014 Keynote Address—Japanese Version," May 30, 2014, https://www.iiss.org/en/events/shangri-la-dialogue/archive/2014-c20c/opening-remarks-and-keynote-address-b0b2/keynote-japanese-af6d.
39. "Fundamental Concepts of National Defense," Ministry of Defense, http://www.mod.go.jp/e/d_act/d_policy/dp01.html.
40. Yoshihide Soeya and Guen Lee, "The Middle-Power Challenge in East Asia: An Opportunity for Co-operation between South Korea and Japan," *Global Asia* 9, no. 2 (Summer 2014): 84–91.
41. Richard J. Samuels, *Securing Japan: Tokyo's Grand Strategy and the Future of East Asia* (Ithaca, NY: Cornell University Press, 2008).
42. This is the central argument of the report of the Council on Security and Defense Capabilities in the New Era set up by the former prime minister Yukio Hatoyama in the Prime Minister's Office: "Japan's Visions for Future Security and Defense Capabilities in the New Era: Toward a Peace-Creating Nation," August 2010, http://www.kantei.go.jp/jp/singi/shin-ampobouei2010/houkokusyo_e.pdf.
43. "Japan-Australia Joint Declaration on Security Cooperation," Ministry of Foreign Affairs of Japan, March 13, 2007, http://www.mofa.go.jp/region/asia-paci/australia/joint0703.html.
44. "Agreement between the Government of Japan and the Government of Australia concerning reciprocal provision of supplies and services between the Self-Defense Forces of Japan and the Australian Defence Force," May 19, 2010, http://www.mofa.go.jp/region/asia-paci/australia/pdfs/agree1005.pdf.
45. "Joint Statement on Enhanced Global and Security Cooperation between Australia and the Republic of Korea," March 5, 2009, http://dfat.gov.au/trade/agreements/kafta/news/Pages/joint-statement-on-enhanced-global-and-security-cooperation-between-australia-and-the-republic-of-korea.aspx.
46. Yoshihide Soeya, *Nihon-no Midoru Pawa Gaiko* [Japan's middle-power diplomacy] (Tokyo: Chikuma Shobo, 2005).
47. Evelyn Goh, *The Struggle for Order: Hegemony, Hierarchy, and Transition in Post-Cold War East Asia* (Oxford: Oxford University Press, 2013).

CHAPTER 14

Can India Balance China in Asia?

JONATHAN HOLSLAG

INTRODUCTION

If there is one prospect that sends the shivers through Asian capitals, it is that of a new Sino-centric order. Even if some governments consider the rise of China as an opportunity, most countries have feared the possibility of a strategic landscape in which they are no longer able to defend their territorial interests, their sovereignty, and their economic autonomy. From that perspective, it has remained critical to keep China's rise in check. Thus far, the United States, flanked by countries like Japan and Australia, has taken the lead. Its military preponderance has been crucial in mitigating strategic uncertainty in the region, but it has of course also prompted China to expedite its search for military power. If China continues to be successful in that endeavor, the America-led balancing formation will inevitably be challenged. In the long run, it thus seems that a rising China can only be checked if another major power stands up, and the most likely candidate is India. India and India alone is able to throw enough ungainly weight onto the scales.

India has always had a strong interest in balancing China. In my book *China and India: Prospects for Peace*, finalized five years ago, I concluded that the two Asian giants will not be able grow together without conflict. But what if one of them fails to perform? This chapter argues that we should not take for granted that India will be able to balance China's rise. Even though there is enough at stake for the country to act as a balancer, it continues to fail to play this role effectively. This is because India has gotten stuck between nonalignment and nonperformance. On the one hand, it resists the prospect of a new coalition that balances China from the maritime fringes of Eurasia, especially if that coalition is led by the United States. On the other hand, it has failed embarrassingly to strengthen its own capabilities. Its military power has come to lag increasingly behind China's, its efforts to reach out to both East and Central Asia ended in disappointment, and its economic reforms have not yielded the expected results. As a result of that economic underachievement, India has found itself also torn between emotional nationalism and paralyzing political fragmentation, which, in turn, will further complicate its role as a regional power.

Earlier on in this volume, Yoshihide Soeya stressed the need for a new form of middle power cooperation to complement with the new great power cooperation that China has proposed to the United States. This paper confirms his conclusion that without solutions for territorial disputes, relations between China and its neighbors will continue to be complicated. However, it questions the ability of the middle powers to stand up to China and to defend their territorial interests in the longer run, if China continues to be successful in balancing security fears against commercial expectations in the short term, and in changing the economic balance of power in the long run. This is not to deny that China has weaknesses. As Zhang Ruizhuang emphasized in his contribution, China has come to face major domestic challenges. But, and this will be the corrective that this chapter proposes, the question is not just how vulnerable a country is, but also whether it can deal with it and, eventually, externalize some of its problems to other countries. China, it will become clear, has been very skilful in doing that. In that regard, the paper also insists that the possibility of coexistence, as Liselotte Odgaard describes it earlier on in this book, should not only be evaluated by looking at China's behavior in security issues, but that it should be considered more broadly.

THE CAUSES OF DISCORD

India has a strong interest in balancing China. It is clear that the balance of power has tilted at India's detriment. China's economy has gotten ahead much more quickly, and that has also allowed it to invest more in its military power and political partnerships in India's neighborhood. But besides the balance of power, there are several factors that made China appear even more as a threat. First among them is the huge need for economic opportunities. Both states remain developing countries with large cohorts of poor people and potentially destabilizing income gaps. Both states have seen political elites tying their destinies to the ability to bring prosperity to the masses. That manifests itself in a much more challenging international economic climate. By 2014, the global economic growth rate had not entirely recovered from the dip of 2009, recording an average of 1.6 percent compared between 2009 and 2013 compared to 3.0 percent between 1990 and 2009.[1] But there is more. Growth is resulting less and less in new employment opportunities.[2] Asia's growth in the last years, for instance, has been largely jobless.[3] A growing body of research also shows that the share of incomes in developed and developing economies is dropping fast. In addition, in many developing countries, the income increases have been erased by high inflation rates.[4] As a result, China and India are still locked in a contest for manufacturing. Manufacturing is deemed particularly important as a driver of job creation, a catalyst of innovation, and a crucial asset to avoid large trade deficits. The two countries have also been locked in fierce competition over natural resources. Since the turn of the century, imports of fuels have been growing by 35 percent per year in India and 37 percent in China, ores by 22 percent in India and 31 percent in China, agricultural products by 14 percent in India and 20 percent in China.[5]

One particular natural resource concerns the shared rivers. China and India struggle with pressing water shortages. If China reached the current development level with 2,093 cubic meters of freshwater annually available for each citizen, India has only 1,184 cubic meters with a population that is set to expand significantly.[6] It comes as no surprise, then, that Delhi has anxiously watched China's infrastructure plans on the upper reaches of the Brahmaputra, which is called the Yarlung Tsangpo until it reaches the contested border with India. More than 185 million people in India and Bangladesh depend on the Brahmaputra for survival. China has continued to build hydropower dams on the river, but these will not have reservoirs so that the water can continue to flow to India and Bangladesh. To reassure India, it signed agreements in 2008, 2010, and 2013 to provide flood-season data. For the time being, a plan to divert over 200 billion cubic meters of water from Tibet to Chinese coastal cities has been put on hold, but experts claim that it is China's right still to go on. Already, and more stealthily, numerous smaller dams and irrigation canals are being built to supply the growing towns and expanding croplands along the eastern part of the Yarlung Tsangpo.

That leads us to perhaps the most sensitive conflict: the border. In 2005, Delhi and Beijing reached an important agreement on political parameters for the settlement of the border disputed in the three sectors—Aksai Chin in the west, the middle sector, and Arunachal Pradesh in the east. But after sixteen rounds of boundary negotiations, no final settlement is in sight. The hope is still for a grand bargain in which China retains control and receives sovereignty over Aksai Chin and India over Arunachal. But this remains politically very sensitive. "Any such swap," a Chinese diplomat avowed, "would be political suicide on the Indian side and very badly received on the Chinese side."[7] Furthermore, differences remain over how to draw the line of actual control. Tensions in the western sector highlighted this. In 2013, India accused China of building bases on its part, in the Daulat Beg Oldi Sector, a barren, unpopulated area in the Depsang plains, but China insisted that the line of actual control was about twenty kilometers further to the southwest. That year, Chinese patrols were also found in Chaglagam, a village about thirty kilometers south of the line of actual control in Arunachal Pradesh.

The territorial dispute has sustained military competition. Indian politicians continue to emphasize China's military modernization as a security threat. Defense Minister AK Anthony commented that the new Chinese leadership would continue to test India's deterrence.[8] In the run-up to the 2014 elections, Narendra Modi called for a strong government to counter the threat from China and Pakistan.[9] Such discourse coincided with shifts in India's military strategy. In December 2009, the India Army Commander, General Deepak Kapoor, acknowledged that he was working on "a proportionate focus towards the western and north-eastern fronts."[10] So, too, has the Indian Navy embarked on a look-east policy, shifting more resources from the Arabian Sea to the Gulf of Bengal.[11] In terms of nuclear doctrine, India has adhered to credible minimum deterrent, and, hence, goes on to invest mainly in survivability and accuracy. The Agni-III intermediate-range missile, commissioned in 2011, has become India's main nuclear deterrent against China, featuring a maneuverable re-entry vehicle and improved navigation. The development of a nuclear missile submarine, that was commissioned in 2016, is another important step to enhance the survivability of India's nuclear deterrence. While India still figures much lower in China's defense priorities, Chinese analysts and military officers have taken notice of the changes in India's military strategizing: said Major General Luo Yuan, one of the PLA's uniformed public affairs commentators, "India is the only country in the world that says that it is developing its military power because of China's military threat."[12]

Status matters too. India still considers itself an important regional power with global interests, a regional power also that has a manifest destiny to dominate the Indian Ocean Rim—from Bab el Mandeb to the Strait of Malacca and from Antarctica all the way to Afghanistan, Nepal, and Myanmar. To some extent, that aspiration is a legacy of India's own turbulent past, the experience of vulnerability when the Indian heartland along the river plains in the north was conquered through the mountain passes to Central Asia and, later on, by European colonialists who arrived by sea—hence Jawaharlal Nehru's assertion, "History has shown that whatever power controls the Indian Ocean, has in the first instance, India's sea borne trade at her mercy, and in the second, India's very independence itself."[13] It is thus crude geopolitics that dictates India must become the dominant power the Indian Ocean Rim, but that has thus also resulted in a more symbolic quest for status. India wants to be a powerful, independent nation. It has tried to advance that objective first through the independence and liberation movement and subsequently through a strategy of nonalignment. In more recent decades, it has translated into a rather inconsistent strategy to side intermittently with the Soviet Union and the United States, a relentless pursuit of nuclear capabilities, a push for its own regional organizations, and a strong desire to be recognized as a peer of China, if not in terms of its actual capabilities then at the very least in terms of its potential power.

Finally, India also has remained concerned about China's growing presence in its periphery. That relates of course first and foremost to Pakistan. Since 2009, China provided the Pakistani armed forces with major arms systems, including four frigates, several dozen JF-17 fighter jets, C-802 antiship missiles, and a batch of modernized Al-Khalid main battle tanks. Beijing and Islamabad also started talks for the delivery of six submarines, corvettes, and air-defense missiles. Meanwhile, China has continued the construction of the four reactors of the Chashma Nuclear Power Complex and offered a $6.5 billion loan for two nuclear power plants in Karachi. Sino-Pakistani cooperation also continued in space, with China launching Pakistan's first communications satellite and Pakistan opting for the Beidou satellite navigation system. India's other neighbor, Bangladesh, also developed closer defense ties with China and ordered various new military systems, including tanks, two corvettes, antiship missiles, and showed interest in purchasing JF-17 fighters and submarines. China emerged as a major supplier of arms to Sri Lanka, most of them delivered via Pakistan, and provided over $3 billion of credit to facilitate the development of railway, telecommunication, and infrastructure at the strategic port of Hambantota.

It does not come as a surprise, then, that public perceptions have been muted at best. As table 14.1 shows, Indian views never recovered after the steep drop between 2004 and 2008. Especially in China, views of India have deteriorated remarkably. Indian politicians also have kept up the pressure on the government to stand strong. Between 2009 and 2013, about 185 questions about China were asked in the Lower House of Parliament, most

Table 14.1 PERCENTAGE OF RESPONDENTS CONSIDERING THE OTHER COUNTRY FAVORABLY (PERCENTAGE). SOURCE: BBC WORLD POLLS 2004–2013.

	Indian Perceptions	Chinese Perceptions
2004	66	56
2005	44	39
2006	36	37
2007	22	45
2008	20	37
2009	30	29
2010	29	30
2011	31	33
2012	30	35
2013	36	23

http://www.bbc.co.uk/mediacentre/latestnews/2017/globescan-poll-world-views-world-service.

of them related to trade disputes and the border issue.[14] This limits the freedom of action of Indian governments. Compromises with China can easily be criticized as an indication of weakness and a lack of leadership. The last two governments of Atal Vajpayee and Manmohan Singh usually veered around this by adopting a highly ambivalent discourse. The prime ministers themselves usually highlighted the need for cooperation, especially economic cooperation, whenever they met their Chinese counterparts, but they responded sharply whenever they were challenged by critical reports in new media or interventions in the parliament related to border incursions or unfair economic competition. The same was true for important cabinet ministers. One day, a minister of defense might praise a joint exercise; the next day, he might call for preparations of a two-front war.[15]

There are several factors that one could expect to mitigate India's rather suspicious attitude and propensity to balance. Liberals would retort, for example, that bilateral trade is on the rise. That is true, but as we will return to later in the chapter, India runs a structural trade deficit with China, and the composition of its exports is disadvantageous as well. It is not likely that China and India will develop a mutually beneficial division of labor either. China is determined to stick to its manufacturing, whereas export-oriented services in India do create a sufficient number of jobs. One could also assume, as Liselotte Odgaard suggests in one of the previous chapters in this volume, that the many nontraditional security threats, like piracy and Islamic terrorism, pave the way for cooperation. The reality, though, is rather that India mistrusts China's efforts to combat these threats in Central Asia, the north of Pakistan, and the Indian Ocean, and reckons that China could use nontraditional security threats as a pretext for ramping up its military presence around China.

Another element that is often expected to temper conflict is the fact that China and India are both part of the Brasil, Russia, India, China and South Africa (BRICS) cooperation platform. It is true that China, India, as well as Brazil and Russia share the interest to reform the way the world is governed, to redistribute power within international organizations, and to restrain American unilateralism. But China remains ambiguous about its support for India to join the UN Security Council, and it its even less clear whether India will, like China, gain from eventual reforms in the International Monetary Fund. Differences also exist with regard to the international trade regime. Until about five years ago, China and India shared a desire to limit the scope of trade liberalization, but as a consequence of its economic success, China is shifting. It already pushes for more free trade in goods, starts to become keener on free trade in services, and continues to mull over the liberalization of its own government procurement and investment. India, meanwhile, is not moving an inch. The same gap becomes visible in financial matters. As China has successfully pushed for a BRIC development fund or bank, mostly to find a new vehicle for its export credit and concessional loans, India is well aware that this could be to the detriment of its own position as economic leader in the Indian Ocean Rim. In short, the more optimistic, liberal arguments fail to hold up. The evidence presented, albeit partially, here suggests that competition and balancing will likely continue to characterize the Sino-Indian relations.

MILITARY BALANCING

In the last five years, India has shown a greater readiness for external balancing. As two middle powers, as they are described by Yoshihide Soeya in this volume, Japan and India share concerns about China's rise. With Japan, India issued a Joint Declaration on Security Cooperation in October 2008, which led to various new exchanges on regional security.[16] In 2009, both sides held their first bilateral navy exercise. India has responded positively to Japan's new emphasis on "Indo-Pacific" security cooperation, and after the elections of 2014, Prime Minister Narendra Modi quickly highlighted the importance of security cooperation with Japan. Yet, Delhi remained reluctant to support Japan's position on freedom of navigation, the Chinese Air Defense and Identification Zone, and even more so on the East China Sea dispute. Mutual frustrations have also built up because of the slow progress in two crucial fields of the strategic partnership: investment promotion and nuclear cooperation. With Vietnam, relations have also been on the increase. In 2010, Defense Minister AK Antony promised that India would help strengthen Vietnam's defense forces' capabilities and that it would stimulate cooperation with the Vietnamese Navy by means of exercises, port calls, and technical support. In 2013, Delhi offered $100 million in credit for defense purchases. Most significant, however, was India's commitment to stay involved in energy exploration activities in parts of the South China Sea that are also claimed by China, despite Chinese resistance and disappointing economic returns. With the Philippines, a first agreement on defense cooperation was signed in 2006, and in 2013 Delhi and Manila confirmed their interest in cooperation in combating nontraditional threats, disaster management, food security, and pandemics. But compared to Vietnam, security cooperation remains modest. In 2013, two defense agreements were signed with South Korea, envisaging the exchange of defense-related information, cooperation on peacekeeping and humanitarian relief, as well as cooperation on defense technologies.[17]

What characterizes all these partnerships is that they have remained limited in scope and substance. They pale in comparison to some of the partnerships established by these partners with one another. One explanation is India's limited capacity. It just does not have the human resources at its Defence and External Affairs Ministries to run a large number of exchanges and practical partnerships. More important, however, is that India seems reluctant to be drawn in the territorial disputes in Eastern Asia. The East China Sea is considered too distant, and Japan's resurgent nationalism is also viewed with concern. With regard to the South China Sea, India did confirm several times that it has an interest in the freedom of navigation on the high seas, but it refuses to take sides. Instead, it called all sides to show restraint and to come to a pragmatic negotiated settlement. Officials vacillated around the question of whether India supports international arbitration, as it is requested for by the Philippines, and stressed that their country would not weigh in on these disputes.[18] "We do not interfere," Indian External Affairs Minister Salman Khurshid said. "We do believe that anything that is a bilateral issue between two nations must be settled by those two nations."[19] This all seems to confirm India's traditional opposition to alliances and the efforts of the Congress-led government to prevent a deterioration of its relations with Beijing. But it also appears to display a concern with possible entanglements in

Eastern Asian disputes at a time that India's immediate security environment shows signs of instability.[20]

These reservations are also clearly discernible with regard to the United States. Indian relations with the United States are much more sensitive, and this sensitivity goes right back to the core of nonalignment, that is, the opposition to entangling alliances with the major powers.[21] Politicians from the left and Hindu parties still scoff at any agreement that makes India look like a deputy of Washington, and they waste few opportunities in Parliament to make government members confirm their allegiance to the nonalignment doctrine. This stance also reflects a more sober-minded calculation that India's interests are best served by maintaining as much strategic autonomy as possible. Indeed, China is considered a security threat, but one that remains, for the time being, manageable, so that there is no need yet for seeking formal security arrangements from others that could lead to more tensions with Beijing and, at the same time, pull India into the strategic rivalry in the Western Pacific. Moreover, even if China's rise is a concern that India shares with the United States, many differences remain, for example, over Pakistan, Iran, Russia, international norms on nuclear energy, global trade, human rights, the Middle East, and so forth. Nor are India and the United States on the same page when it comes to one of the most divisive issues in the maritime disputes in East Asia: India disapproves America's claim that foreign military vessels are allowed to enter exclusive economic zones (EEZ) as they please, and it lodges a complaint each time an American military vessel enters its own EEZ. The Indian military is also loath to enhance interoperability and has therefore opposed agreements that provide for the use of Indian facilities during military operations, the use of NATO-encrypted communication and hardware, geospatial cooperation, and technical standards in developing new armaments. As a result, India will likely remain reluctant to join efforts of the United States to enlist it in a grand alliance.

India is not the only country that seeks to avoid strategic alignment or entanglement. Its reluctance to ally with the United States is similar to the foreign policy orientation of countries like Vietnam and Indonesia. Because of growing tensions in the South China Sea, Vietnam was one of the first states in the region to seek closer relations with the United States. The two established regular exchanges on security, and Vietnam received various port calls of US Navy ships. Vietnam also actively pursues American investments. However, it has simultaneously engaged other regional powers, including a major challenger of the West: Russia. Russia has become the country's main supplier of military equipment and equally makes regular port calls. Russia has also emerged as an important security partner of Indonesia, supplying arms and participating in frequent high-level meetings—all simultaneous with growing security relations between Jakarta and Washington. What thus characterizes the behavior of India and other important countries is an effort to diversify security relations. The United States is certainly the main military counterweight to China, but partners like Russia are cherished for practical reasons, like the supply of weapons, and symbolic reasons, notably the signaling that they do not want to be caught in a bipolar world order dominated by two superpowers.

India has hesitated to engage in external military balancing against China, and it sticks to a policy of nonalignment and strategic autonomy. The quest for autonomy inevitably brings a greater need for internal balancing. India has to strengthen its own military capabilities if it wants to maintain its security without the entangling and polarizing alliances. But here India enters the arena with severe constraints as well. A first limitation concerns the official defense budget. In the years 2009–2014, defense spending hardly increased, whereas China's grew by 32 percent. In 2013, China's defense budget was almost four times larger than India's. That year, Beijing increased spending by 11 percent, whereas Delhi sliced 8 percent from the budget for 2012–2013. The consequences for India's military power are felt across all branches of the armed services.

To defend the "line of actual control" with China, Indian ground forces have long been in a disadvantageous position. In the last decade, China has been much faster in developing its infrastructure in the border area, paving roads and building barracks. India has tried to catch up and has successfully accelerated the establishment of its own network of roads and patrol trails, especially in the western sector. The whole of Ladakh is now strewn with small observation posts and flimsy trails that move up to strategic passes and heights. Still, China is able to project off its capabilities more forcefully. It has dispatched helicopters, patrol boats, and radar installations all along the most sensitive parts of the line of actual control. Furthermore, on the Tibetan plain, Chinese railways, airports, and roads have been developing fast, so that troops can be transferred from large bases further north with ease. A lot of excitement followed the decision in 2013, after several years of delay because of budget constraints, to raise an Indian mountain strike corps of nearly forty thousand troops for the disputed China border by the end of 2016. The corps will consist of two infantry divisions specialized in mountain warfare, an air defense brigade, two artillery brigades, and one engineering brigade. It was reported that it would be supported by newly ordered light artillery, attack helicopters, and heavy lift helicopters.[22] But these orders were again pushed into the future because of budgetary constraints. In 2014, the defense acquisition committee postponed the order of M-777 light howitzers, twenty-two attack helicopters, and fifteen heavy lift helicopters in all. India is also known for the poor state of its infantry combat equipment, ranging from assault rifles, communication equipment, to infantry combat vehicles. Since 2012, the government started to fill some of these gaps, but at a slow pace and in small batches. The Comptroller and Auditor General (CAG) has repeatedly pointed to the lack of modern artillery, antitank capabilities, and insufficient ammunition stocks for Indian tanks.[23]

The Indian Navy has embraced checking China's presence in the Indian Ocean as one of its main duties. The construction of the large Varsha Navy Base, near Rambili, on the eastern coast, and the modernization of facilities at the Nicobar Islands are all meant to showcase the rebalancing of the navy's capabilities to the east. Spending cuts have also hit the Indian Navy hard. Between 2009 and 2013, it only commissioned six major surface ships: one Kolkata Class destroyer, two Talwar B class frigates, and three Shivalik Class frigates. In the same period, China commissioned twenty-three large surface combatants: six destroyers, three large landing platform docks, and fourteen advanced frigates. The ageing fleet and the failure to replace old ships have led to a loss of thousands of days of operational readiness.[24] These ships have also been plagued by accidents, killing over twenty sailors in 2015 alone. Likewise, China commissioned eighteen new submarines, mostly conventional ones, whereas India only built one . . . and lost one: a potent Kilo submarine that was destroyed in a fire. In 1999, India released a thirty-year submarine building program that aims for the construction of twenty-four new submarines, but only fourteen of these vessels were actually added, purchased from Russia.[25] Most of these Kilo-class submarines have already been modernized, but readiness rates for India's existing submarine fleet sit below 40 percent, meaning that only six to seven of them can be deployed simultaneously. In 2011, the Auditor General warned that the Navy's force levels were on the decline. "The strength of warships in the Indian navy has been stagnating and despite construction of warships indigenously, the Indian navy is facing large shortfalls against its planned levels."[26] The Auditor General also reported that the Navy's aviation was only at 26 percent of its required force level, that reconnaissance activities were curtailed due to ageing patrol aircraft, that no antisubmarine aircraft besides two potent P8 Poseidons had been inducted since 1990.[27] The government has not been able to approve new orders to replace the twenty-eight dilapidated antisubmarine helicopters. In the same vein, it could not build up large enough stocks of air-defense missiles for its surface combatants.[28] The two new aircraft carriers have been plagued by delays, and no armaments were ordered for the MiG 29K fighters that will spearhead their air wing.

The Indian air force has deployed its newest capabilities in the region of the disputed border with China. The strengthening of Eastern Air Command's capacity has been impressive. The Indian government decided to base squadrons of its most potent fighter jets, the Su-30MKI, in the Eastern Sector from 2009 onward. The first two squadrons with thirty-six fighters were based at Tezpur airbase. The shelters and runway of this base were recently renovated.[29] In addition to Tezpur, the Indian Air Force is also in the process of upgrading its other airbases in the Eastern Sector. The length of runway at the base in Kalaikunda in West Bengal state has been extended to back forward operations in Arunachal.[30] The Command is also refurbishing its forward airbases at Chabua, Jorhat, and Hash Mara airbases. Yet, capabilities are still wearing thin. The Indian Air Force reports that it requires fifty squadrons to fight a two-front war, but it only has thirty-four squadrons compared to the forty-two it is supposed to operate, and it will have thirty of them equipped with advanced Su-30MKI. The order for 126 Rafale fighters is suffering delays, and costs soared from $10.6 billion in 2007 to over $25 billion.

Air defense is a further stumbling block for India. The country's air defenses remain highly centred on zones and bases and only allows for partial air denial. It is just starting to lay out Integrated Air Command and Control Systems and to unfold a Multi-Function Control and Long Range Tracking Radar network. India has developed a medium-range Ashkash, and a longer range Prithvi Air Defense (PAD) and Advanced Air Defense (AAD) missile. It will take years, still, before these will be fully deployed.

India has tried to balance China across the full range of military capabilities. One could assert that it is more effective to balance selectively, for instance, by building up capabilities where China is the most vulnerable—along its maritime trade routes to the Middle East and Africa. India has certainly attempted to position itself as the gatekeeper to the Indian Ocean, but that cannot suffice. First of all, its naval capabilities remain too limited, and China too is trying to reduce its vulnerability. More important is that the land border with China is also politically more sensitive, so that Delhi just cannot afford to be seen as losing ground. India has thus to balance comprehensively, and that, we have seen, comes as a tremendous challenge.

DIPLOMATIC BALANCING

If India has been reluctant to pursue external military balancing, it has attempted to respond to China's growing influence in its neighborhood by setting up multilateral partnerships of its own. To some extent, these harken back to the Look East Policy that was initiated in 1992, but more efforts have been made in the last decade. Important in that regard are the overtures to the Association of Southeast Asian Nations (ASEAN). "We understand India's potential role as a soft balancer," an Indonesian official remarked, "but we have thus far rather seen it as a weak balancer."[31] That weakness obviously concerns India's role as a trade partner. If China's share in ASEAN's exports increased from 6 to 11 percent between 2003 and 2012, India's share grew only from 2 to 3 percent.[32] During the free trade negotiations with the grouping, the Indian government was also not in a position to offer the same early harvest facilities as China presented to some smaller countries. Early harvest refers to concessions offered to partner countries to have some earlier benefits from trade liberalization. But weakness also relates to political and security cooperation. Officials from the region lament that India is unable to match China's involvement from the highest-level heads of state gatherings to the informal meetings between experts. One indicator that appears to confirm this observation is India's diplomatic presence in different capitals in the region: a Chinese embassy counts on average three to four times as many diplomats as an Indian embassy.[33] Resources also play a role in military diplomacy. In 2013, for instance, the Chinese Navy made port calls to eight ASEAN member states, India to five countries. Most important, however, is that Indian leaders have pointedly avoided criticizing China's behavior in the South China Sea. India has expressed its support for a Code of Conduct for the South China Sea, but in much less forceful wording and much less frequently than, say, Japan, the United States, or Australia.[34] In the East Asia Summit too, India has called for peace in the South China Sea, but much more by highlighting the need for consensus. Delhi also considers the main objective of the venue to be the promotion of economic development, rather than security issues.

Another forum concerns the Bay of Bengal Initiative for Multi-Sectoral Technical and Economic Cooperation (BIMSTEC), which includes Bangladesh, Bhutan, Myanmar, Nepal, Sri Lanka, and Thailand. BIMSTEC was set up in 2004, at a time that the Indian government became increasingly concerned about China's growing influence and sought to include the landlocked northeast in its neighborhood-policies. A free trade agreement was to be put in place by 2006. Eight years later, however, an agreement remains deadlocked. The same was true for most of the other thirteen areas of cooperation. Southeast Asian countries, especially Thailand and Myanmar, do take an interest in BIMSTEC as an opportunity to hedge against China's rise. There are several explanations for its lack of progress. First, the countries that it gathers are not known for cordial relations with each other. Relations between India and Bangladesh are complex. So are ties between India and Sri Lanka. Relations between Myanmar and Bangladesh are marred by Yangon's persecution of the cross-border Rohindra minority. Second, its members often compete in the same agricultural sectors. Third, the land bridge between the Indian subcontinent and Southeast Asia is one of the most unstable parts of Asia. Rebel groups, organized crime, and terrorism make it very difficult to deepen trade relations. Yet, still, China did manage to overcome similar stumbling blocks in its cooperation with the Mekong countries. It spearheaded security cooperation and now even guards the whole Mekong River against armed gangs. It has solved the connectivity constraints by sinking billions into transportation infrastructure. China has also overcome its neighbors' fear of competition with the farmers from Yunnan, a province that produces many of the crops on which farmers south of the border also depend, by offering loans, promising investment, and facilitating access to its market. India appears incapable of displaying the same degree of active leadership in BIMSTEC.

ECONOMIC COMPETITION

The new Congress-led cabinet arrived with a promise to decisively break with the sluggish Hindu rate of growth that marked the 1990s for India. Economic reforms would be carried out with more vigor, and India was expected to grow at 9 percent per year.[35] If anything characterized the government led by Manmohan Singh, it was confidence. At that point in time, it was also assumed that India and China could grow perfectly without competition. Between 2004 and 2007, Indian leaders consistently emphasized the emerging of a mutually beneficial division of labor. The Indian Chamber of Commerce and Industry (FICCI) calculated that China would replace the United States as India's largest trading partner. In answer to anxiety about Chinese goods harming domestic producers, Prime Minister Manmohan Singh stated, "There is a misconception that India and China are competitors. This is not true."[36] The influential Minister of Industry and Trade, Kamal Nath, put it this way: "It is not an issue of China versus India. It's India and China. We have our genius, they have theirs. While the sheer population numbers alone present an opportunity for both India and China, it is India's demographic profile that holds the key to the future. The India of tomorrow is an India of savers and spenders."[37] "We are pretty much on the same trajectory from now on," asserted the Chairman of the Planning Commission.[38]

The Eleventh Indian Five-Year Plan (2007–2012) confirmed that confidence, but the ten years of economic promises have ended in disappointment. China might have its own problems, but India's performance has come to lag increasingly behind. There were specific failures. The special economic zones, established to attract foreign investment, remained largely empty. In 2013, only 158 out of 558 approved zones were operational. Between 2004 and 2013, India attracted $23 billion in foreign direct investments, China $74 billion. The schemes to tackle poverty were flawed too. Poverty rates did drop, but that was only achieved by means of large subsidy campaigns that drove the government deeper in the red. By 2013, subsidies for farmers equalled 3 to 4 percent of India's GDP. Meanwhile, the quality of primary and secondary education only improved slowly. The campaign against corruption, another priority on the agenda of the incoming government, turned into another disappointment. The World Bank's governance indicators database, which aggregates many other databanks, reveals a percentile rank on the "control of corruption" of 39 percent for China and 35 percent for India.[39] For "regulatory quality," this is 44 and 34 percent.

If Indian politicians were still confident in 2004 that they could stand the comparison with China, frustration and disappointment now prevail. Between 2004 and 2014, India's GDP grew by 170 percent, China's by 350 percent. On a per capita basis, this performance gap is even larger. But there were also important differences in the way growth was generated. In China, investment and current account surpluses drove growth; India's GDP was dominated by household consumption and current account deficits. This had several consequences. To begin with, China's external debt shrank between 2004 and 2013, whereas India's external debt grew from 17 to 21 percent. China's infrastructure developed rapidly. It invested nine times as much in its manufacturing sector as India. The total length of its railways grew five times more than India's, its total length of roads two times. It was also the Chinese economy that became much more connected to the Internet. By 2013, it had four times as many Internet subscribers per 100 inhabitants than India. Its investment in research and development was seven times larger.

That was also reflected in their bilateral trade. Out of a total bilateral trade volume of $65 billion, India ran a deficit of $34 billion. And even the composition of India's exports remained problematic. About 70 percent of India's exports in 2013 consisted of raw materials: mostly ores and agricultural products. As much a 96 percent of China's exports consisted of manufactured goods: machinery, electronics, vehicles, and . . . much of the fertilizer on which the Indian government relies to keep the countryside stable. One could have expected India to gain in labor-intensive manufacturing, as the wages for its rapidly growing cohorts of workers remain lower than in China. But that was not the case. In 2013, China exported $6 billion of labor-intensive goods to India, whereas India only shipped for $1.4 billion of those same goods to China. Between 2004 and 2013, China's total labor-intensive exports grew by $300 billion, India's by $20 billion. Interestingly enough, Indian companies deemed China's economy more interesting than the other way around. In 2012, the Chinese government reported a Chinese investment stock of $657 million in India, whereas Indian companies had invested $723 million in China.[40]

This had important consequences. Asked whether they were satisfied with the country's economic situation, over 80 percent of Chinese citizens answered yes, compared to less than 50 percent in India.[41] The main concerns relate to employment and inflation. Indeed, between 2003 and 2013, China has created far more jobs and also many more jobs in the formal sector. Manufacturing has made an important difference. Between 2004 and 2011, China generated 16 million manufacturing jobs on top of the initial total of 112 million, whereas India generated only 3 million on an initial total of 11 million.[42] As regards inflation, the impact on Indian citizens was also significantly larger. Between 2004 and 2013, average growth per capita was 6 percent, but the average inflation rate was 9 percent. In China, this was 10 versus 3 percent.[43] This had repercussions at the political level. Chinese citizens also appear to have far more trust in their government than Indians.[44] Economic disappointment may also explain why the two main parties—Congress and the BJP—have seen their combined share drop election after election: from 94 percent in 1999 to 56 percent in 2009. That meant more fragmentation and more difficulties in reaching consensus about economic reforms. The 2014 elections did not change that. Due to the seat allocation system, Modi's BJP ended up with a majority of the seats, but he still only attracted 31 percent of the votes. The combined share of the BJP and Congress dropped to a new low of 50 percent.

It comes as no surprise, then, that after a few years of enthusiasm about "Chindia," Delhi became more frustrated with the unbalanced partnership. Indian officials acknowledge that their economic policy has failed, but they also point at unfair competition from China. In 2012 and 2013, in its second term, the government has had to respond to one question related to the trade relations with China in the lower house each week.[45] Since 2009, the Indian government slapped as many as forty-one anti-dumping duties imposed on Chinese imports.[46] Premier Manmohan Singh also raised the trade deficit with China several times. Yet, India is able to respond to China's industrial policy or its efforts to continue to prop up export-oriented industries. On the one hand, India is not able to join a large trade scheme like the Trans-Pacific Partnership, because it does not consider comprehensive liberalization in the interest of its economy. In other words: Delhi cannot make the concessions needed to present itself as an interesting partner in such trade blocs. Even in positioning itself as an alternative investment market to countries like Japan, India has been disappointing. Of the tens of billions of Japanese investments that were expected at the beginning of Premier Singh's first term, only a small part has actually found its way to India. In fact, between 2004 and 2013, Japan's investments in China grew annually by an average of $8.1 billion, but in India they grew only by $1.4 billion.[47]

Weakness is the first element that holds India back from challenging Chinese policies that distort trade; fragmentation is the other. In recent years, China has spared no effort in establishing relations with local elites in the Indian states, and in presenting itself as a potential investor and export market. Consider India's largest state. To Bihar, China promised investment in agribusiness to set up a train manufacturing plant, and to donate $1 million to a university.[48] Local ministers were also invited to trade fairs in China.[49] Uttar Pradesh was cajoled with an offer to purchase more of its mangoes and to set up an industrial park.[50] But Uttar Pradesh was not the only state where China offered to build an industrial park. In fact, about six states were pitted against one another for the same park, including the third-largest state, Maharashtra.[51] West Bengal was wooed by the prospect of becoming a major trade bridge between China and the rest of India. In Andhra Pradesh, the local government expected to attract Chinese investors in the telecom sector.[52] There were euphoric news reports when a mysterious businessman promised $160 billion of investment in the state.[53] Madhya Pradesh was approached with possible opportunities to export traditional pharmaceutical goods, fruits, and . . . buffalo meat.[54] Even Narendra Modi, known for his saber rattling on the border dispute, has been remarkably soft on China. As head of the state of Gujarat, he too was keen to attract Chinese investors and was one of the five states to bid, together with Maharashtra and Uttar Pradesh, for the famed Chinese industrial park.

Instead of a comprehensive strategy that targets Chinese economic power politics, India shows a greater tendency to become an object of that power politics. By no means has India been able to match China's robust industrial and trade strategies, and with the growing political fragmentation, that might be less the case in the future, so that local governments will display even more impatience to attract Chinese investors.

CONCLUSION

The question that arises from the previous sections is whether India can get its act together before it crumbles. There is no doubt that India has an interest in balancing China. There is the long-standing border dispute that affects its strategic interests and the prestige of its leaders. There is the contest for prosperity in a context where economic growth globally generates relatively less benefits in terms of jobs, wages, and government incomes. There is the concern that China will turn its growing economic presence in India's neighboring countries into political leverage. Indian citizens and politicians do worry about these issues, hence the decreasing levels of trust in China, the numerous questions in Parliament, the antidumping procedures, and the military reinforcements along the border. In the run-up to the elections of 2014, the main parties all vowed to address the unbalanced partnership. "We want India to challenge China as the manufacturing capital!" proclaimed Rahul Gandhi.[55] "I swear by this land that I will not let this nation be destroyed, I will not let this nation be divided, I will not let this nation bow down," Narendra Modi cried. "China should give up its expansionist attitude and adopt a development mind-set."[56] "Pakistan and China are constantly posing a threat to our national borders," the frontrunner of the Indian National Lok Dal Party declared at a rally.[57]

But we have heard such nationalistic outcries before, in 2004 and 2009. The truth is that India has remained unable to bridge the gap between discourse and deeds, between Sinophobia and impotence. There are no indications that it will change after the elections, mostly because the deteriorating economic climate and political fragmentation will complicate reforms. All the rest—military modernization and regional leadership—depend on the success of these reforms and the ability to create better jobs for the poor. Meanwhile, India's labor force is set for a rapid expansion. Between now and 2030, the labor force will expand by about 6.5 million workers: 6.5 million workers each year. It is also uncertain what China will do. Its growth is under pressure, so much is clear, but it still manages to externalize many of its problems. Consider the overcapacity in its industry. For all the trade frictions in the last years, the share of its manufacturing output that was exported grew from 18 percent in 2004 to 34 percent in 2013.[58] The eagerness of Indian states to do business with China and the ease with which China cultivates the expectations hint that its efforts to dump the glut of its factories on other markets are not likely to hit major barriers any time soon. So even if India and China are both plagued by economic imbalances and vulnerability, China still seems to be better equipped to keep India at bay as a possible economic rival and thus also to undermine its role as a balancer.

NOTES

1. World Development Indicators Database. http://data.worldbank.org/data-catalog/world-development-indicators
2. International Labor Organization, *Global Wage Report* (Geneva: ILO, 2013), 41–50.
3. ADB, *Key Indicators for Asia and the Pacific 2011* (Manila: ADB, 2011), 15–32.
4. Between 2009 and 2012, the average annual income growth was 2.2 percent, the inflation rate 3.8 percent. Source: World Development Indicators Database. Source: http://data.worldbank.org/data-catalog/world-development-indicator
5. UNCTAD Statistical Database, merchandise trade matrix: Fuels (SITC 3), Ores and metals (SITC 27 + 28 + 68), and Agricultural raw materials (SITC 2 less 22, 27, and 28). Source: http://unctad.org/en/Pages/statistics.aspx
6. Statistical Database of the Food and Agriculture Organization, Renewable internal freshwater resources per capita in cubic meters for 2011. Source: http://www.fao.org/statistics/en/
7. Conversation with Chinese official, Brussels, March 4, 2013.
8. Rajat Pandit, "Antony Warns Army against Threats from China, Pakistan," *India Times*, April 9, 2013.
9. "Modi Gives a Call for Change; Says If Govt Is Strong, China, Pak Can Never Threaten India," *Hindustan Times*, September 15, 2013.
10. Rajat Pandit, "Army Reworks War Doctrine for Pakistan, China," *Times of India*, December 30, 2009.
11. Ministry of Defense, *Freedom to Use the Seas: India's Maritime Military Strategy* (Delhi: Ministry of Defense, 2007).
12. "Chinese General Warns India against Sparking New Trouble," *South China Morning Post*, July 4, 2013.
13. Jonathan Holslag, China and India: Prospects for Peace (New York: Columbia University Press, 2010), p. 129.
14. Questions in the Lok Sabha: 2004: 20; 2005: 48; 2006: 28; 2007: 34; 2008: 37; 2009: 26; 2010: 51; 2011: 35; 2012: 42; 2013: 31. Source: http://164.100.47.132/LssNew/psearch/qsearch15.aspx.
15. Rajit Pandit, "Army Reworks War Doctrine for Pakistan, China," *Times of India*, December 30, 2009.
16. "Joint Declaration on Security Cooperation between Japan and India," Ministry of Foreign Affairs of Japan, October 22, 2008, http://www.mofa.go.jp/region/asia-paci/india/pmv0810/joint_d.html.
17. "India and South Korea Sign Two Landmark MoUS to Boost Defence Cooperation," Press Information Bureau, Government of India, September 3, 2010, http://pib.nic.in/newsite/erelease.aspx?relid=65522.
18. "Arbitration is one answer. I hope it works. But at the end of the day, whatever the institutional response is . . . it is the will of the people of the region that is very important, and that will of the people of the region is there should be a peaceful resolution." See Tarra Quismundo, "India Backs PH Arbitration Bid to Solve Sea Dispute," *Inquirer*, October 24, 2013.
19. "We won't interfere in China's sea disputes, says Indian minister," *South China Morning Post*, 23 October 2013.
20. Harsh Pant, "India in the Asia-Pacific: Rising Ambitions with an Eye on China," *Asia-Pacific Review* 14, no. 1 (2007): 54–61; Abanti Bhattacharya, "China's

Discourse on Regionalism: What It Means for India," *Asia-Pacific Review* 17, no. 1 (2010): 97–101.
21. Shrikant Paranjpe, "United States in India's Changed Strategic Perspective," *Post-Cold War Era India Quarterly: A Journal of International Affairs* 69, no. 1 (March 2013): 1–12.
22. "India's New Mountain Corps Cannot Match China's Military Capabilities across LAC," *Times of India*, July 18, 2013.
23. CAG, *Audit Report n° 24 on Union Government, Defence Services Tabled in Parliament under Article 151* (Delhi: CAG, December 2012), 14–15.
24. CAG, *Performance Audit of Planning and Management Refits of Indian Naval Ships* (Delhi: CAG, 2014), chap. 4.
25. Ranjit Bai, "Indian Navy's Second Submarine Line Will Witness Strong Competition," *India Strategic*, May 2011, p. 29–32.
26. "Auditor slams Indian navy," *Financial Times*, 28 March 2011.
27. CAG, *Audit Report No. 7* (Delhi: CAG, December 2012), 35–53.
28. Rajat Pandit, "Govt Drags Feet on Anti-Submarine Chopper Deal," *Times of India*, October 3, 2013.
29. "Sukhoi Base in the East to Counter China," *Times of India*, September 28, 2007.
30. Bappa Majumdar, "China in Mind, India to Boost Eastern Air Power," *Straits Times*, August 8, 2007.
31. Conversation with Indonesian official, Brussels, March 19, 2014.
32. UNCTAD Stats Database. http://unctad.org/en/Pages/statistics.aspx
33. Ministry of Foreign Affairs, Singapore, 2014. Diplomatic and consular list; ROK Ministry of Foreign Affairs, 2013. Diplomatic list; Ministry of Foreign Affairs, Thailand, 2014. Diplomatic List: http://www.mfa.go.th/main/en/information/1694/25862-INDIA.html; Ministry of Foreign Affairs, Malaysia, 2014. Diplomatic List: http://www.kln.gov.my/web/guest/foreign-mission-in-malaysia1.
34. "India Advocates Stable Maritime Environment in South China Sea," *Hindu*, October 10, 2013.
35. Isher Ahluwalia and I. M. D. Little, *India's Economic Reforms and Development* (Delhi: Oxford University Press, 2012).
36. "Singh: India, China not rivals," *China Daily*, 12 December 2005.
37. Pranay Gupte, "World Sees India as Tomorrow's Tiger," *Forbes Asia*, November 17, 2006.
38. Adil Zainulbhai, "Clearing the Way for Robust Growth: Interview with Montek Singh Ahluwalia," *McKinsey Quarterly*, May 2007: 26–31.
39. See "Worldwide Governance Indicators," The World Bank Group, 2017, http://data.worldbank.org/data-catalog/worldwide-governance-indicators.
40. Ministry of Commerce, Statistical Bulletin of China's Outward Foreign Direct Investment (Ministry of Commerce, Beijing, 2011), p. 79.
41. "Country's Economic Situation: Is the Country's Economic Situation Good or Bad?," for 2012 and 2013, Pew Research Center, June 2016, http://www.pewglobal.org/database/indicator/5/survey/15/.
42. ILO Labor Statistics Database. http://www.ilo.org/global/statistics-and-databases/lang--en/index.htm.
43. WDI Statistical Database. http://data.worldbank.org/data-catalog/world-development-indicators.

44. For 2011 and 2012, the Edelman Trust Barometer stands at 88 and 75 for China and 44 and 53 for India. Edelman, *Edelman Trust Barometer* (New York: Edelman, 2012).
45. 2009: 34; 2010: 44; 2011: 29; 2012: 33; 2013: 35. Lok Sabha database of questions: http://loksabha.nic.in/.
46. "Statistics on Anti-Dumping," World Trade Organization, http://www.wto.org/english/tratop_e/adp_e/adp_e.htm.
47. Jetro, "Japan's Total Outward FDI by Country/Region . https://www.jetro.go.jp/en/reports/statistics/
48. Faizan Ahmad, "China to Cooperate with Bihar in Several Sectors," *Times of India*, January 21, 2011; Rajat Arora, "Chinese Cos Queue Up for Bihar Loco Plant Project," *Indian Express*, September 21, 2013.
49. Anand Raj, "Minister China-Bound to Attract Investors to Bihar," *Telegraph*, August 30, 2013.
50. "Govt Nod for 4 Agri-Export Zones—China Keen on MoU to Import Mangoes," *Hindu*, August 9, 2002; "China Eyes Uttar Pradesh to Expand Trade in India," *Hindustan Times*, August 4, 2013.
51. "Maharashtra Pitches for Chinese Industrial Park," *Rediff*, April 25, 2014.
52. "Ponnala Wants Chinese Companies to Invest in Andhra Pradesh," ITSAP, October 19, 2012.
53. "China Ready to Invest $160 Billion in Andhra Pradesh," *Times of India*, July 21, 2013.
54. Shashikant Trivedi, "China Plans to Enter Agri, Pharma Sectors in MP," *Business Standard*, September 22, 2013; "Madhya Pradesh's China Syndrome," *Business Standard*, January 18, 2012.
55. P. Sudhakaran, "We Want India to Challenge China as Manufacturing Capital: Rahul Gandhi," *Times of India*, April 4, 2014.
56. Victor Mallet, "Modi Hits Out at Chinese Expansionism," *Financial Times*, February 24, 2014.
57. Vishal Joshi, "Badal Campaigns for INLD," *Hindustan Times*, April 8, 2014.
58. Clarification: this figure concerns the surplus, i.e., (export-import)/manufacturing coutput*100. Source: World Development Indicators and UNCTAD Statistical Database.

CHAPTER 15

Axis of Opposition

China, Russia, and the West

MICHAEL COX

Western assessments of the China-Russia relationship generally reach one of two conclusions: hyperventilation about a Beijing-Moscow alliance that aims to upend the existing international order or a blithe dismissal of a temporary meeting of minds and interests.
—Yun Sun[1]

INTRODUCTION

It is often remarked that understanding the past is difficult enough without then attempting the near-impossible task of trying to predict the future. Nonetheless, a reasonably intelligent analyst back in the mid-1980s could be forgiven for making at least two predictions with some degree of confidence: one, that the USSR would remain in its essentials the same—that is, economically inefficient, politically repressive, globally challenging, but strategically incapable or unwilling to give up its increasingly costly possessions in Eastern and Central Europe; and two, that even if China could look forward to better times in a post-Mao age—difficult to imagine otherwise—it would take generations before it could ever become a serious actor on the world stage. Few back then could have imagined, and none as far as we know did, that the Soviet system of power would implode in little under ten years; or that backward, communist-led China would have become the second-largest economy in the world in just over twenty. Of course, China was beginning to change by the late 1980s. Incomes were rising. Foreign investors were beginning to take note. Growth was on the up. The country was clearly on the move—so much so that even the *Economist* could talk in November 1992 of "one of the biggest improvements in human welfare anywhere at any time," and six months later *Business Week* of "breathtaking changes." Still, all this was taking place in a country where hundreds of millions of ordinary Chinese were poor, where China's overall weight in the international economy remained pathetically low, where an inefficient state sector remained dominant, and where all manner of obstacles still stood in the way of further economic reform.[2]

For all these reasons, and no doubt a few more besides, most experts would more likely have put their money on Russia succeeding than China. With its vast energy wealth, educated work force, proximity to Europe, and emerging democratic polity, Russia's future looked decidedly more rosy than that of China with its limited resources, aging population, sclerotic party leadership, and huge rural hinterland. Certainly the events of Tiananmen Square did not encourage much optimism about China's future. Singaporean leader Lee Kuan Yew may have gotten China right.[3] But his was only one voice among many during the 1990s; and even a few years after he had made his optimistic forecast, there were still people warning us not to buy into the hype then being propagated about a new China rising within the most dynamic region in the world. The so-called Asian miracle was nonsense on stilts according to leading economist Paul Krugman.[4] Moreover, all this frenzied talk about China's rise was so much hot air, claimed Gerald Segal in a much quoted-article. Segal was insistent. China was, and would remain, a middle-ranking power that had the rhetorical potential to frighten a few of its insecure neighbours. But it had little chance of ever becoming a serious international actor. The world could rest easy. China was not about to shake things up in spite of Napoleon's much earlier warning that one day it might.[5]

The quite unexpected decline of one communist superpower and the exponential rise of another raises all sorts of interesting and difficult questions. Much of course has been written about why Sovietologists failed to anticipate the decline of the Soviet system.[6] But much the same might be said about the failure of many Sinologists to predict the opposite about China. One can only speculate. Were analysts so mesmerized by their own liberal prejudices that they could not contemplate the possibility of a communist-led polity managing a successful economy?[7] Or did the end of the Cold War itself lead many in the West to think that history really had come to an end and that liberalism had triumphed? Either way, the speedy and dramatic transformation of China from economic backwater to the world's number-two economy was something that only a few foresaw.[8] Moreover, many of those who did talk in the 1990s of China "awakening" or the dragon "roaring" could not have envisaged how far China would rise or the impact this would then have on the international system.[9] Certainly, nobody in the 1990s speculated (as some did a decade later) of China one day "ruling the world."[10]

The sheer speed of China's ascent over the past twenty years has produced two very distinct literatures. On the one side stand what might loosely be called the "economists." Almost to a man (and a woman) they have been uniformly enthusiastic about China's economic rise. And for several good reasons. First, China's economic ascent, they point out, has helped the rest of the international economy remain on course during some very turbulent times. By mass-producing cheap goods, China has also improved choice for millions of people around the world while helping keep global inflation in check. China moreover has spawned an extraordinarily large, cash-rich middle class who appear to have become hooked on high-end Western products from Armani to the top-five French Bordeaux. Finally, for those in the field of development economics, China has shown the way and in the process taken more than 400 million ordinary Chinese out of poverty. Indeed, so important has the Chinese economy become for all of us that the biggest worry today is not whether China can keep on growing but what might happen to the world economy as a whole if—as is now the case—it starts to slow down.[11]

Scholars of international relations (IR) (or at least those of a strongly realist disposition) have been altogether less sanguine. China's economic transformation might have produced more wealth. However, it has also increased the power of the Chinese state in the international system; and this, it has been suggested, could be, and for some is already becoming, a serious worry.[12] How much of a worry might be best measured by the kind of questions students of IR have been asking of China over the past few years. First, they ask, how long can China keep on rising?[13] Secondly, what will happen to the world once it has risen?[14] Thirdly, can it continue to rise peacefully?[15] Fourthly, what do the Chinese themselves think about their rise?[16] And finally, how will rising China relate to other actors in the international system, especially the last remaining superpower with which China has had a long, complicated, and sometimes very difficult relationship: namely the United States of America?[17] There is no easy answer. But one does not need to have a deep knowledge of Chinese debates to know how much time Chinese foreign policy elites spend thinking about this question. Equally, one does not need to talk to too many American officials in Washington to discover how preoccupied they are with China. And one can readily understand why.[18] China after all is a nuclear weapon state, a permanent five member of UN Security Council, a big purchaser of US debt, and a key player in addressing larger global issues—not to mention a major supplier of highly motivated and generally wealthy students to American campuses. But more important still, China among all the rising powers is really the only one with the potential to challenge American hegemony in the Asia-Pacific region. How then to deal with this challenge has become the number-one question in Washington, with liberals on one side reassuring policy makers that China was only rising because it had bought into the established order and would therefore be loathe to upset it,[19] and realists on the other warning that we were fast heading into some decidedly choppy international waters—not, they hastened to add, because China was communist or sought war, but rather because this is what always happens when there is a power transition.[20]

If China's modern relationship with the United States has received more than its fair share of attention—too much, some might complain in Europe[21]—the same could not be said until very recently of its complex relationship with another important state with which it has had an even closer history: Russia. This is surprising. After all, the two countries share one of the longest land borders in the world. The old USSR was for many years a close ally of the Chinese Communists. And though Russia may have abandoned communist rule—while China has not—the two countries today appear to be on excellent terms, so much so that China is now regarded by Putin as Russia's indispensable friend, while Russia and its much fêted leader is now viewed in China in the most positive terms imaginable.[22] But in spite of the mounting evidence that the two have formed what they themselves see as a very close partnership built on nearly twenty years of increased cooperation, there are many who still doubt whether the relationship is an especially secure one. Indeed, according to what might be called the majority view, things still seem to be what they were some time back:[23] namely that even though relations might have improved, more will always divide the two countries than unite them.[24] As one expert noted only a few years ago, even though things between the two sides had gotten better, the relationship would, and could, never become a close one.[25] Nor was this his view alone. As another writer suggested in a much-cited study followed two years later by a wide-ranging paper on the same subject, the relationship would forever remain "non-committal and asymmetrical": "convenient" for both sides to be sure, but nothing we should be especially impressed by.[26] In fact, Bobo Lo's underlying argument—that the character, culture, history, and interests of these two countries were just too different for them to make common cause—is one that seems to have been adopted by most experts. Thus we are regularly informed that the two countries are less friends than rivals (especially when it comes to Central Asia),[27] that the Russians and the Chinese just do not like one another, (call it cultural misunderstanding if you will), and that while many policy makers in Beijing view the Russians with a degree of contempt, the Russians themselves view China with a mixture of awe (because of its economic success) and fear (because it is doing so much better than Russia).[28] Nor, we are told, does the economics work. Trade between the two countries may have risen. On the other hand, neither would be prepared to sacrifice their more important ties with the Western capitalist economies for the dubious benefits of working closely with the other. Their own economies are not especially complementary either.[29] And to cap it all off, there is, we are informed, a growing and deepening power gap between the two that must inevitably push them apart. Geoff Dyer has perhaps expressed this idea more eloquently than most. China and Russia, he notes, are both power-obsessed states. But one of those powers is on the up—obviously China—while the other, Russia, is on the way down. This, he then goes on to argue, can only feed Russian anxieties; and as those anxieties grow, Russia will pull back from a dependency relationship on a China it once regarded as its little brother and whose rising power it now fears. The two are thus destined to be very uneasy bedfellows, rivals at worst. All talk of a new strategic partnership between a new axis of authoritarian powers is so much hot air.[30]

In what follows, I want to challenge this still-dominant view.[31] I do so not because I believe there are no differences between China and Russia or because I am unaware of the potential for competition and rivalry. Rather, I do so for an altogether different reason—which is to explain what the various skeptics seem unable to: why it is that these two great powers have managed to form an increasingly close relationship in spite of all their obvious differences and in spite of what most experts predicted. Nor can the relationship simply be understood in its own bilateral terms. In other words, it has to be understood in terms of its opposition to something else—and that something, quite obviously, is the West, or more precisely the West's liberal values and the way in which the West continues to dominate the international system (in spite of all the loose talk of late about there having been a power shift away from the West). Some of course will still insist that that this does not add up to classic balancing behavior;[32] that neither China nor Russia has a positive vision of a new world order;[33] that there are subtle and sometimes not-so-subtle differences in the ways in which Russia and China conduct themselves abroad; and that the two prefer to think of themselves as partners rather than formal allies.[34] Nor can it be ruled out that their different national identities might still force them apart in the future.[35] Clearly, this is still a work in progress. Nonetheless, it is impossible to ignore the by now self-evident fact that what increasingly binds the two together—more so than ever since the great financial crash of 2008 followed a few years later by a breakdown in relations between Russia and the West—has become more important than what separates them. Naturally, this does not mean they do not have other interests, including in China's case a very great interest in exporting as much of its capital and goods to the rest of the world. Nor, it seems, does either want to challenge world capitalism as an economic system. But this does not detract from the main argument being advanced here: namely, that China, which has so few serious friends in the world today, appears to have found something close to one in Russia, and that Russia—increasingly isolated from the West and in need of as much support as it can muster—has clearly discovered one in China.[36]

To make good on my claim I have divided the essay into several parts. In the first section, I examine the collapse of the USSR and why this cataclysmic event has such importance for the ways in which contemporary Russia and modern China together view the world and each other. In part 2, I then look at their positions on international affairs, focusing in particular on their critique of American power and US policies in the world system. In part 3, I go on to look at four key areas where China and Russia now cooperate regularly: inside the permanent five (P5) of the UN; as part of the Shanghai Co-operation Organization; within the BRICS organization; and over their preferred trade architecture for the Asia-Pacific. Finally, I reflect on the future in the light of the crisis in Ukraine. Here I differ from those who seem to think that the crisis has exposed deep fault lines in the Sino-Russian relationship. I take a rather different view, which, stated bluntly, is that the crisis has revealed something quite different: namely, that China has been prepared to abandon certain basic principles in order to maintain its relationship with Russia, while Russia has been more than willing to appease China in order to make sure it can keep the Chinese on their side. Nothing of course is predetermined. But if one were to make a prediction (a fool's errand to be sure), it would be that a Russia increasingly under siege from what it now perceives as being a permanently hostile West, and a China still confronted by an America that stands as the principal obstacle to its ambitions in the Asia-Pacific, have come to the not illogical conclusion that there is nothing to lose, and probably much to be gained, from moving even closer together. That this presents a challenge to the West is obvious: though whether or not it constitutes a serious threat is much less clear. This, I believe, will in part depend just as much on how the West responds to what is happening as it will on policies devised in either Moscow or Beijing. In an age of improving Sino-Russian relations, there is still much the West can do to shape the future. But it will only be able to do this if it abandons the now-outdated view that the relationship is "vulnerable, contingent and marked" only "by uncertainties." In short, it will only be able to think straight about China and Russia together when it abandons what I would term here old ways of thinking about their emerging relationship.[37]

UNITED BY HISTORY

The People's Republic of China and Russia are more aware of the world's problems than the United States because they have gone through terrible wars unleashed by the blind egoism of fascism.

—Fidel Castro[38]

One of the basic reference points in the ongoing debate about the durability of the China-Russia relationship is of course what happened in history—or more exactly what happened in their history—to create what many still believe is a serious barrier to the establishment of trust between the two. The list of grievances on the Chinese side in particular is indeed a long one, going right back to the unequal treaties of the nineteenth century, through Stalin's efforts to stop the CCP coming to power in 1949, and on to the great split between the two communist states between the early 1960s and the late 1980s. Yet history, as we know, is always contested terrain, and one could just as easily make the case that the past has the potential to unite rather than divide. After all, if it had not been for the USSR, the Chinese Communist party would never have come into being in the first place; and though Stalin was never less ambiguous about Mao, in the end the Soviet Union did provide the PRC with massive support in its early formative years. Moreover, the USSR and China did fight on the same side in World War II, a fact the world was graphically reminded of in the spring of 2015 when the Chinese president was the guest of honor in Moscow standing next to Putin as the tanks and troops rolled by during the victory parade, and four months later when Putin attended another massive event in Beijing celebrating China's victory over Japan. The two leaders moreover used both occasions not just to recall times gone by, but to demonstrate how far their relationship had improved. Indeed, Xi's visit to Russia and his appearance at the Moscow commemorations, according to one Chinese official, "pushed the China-Russia all-round strategic partnership relationship to a new level," while Russia's equally active participation in China's celebrations, according to Putin himself, marked yet another major step forward in a fast-maturing relationship.[39]

But it is not just the war that unites the two. So too does a more recent event: the collapse of the Soviet project itself between 1989 and 1991. The reasons why a once mighty superpower with an extensive industrial base, a huge military capability, and a powerful apparatus of controls finally imploded has been analyzed at length in the West. However, the collapse of Soviet communism has perhaps been of even greater interest to those states directly and indirectly involved themselves, namely Russia and China. The official line in Russia initially was that the end of the Cold War and the implosion of the USSR were more or less inevitable given the burdens of empire and the more efficient character of their capitalist competitor. But all was not lost, it was felt. Indeed, precisely because these seismic changes appeared to open up the way to deep economic reform at home and a much-improved relationship with the West, there was good reason to think they would lay the foundation for greater prosperity at home and huge economic opportunities abroad. In fact, for a while, with a ostensibly liberal and democratic president in the White House calling for a deep strategic partnership with Russian reform, there looked to be every chance that Russia would be able to come to terms with its much-reduced role in world politics, not to mention its diminished influence in its former imperial space.[40]

Whether there was ever any chance of a new cooperative relationship being built between postcommunist Russia and the United States remains an open question. What is not open to question is how quickly this early vision of a new deal began to lose its allure. The shift from what has been described as the pro-Western phase in Russian thinking to something quite different evolved through several stages. In simple chronological terms, however, the decline in the relationship began as early as 1990 when the West refused large-scale economic aid to Russia; it then continued after 1993 with the enlargement of NATO; the relationship was further compromised as Russian nationalists and communists began to mobilize their not inconsiderable base of support at home; and it was finally provided with a more material form as the Russian economy imploded because of what many in Russia saw as a deliberate Western plan to reduce the country to the status of a Third World country. Certainly, long before Putin assumed office, there was a sizeable group of Russians who insisted that having given away everything to the West between 1989 and 1991, Russia had gotten nothing back in return other than broken promises and a raft of policy suggestions that had impoverished the majority and allowed a narrow band of oligarchs to seize control of the nation's assets.[41]

In terms of his policies, Putin did not at first seem to represent a break with those pursued by his predecessor, Yeltsin. But very soon it became clear that he had a strategy of sorts at the heart of which was a drive to consolidate as much power in his own hands while aligning his own political fortunes with those of Russian state power.[42] Though not opposed to working with the West, or even the United States, his basic outlook was infused with an underlying suspicion of the Western world and what he appeared to view as a Western desire to ensure that Russia remained weak and dependent. The consequences of this for both Russia and its near abroad—not to mention Russia's relations with the United States and the European Union—were deeply significant. Putin also added a "dash of history" to justify his new stance and did so by turning to a group of patriotic "Eurasianists," who were more than happy to provide him with a story that best suited his purpose. At the heart of this was the very strong belief that Russia was not merely different from the "liberal" West: the West, it was argued, was almost congenitally hostile to Russia. This had been true for the greater part of the nineteenth century. It remained true for the whole of the Soviet period. And it continued to be true into the twenty-first century. In fact, according to Putin's apologists, the end of the Cold War and the collapse of the USSR itself were all part of a larger Western plan to ensure the West's and the United States' continued primacy. This is why 1989 and what followed in 1991 were not the progressive "liberating" events portrayed in much Western literature but rather well-organized regime-changing plots backed by certain traitors at home like Gorbachev.[43]

Unsurprisingly, this particular narrative was one that found a ready audience in China. In fact, the Chinese had been saying very much the same ever since the collapse of Soviet power back in 1989—in part because they opposed political reform per se and in part because Gorbachev's reforms had posed a very real danger to Chinese communist rule itself. Indeed, as we knew then (and have found out more since) during that fateful year, Beijing did as much as it was then possible for it to do to prevent the collapse from happening; and, when that proved impossible, they then took their own draconian measures in the June of 1989 to ensure that the contagion did not bring down communist rule at home. Always hostile to Gorbachev, and from the outset opposed to what they viewed as his dangerously destabilizing efforts to liberalize the Soviet system—Deng later commented that even though Gorbachev may have looked "smart," he was in fact "stupid"—the Chinese had little trouble in agreeing with Putin's less than positive analysis of both 1989 and the final denouement of Soviet power later in 1991. And why not? After all, what had happened to the USSR could just as easily have happened to China itself.[44]

In rather typical Stalinist fashion, the Communist Party then went on to draw all sorts of "lessons" about how to make sure that what had happened to the Soviet Union did not happen to China.[45] This was not a task they took lightly. Commissions were set up and study groups created tasked with the crucial job of explaining what had destroyed the other communist superpower. As has been observed, the collapse of the Soviet Union following hard on the heels of communist collapse in Eastern Europe and East Germany "was a deeply disturbing experience for the Chinese communists."[46] It was also a deeply complicated problem, which might in part explain why it took a several study groups over many years (not to mention An eight part television series called Preparing for Danger in Times of Safety—Historic Lessons Learned from the Demise of Soviet Communism (Ju'an siwei)) before they could come to any firm conclusions. Even then, the conclusions at which they arrived at were not entirely consistent. Nor did they necessarily agree with Putin that the collapse of the Soviet Union had been a catastrophe. After all, once the USSR had disintegrated, China itself no longer faced a united rival on its northern and eastern borders. That said, China in the end did concede that what had happened contained lessons for both states: the first was that while economic reform might be necessary (and in China's case, essential), one should make sure that this did not threaten the integrity of the state; and the second was that one should forever remain wary of the West's intentions, especially when the West—as it tended to—dressed up its geostrategic ambitions in liberal rhetoric. Herein lay the most obvious lesson of all: namely, that whatever else may have divided them in the past, and might divide them in the future, both states had a very strong interest in supporting the other against those who challenged their sovereign right to rule in a particular way. By so doing, they would not only be protecting themselves at home from dangerous ideas born in the West. They would, ironically, also be upholding the fundamental Westphalian principle of noninterference upon which the whole international system had rested for centuries and would hopefully continue to do so for decades to come.[47]

UNIPOLARITY AND ITS DANGERS

China opposes hegemonism and power politics in all their forms, does not interfere in other countries' internal affairs and will never seek hegemony or engage in expansion.
—Xi JinPing at the 18th Party Congress (2012)

The lessons drawn from the collapse of Soviet power thus provided, and still provides, China and Russia with a common point of historical reference. But it was the structure of the new international system that concerned them more. Both of course recognized that with the passing of the old order the world had changed forever; and both would now have to sink or swim in a word dominated by the market. There could be no going back to the past. On the other hand, the world as seen from Beijing and Moscow was not one in which either could feel especially comfortable. For one thing, the established rules governing the world had all been written by the West. The metaphorical table around which the main players then sat was also made and designed in the West. And sitting at the top of the table of course was the established hegemon: the United States.

To add material insult to injury, in this world the United States not only possessed a vast amount of power—soft and hard—but an extensive alliance system as well. Its very existence not only reminded China and Russia of how few genuine friends they had themselves; it also contributed in significant ways to America's ability to place pressure on the two countries. The United States may have proclaimed its innocence, insisting that the last thing it was thinking about when it enlarged NATO was to encircle Russia, or that when it tilted to Asia it was looking to contain China rather than engage it. However, that is not how things were viewed in either Moscow or Beijing. Indeed, for the Chinese, the so-called tilt (accompanied as it was by what they saw as a change in US military doctrine)[48] was seen as a highly aggressive act; and the only legitimate response, it was felt, was to fight fire with fire, which it did with an "outpouring" of increased "anti-American sentiment" in China itself followed up by what looked to many as a final abandonment in practice, if not in theory, of the tried and true Deng principle of keeping a low profile.[49] To underscore the point, it also began to refer to the US less frequently as a global partner—though such language did not disappear entirely from the Chinese foreign policy discourse[50]—and more as a potential rival that would forever seek to maintain its position of primacy in Asia through the manipulation of its still highly dependent allies.[51]

This in turn connects to a wider debate in which China and Russia have been engaged for some time about the structure of the world system after the Cold War; and one thing has emerged from these: neither feels that their interests, singly or collectively, are best protected in a system in which power is so heavily concentrated in the hands of a single "hegemon," especially when that hegemon happens to be a liberal power like the United States of America.[52] This not only flows from their very strongly held realist belief that hegemony by definition confers great status on the hegemon. The concentration of power in the hands of a single power, they argue, is also likely to encourage greater assertiveness. Clinton may have resisted the temptation for a while, though not entirely as the NATO-led bombing of Kosovo showed. But post-9/11, the situation changed dramatically, and buoyed up by a American public fearful of yet another attack, and taking full advantage of the freedom afforded it by the much-debated unipolar "moment," the United States launched a war on terror with the ostensible goal of combating global jihad (of which the Chinese and Russians approved) but with the unwritten purpose (to which they did not) of reasserting US power after what many on the Republican political right saw as a post-Cold War decade of drift.[53] The lesson drawn in China and Russia from all this was obvious: until and when the distribution of power in the international system had become more evenly distributed—in short had become "multipolar"—then the world would not only remain a deeply disturbed place but one in which their voices would remain marginal at best, insignificant at worst.[54]

China and Russia's various efforts to challenge what they saw, and still see, as America's global preeminence has also brought both into direct opposition with what they view as something equally challenging: the Western idea of "humanitarian intervention," or to give its more official title, the international community's right to protect individuals when sovereign states fail to uphold certain basic norms. The story, of course, is not a simple one. Indeed, in theory, neither power is by definition opposed to the basic principles of the *Responsibility to Protect* (R2P). That said, the two clearly feel deeply uncomfortable with the whole drift in Western thinking that they insist allows the West to bring outside pressure to bear on what they see as recalcitrant states. This, they argue, not only undermines the UN system based on the original Charter of 1945 and the principle of sovereignty. It also provides a green light for the West to force change from without on states with whom the West either happens to disagree or with whom both China and Russia may have significant economic and strategic relations.[55] But this is not all. Their even greater fear, one suspects, is that if the democratic West is given the green light to change or overthrow dictatorial regimes in, say, Iraq, Libya, or Syria, this opens up the theoretical possibility at least of them legitimately demanding change in Russia and China as well. In this sense, their hostility to intervention is not just because they look at the world differently: it is because they worry that under the guise of advancing the rights of the human, or protecting peoples from their less than perfect governments, the West could use the doctrine of humanitarianism as a Trojan Horse with the purpose of weakening their own control at home.[56]

This would be less important, of course, if either China or Russia, or both, happened to agree with the kind of values that America and most of its allies have sought to promote over the past twenty-five years. But this is clearly not the case. Indeed, viewed from the vantage point of Putin's

Kremlin or China's leadership compound in Beijing, Zhongnanhai, the values espoused by the West in general look deeply problematic. It is one thing doing business with the West. It is something else altogether when engagement with the West leads, as the Chinese and Russians clearly fear it has, to ideological contamination. The market may be neutral politically, but the West as a project is not; and faced with such a challenge, the two countries together have taken different, but not entirely dissimilar, countermeasures.[57] These have included in the Chinese case an extensive system of censorship reinforced in the age of the web by an increasingly intrusive set of controls over the internet.[58] Russia may not have the same system of controls. Nevertheless, under Putin, the flow of information has been severely curtailed by a media that is now either completely state controlled or run by the friends of the president. Like the Chinese, the Russians have also spent an inordinate amount of time and effort trying to curtail flows of information from the outside world in an attempt to uphold what some Russians now call "internet sovereignty."[59] Those close to Putin have even spoken of the West having launched what they call an "'information war' against Russia," one that they have no intention of losing. Indeed, in one typically forceful statement (one of several), the Russian Foreign Minister not only linked US aggression back to the Cold War and an unreformed Cold War mentality, but to American exceptionalism and what he termed the belief by Americans that they possessed an "eternal uniqueness," one that allowed them to resist any form of external interference into their affairs but made it perfectly acceptable for them to become deeply involved in the affairs of others.[60]

Finally, in this ongoing ideological battle against the liberal West, both China and Russia have tended over the years to identify any form of internal dissent with some assumed Western plot to undermine their respective systems. In the case of Russia, the presumed link between opposition at home and the machinations of some unnamed Western agencies is now regularly made in the media. Indeed, in 2014, a TV program was put out (hosted by the same individual who allegedly murdered Litvinenko in London) purporting to show that there were still many traitors in Russia, all of them—including a number of NGOs—being supported by (and obviously working for) the West. Others are portrayed in harsher terms still, most notably the Ukrainians, who are now systematically portrayed in the wider Russian press as being little more than stalking horses for the Americans and their dangerous allies in Brussels. China may have adopted a somewhat (though only somewhat) less bellicose approach. Nonetheless, in its own ongoing struggles against all those who would challenge the idea of the "harmonious society," it has rarely, if ever, been reluctant not to associate dissent at home with acts of subversion from abroad. Nor has it been backward in coming forward in sanctioning those in the West who they deem to have overstepped the ideological mark—as Norway found out to its cost back in 2010 when the Nobel Peace Prize committee had the temerity to award the prize to the jailed human rights activist, Liu Xiabo. Whether or not Beijing viewed the award as a Western plot remains unclear. What is clear is the impact it had on the official mind in China, reinforcing its basic belief that Western countries (even small ones like Norway) were engaged in subtle and sometimes not-so-subtle forms of subversion whose ultimate purpose was political change in China.[61]

CHINA AND RUSSIA—INTERNATIONAL COOPERATION

Russia and China attach great importance to cooperation within multilateral formats, including the UN, G20, BRICS, the SCO.
—Russian Foreign Minister Sergei Lavrov[62]

If, as I have suggested here, China and Russia adhere to a broadly similar view of the world while together asserting their right to protect themselves from what they both regard as that bearer of ideological contamination known as the liberal West, how has their increasingly close strategic partnership manifested itself at the international level? Here again, the by now standard answer is that in spite of a certain tactical convergence on specific issues, one should not overstate the extent of their collaboration. Not only do big divisions remain. China has also become far too respectable—too much of a "stakeholder"—to be drawn into an ever-closer diplomatic relationship with its less than respectable neighbor, especially when the neighbor in question has, it is argued, little to offer.[63] Indeed, in the midst of the crisis occasioned by the Russian intervention in Ukraine, one respected Western newspaper made a very direct comparison between the "constructive" approach being pursued by the Chinese and the "increasingly dangerous" approach adopted by the Russians. It is high time, the paper went on, for the "provocative" Russians to learn something from the more pragmatic Chinese. Whether Putin ever read the advice coming from the *Financial Times* is of course unknown. But one suspects that if he had, he might have wondered why the editorial made no mention of the tacit support he was already receiving from the Chinese in his efforts to undermine Ukrainian sovereignty. He may have also noted that the editorial also forgot to mention the fact that in the years leading up to the Ukrainian crisis, the apparently "irresponsible" Russians and the "well-behaved" Chinese had been working increasingly closely together on a range of significant international issues in a number of key international forums.[64]

The first, and perhaps most important, arena where China and Russia had been working closely together was at the United Nations, where both occupied seats as Permanent Members of the UN Security Council. Their approaches were not identical, to be sure. Indeed, China appeared to be less willing than Russia to deploy its veto, usually preferring to use the less controversial strategy of abstention when faced with resolutions it opposed. Moreover, on some issues involving international security (Iran's nuclear program, for example) China was willing to support measures such as sanctions. Nonetheless, like Russia, it consistently resisted the use of force by the West against recalcitrant regimes if the purpose was regime change; and more generally, it opposed any form of economic pressure being applied to states deemed to be guilty of human rights abuses. The record speaks for itself. Thus in 2006, it effectively prevented any action being taken against Sudan over its genocidal behavior in Darfur. In 2007 it then stymied the UN over Myanmar. And a year later, it acted once again to protect Mugabe's Zimbabwe from censure. But more was to follow when China, together with Russia, repeatedly vetoed UN motions aimed to censure Russia's close (and only) ally in the Middle East, Syria. In 2011, for example, both vetoed a resolution condemning the Syrian regime's handling of antigovernment street protests. A year later, they vetoed an Arab League Plan calling for political change. Resolutions calling for sanctions against Assad were also vetoed, as was a UN draft resolution in May 2014 backed by sixty-five countries calling for the crisis in Syria to be referred to the International Criminal Court.[65] And so it went on, causing something close to a storm in the UN and the wider Arab world. One writer even accused the two of "kneecapping" the Security Council.[66] But all to no avail. In fact, at a 2014 meeting in Beijing, the two both appeared to congratulate the other for having prevented a Western intervention, which in their view would not only have made matters much worse, but would have undermined any moves toward a peaceful resolution of the conflict.

If increased political cooperation in the United Nations points to more than just a coincidental meeting of minds over specific issues, then China and Russia's formal membership of the sometimes underestimated—and often understudied—Shanghai Co-operation Organization (SCO) points to something of equal significance: a proven longer-term ability to cooperate in matters relating to hard security. Of course, the SCO was not, and was never intended to be, the Eurasian equivalent of NATO. However, over time it soon became more than the sum of its disparate parts. A Chinese initiative in the first instance with the purpose of promoting some degree of regional coordination where before there had been none, the SCO has since its foundation in 2001 taken on several roles that now include a counterterrorism function, a sharing of intelligence, and an increasingly high degree of military cooperation—especially between China and Russia.[67]

Initially, China was keen to stress that even if no Western power was likely to play a role in the organization, this did not mean that its purpose was anti-Western or anti-American as such. However, even if the SCO sought "no open confrontation" with the United States, it was difficult to think of the SCO as not having some broader strategic purpose, especially after 9/11, when the United States began to increase its presence in Central Asia. This certainly worried the ever-sensitive Chinese, though given their own concerns about terrorism, they were prepared to concede some temporary US presence. The Russians too conceded some US role for the time being. But as time passed, the Russian position changed. Indeed, the longer the United States remained in Central Asia, the more concerned the Russians became with what they saw as an American attempt to establish a long-term presence in countries that had once formed part of the USSR. In the end, things came to a head, and in July 2005 it managed to get its SCO partners—including China—to demand of the West and the US that they remove their forces from SCO members' territories. They in turn linked this specific demand to a wider debate about the kind of international system they sought and the role the SCO might play in creating a new "world order," one in which no single power (here meaning the United States) would have a "monopoly in world affairs" or be able arrogate to itself the right to interfere "in the internal affairs of sovereign states." Furthermore, at its various meetings, China and Russia started to behave as if the SCO formed the kernel of a powerful new security organization constructed on principles very different from those found in the liberal and democratic West. Underwritten politically by what has become known as the "Shanghai spirit," with its strong emphasis on noninterference, stability, and diversity, the SCO thus soon came to form part of wider Chinese and Russian strategy with the purpose of establishing deeper cooperation between the two powers. Of course, the SCO still only has a limited impact on the security situation in Eurasia more generally; and the organization it has accepted has been unable to "sustain or even execute many of the agreements it reaches at meetings due to conflicting national regulations, laws, and standards." There are also ongoing complaints that some SCO members have so far been unwilling to "supply the collective SCO bodies" with the resources necessary to make them function effectively.[68] That said, a body that did not exist some time ago exists today; and it exists with the broad overarching purpose of allowing both Russia and China to find a united and separate voice in a part of the world from which they seek to minimize or even exclude the Americans.

If both China and Russia have invested much in maintaining and strengthening SCO as a regional security organization, the same could just as easily be said of an even more famous organization, which started life back in 2001 as an acronym invented by Goldman Sachs economist Jim O'Neill.[69] Initially, of course, the idea of the BRICS was pooh-poohed by most conventional economists; and even after the organization had begun to take on a life of its own, there were still those who repeated the line that the countries who constituted the BRICS were too different to be viewed as a united bloc. Even so, the simple idea of the BRICS not only helped redefine the way many people came to see the world—contributing in no small part to the notion that power was shifting away from the West. As an organization, it also showed enormous creativity, especially after financial crash of 2008 helped undermine the belief that only the West had answers to the economic challenges facing the world.[70] Certainly, ever since its first summit in 2009, the BRICS has assumed ever-greater importance; and within the BRICS organization itself, China and Russia have worked closely together, fashioning common positions attacking in one breath Western-style structural reforms, and then, in another, the unequal character of the world's financial system and the privileged role enjoyed by the US dollar. They have been equally vocal on global governance issues, arguing that the current distribution of voting power on the IMF and the World Bank is much too heavily weighted in favor of the Europeans and the Americans. Not only have they been critical, however. At the Brazil summit in 2014, the two also helped the BRICS establish two banks that would, they hoped, challenge the primacy of the International Monetary Fund and the World Bank. Now, whether or not these various efforts could ever weaken, let alone undermine, the West's grip on the levers of financial power was not at all clear. Still, it was not without significance (or irony) that a body that had been invented in the West by a Western economist working for a Western investment Bank, many years later looked like it was now providing both China and Russia with a platform from which they were able to launch a critique of the West.[71]

Of course, the BRICS, like the SCO, is a work in progress. But in spite of the problems currently facing some of its members, what may once have been defined (and dismissed) as a mere "club" has over time taken steps "towards becoming an organization" with a life all of its own. Perhaps there is no clear idea yet of what each of the five members wants the BRICS to become. And there is real doubt, even among some of its strongest supporters, whether it really exists to challenge the West or to express discontent with the way in which the West currently manages global affairs. Nonetheless, a body that was for the first few years of its existence virtually ignored by most experts in the West, or simply written off as being little more than an acronym, has assumed a significance that few ever believed possible. And in an age of economic uncertainty where the West's own institutions hardly look robust, there is every chance that the BRICS could assume an ever more important role in the future.[72]

Finally, in any assessment of the China-Russian relationship, one should not underestimate the importance of wider trade questions relating to the Asia-Pacific region. Indeed, in what has rapidly become a battle between the United States and China over which body should define the trade agenda around the Pacific, it is not insignificant that Russia has rushed into support China—which favors the Asia-Pacific economic cooperation (APEC)—while taking great exception to American efforts (now abandoned) to establish its own parallel organization in the shape of the Trans-Pacific Partnership (TPP).[73] Not only has it done so because both countries were at first excluded from TPP. It has acted thus because, like China, it seeks to thwart America's much-vaunted "tilt to Asia," of which TPP is seen as being a vital part. Making its own very strong claim to be as much an Asian power as a European one—some have even talked of a Russian tilt to Asia—Russia has certainly been highly active on the diplomatic front of late. Indeed, at the APEC summit hosted by the Chinese in Beijing in November 2014, it could not have been more active or Putin more vocal. It was quite "obvious," Putin noted in one interview, that the TPP was nothing more than "just another American attempt to build an architecture of regional economic co-operation" from which the US in particular "would benefit." But the effort would fail, he continued, and would do so in large part because the Americans had gone out of their way to exclude "two regional players" in the shape of Russia and China. Thus having stressed the dubious motives of the Americans, Putin then emphasized how close Russia now was to China, noting that "relations between the two countries" had never been better. Indeed, according to Putin, they had "reached the highest level" in our "entire history."[74] The Chinese president did not appear to digress from this assessment. Nor did the official Chinese press, who continued to rail against what they saw as an American-led strategy of returning to Asia by opening "the door" to the Asian "market" as part of an even wider, and more insidious, effort to encircle China itself.[75]

Of course, this jaundiced view of US policy was strongly denied by officials in Washington; and indeed at the same APEC summit—and at later forums in 2015 and 2016—Obama went out of his way to stress that the TPP was definitely not an "anyone but China club."[76] Indeed, in 2015 he even invited Russia and China to join. But neither the Russian leadership nor the Chinese seemed to be won over. Indeed, Putin continued to see all this as part of a larger American plan to either undermine or surround Russia, even though some Russian analysts argued that TPP might have positive results for the country.[77] The Chinese president appeared to be equally aggrieved, even though certain reformers in China appeared to be in favor of joining.[78] Either way, both stuck to the original official line that TPP was a direct challenge, and that the only thing that could hold it back (aside from opposition to it coming from the American people themselves!) was an ever-closer partnership between a China that was more than happy to have Russia making the case against America on its behalf, and a Russia that was now more keen than ever to strengthen its ties with China in a period when its own relations with the West had moved from being poor to bad to near disastrous following events in Ukraine.[79]

CONCLUSION: CHINA, RUSSIA, UKRAINE, AND BEYOND

China does not want the South China Sea dominated by Americans. Russia does not want the West—the United States and Europe—to penetrate what Moscow perceives as "its sphere of influence." In short, Russia and China do not want a world dominated by the United States.[80]

Though the crisis in Ukraine might be seen as being the immediate cause of what some are now claiming, rather spuriously, is a "new" Cold War between Russia and the West, its deeper origins can be traced back to the disintegration of the USSR in 1991 and the traumatic effect this then had on Russian power and Russian identity.[81] Squeezed, as Russia then felt that it was, between on the one hand an unsympathetic and predatory West determined to spread its liberal values, and on the other by a rising tide of nationalist sentiment in its former republics, Russia was bound, in the end, to try and call a halt to what Putin came to see as the country's precipitate decline. The material foundation for this was in the first instance provided by a near ten-fold increase in the price of oil and gas. But Russia's rebooting also took a more direct form, firstly in Georgia in 2008, when it intervened directly to punish a Georgian government looking westward toward NATO, and then, more seriously, in 2013, when Ukraine took what now looks like a tipping-point decision to establish a much closer relationship with the European Union. What followed is by now well known, with revolt breaking out in Kiev, Russia's chosen political proxy in Ukraine taking flight, Crimea then seceding from Ukraine, followed in turn by ongoing Russian-inspired interventions in East and Southeast Ukraine.[82]

As we now know, this unprecedented crisis has not only had a major impact on Russia's relationship with the West. It has also posed a serious problem for China. Naturally enough, Beijing was following these events with enormous interest, fully aware that what Russia had done and was doing—organizing a secession and then continuing to interfere in the internal affairs of another state—ran directly counter its own cherished foreign policy principles. Indeed, there is some evidence to suggest that some Chinese officials may have disapproved (in private) of Russian actions. Moreover, Beijing (to be fair) did issue a number of statements that, though not directly critical of Russia, did repeat their by now standard foreign policy position that matters should be settled through negotiation, not force, and that all parties to the conflict should recognize each other's sovereign rights. But to many observers, this looked like so much window dressing.[83] Indeed, while Russian-led or Russian-backed forces continued to operate in southern and eastern Ukraine, China seemed to be doing its best to support Russia diplomatically while hiding behind a curtain of studied diplomatic neutrality, albeit not always very successfully. In fact, as the crisis unfolded, China appeared to suggest that if anybody was to blame, it was not so much their close friend Putin but a meddling West that had failed to understand history or the "complexities of the Ukrainian issue." Furthermore, far from attacking Russia, China went out of its way two months later at the BRICS summit in Brazil to ensure that it escaped any form of censure at all.

China's diplomatic attempts to sound even-handed in public while scolding the West for acting irresponsibly undoubtedly helped the Russians in their moment of diplomatic need. China meanwhile took full advantage of the situation to enhance its own position by exploiting Russia's self-evident need for diplomatic and economic cover. Certainly, the much-vaunted gas deal signed in May 2014 was one that worked to China's advantage. Indeed, as was observed at the time, China had driven an espcially "hard bargain."[84] But with the Russian economy now under increased pressure, China was perfectly happy to exploit the new situation by drawing ever closer to Russia. Nor did the diplomatic initiatives end there. Indeed, as if to make the point even "clearer than the truth" to those who may have been wondering about the health of the relationship, the two countries signed yet another energy deal in November! Then, as if to drive the point home, they confirmed they were planning even more naval exercises together, this time however in the Mediterranean, not off the Chinese mainland.[85] At around the same time, China also signed a major new arms deal with Russia. Certainly, if China was feeling uncomfortable in supporting Russia, as some Western analysts speculated at the time, it was certainly not showing.[86]

Naturally enough, none of this seemed to make much difference to those who had always doubted the staying power of the relationship. Thus, a short while after China and Russia had signed a massive new gas deal, one analyst was still reassuring his readers that the relationship was still "more superficial than strategic."[87] A few months later, another pundit was claiming that the Russian and Chinese leaders were not really "buddies."[88] And by the beginning of 2015, yet another writer was suggesting that even if China and Russia might have looked like they were getting on extraordinarily well, the relationship with China could not deliver what Russia really needed.[89] Nor, it seemed, could it deliver on what either needed. Indeed, with the economic slowdown in China and the collapse of energy prices in Russia, it once again looked to the skeptics as if the relationship was about to take a tumble.[90] But nothing of the sort happened. Indeed, far from sputtering or coming to a halt, the relationship continued to move forward, and did so, as leaders in both Moscow and Beijing pointed out, for a very simple reason: it was in their interest for it to do so. As Putin made clear—and Xi did not demur—the continued "expansion of the Russian-Chinese partnership" met and presumably would continue to "meet the interests and strategic goals of our two countries."[91]

The question then remains, How might the relationship evolve in the future? As I have earlier indicated, there is no easy way of predicting what might happen over the longer term. Our numerous skeptics obviously think, and continue to insist, that underlying tensions will in the end make the relationship—whose significance they doubt anyway—either less important or undermine it altogether. But this is certainly not a view supported by the evidence at the moment. Nor is there much to suggest they will be pulling apart any time soon. Indeed, why should they? After all, the relationship has already realized major strategic and political gains for the two sides. It has provided both with important diplomatic cover at crucial moments. It has led to increased political and military cooperation (if not a formal military alliance). And though there are still problems in the economic relationship, it is worth recalling that whereas trade back in the 1990s was negligible, by 2016 China had already become Russia's single-biggest trade partner and Russia had become an important source of energy for China. More important still, the partnership permitted the two countries to confront together what both agreed was their biggest joint problem: namely, an American-led global alliance that not only tried to limit their ambitions but put into doubt the very legitimacy of their respective regimes. Theoretically, of course, things could change. They could both adopt Western-style human rights reforms. Russia and China could come to accept the international order as it is. Russia could stop acting in the way it has been acting in Ukraine. The West could accept the annexation of Crimea. China could give up on its goals in the East and South China seas. It might even accept that the United States has a right to be an Asian power. But as we know, the chances of any of this happening in practice are virtually nil. The scene is thus set for a continued standoff, one consequence of which will be to reinforce the belief in Moscow and Beijing that in a hostile international environment, one should stick close to one's friends (however imperfect they may be) because in an insecure world such friends (warts and all) are central to achieving what both are still striving to achieve: namely, greater political security at home, fewer obstacles to their ambitions in their own neighborhood, and a more equal world system in which the United States and its allies have less control over what happens. So long as they continue to share these basic goals—and there is no reason to think these are going to change any time soon—there is every chance the two will continue to travel together along the same, sometimes rocky, path they have been moving along since the beginning of the twenty-first century.[92]

NOTES

1. Quote from Yun Sun, "China-Russia Relations: Alignment without Alliance" https://www.csis.org/analysis/pacnet-67-china-russia-relations-alignment-without-alliance.
2. This section draws heavily from Liu Binyan and Perry Link, "A Great Leap Backward?," *The New York Review of Books*, October 8, 1998. http://www.nybooks.com/articles/1998/10/08/a-great-leap-backward/.
3. Zuraidah Ibrahim "Lee Kuan Yew Was Ahead of the Curve when He Predicted China's Emergence," *South China Morning Post*, March 24, 2015, http://www.scmp.com/news/asia/article/1745715/lee-kuan-yew-was-ahead-curve-when-he-predicted-chinas-emergence.
4. Paul Krugman, "The Myth of Asia's Miracle," *Foreign Affairs*, December 1994, pp. 62–78.
5. Gerald Segal, "Does China Matter?," *Foreign Affairs*, (September–October 1999): 24–36
6. Michael Cox, ed., *Rethinking the Soviet Collapse: Sovietology, the Death of Communism and the New Russia* (London: Pinter Publishers, 1998).
7. Will Hutton, *The Writing on the Wall: China and the West in the 21st Century* (London: Little, Brown, 2006).
8. No doubt some will claim they foresaw China's economic rise a quarter of a century before it happened; and no doubt a few were better positioned to see the economic writing on the wall before the beginning of the great economic takeoff. Among some of the more perceptive Sinologists, see the work of Allen Whiting, Steven Fitzgerald, and Stuart Harris, who did, to be fair, foreshadow a more positive economic future for China, despite the massive domestic challenges and international skepticism that continued to prevail during the 1980s and 1990s.

9. Nicholas D. Kristof and Sheryl Wudunn, *China Wakes: The Struggle for the Soul of a Rising Power* (London: Nicholas Brealey Publishing, 1994). See also Daniel Burstein and Arne de Keijzer, *Big Dragon: The Future for China: What It Means for Business, The Economy and Global Order* (New York: Touchstone, 1999).
10. Martin Jacques, *When China Rules the World: The Rise of the Middle Kingdom and the End of the Western World* (London: Penguin / Allen Lane, 2009).
11. See Peter Goodwin, "In Davos: Deepening Worries about China and the Global Economy," *International Business Times*, January 22, 2016, http://www.ibtimes.com/davos-deepening-worries-about-china-global-economy-2276048.
12. Michael Cox, "Power Shifts: Economic Change and the Decline of the West?," *International Relations* 26, no. 4 (2012): 369–88.
13. James Kynge, *China Shakes the World: The Rise of a Hungry Nation* (London: Phoenix, 2006).
14. Susan Shirk, *China: Fragile Superpower* (New York: Oxford University Press, 2008).
15. Barry Buzan and Michael Cox, "China and the US: Comparable Cases of 'Peaceful Rise,'" *The Chinese Journal of International Politics* 6 (2013): 109–32.
16. Mark Leonard, *What Does China Think?* (London: Fourth Estate, 2008).
17. Ted C. Fishman, *China Inc.: How The Rise of the Next Superpower Challenges America and the World* (New York: Scribner, 2006).
18. A. Bader, *Obama and China's Rise: An Insider's Account of America's Asia Strategy* (Washington, DC: Brookings Institution Press, 2012).
19. G. John Ikenberry, "The Rise of China and the Future of the West: Can the Liberal System Survive?," *Foreign Affairs*, January/February 2008, 23–37.
20. John Mearsheimer, *The Tragedy of Great Power Politics*, 2nd ed. (New York: W. W. Norton, 2014).
21. On EU, see Paul Irwin Crookes, "Resetting EU-China Relations from Values-Based to an Interest-Based Engagement," *International Politics* 50, no. 5 (2013): 639–63.
22. See Jeremy Page, "Why Russia's President Is 'Putin the Great' in China," *Wall Street Journal*, October 1, 2014, http://www.wsj.com/articles/why-russias-president-is-putin-the-great-in-china-1412217002.
23. Rajan Menon, "The Strategic Convergence between Russia and China," *Survival* 39, no. 2 (1997): 101–25.
24. For a strong refutation of at least four of the more comforting Western myths about the China-Russian relationship and why it will always fall afoul of various obstacles according to this account, see Alexander Korolev, "The Strategic Alignment between Russia and China: Myths and Reality," *The ASAN Forum*, April 30, 2015, http://www.theasanforum.org/the-strategic-alignment-between-russia-and-china-myths-and-reality/.
25. Rajan Menon, "The Limits of the Chinese-Russian Partnership," *Survival* 51, no. 3 (2009): 99–130.
26. Bobo Lo, *Axis of Convenience: Moscow, Beijing and the New Geopolitics* (Washington, DC: Brookings Press, 2008); and his *How the Chinese See Russia*. Russie.Nei. Reports no. 6. IFRI. Russia, NIS Center, December 2010, 1–30. https://www.ifri.org/sites/default/files/atoms/files/rnr6chinaloengdec2010.pdf.
27. "Russia and China: An Uneasy Friendship," *Economist*, May 9, 2015.
28. David Shambaugh, *China Goes Global: The Partial Power* (New York: Oxford University Press, 2013), esp. 78–86.

29. On some of the many problems facing economic relations between China and Russia, see Bjorn Alexander Duben, "Why Russia's Turn to China Is a Mirage" *The Great Debate* (blog), July 8, 2015, http://blogs.reuters.com/great-debate/2015/07/08/why-russias-turn-to-china-is-a-mirage/; Michael Schuman, "Thaw in China-Russian Relations Hasn't Trickled Down," *New York Times*, December 15, 2015, http://mobile.nytimes.com/2015/12/16/business/international/thaw-in-china-russia-relations-hasnt-trickled-down.html?referer=&_r=0; and Jacopo Dettoni, "Trades Misses Targets Despite Political Deals," *Nikkei Asian Review*, January 20, 2016, http://asia.nikkei.com/Politics-Economy/International-Relations/Trade-misses-targets-despite-political-deals.
30. Geoff Dyer, *The Contest of the Century: The New Era of Competition with China* (London: Allen Lane, 2014), 212.
31. For an exposition of a view close to the one expressed in this essay, see, however, Gilbert Rozman, "The Sino-Russian Partnership Is Stronger Than the West Thinks," *World Post*, January 11, 2015, http://www.huffingtonpost.com/gilbert-rozman/sino-russia-partnership_b_6140358.html.
32. Putin denies that "China and Russia are . . . creating any military blocs or alliances against anybody," but he does admit that "we are in the process of building an alliance to safeguard our national interests." See "Russia, China Do Not Form Blocs against Anyone: Putin," *China Daily* (USA), June 20, 2015.
33. See Daniel Drezner, "The System Worked: Global Economic Governance during the Great Recession." World Politics 66 (January 2014): 123–164.
34. Feng Zhan, "China's New Thinking on Aliances," *Survival* 54, no. 5 (2012): 129–48.
35. See Gilbert Rozman, *The Sino-Russian Challenge to the World Order* (Stanford, CA: Stanford University Press, 2014).
36. Benni Avni, "Vladimir Putin's Budding Bromance with China's Xi JinPing." *Newsweek*, 05/16/15 http://europe.newsweek.com/vladimir-putin-xi-jinping-32 See 7392?rm=eu.
37. Quotes from Fu Ying, "How Russia Sees China: Beijing and Moscow Are Close but Allies," *Foreign Affairs*, January/February 2016, https://www.foreignaffairs.com/articles/china/2015-12-14/how-china-sees-russia.
38. Castro's statement can be found at "Fidel Castro: Russia, China Will Do Their Best to Preserve Peace," *Sputnik News*, December 12, 2015, http://sputniknews.com/latam/20151212/1031630092/-castro-russia-china-peace.html#ixzz45hu3nRtz.
39. See "China Invites Russian Troops to Second World War Parade in Beijing," *Guardian*, May 11, 2016, http://www.theguardian.com/world/2015/may/11/china-invites-russian-troops-to-second-world-war-parade-in-beijing; and "Russia and China Celebrate Japanese Surrender in World War II," *Moscow Times* http://old.themoscowtimes.com/multimedia/photogalleries/russia-and-china-celebrate-japanese-surrender-in-world-war-ii/5859.html.
40. Michael Cox, "The Necessary Partnership? The Clinton Presidency and Post-Soviet Russia," *International Affairs*, October 1994, 635–58.
41. Stephen Kotkin, *Armaggedon Averted: Soviet Collapse, 1970–2000* (New York: Oxford University Press, 2008).
42. Masha Glesson, *The Man without a Face: The Unlikely Rise of Vladimir Putin* (New York: Riverhead Books, 2012).
43. David Satter, *It Was a Long Time Ago, and It Never Happened Anyway: Russia and the Communist Past* (New Haven, CT: Yale University Press, 2012).

44. Jonathan Fenby, *China: The Fall and Rise of a Great Power, 1850 to the Present* (London: Penguin Books, 2013), 574–637.
45. Odd Arne Westad, *Restless Empire: China and the World since 1750* (London: The Bodley Head, 2012), 427–28.
46. David Shambaugh, *China Goes Global: The Partial Power* (New York: Oxford University Press, 2013), 79.
47. David Shambaugh, *China's Communist Party: Atrophy and Adaptation* Berkeley, UC Press; Washington, Woodrow Wilson Center Press, 2008.
48. Amitai Etzioni, "Air Sea Battle Concept: A Critique," *International Politics* 51 (September 2014): 577–96.
49. Bonnie S. Glaser, "Pivot to Asia: Prepare for the Unintended," *Center for Strategic and International Studies Forecast* (2012): 22–24, http://csis.org/files/publication/120413_gf_glaser.pdf.
50. See the comments delivered by Chinese foreign minister Wang Yi at the CSIS in Washington in February 2016. He noted, "The surmise that China will become a major rival of the US and even supersede the US is a false proposition." See "Wang: China Won't Be a Rival to the U.S.," US-China Perception Monitor, February 26, 2016, http://www.uscnpm.org/blog/2016/02/26/wang-china-wont-be-a-rival-to-us/.
51. On partnership and rivalry in the US-China relationship, see Wendy Dobson, *Partners and Rivals: The Uneasy Future of China's Relationship with the United States* (Toronto: University of Toronto Press, 2013).
52. Deborah Welch Larson and Alexei Shevchenko, "Status Seekers: China and Russia's Response to U.S. Primacy," *International Security* 34, no. 4 (Spring 2010): 63–95.
53. See Michael Cox, "The Empire's Back in Town: Or America's Imperial Temptation—Again," *Millennium* 32, no. 1 (February 2003): 1–27.
54. On Russia, see Thomas Ambrosio, *Challenging America's Global Pre-eminence: Russia's Quest for Multipolarity* (London: Ashgate, 2005). On China, see Jenny Clegg, *China's Global Strategy: Towards a Multipolar World* (London: Pluto Press, 2009; and Randall L. Schweller and Xiaoyu Pu, "After Unipolarity: China's Visions of International Order in an Era of U.S. Decline," *International Security* 36, no. 1 (Summer 2011): 41–72.
55. Gregory Chin and Ramesh Thakur, "Will China Change the Rules of the Global Order?," *Washington Quarterly* 33, no. 4 (2010): 119–38.
56. Theresa Reinold, "The Responsibility to Protect—Much Ado About Nothing," *Review of International Studies* 36, no. 1 (October 2010): 55–78.
57. For a recent overview, see Alexander Gabuev, "How Russia and China see the Internet," *World Economic Forum*, December 16, 2015, https://www.weforum.org/agenda/2015/12/how-china-and-russia-see-the-internet/.
58. On China, see 'Internet in China. Government Plans further tightening of controls on search engines and new outlets', Reuters. 5/07/17. http://www.newsweek.com/china-internet-control-censorship-news-search-engine-595928
59. On Russia, see Andrei Soldatov and Irina Borogan, 'Putin brings China's Great Firewall to Russia in cybersecurity pact' *The Guardian*, https://www.theguardian.com/world/2016/nov/29/putin-china-internet-great-firewall-russia-cybersecurity-pact.
60. F. M. Lavrov, "USA's 'Exceptionalism' Is a Global Threat." pravda.ru, December 25, 2014, http://english.pravda.ru/russia/kremlin/25-12-2014/129391-sergei_lavrov_usa-0/.

61. See Benjamin David Baker, "Sino-Norwegian Relations 5 Years after Liu Xiaobo Nobel Peace Prize." *The Diplomat*, January 4, 2016, http://thediplomat.com/2016/01/sino-norwegian-relations-5-years-after-liu-xiaobos-nobel-peace-prize/.
62. Lavrov quote from "Lavrov Outlines the Way Forward for Relations," *China Daily*, April 14, 2014, http://www.chinadaily.com.cn/world/2014-04/14/content_17433463.htm.
63. Fiona Hill and Bobo Lo, "Putin's Pivot: Why Russia Is Looking East," *Foreign Affairs* (online), July 31, 2012, https://www.foreignaffairs.com/articles/russian-federation/2013-07-31/putins-pivot.
64. China's Lesson for Putin in How to Do Diplomacy," *Financial Times*, November 15, 2014.
65. Ian Black, "Russia and China Veto UN Move to Refer Syria to International Criminal Court," *Guardian*, May 22, 2014.
66. George A. Lopez, "Russia and China: Sabotaging U.N. with Vetoes," CNN.com, February 8, 2012, http://edition.cnn.com/2012/02/08/opinion/lopez-russia-sanctions-cold-war/index.html
67. On the SCO see Weiquing Song, "Feeling Safe, Being Strong: China's Strategy of Soft Balancing through the Shanghai Cooperation Organization," *International Politics* 50, no. 5 (September 2013): 664–85.
68. Richard Weitz, "Shanghai Cooperation Organization's Growing Pains," *The Diplomat*, September 18, 2015, http://thediplomat.com/2015/09/the-shanghai-cooperation-organizations-growing-pains/.
69. Jim O'Neill, *Growth Map: Economic Opportunity in the BRICS* (London: Penguin Books, 2011).
70. Zaki Laidi, "BRICS: Sovereignty, Power and Weakness," *International Politics* 49, no. 5 (2012): 614–32.
71. Robert J. Lieber, "The Rise of the BRICS and American Primacy," *International Politics* 51, no. 1 (2014): 137–54.
72. Alexey Timofeychev, "BRICS Now a Full Fledged Organization," *Russia and India Report*, July 10, 2015, http://in.rbth.com/world/2015/07/10/brics_now_a_full_fledged_organization_44171.
73. Alexander Gabuev, "Russia's Uneasy Relationship with China," *International New York Times*, November 26, 2014.
74. "US-Backed TPP to Be Ineffective without Russia, China—Putin," *RT Business*, November 6, 2014.
75. Aurelia George Mulgan, "Japan, US and the TPP: The View from China," *East Asia Forum*, May 5, 2013.
76. Carol E. Lee and Jeremy Page, "Obama Seeks Common Ground with China at APEC," *Wall Street Journal*, November 10, 2014.
77. See for example Vladimir Salamatov, "Why the TPP Is Not a Threat to Russia," *Russia Direct*, November 20, 2015, http://www.russia-direct.org/opinion/why-tpp-not-threat-russia.
78. On Chinese views on TPP, see for instance Paul Bowles, "China Debates the TPP," East Asia Forum, March 20, 2014, http://www.eastasiaforum.org/2014/03/20/china-debates-the-tpp/.
79. For a discussion of what the TPP might mean in general, see Robert A. Manning, "Myths and Realities of the Trans-Pacific partnership," *National Interest*, October 26, 2015.

80. Quote from "The Real Winner of the Ukraine Crisis Could Be China," *Washington Post*, February 24, 2015, https://www.washingtonpost.com/posteverything/wp/2015/02/24/the-real-winner-of-the-ukraine-crisis-could-be-china/.
81. For background on the so-called new Cold War, see the 2016 LSE IDEAS Report edited by Christian Nitoiu, *Avoiding a New "Cold War": The Future of EU-Russian Relations in the Context of the Ukraine Crisis*, http://www.lse.ac.uk/IDEAS/publications/reports/SR20.aspx.
82. For two rather different discussions of the Ukraine crisis, see Andrew Wilson, *Ukrainian Crisis: What It Means for the West* (New Haven, CT: Yale University Press, 2014); and Richard Sakwa, *Frontline Ukraine: Crisis in the Borderlands* (London: I. B. Tauris, 2014).
83. Lyle J. Goldstein, "What Does China Really Think about the Ukraine Crisis?," National Interest, September 4, 2014, http://nationalinterest.org/feature/what-does-china-really-think-about-the-ukraine-crisis-11196.
84. Wayne Ma., "Why China is Driving a Hard Bargain with Russia Over Gas" *The Wall Street Journal*, May 19, 2014, https://blogs.wsj.com/chinarealtime/2014/05/19/why-china-is-driving-a-hard-bargain-with-russia-over-gas/.
85. Gideon Rachman, "China, Russia and the Sinatra Doctrine," *Financial Times*, November 24, 2014.
86. Roger Boyes, "Why This Old Pals' Act Should Alarm the West," *Times*, August 27, 2014.
87. Ali Wyne, "The Limits of China-Russia Cooperation," *Wall Street Journal*, May 22, 2014, https://www.wsj.com/articles/wyne-the-limits-of-china-russia-cooperation-1400776434.
88. Mark Landler, "Obama, Xi and Putin: Not Buddies," *International New York Times*, November 1, 2014.
89. Kathryn Hille, "Dangers of Isolation," *Financial Times*, January 9, 2015.
90. Jane Perlez and Neil MacFarquhar, "Friendship between Putin and Xi Becomes Strained as Economies Falter," *Asia-Pacific News*, September 3, 2015, http://www.cnbc.com/2015/09/03/friendship-between-putin-and-xi-becomes-strained-as-economies-falter.html.
91. See "Russia-China Relations at 'Historic Peak' Despite 'Illegitimate Western Restrictions'—Putin," *RT*, September 1, 2015, https://www.rt.com/news/313998-putin-china-visit-xinhua/.
92. Andranik Migranyan, "Washington's Creation: A Russia-China Alliance," *National Interest*, July 10, 2014.

CHAPTER 16

How Should the US Respond to a Rising China?

STEVEN E. LOBELL

INTRODUCTION

Recent books, reports, and statements on power trends warn that the United States will be surpassed by China or some combination of the BRICS (Brazil, Russia, India, China, and South Africa) in the coming decades.[1,2] These findings raise a number of important questions that are discussed in the introductory chapter.[3] Is great power competition, counterbalancing, and contestation an unfortunate tragedy of great power politics, and is it occurring already between a declining United States and an emerging China?[4] Is the "Thucydides Trap" of hegemonic war inevitable, or are President Xi Jinping and some American officials correct that a New Model of Major Power Relations (NMMPR) is possible between the United States and China?[5] Is the American pivot or rebalancing to Asia and the Air-Sea Battle (ASB) strategy a form of economic and military containment, as Chinese officials maintain?[6] Will China's One Belt, One Road Initiative or Belt and Road (B&R) collide with US interests? To answer these questions, I advance Components of Power theory—a granular understanding of how foreign policy leaders gauge power relations and how they react to shifts in the power bases of other states.[7]

The United States is a Pacific great power. Beginning in 2009, President Obama made the strategic choice to rebalance and shift US foreign policy priorities toward Asia and the Pacific. The pivot or rebalance strategy to Asia builds on more than a century of US engagement in the region.[8] Under President George W. Bush, the United States strengthened alliances, concluded a free trade agreement with South Korea, brought the United States into the twelve-nation Trans-Pacific Partnership trade agreement negotiations (which President Trump has withdrawn from), and into new relations with both India and Vietnam. The US pivot policy was further articulated by President Obama in 2011, at a speech addressing the Australian Parliament, where he announced that "the United States will play a larger and long-term role in shaping this region and its future,"[9] and in Secretary of State Hillary Clinton's *Foreign Policy* article on "America's Pacific Century."[10] Former National Security Advisor Thomas Donilon wrote that the rebalance policy is neither containing China nor simply a shift in military forces, but is rather "an effort that harnesses all elements of US power—military, political, trade and investment, development and our values."[11]

The Obama administration's pivot to Asia reflected heightened US economic, diplomatic, security, and military attention to the Asia-Pacific region. The pivot entailed boosting the US presence in the Pacific, including new troop deployments to Australia, new naval deployments to Singapore, and US military personnel stationed in the Philippines, and to possibly include air or naval forces; new agreements such as the US-Singapore agreement to allow for four US warships, the new Littoral Combat Ship (LCS); reaffirming existing alliance agreements; a commitment by the Navy to deploy 60 percent of its fleet in the Pacific rather than 50 percent; the development by the Navy and Air Force of a joint operating concept known as the ASB strategy to better integrate surveillance and airstrike platforms to attack coastal powers; and greater US engagement with multilateral institutions in the Asia-Pacific region including membership in the East Asia Summit (EAS), enhanced commitment to the Association of Southeast Asian Nations (ASEAN) including a permanent ambassador, the US-Korea Free Trade Agreement, and negotiation of the now defunct TPP. The pivot also signaled that the United States is balancing its historic involvement in Northeast Asia with a renewed emphasis to countries in Southeast Asia, including Indonesia, Malaysia, the Philippines, and Vietnam.[12]

Though Sino-American relations have witnessed an uptick in competition, it does not mean that conflict or hegemonic war—or, more broadly, the tragedy of great power politics—is inevitable.[13] In February 2012, then Vice President Xi Jinping introduced the concept of a "new model of major power relations (NMMPR)."[14] Hillary Clinton later stated that "together the United States and China are trying to do something that is historically unprecedented, to write a new answer to the age-old question of what happens when an established power and a rising power meet?"[15] The idea of an NMMPR "rejects the debate over whether a rising power and an established power are destined to clash."[16] In an interview with Evan Medeiros, the Senior Director for Asian Affairs in the National Security Council, he emphasized the concept of a new model of great power relations:

> We see the concept as a way to encourage—to ensure that China's rise is a force of stability in the region . . . . When we say a 'new model,' the question is, what's new? And my point is it's new only insofar as we are able to develop patterns of interaction and habits of cooperation that allow us to avoid the historic trap of an established power and a rising power inevitably coming into conflict."[17]

Hegemonic and balance of power theories or aggregate power realism (APR) challenge the optimism of NMMPR and reflect a return to great power politics.[18] Deep engagement entails maintaining and possibly expanding America's hegemonic leadership. Proponents contend that America's military and material preponderance of power in Asia dissuades China from territorial expansion and from challenging US leadership, and reassures allies such as South Korea, the Philippines, Australia, and Japan. Any drawdown of US commitments will contribute to doubts about the long-term prospects for the US presence in the Pacific. In commenting on the American pivot, Kevin Rudd, the former prime minister of Australia, states, "Without such a move, there was a danger that China, with its hard-line, realist view of international relations, would conclude that an economically exhausted United States was losing its staying power in the Pacific."[19] A Congressional Research Service (CRS) report makes a similar claim. The report states, "Many if not most Asian foreign policy officials and experts see a deep U.S. presence in the region as critical to stability, and many seek U.S. support for stronger rules-based security and economic structures."[20]

An alternative realist strategy is offshore balancing, which calls for American retrenchment in Europe, Asia, and the Middle East. Proponents argue that the concentration of American power in Asia, including the pivot, the ASB, and the now defunct TPP is self-defeating, and is antagonizing and provoking soft and even hard balancing by China, including Beijing's Anti-Access/Area Denial or (A2/AD) asymmetric strategy.[21] For instance, the CRS warns that with the pivot, the "PLA [People's Liberation Army] will become more determined to strengthen China's anti-access capabilities and more assertive about defending China's territorial claims, rather than less."[22] Also, the impression that the United States is containing China will make it more difficult to gain Beijing's cooperation in other issue-areas. Finally, supporters counter that deep engagement is expensive, contributes directly to American economic decline, and encourages both free riding by wealthy allies and their reckless behavior.

A New Model of Realist Major Power Relations (NMRMPR) is possible.[23] Below I present Components of Power theory—a more finely tuned understanding of how leaders unpack power relations.[24] Specifically, state leaders ask themselves, which specific components or elements of China's national power are increasing, and will they challenge vital American interests? Does China have the appropriate or necessary elements of power to challenge the United States?[25] Which elements, if any, should Washington target its counterbalancing against?

First, rather than aggregate measures and metrics of power and the relative distribution of material capabilities, what matters in assessing power trends is the specific components or elements of a state's national power and whether they challenge vital interests. For the United States, the foundation of its security rests on its Command of the Commons, including the globe's sea, space, and air. In disaggregating power trends, whether China's "peaceful rise" or "peaceful development" to great power status will provoke the United States to counterbalance will depend on which components or elements of its power are emerging and whether they threaten vital US geostrategic interests.[26] Specifically, the United States should respond differently if Beijing moves to develop the real assets necessary to build an ambitious blue-water naval program or if Beijing continues to favor the land-based People's Liberation Army.[27] Similarly, China's Belt and Road Initiative calls for establishing relations among countries primarily in Eurasia. It consists of two elements: the land-based Silk Road Economic Belt and the oceangoing Maritime Silk Road. The import is that whichever element of power Beijing pursues will affect whether (or not) China and the United States will clash.[28]

Second, aggregate power is rarely fungible across issue-areas or elements of power. More important than increases in China's relative share of material and military capabilities is whether Beijing has or will have the appropriate real assets including the technology, knowledge, industry, and equipment to develop and construct anti-ship ballistic missiles, antiship cruise missiles, quiet diesel-powered submarines, stealthy combat aircraft, and cyber-warfare capabilities to keep US forces at a distance from its coast and over the horizon. One element of concern for Washington is that Beijing is acquiring anti-access and area denial capability.[29] A2/AD capabilities "threaten the ability of the U.S. and allied forces to both get to the fight and to fight effectively once there."[30]

Finally, when states balance, they target their counterbalancing against the specific threatening elements of a rival's power rather than against its aggregate power. For the United States, while there has been much discussion of the policy of pivoting or rebalancing to Asia, there have been few concrete military steps besides restructuring regional security arrangements to allow for more dispersed US forces across Asia-Pacific. One reason is that China is primarily a land power, and few elements of its national power challenge US vital interests. If China does develop the real assets to become a maritime power or pursues the Maritime Silk Road strategy, then American-targeted balancing might include a combination of naval construction to outbuild Beijing, technology such as anti-ballistic missile and anti-rocket defense, cyber-warfare capabilities, and stealth strikes to destroy its anti-ship missiles, submarines, destroyers, and fighters.[31] Concomitantly though, China's asymmetric A2/AD strategy does not require that Beijing become a peer competitor or even a near-peer competitor to pose a danger to America and its allies.

The import of Components of Power theory in understanding Sino-American relations in the coming decades is several-fold. First, in contrast to the expectations of APR, if no components or elements of China's power challenge America's interests in Asia, then it should not provoke counterbalancing in the short time, even if Beijing has a high aggregate capability score. Second, when assessing threats, a weaker overall state with a much lower military capability score might be more threatening, depending on the mix of its components of power. Third, in contrast to arguments that emphasize aggregate shifts in power alone, China does not need to become a peer or even a near-peer competitor to pose a major danger.[32]

The first section of this chapter discusses rising Sino-American competition. The next section examines two alternative APR grand strategies for the United States in the post-Cold War period: offshore balancing and deep engagement. The final sections develop NMRMPR and applies it to understand the America's grand strategy toward China and the Asia-Pacific.

INCREASING SINO-AMERICAN COMPETITION

US-Chinese territorial, economic, and military competition is on the rise. Moreover, beginning in 2013, the Obama administration responded more forcefully to China's territorial claims and even more so following Russia's annexation of the Crimea.[33] From China's perspective, the Obama administration's policies such as the TPP, the pivot, and the ASB reflected elements of a new American containment strategy and is intended to encircle China, divide China from its neighbors, and keep its military capability in check.[34]

The Obama administration denied these policies targeted China and sought to reassure Beijing that the United States is not seeking to contain China.

In terms of Sino-American territorial and maritime disputes, one point of contestation is China's unilateral change to the status quo in the form of the nine-dashed map that includes a U-shaped line (the so-called nine-dash line) that claims the bulk of the South China Sea as China's.[35] In March 2014, Daniel Russel, the assistant secretary of state for East Asian and Pacific Affairs, criticized China's nine-dash line claim. In testimony before the House Committee on Foreign Affairs, he stated that "any use of the 'nine-dash line' by China to claim maritime rights not based on claimed land features would be inconsistent with international law. The international community would welcome China to clarify or adjust its nine-dash line claim to bring it in accordance with the international law of the seas."[36] Russel argued that claims to the sea must be based on genuine land features rather than just rocks that can be covered at high tide. Under the UN Convention on the Law of the Sea (UNCLOS), a country can claim a two hundred kilometer economic zone around islands. More recently, China has engaged in building islands and arming them in the South China Sea. For China, this bolsters its claims to the South China Sea and extends its ability to project its military capabilities.

Another recent Sino-American territorial dispute is China's unilateral declaration of the East China Sea Air Defense Identification Zone (ADIZ). An ADIZ is airspace over land or water where identification, the location, and the control of civil aircraft are required due to national security. ADIZs extend beyond a state's legal airspace to give early warning about hostile aircraft before it enters its territory. In 2013, China announced the new East China Sea ADIZ with the disputed Paracel Islands as the center. One of China's goals in establishing this ADIZ is to bolster its administrative control over the disputed Senkaku Islands with Japan. US officials assailed China's steps as unilateral. The Obama Administration, including Secretary Kerry and Secretary of Defense Chuck Hagel, warned China not to undertake "destabilizing, unilateral actions" to create a South China Sea ADIZ, where China has disputes with Vietnam and the Philippines.[37] According to Russel, "There are growing concerns that this pattern of behavior in the South China Sea reflects incremental effort by China to assert control over the area."[38]

In addition to increased territorial disputes, Sino-American military contestation is also on the rise. Since the 1990s, rather than directly challenging the United States, China has advanced its anti-ship missiles, short- and medium-range ballistic missiles, cruise missiles, stealth submarines, and cyber and space arms to challenge US naval and air superiority, especially in

China's littoral waters. These anti-access/anti-denial asymmetric weapons raise the cost for the United States in projecting American force by undermining fixed bases in Japan and Guam, and threatening American aircraft carriers in the Pacific.[39]

Economically, Sino-American contestation has resulted in competing trade organizations. China is pushing to advance the Regional Comprehensive Economic Partnership (RCEP) and has financed the Asian Infrastructure Investment Bank (AIIB). The RCEP is a free trade agreement between the ASEAN member states and six additional states, including Japan and Australia. The AIIB is a development bank to build infrastracutre in the Asia-Pacific region. These new Beijing-led financial institutions compete with and complement the US dominated World Bank (WB) and International Montetary Fund (IMF), and the Asian Development Bank (ADB).[40]

OFFSHORE BALANCING VERSUS DEEP ENGAGEMENT STRATEGIES

In the debate over the direction of America's post-Cold War grand strategy, two alternative APR grand strategies for the United States challenge the optimism of Xi Jinping's NMMPR.[41] Offshore balancing maintains that the concentration of US power has provoked China to counterbalance through soft balancing such as the AIIB and RCEP and hard balancing through an A2/AD asymmetrical strategy. A more forward US military and economic posture such as stationing troops in Australia, tightening treaty commitments with Japan, joint exercises and training with US forces, and a new agreement allowing for deploying Littoral Combat Ships to Singapore are criticized as provocative and destabilizing.

Alternatively, deep engagement maintains that American primacy in Asia discourages China from moving beyond an A2/AD asymmetrical strategy to build a blue-water navy. Moreover, American allies have complained that Washington needs to play a more engaged role in the region, including new naval deployments and new military cooperation.

Offshore Balancing: For the United States, offshore balancing entails that Washington engage in a policy of global restraint wherever possible.[42] Based on the premise of balance of power theory, offshore balancing translates into US retrenchment though not a complete withdrawal and retreat of treaty commitments from theaters including Europe, the Middle East, the Persian Gulf, and Asia, and renegotiating security treaties with Japan, South Korea, and NATO.

American offshore balancing means regional states will play a larger role in counterbalancing China. Specifically, China's rise will be countered by India and Russia, as well as Japan, South Korea, and Vietnam. American retrenchment from Asia is particularly easy since there is no imminent regional hegemon and therefore time for local states to form a counterbalance. If the local states are unable to restore the balance, then the United States will intervene. Otherwise, the United States can assist the weaker states by building up their economic strength and military capability.

For offshore balancing proponents, a strategy of deep engagement or extending America's Pacific leadership is self-defeating for three reasons.[43] First, the accumulation of American power, including a strong US military pivot to Asia and the ASB concept provokes soft and hard counterbalancing by China.[44]

Second, deep engagement encourages reckless behavior on the part of America's allies. Based on the logic of moral hazard, US treaty and security commitments embolden allies to act more recklessly and aggressively than if they had no security commitments. Moreover, they risk pulling the United States into their local disputes.

Third, deep engagement is expensive and contributes directly to American economic decline. The logic is twofold: first, military expenditure squeezes out and diverts resources (both financial and human capital) available for domestic investment, which reduces the size of the pie for future spending, including military and entitlement programs. Second, deep engagement encourages free riding and discourages burden sharing by allies.

Deep Engagement: Alternatively, a deep engagement and primacy strategy calls for Washington to extend America's leadership and preponderance of power to ensure security and prosperity for the United States and its Pacific allies.[45] America's military spending, foreign security ties, and overseas bases and rights in the Asia-Pacific region serve several roles. First, America's huge lead in military power will discourage China from challenging the United States in a military arms race. Specifically, America's military preponderance is intended to convince China that it cannot compete militarily with the United States. With no chance of catching up and the likelihood that the United States would outpace China in an arms race, Beijing is dissuaded from competing.

Second, to be the security partner of choice by regional states requires that the United States remain powerful and engaged in Asia. According to Medeiros, there is a "strong demand from allies for further enhanced US engagement."[46] Medeiros continues that "an important part of that rebalancing strategy is ensuring that our relationships with our allies and partners in the region are strong in order to meet the principal security challenges facing us." Moreover, as the CRS report notes, "If the United States can convince the region it is committed for the long haul it may get deeper cooperation from partners."[47]

Third, by extending America's security umbrella to its Pacific allies, they do not need to provide as much of their own security. By keeping their own military spending artificially low, they do not provoke the security dilemma among each other. Moreover, this strategy discourages strategic independence and regional hegemonic aspirations.

Deep engagement proponents challenge the claims of offshore balancing.[48] First, they challenge the assertion that both soft balancing and hard balancing are occurring against the United States.[49] Soft balancing in particular is discounted as simply diplomatic differences that occur among states.[50] Second, deep engagement supporters argue that the amount of savings from retrenchment is less than clear. Moreover, shipping US overseas commitments to bases in the United States will not save money, and the United States will lose the contributions that its allies make to the cost of basing American troops on their territory. Finally, deep engagement proponents do not accept the claim that military spending contributes to imperial overextension, overstretch, and decline. First, they argue that the United States is a wealthy country and can afford to spend on defense. Second, they discount the claim that there is a direct connection between military spending and economic decline.

NEW MODEL OF REALIST MAJOR POWER RELATIONS (NMRMPR)

The "Thucydides Trap" and the tragedy of great power politics between the United States and China are not inevitable. In testimony before Congress, Daniel Russel stated that "there are those who argue that cold war-like rivalry is inevitable and that the United States and China are condemned to a zero-sum struggle for supremacy, if not conflict. I reject such mechanistic thinking."[51] Of course, Medeiros and other American officials are correct to argue that there are "serious sources of competition in the U.S.-China relationship and that these need to be managed."[52] Moreover, the intent is not a G-2 Sino-American model of cooperation but rather to "ensure that China's rise is a force of stability in the region."[53]

The Obama administration sought to broaden and deepen the channels of communication with China, including high levels of Sino-American trade, military-to-military talks, and greater transparency. Moreover, the United States and China were able to cooperate on important issues such as sanctions on Iran (until they were lifted) and on the UN resolution authorizing military action in Libya, on anti-piracy efforts in the Gulf of Aden, and in important bilateral forums for the world's two largest economies, such as the US-China Strategic and Economic Dialogue (S&ED), the US-China Asia-Pacific Consultations (APC), and the US-China Strategic Security Dialogue.

A New Model of Realist Major Power Relations (NMRMPR) is possible, but in its current form it is underdeveloped. Specifically, the extant APR approaches miss how states assess power trends, the fungibility and usefulness of aggregate material capabilities, and whether states balance against accumulations and concentrations of power. In the next sections, I advance these three important fixes to APR to develop a New Model of Realist Major Power Relations.

DISAGGREGATE POWER

When American decision-makers assess China's power trends to forecast power projections and enmities, they ask themselves several questions. First, which components or elements of China's national power are increasing, and will they peak above or below America's own components of national power? The four general categories of national power include changes in political leadership or ideology; shifts in territory or population; growth in real assets including equipment, plant, knowledge, technology, and inventory; and increases in land-based military, naval, and air power.[54] For instance, in terms of political leadership, does the Communist Party of China have the capacity to sustain its political monopoly, and if not, will this impact the ability the state has to extract and mobilize societal resources and convert it into military power? Similarly, in terms of real assets, the 2014 Quadrennial Defense Review (QDR) emphasizes that the United States will sustain its priority investment in science, technology, research, and development in the defense sector—all real assets in which America holds a commanding lead over China.[55] Moreover, in assessing trends, state leaders ask themselves whether specific components of China's power will peak above critical thresholds and redlines of power. Finally, state leaders will ask, how interchangeable are resources intended for one element of power for use with another?[56]

For the United States, the foundation of its military security is its Command of the Global Commons.[57] Command of the Commons allows Washington to extend its reach far beyond its waters' edge. Command of the Commons represents the United States' command over the globe's sea, space, and air. According to Barry Posen, this is supported by nuclear attack submarines, surface fleet and aircraft carriers, satellite communication and anti-satellite technology, fighters and bomber aircraft, air and sea lift capacity, and missile and anti-missile technology. Command of the Commons is further supported by a deep and thick network of bases, landing and air rights, and combat centers. This includes defense treaties, strategic partnerships, major bases, and new arrangements with regional states.

In contrast to the expectations of balance of power theory, components of power can explain why there is no significant Asian counterbalancing against the United States despite its unprecedented aggregate capability. First, continental land powers such as Russia do not assess America's Command of the Commons as a major challenge to their vital interests. Moreover, they will not use significant resources to target their balancing against this element of American power.[58] For continental powers, counterbalancing against America's Command of the Commons is an inefficient use of resources that can better be directed toward interior border security and against land-based proximate threats.[59]

Second, China's barrier to entry to developing a naval capability of command of the global commons is high. In disaggregating US power, the real assets for Command of the Commons include specific weapons and platforms that are expensive and require a huge scientific and industrial base.[60] According to Posen's findings, in 2001, the research and development for the US military was equivalent to the defense spending of France and Germany. In addition to the large-scale industrial projects, Command of the Commons requires the development of new weapons platforms and tactics, and skilled military personnel.

Third, China is a continental land power and shares borders with fourteen neighboring states, some of whom have nuclear weapons and large land armies, and whom Beijing has engaged in border disputes and wars. Moreover, China faces both interior border disputes on its northern and western frontiers, and internal security challenges including terrorism, separatism, and extremism. Historically, land powers including France, Germany, and Russia have failed to secure a maritime blue-navy. Instead, as continental powers, they have pursued a maritime asymmetric strategy of access-denial capability to defend maritime approaches and shores.

As a land power, the PLA's demand for interior and internal security and defense against contiguous major powers will constrain the development of the real assets necessary to become a blue-water maritime power. According to Robert Ross, China allocates the bulk of its defense spending to the PLA with about one-tenth going to the People's Liberation Army Navy (PLAN).[61] By comparison, in 2006, as a maritime powerhouse, the

US Navy and Marines constituted nearly 40 percent of total US forces. Moreover, the United States requires three carriers to be assured of having one carrier on deployment.[62] China has one carrier, and as a scholar notes, "the construction of carrier [s], other ships in the strike force, their onboard equipment and technologies will all strain China's defense budget, especially given the multiple other missions assigned to the PLA."[63]

In disaggregating China's power, one element of concern for Washington is that Beijing is acquiring access and area denial capability.[64] Starting in the 1990s, China's investment in anti-Ship missiles, short- and medium-range ballistic missiles, cruise missiles, stealth submarines, and cyber and space arms began to challenge US superiority, especially in China's littoral waters. China's intent is to keep US forces at a distance from its shore and over the horizon. Specifically, for the United States, China's A2/AD capabilities mean that operating in close proximity to Chinese territory during a conflict is more costly and complicates the deployment of carriers near China, thereby pushing them further offshore. Also, China's A2/AD strategy increases the vulnerability of American bases in Okinawa and Guam to attack by Chinese land-based missiles. It might also undermine the resolve of America's allies in the Pacific, encourage bandwagoning with China, and lead Beijing to believe that the United States will abandon its allies. Finally, this asymmetric strategy limits the ability of the United States to project power deep into China's territory.

Concomitantly, though China is a land power, Beijing does not need to become a peer or even a near-peer naval competitor with the United States and its allies to pose a major threat. In contrast to the expectations of power transition and long cycle theories, China will not necessarily wait until its GDP or military capability approaches America's to challenge its leadership in the Pacific. States are driven by windows of opportunity and vulnerability in terms of specific components of power. Washington should not ask if increased competition and conflict between the United States and China will occur around the point of a power transition. Instead, China might challenge the United States when it believes it has sufficient strength in a particular element of power and much sooner than the expectations of power transition theory.

Second, if American statesmen expect a major hegemonic war to only occur near the intersection of the aggregate power curve of the rising and declining great powers, then they will be too late in preparing for war. For this reason, Avery Goldstein is wrong to identify China as "one of a small handful of states that may have the necessary ingredients to emerge one day as a peer competitor . . . . The distance China must travel before it has the economic and military foundation of power comparable to those of the United States is great, however . . . . While China's capabilities have grown impressively compared with its own past, the strides it is making in 'closing the gap' with the United States are so far rather small."[65] Similarly, Posen is mistaken to state that "the U.S. military advantage in the sea, in the air, and in space will be very difficult to challenge—let alone overcome."[66] China does not need to overcome the United States. Instead, as discussed in the next section, in disaggregating China's power, what matters is whether China has the appropriate elements of power to challenge the United States.

APPROPRIATE ELEMENTS OF POWER

More important than aggregate capability scores or a composite index of power in assessing China's power trends is whether Beijing has the appropriate or necessary components of national power to pose a major danger to the United States. Specifically, aggregate material capability is rarely funigible across issue-areas or elements of power.

China's military power is increasing relative to past levels and at a faster ratio according to reports by the Defense Department and Jane's.[67] Some scholars and policy makers have identified the PLAN as a "limited blue water" navy which means it has restricted expeditionary capabilities because it can operate out to the second island chain including all of the South China Sea down to Indonesia and East Timor (the first island chain includes the Kurile Islands in the north down through Japan, the Senkaku and Ryuku Islands, Taiwan, and some of the South China Sea). A green-water navy entails destroyers and frigates for regional tasks, and a blue-water navy, which could operate throughout the Pacific, includes aircraft carriers and the supporting ships. However, China's military power does not necessarily translate into outcomes; China needs the appropriate elements of power to pose a credible threat to US interests in the Pacific. In disaggregating China's national power and given that Beijing does not have a blue-water navy but just commissioned its first aircraft carrier, its first at-sea landings, and has no integrated carrier task group, Washington should not exaggerate China's challenge.

A number of scholars and policy makers call for the United States to have a preponderance of military capability in Asia to deter China. US military capability must also be appropriate or targeted. Washington should monitor China's naval power trends and specifically the supporting production, plant, skilled labor, and capacity to construct a green- or a blue-water navy to determine whether Beijing is in fact challenging America's Command of the Commons.[68] Moreover, Washington should ask whether China's specific elements are increasing and whether they will peak above or below America's components of national power and above critical thresholds and redlines.

TARGETED BALANCING

States regularly target their balancing against specific elements of a rival's power that threaten their vital interests.

In disaggregating China's material and military power, one element of concern for Washington is that Beijing is acquiring access and area denial capability. America's balancing against this element of China's power should not entail balancing against non-threatening elements too. US target balancing entails a combination of naval construction to maintain naval supremacy, technology such as anti-ballistic missile and anti-rocket defense, blinding cyber-warfare capabilities, and stealth attacks to destroy its antiship missiles, submarines, destroyers, and fighter Planes. Specifically, in 2009, Secretary of Defense Robert Gates initiated work on the AirSea Battle concept to address this asymmetrical danger. The idea is to "develop a joint air-sea battle concept . . . [to] address how air and naval forces will integrate capabilities across all operational domains —air, sea, land, space, and cyberspace—to counter growing challenges to US freedom of action."[69] The campaign begins with a "blinding attack" against targets in mainland China to allow the United States to enter contested zones and allow the United States to bring to bear the full force of its material and military advantage.

Reflecting targeted US balancing and the greater priority to the US Navy, the Department of Defense under President Obama minimized the cuts in the size of the Navy, with US force reductions focused on Army and Marine ground forces. Other targeted balancing steps included the Navy deploying 60 percent of its fleet in the Pacific rather than 50 percent, more destroyers and amphibious ships ported in the Pacific, and LCS rotated through Singapore.[70]

CONCLUSION

The US pivot or rebalancing represents an enhanced economic, military, and diplomatic presence in Asia. However, it does not mean that the United States and China are destined for strategic rivalry, confrontation, or hegemonic war. As Evan Medeiros notes, "[O]ur approach to China has always had elements of cooperation and elements of competition."[71]

In this chapter, I advance a New Model of Realist Major Power Relations. The import of this model for understanding what role America sees for China is fourfold. First, if no components or elements of China's power pose a threat to US interests in the Pacific, then Washington should not counterbalance, despite Beijing's growing material capabilities. For now, much of China's defense spending remains focused on interior border security, internal security, and the People's Liberation Army, rather than on the People's Liberation Army Navy or the People's Liberation Army Air Force—all elements and power trends that do not directly challenge US vital interests. Second, when assessing threats, a weaker state with a lower military capability score might be more threatening to the United States than China, depending on the mix of its components of power. For instance, it is possible that a lesser power such as North Korea could prove to be more dangerous in Asia-Pacific. Third, in contrast to APR, China does not need to become a peer or even a near-peer competitor to pose a major danger to the United States. Dissimilar to David Shambaugh's findings, China does not need to possess a comprehensive toolbox of capabilities. Rather, as a partial power, what matters is whether China has the correct elements of power to threaten vital US interests.[72] Fourth, American leaders should assess power trends based on components or elements of national power. Specifically, relative American military or economic decline and even the possible surpassing of the United States by China in 2027 or 2035 does not mean that America is necessarily less secure.[73] Nor, does pouring more money into defense spending or boosting overall military capability necessarily make the United States more secure, especially if it is directed against the wrong elements of China's power.

NOTES

1. Stephen M. Walt, "The Enduring Relevance of the Realist Tradition," in *Political Science: State of the Discipline*, ed., Ira Katznelson and Helen V. Milner (New York: W.W. Norton and Co., 2002): 197–230; Joseph M. Parent and Sebastian Rosato, "Balancing in Neorealism," *International Security* 40, 2 (2015): 51–86.
2. On the rise of the rest, see Fareed Zakaria, *Post-American World and the Rise of the Rest* (New York: Penguin Books, 2009); Charles A. Kupchan, *No One's World: The West, the Rising Rest, and the Coming Global Turn* (New York: Oxford University Press, 2012); Henry R. Nau and Deepa Ollapally, *Worldviews of Aspiring Powers: Domestic Foreign Policy Debates in China, India, Iran, Japan, and Russia* (New York: Oxford University Press, 2012); Kristen P. Williams, Steven

E. Lobell, and Neal G. Jesse, eds., *Beyond Great Powers and Hegemons: Why Secondary States Support, Follow, or Challenge* (Stanford, CA: Stanford University Press, 2012); T.V. Paul, ed., *Accommodating Rising Powers: Past, Present, Future* (Cambridge: Cambridge University Press, 2016).

3. In contrast, for arguments that challenge the rise of the rest thesis, see Michael Cox, "Power Shifts and the Death of the West? Not Yet!," *European Political Science* 10, no. 3 (2011): 416–24; Gideon Rachman, "Think Again: American Decline," *Foreign Policy*, January–February 2011, 59–63; Michael Beckley, "China's Century? Why America's Edge Will Endure," *International Security* 36, no. 3 (Winter 2011–2012): 41–78.

4. Aaron Friedberg, "Ripe for Rivalry: Prospects for Peace in a Multipolar Asia," *International Security* 18, no. 3 (1993): 5–33; John J. Mearsheimer, *The Tragedy of Great Power Politics* (New York: W. W. Norton, 2001), 397–402; Aaron L. Friedberg, *A Contest for Supremacy: China, America, and the Struggle for Mastery in Asia* (New York: W. W. Norton, 2011); Denny Roy, *Return of the Dragon: Rising China and Regional Security* (New York: Columbia University Press, 2013); Ashley J. Tellis, "U.S.-China Relations in a Realist World," in *Tangled Titans: The United States and China*, ed. David Shambaugh (New York: Rowman and Littlefield, 2013), 75–100.

5. Robert Gilpin, *War and Change in World Politics* (Cambridge: Cambridge University Press, 1981). For recent applications of power transition theory to China's rise, see Douglas Lemke and Ronald Tammen, "Power Transition Theory and the Rise of China," *International Interactions* 29, no. 4 (2003): 269–71; Steve Chan, "Is There a Power Transition between the U.S. And China? The Different Faces of National Power," *Asian Survey* 45, no. 5 (2005): 687–701; Ronald Tammen and Jacek Kugler, "Power Transition and China-U.S. Conflicts," *Chinese Journal of International Politics* 1, no. 1 (2006): 31–55; Steven E. Lobell, "Can the United States and China Escape the Thucydides Trap?" *China International Strategy Review* (Beijing: Foreign Language Press, Co., 2016): 81–94; Graham Allison, *Destined for War: Can America and China Escape the Thucydides's Trap?* (New York: Houghton Mifflin Harcourt Publishing, 2017).

6. On the pivot to Asia, see President Obama's address to the Australian Parliament, November 17, 2011, accessed at http://www.whitehouse.gov/the-press-office/2011/11/17/remarks-president-obama-australian-parliament; Mark E. Manyin, Stephen Daggett, Ben Dolven, Susan V. Lawrence, Michael F. Martin, Ronald O'Rourke, and Bruce Vaughn, *Pivot to the Pacific? The Obama Administration's "Rebalancing" toward Asia*, Congressional Research Service Report (Washington, DC, March 29, 2012); "Sustaining US Global Leadership: Priorities for 21st Century Defense," US Department of Defense (Washington, DC, January 3, 2012); *2014 Quadrennial Defense Review*, United States Department of Defense (Washington, DC: Government Printing Office, 2014); David Shambaugh, "Assessing the US 'Pivot' to Asia," *Strategic Studies Quarterly* 7, no. 2 (Summer 2013): 10–18.

7. Steven E. Lobell, "Threat Assessment, the State, and Foreign Policy: A Neoclassical Realist Model," in *Neoclassical Realism, the State, and Foreign Policy*, ed. Steven E. Lobell, Norrin M. Ripsman, and Jeffrey W. Taliaferro (Cambridge: Cambridge University Press, 2009), 42–74; Steven E. Lobell, "A Granular Theory of Balancing," *International Studies Quarterly* (forthcoming).

8. Kurt M. Campbell and Ely Ratner, "Far Eastern Promises," *Foreign Affairs*, May/June 2014, 106–16.

9. "Remarks by President Obama to the Australian Parliament" (Parliament House, Canberra, Australia, November 17, 2011, http://www.whitehouse.gov/the-press-office/2011/11/17/remarks-president-obama-australian-parliament; accessed on July 17, 2017).
10. Hillary Clinton, "America's Pacific Century," *Foreign Policy*, November 2011, http://foreignpolicy.com/2011/10/11/americas-pacific-century; accessed on July 17, 2017.
11. Benjamin H. Friedman, "What Asian Pivot?," *China-US Focus*, November 13, 2013, http://www.cato.org/publications/commentary/what-asian-pivot; accessed on July 17, 2017.
12. Campbell and Ratner, "Far Eastern Promises."
13. Mearsheimer, *The Tragedy of Great Power Politics*.
14. Rudy deLeon and Yang Jioemian, eds., "U.S.-China Relations: Toward a New Model of Major Power Relationship," Center for American Progress, February 2014, 1–106, http://cdn.americanprogress.org/wp-content/uploads/2014/02/ChinaReport-Full.pdf; accessed on July 17, 2017.
15. DeLeon and Jiemian, "U.S.-China Relations," 23.
16. DeLeon and Jiemian, "U.S.-China Relations," 7.
17. Evan Medeiros, "China's Attempt to Isolate Japan Worsens Bilateral Relations," *Asahi Shimbun*, April 6, 2014.
18. On realism and optimists and pessimists, see Thomas J. Christensen, "Fostering Stability or Creating a Monster? The Rise of China and U.S. Policy toward East Asia," *International Security* 31, no. 1 (Summer 2006): 81–126.
19. Kevin Rudd, "Beyond the Pivot: A New Road Map for U.S.-Chinese Relations," *Foreign Affairs*, March/April 2013, 9–15.
20. *Pivot to the Pacific?*, 9.
21. Robert S. Ross, "International Bargaining and Domestic Politics: U.S.-China Relations since 1972," *International Security* 38, no. 2 (1986): 255–87. On the effect of unipolarity on a rising China, see Zhu Feng, "China's Rise Will Be Peaceful: How Unipolarity Matters," in *China's Ascent: Power, Security, and the Future of International Politics*, ed. Robert S. Ross and Zhu Feng (Ithaca, NY: Cornell University Press, 2008), 34–54; Avery Goldstein, "Parsing China's Rise: International Circumstances and National Attributes," in *China's Ascent: Power, Security, and the Future of International Politics*, ed. Robert S. Ross and Zhu Feng (Ithaca, NY: Cornell University Press, 2008), 55–86.
22. *Pivot to the Pacific?*, 8.
23. Norrin M. Ripsman, Jeffrey W. Taliaferro, and Steven E. Lobell, *Neoclassical Realist Theory of International Politics* (Oxford: Oxford University Press, 2016).
24. On Components of Power theory, see Steven E. Lobell, "Britain's Grand Strategy during the 1930s: From Balance of Power to Components of Power," in *The Challenge of Grand Strategy: The Great Powers and the Broken Balance between the World Wars*, ed. Jeffrey W. Taliaferro, Norrin M. Ripsman, and Steven E. Lobell (Cambridge: Cambridge University Press, 2012), 147–70.
25. T. V. Paul, *Asymmetric Conflicts: War Initiation by Weaker Powers* (Cambridge: Cambridge University Press, 1994); David Shambaugh, *China Goes Global: The Partial Power* (New York: Oxford University Press, 2013).
26. Stephen M. Walt, *The Origins of Alliances* (Ithaca: Cornell University Press, 1987).
27. On China as a unipolar power by 2030, see Arvind Subramanian, "The Inevitable Superpower: Why China's Dominance Is a Sure Thing," *Foreign Affairs*, September/October 2011, 66–78.

28. Wu Zhengyu, "Toward 'Land' or Toward 'Sea,'" *Naval War College Review* 66, no. 3 (Summer 2013): 53–66.
29. Robert S. Ross, "China's Naval Nationalism: Sources, Prospects, and the US Response," *International Security* 34, no. 2 (Fall 2009): 46–81.
30. "Service Collaboration to Address Anti-Access and Area Denial Challenges," Air-Sea Battle Office, May 2013, http://archive.defense.gov/pubs/ASB-ConceptImplementation-Summary-May-2013.pdf; accessed on July 17, 2017.
31. Lyle Goldstein and William Murray, "Undersea Dragons: China's Maturing Submarine Force," *International Security* 28 (Spring 2004): 161–96.
32. David Shambaugh, "China Engages Asia: Reshaping the Regional Order," *International Security* 29, no.3 (Winter 2004–2005): 64–99.
33. Bonnie Glaser and Jacqueline Vitello, "US-China Relations: China's Maritime Disputes Top the Agenda," *Comparative Connections* 16, no. 1 (May 2014), https://www.csis.org/analysis/comparative-connections-v16-n1; accessed on July 17, 2017.
34. *Pivot to the Pacific?*, 8.
35. In 2009, China submitted to the UN a historical map that claims up to 90 percent of the South China Sea.
36. Jeffrey A. Bader, "The US and China's Nine-Dash Line: Ending the Ambiguity," *Brookings*, February 6, 2014, https://www.brookings.edu/opinions/the-u-s-and-chinas-nine-dash-line-ending-the-ambiguity/; accessed on July 17, 2017.
37. "US, Japan Blast China Over Asia Security," *Wall Street Journal*, May 30, 2014.
38. Testimony before the House Committee on Foreign Affairs on February 5, 2014.
39. Air-Sea Battle, "Service Collaboration."
40. Rebecca Liao, "Out of the Bretton Woods—How the AIIB is Different," *Foreign Affiars* (July 27, 2015).
41. Robert J. Art, *A Grand Strategy for America* (Ithaca, NY: Cornell University Press, 2003).
42. Barry R. Posen, "Pull Back," *Foreign Affairs*, January/February 2013, 116–28; Barry R. Posen, *Restraint: A New Foundation for U.S. Grand Strategy* (Ithaca: Cornell University Press, 2014).
43. Christopher Layne, "From Preponderance to Offshore Balancing: America's Future Grand Strategy," *International Security* 22, no. 1 (Summer 1997): 86–124.
44. T. V. Paul, "Soft Balancing in the Age of U.S. Primacy," *International Security* 30, no. 1 (2005): 46–71. Also, see Robert Ross, "The Problem with the Pivot: Obama's New Asia Policy Is Unnecessary and Counterproductive," *Foreign Affairs*, November/December 2012, 70–82.
45. G. John Ikenberry, Michael Mastanduno, and William C. Wohlforth, *International Relations Theory and the Consequence of Unipolarity* (Cambridge: Cambridge University Press, 2011); Stephen G. Brooks, G. John Ikenberry, and William C. Wohlforth, "Lean Forward," *Foreign Affairs*, January/February 2013, 130–42.; Nuno Monteiro, *Theory of Unipolar Politics* (Cambridge: Cambridge University Press, 2014).
46. "US Foreign Policy in the Asia Pacific Region" (US State Department Briefing, New York, September 27, 2013, https://2009-2017-fpc.state.gov/214866.htm; accessed on July 17, 2017.
47. *Pivot to the Pacific?*, p. 7.
48. Charles P. Kindleberger, *The World in Depression, 1929–1939* (Berkeley: University of California Press, 1973); George Modelski, "The Long Cycle of Global Politics and the Nation-State," *Comparative Studies in Society and History* 20

(April 1978): 214–35; William Wohlforth, "The Stability of a Unipolar World," *International Security* 24, no. 1 (Summer 1999): 5–41.
49. Stephen G. Brooks, G. John Ikenberry, and William C. Wohlforth, "Don't Come Home, America: The Case against Retrenchment," *International Security* 37, no. 3 (Winter 2012–2013): 7–51; Brooks, Ikenberry, and Wohlforth, "Lean Forward."
50. Kier A. Lieber and Gerard Alexander, "Waiting for Balancing: Why the World Is Not Pushing Back," *International Security* 30, no. 1 (Summer 2005): 109–39.
51. Daniel R. Russell, "The Future of US-China Relations," Testimony before the Senate Foreign Relations Committee, Washington, DC (June 25, 2014).
52. Peter Lee, "Obama Admin Pushes Back Against Japan Lobby," *International Policy Digest*, February 2, 2014.
53. Ibid. China participated in the 2014 Rim of the Pacific Navy Exercise (RIMPAC) off of the Hawaiian Islands. RIMPAC is a high-level military exchange to build up transparency and discussions with China about operational safety and confidence-building mechanisms in the region, and to foster new rules and guidelines for resolving disputes and avoiding crises. DeLeon and Jiemian, "U.S.-China Relations," 9.
54. Jack S. Levy and William R. Thompson, "Balancing on Land and at Sea: Do States Ally Against the Leading Global Power?" *International Security* 35, no. 1 (Summer 2010): 7–43.
55. *2014 Quadrennial Defense Review*, vii.
56. For instance, a naval power will view naval construction of another state as a threat, while a land power will view the land component of another power as a threat. Thus, "a state with a comparative advantage in the production of sea power may stress naval balances, while one with advantages in land power may highlight its geographical position and large army." William Wohlforth, *The Elusive Balance: Power and Perceptions during the Cold War* (Ithaca, NY: Cornell University Press, 1993), 303.
57. Barry R. Posen, "Command of the Commons: The Military Foundation of U.S. Hegemony," *International Security* 28, no. 1 (Summer 2003): 5–46.
58. Levy and Thompson distinguish between naval and land powers. Jack S. Levy and William R. Thompson, "Balancing on Land and Sea: Do States Ally against the Leading Global Power?," *International Security* 35, no. 1 (Summer 2010): 7–43. In contrast, Layne anticipates that US primacy will provoke balancing. See Christopher Layne, "The Unipolar Illusion Revisited: The Coming End of the United States' Unipolar Moment," *International Security* 31, no. 2 (Fall 2006): 7–41.
59. Walt, The Origins of Alliances, 21–28.
60. Posen, "Command of the Commons," 10.
61. Robert S. Ross, "China's Naval Nationalism Sources, Prospects, and the U.S. Response," *International Security* 34, no. 2 (Fall 1990): 46–81.
62. Ibid., 75.
63. Ibid.
64. Roger Cliff, Mark Burles, Michael S. Chase, Derek Eaton, and Kevin L. Pollpeter, *Entering the Dragon's Lair: Chinese Anti-Access Strategies and Their Implications for the United States* (Santa Monica, CA: RAND Corporation, 2007).
65. Goldstein, "Parsing China's Rise," 61.
66. Posen, "Command of the Commons," 21.
67. "China to Exceed Combined Defence Budget of All Other Key Defence Markets in APAC by 2015," *IHS Markit*, February 14, 2012, http://press.ihs.com/

press-release/defense-risk-security/china-exceed-combined-defence-budget-all-other-key-defence-marke; accessed on July 17, 2017.
68. Zhengyu maintains that China will pursue a continental strategy of investing in high-speed rail and westward expansion toward the Eurasian landmass. Zhengyu, "Toward 'Land' or Toward 'Sea.'"
69. *2014 Quadrennial Defense Review*, 32.
70. *2014 Quadrennial Defense Review*, 2014.
71. Yoichi Kato, "Interview/Evan Medeiros: China's Attempt to Isolate Japan worsens Bilateral Relations," *The Asahi Shimbun* (April 6, 2014). Available at: ajw.asahi.com/article/views/opinion/AJ201404060018; accessed July 29, 2015.
72. David Shambaugh, "China Engages Asia: Reshaping the Regional Order," *International Security* 29, no.3 (2004): 94.
73. "The Long-Term Outlook for the BRICS and N-11 Post Crisis," *Global Economics Paper No. 192*, December 4, 2009, http://www.goldmansachs.com/our-thinking/archive/brics-at-8/brics-the-long-term-outlook.pdf; accessed July 17, 2017.

INDEX

Note: References to figures and tables are denoted by 'f' or 't' in italics following the page number.

Abe, Shinzo, 290–92
aggregate power realism (APR), 351, 353
Allison, Graham, 1, 81–82, 211
America. *See* United States
Angell, Norman, 111
Anglo-German rivalry, 123–38
Aron, Raymond, 1
Association of Southeast Asian Nations (ASEAN), 89, 153, 154–55, 311, 355
Asia, 68
   American military power in, 351
   conflict in, 22–27
   dominance of China in, 81
   India as a balance to China in, 299–316
   regional stability in, 13, 166, 312
   the rise of China in, 277–94
   See also East Asia; Southeast Asia
Asian Development Bank (ADB), 355
Asian Infrastructure Investment Bank (AIIB), 355
Asia-Pacific economic cooperation (APEC), 338
Australia, 292–93, 299, 351

balance of power
   and the risks of war, 14–19
   shifts in the, 17–19, 164, 300
   theories of the, 351
Bangladesh, 311–12
Bay of Bengal Initiative for Multi-Sectoral Technical and Economic Cooperation (BIMSTEC), 311–12

Beijing, 195. *See also* China
Bergsten, Fred, 280
Bhutan, 311
Brazil, 305
BRICS cooperation platform, 305, 337, 340, 349
Britain, 1, 21, 46, 60, 67, 81, 106, 111–12, 123–38, 143
Brooks, Steve, 67
Bush, President George W., 145, 350

Calleo, David, 138
Campbell, Kurt, 85
capitalism, 167
   crony, 179
   global neoliberal, 188
Carr, E. H., 4, 61, 74, 135–37
Castro, Fidel, 327
censorship, 185–204
   digital, 189, 194
   online, 190–93, 333
   See also media; repression
Central Asia, 300, 325. *See also* Asia
Chan, Steve, 83
Chen Guangcheng, 175
China, 1, 14, 79, 81, 117, 149, 196
   ageing society of, 170–71
   communist leadership of, 144, 163
   competition of the United States and, 353–55
   cooperation with Russia of, 334–39
   cooperation with the United States of, 109–11

China (cont.)
  Cultural Revolution of, 156, 167
  defense spending of, 114–15
  and the democracies, 47–51
  the demographic dividend of, 168–69
  as a developing country, 224–25
  diplomatic power of, 214–17
  discord with India of, 300–5, 304t
  economic growth of, 28, 65, 93, 168–71, 176, 179, 232–36
  economic power of, 221–24, 240, 312–16
  environmental problems of, 169–70, 237
  foreign policy of, 68
  GDP of, 68, 237, 245, 313
  and the global economy, 167–68, 170
  as a global power, 5, 280–83
  and the history problem, 283–85
  internal migration in, 169
  and the international order, 231–47
  media entrepreneurs in, 192–95
  military power of, 217–19, 299, 361
  patronage and co-optation in, 171–74, 179
  peaceful rise of, 22–29, 127–29, 231, 352
  policy of a normal Japan of, 287–90
  poverty in, 237
  realism and the rise of, 104–5
  reforms in, 93, 167–68
  as a regional power, 280–83
  relations with other Asian nations of, 5, 92, 143–57
  relations with Russia of, 321–42
  relations with the United States of, 349–63
  repression in, 174–76
  rural, 198, 200
  social protest in, 197, 200
  soft power of, 219–21, 220t
  as a superpower, 73–74, 185, 211–28
China Model, 166. See also China
Chinese Communist Party (CCP), 171–77, 185, 188–91, 195, 204, 327
Churchill, Winston, 129
climate change, 86
Clinton, Secretary of State Hillary, 85, 137–38, 350

coexistence, 253–71
  and legitimacy, 256–58
  and regional security, 258–63
Cold War, 47, 63, 68, 82, 127, 138, 143, 157, 280, 287, 322, 331–33
Components of Power theory, 353
conflict
  in Asia, 22–27, 157
  in the China-US relationship, 79–95, 137, 143, 163, 226–28
  See also war
containment, 136
Copeland, Dale, 14
corruption, 166, 172–73, 186, 188
Cox, Michael, 7, 9
Crick, Bernhard, 188
Crimea, 86, 339
Crimean War, 61
Crowe, Eyre, 1
cyber security, 86

democracy, 47–51, 132, 134
  rural, 200–1
  transition to, 180
  weak, 93
  Western, 132, 164, 186–87
Deng Xiaoping, 152, 167, 179, 280, 283, 329. See also China
Diaoyu/Senkaku Dispute, 8, 125, 133, 138, 178, 258–63, 285–87
Ding Jian, 195
diplomacy, 214–17
Doran, Charles, 14
Dyer, Geoff, 325

East Asia, 105, 123, 125, 300
  American power in, 132–34
  Chinese dominance in, 144–51
  regime change in, 134
  See also Asia
East China Sea, 281
East Germany, 330. See also Germany
economic growth
  of China, 28, 166–69, 179
  slowdown of Chinese, 176
  See also economy
economy
  domestic, 93–94
  global, 90–93
  interdependence and, 90–93

[370] *Index*

liberalization of the, 167
    See also economic growth
energy, 113, 170, 341
environmental degradation, 169–70, 188, 237
European Union, 155

Foot, Rosemary, 6, 8, 68, 163
foreign direct investment (FDI), 167
France, 1, 106
French Revolution, 60
Friedberg, Aaron L., 81, 105, 134

Gaddis, John Lewis, 126
Gandhi, Rahul, 316
Gates, Secretary of Defense Robert, 115, 117, 137, 362
geography, 44–46
Georgia, 73, 339
Germany, 1, 34, 65, 67, 81, 83, 106, 111–12, 123–38, 143, 231
Gibbon, Edward, 1
Gilpin, Robert, 6, 14, 37–38, 59–60, 62–64, 69, 81, 129
Global Financial Crisis of 2008, 93
Goldstein, Avery, 360
Gorbachev, Mikhail, 329
Gross Domestic Product (GDP)
    American share of global, 65, 66*f*
    Chinese economic growth and, 65
    Chinese share of global, 66*f*
Gulf of Aden, 264–68

Hagel, Secretary of Defense Chuck, 86–87, 137
hegemony, 59–64, 81, 133, 135–36
    incumbent, 135
    regional, 105
Hirschman, Albert, 189, 202
history, 6–7, 187
    of the China-Russia relationship, 327–30
    diplomatic, 125
    the record of, 19–22
    and theory, 127
    the uses of, 103–18
    wars of, 64
Holslag, Jonathan, 9
Hu Jintao, 84, 145
human rights violations, 176–77

Hunt, Michael, 126
Huntington, Samuel, 47
Hurrell, Andrew, 84

ideology, 4
Ikenberry, G. John, 6–8, 59–63, 68, 73, 81, 83, 109, 125, 135, 164, 186–87, 280
India
    as a balance to China in Asia, 299–316
    diplomatic balancing of, 310–12
    discord with China of, 300–5, 304*t*
    economic competition with China of, 312–16
    GDP of, 313
    military balancing of, 305–10
    relationship of the United States and, 350
    and the rise of China, 300–5, 356
    structural trade deficit with China of, 304
international law, 165
International Monetary Fund (IMF), 117, 243, 355
international order, 5–6, 33–53, 57–74, 135, 164
    bipolar, 1
    challenge of China to the, 231–47
    change to the, 240–245
    liberal, 186–87, 280, 293–94
international relations theory, 125–26, 135
Internet Society of China (ISOC), 197
Iran, 86

Japan, 7, 20, 27, 83, 87–88, 147, 231, 351, 356
    and the history problem, 283–85
    relationship with China of, 92, 190, 283
    and the rise of China, 277–94, 299
    security guarantees with, 133, 290–93
    unconditional surrender of, 106
Japanese Self Defense Forces (SDF), 287
Jervis, Robert, 4

Kennan, George F., 1, 4
Kennedy, Paul, 1, 6, 130
Kerry, Secretary of State John, 22, 88
Kirshner, Jonathan, 82–83

Index [371]

Kissinger, Henry, 105
Korean peninsula, 8, 29, 144–51. *See also* North Korea; South Korea
Krugman, Paul, 322
Kugler, Jacek, 14, 211

Lagerkvist, Johan, 8, 211
Lagerkvist, Lars, 165
Lavrov, Sergei, 334
Layne, Christopher, 6–8, 58, 65, 105
Lee Kuan Yew, 322
Leffler, Melvyn, 126
legitimacy, 7–8, 163–65, 180, 185–204, 256–58
Levine, Steven I., 126
Lieberthal, Kenneth, 132
Li Keqiang, 187
Linz, Juan, 203–4
Lipset, Seymour Martin, 188
Liu Xia, 175
Liu Xiabo, 175–76, 334
Lobell, Steven, 7, 9, 105
Lundestad, Geir, 7–8, 126

Macmillan, Margaret, 128
Malaysia, 88
Mao Zedong, 152, 232, 327
maritime security, 253–71
Maritime Silk Road, 352–53. *See also* China
May, Ernest R., 103–4
McDougall, Walter, 126
Mearsheimer, John J., 5, 15, 22, 81–82, 105
media, 199–201
 control of, 189
 digital, 199, 204
 international, 194, 198, 200
 See also censorship
Mexico, 21
Middle East, 79, 85
Minxin Pei, 187, 190, 211
Monroe Doctrine, 22
Morgenthau, Hans, 4
Myanmar, 311–12

Nathan, Andrew, 134, 186
nationalism, 81, 83, 93, 146–47, 166
 appeals to, 189–90
 of China, 227
 of India, 316
 manipulation of, 176–80
 regressive Japanese, 290
National People's Congress, 202
National Security Commission, 186
Nepal, 311
North Atlantic Treaty Organization (NATO), 63, 73, 268, 328, 331, 339
New Model of Realist Major Power Relations (NMRMPR), 7, 349–52, 355–63
Newtonian Theory of Geopolitics, 133
Nixon, Richard, 85
nongovernmental organizations (NGOs), 185–86
Northeast Asia, 156. *See also* Asia
North Korea, 86, 145–49. *See also* Korean peninsula
Norway, 334
Nuclear Security Summit, 86
nuclear weapons, 127, 323

Obama, President Barack, 85–86, 94, 137, 154, 281–82, 338, 349, 362
Odgaard, Liselotte, 9, 68, 300
organized crime, 312
Organski, Kenneth, 14, 211

Pakistan, 316
Pax Americana, 6, 62, 65, 133, 137–38
Pei, Minxin, 8
People's Liberation Army (PLA), 351–52, 359, 363. *See also* China
Philippines, 88, 350–51
piracy, 264–68
Politburo Standing Committee, 194
politics
 domestic, 4
 great power, 349–50
 world, 59–74
 See also power; rising powers
power
 bilateral rivalries of, 130–32
 China as a global, 211–28, 231–47
 disaggregate, 358–61
 elements of, 361–62
 national, 236–37, 358
 rise and fall of, 103–18
 shifts of, 57–74

transitions of, 36–40
See also rising powers
Power Transition Theory, 79–95
propaganda, 190
Putin, Vladimir, 74, 324, 327–30, 332–33, 340. *See also* Russia

realism, 13–29, 81, 104–5
   neoclassical, 125–27
   and Waltzian international relations theory, 125
Regional Comprehensive Economic Partnership (RCEP), 355
regional order, 87–90
repression, 174–76. *See also* censorship
Rice, National Security Advisor Susan, 282
riots, anti-Japanese, 178
rising powers
   and the liberal international order, 40–43
   peaceful, 127–29, 277–94, 349–63
   and power transitions, 36–40
   restrictions on, 157
   and the risks of war, 13–29
   See also power
Ruizhuang, Zhang, 9
Russel, Daniel, 85–86
Russia, 4, 44, 49, 60, 86, 145, 177, 196, 305, 321–42, 356. *See also* Soviet Union

Sanders, Bernie, 94
Schroeder, Paul, 61, 106
Schweller, Randall, 59–60, 73
Scobell, Andrew, 134
security, 7–8, 15–16, 163–65
   domestic, 176
   national, 165
   regime, 165
   regional, 305
Segal, Gerald, 322
Shambaugh, David, 6, 9, 67, 113–14, 117, 125, 195, 203, 363
Shanghai, 195
Shanghai Co-operation Organization (SCO), 326, 335–37
Silk Road Economic Belt, 352. *See also* China
Sina Weibo, 190–200

Singh, Manmohan, 312
Sino-American relations, 9, 81, 123–38
   damage to, 178
   the future of, 126
   realist view of, 13–29
   rivalry and, 43–47, 130–32
   and the Sino-American Strategic and Economic Dialogue of 2012, 84
Sino-Japanese relations, 7, 180
Snowcroft, Brent, 16
Snowden, Edward, 187
social inequality, 47, 188
social media, 190–91, 193–94, 201–2
social protest, 169, 185–204
social sciences, 103–4, 213
Soeya, Yoshihide, 7–9, 300, 305
Solnick, Steven, 196
South Africa, 305
South China Sea, 8, 86–87, 89, 116, 125, 138, 155, 177, 235, 281, 285–86, 339
Southeast Asia, 88, 125, 132, 134, 144, 311
   China's relations with, 151–56, 277, 312
   free trade agreement of China with, 145
   security measures in, 312
   See also Asia
South Korea, 27, 92, 138, 145–49, 180, 293, 350–51, 356. *See also* Korean peninsula
Soviet Union, 1, 103, 196, 321
   in the Cold War, 68, 143
   collapse of the, 16, 105, 127, 167, 329–30
   rise of the, 106
   superpower status of the, 62–65
   See also Russia
Spain, 21, 143
Sri Lanka, 311
stability, 7–8, 165
   of China, 178, 237–40
   of the current international system, 163–64
   and the United States, 132–35
Stalin, Josef, 327
status quo, 15–17, 69, 135
Strange, Susan, 1
strategic incentives, 69–73

Taiwan, 8, 29, 49, 87, 94, 125, 134, 137, 177, 180. *See also* China
Tencent Weibo, 194–99
Thailand, 311
Thucydides, 1, 4, 14, 104
Thucydides trap, 80–81, 84–86, 163, 211, 349
Tiananmen Square crackdown (1989), 176, 192, 322
Tibet, 93, 138, 174
Trachtenberg, Marc, 126
Trans-Pacific Partnership (TPP), 87, 338
Trump, President Donald, 86–87, 94, 154
Twain, Mark, 126

Ukraine, 73, 326, 339–42
unipolarity, 330–34
United Nations, 332
United Nations Peace Keeping Operations (PKO), 287
United Nations Security Council, 305, 323
United States, 1, 4, 79, 113–17, 125, 323
    competition of China and the, 353–55
    cooperation of China with the, 109–11
    deep engagement strategy of the, 355–57
    exceptionalism of the, 138
    foreign policy of the, 137, 349–53
    hegemony of the, 331
    liberal ideology of the, 132–33, 138
    military of the, 349–50, 356, 359
    offshore balancing strategy of the, 355–57
    response to China's rise in the, 6–7, 164, 349–63
    the rise of the, 21–22, 105–6, 299
    stability and the, 132–35
    war on terror of the, 332
US-China Business Council, 91

Vietnam, 92, 153–54, 350, 356

Walt, Stephen M., 7–8, 82, 104–5, 125, 163, 187, 280
Waltz, Kenneth, 104, 106
Wang Gungwu, 156
Wang Jisi, 132
Wang Yang, 200, 202
Wang Yi, 84–85
war
    hegemonic, 59–64
    interdependence and, 111–13
    opportunistic, 17–18
    preventive, 17–18
    rise, decline, and, 105–9
    risks of, 13–29
    See also conflict
Washington. *See* United States
Westad, Odd Arne, 7–8, 67, 190, 294
White, Hugh, 81, 227
Wohlforth, William C., 6, 8, 83, 105, 125, 138, 164
World Bank, 169, 237, 243, 245
world order. *See* international order
world peace, 163–80
World Trade Organization (WTO), 167–68
World War I, 21, 61, 81, 103, 107, 111, 127, 137
World War II, 62–63, 88, 103, 107, 236
Wukan incident, 189, 197–201, 203

Xi Jinping, 86, 90, 93, 148, 155, 169, 186, 190, 194, 199, 237, 282, 330, 349–50
Xinjiang, 138, 174

Yuan Yulai, 200

Zhang Ruizhuang, 300
Zhao Yuezhi, 189
Zhu Xi, 146

CPSIA information can be obtained
at www.ICGtesting.com
Printed in the USA
BVHW041532180922
646945BV00001B/3

9 780190 675394